PUBLIC LIBRARY
Stoneham, MA

S0-CEX-179

The Hollywood Western

SALOON
THE
LAST FRONTIER
MATT GARSON, PROP.

A CITADEL PRESS BOOK
Published by Carol Publishing Group

THE HOLLYWOOD WESTERN

90 Years of Cowboys and Indians,
Train Robbers, Sheriffs and Gunslingers,
and Assorted Heroes and Desperados

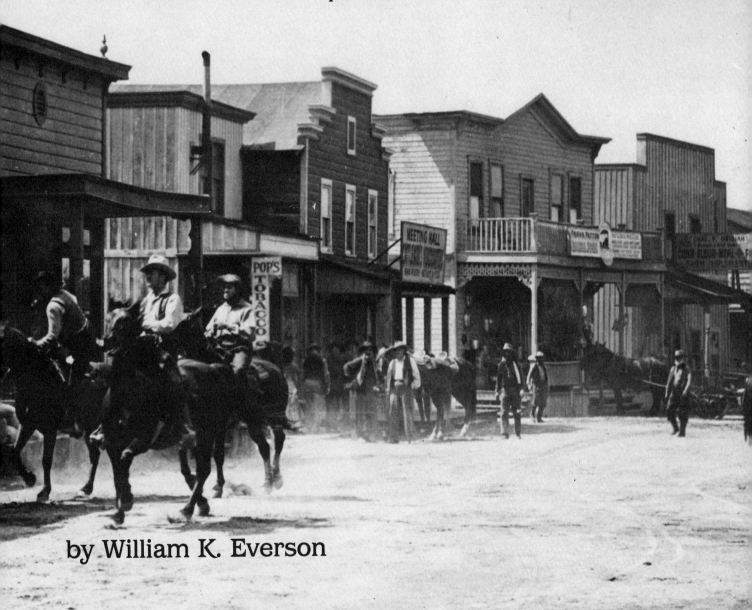

by William K. Everson

791.4362
Everson
1992

SEP 1992

Dedicated to my children,
BAMBI and GRIFFITH,
who, born and raised in an era
of super-spies and rocketships,
still appreciate and prefer
William S. Hart and Gene Autry

ACKNOWLEDGMENTS

For their unstinting cooperation in many ways but especially for supplying many of the rarest stills in this volume, I wish to thank James Card, motion picture curator of the George Eastman House in Rochester, N.Y., and producer Alex Gordon. Grateful thanks are also extended to George Pratt of the George Eastman House; Jacques Ledoux of the Royal Film Archive, Belgium; Janus Barfoed of the Danish Film Archive; William Kenly of Paramount Pictures; and Howard and Ronald Mandelbaum of Photofest.

Copyright © 1969 and 1992 by William K. Everson
All rights reserved. No part of this book may be reproduced in any form, except by a newspaper or magazine reviewer who wishes to quote brief passages in connection with a review.

A CITADEL PRESS BOOK
Published by Carol Publishing Group
CITADEL PRESS is a registered trademark of Carol Communications, Inc.

Editorial Offices: 600 Madison Avenue, New York, N.Y. 10022
Sales & Distribution Offices: 120 Enterprise Avenue, Secaucus, N.J. 07094
In Canada: Canadian Manda Group, P.O. Box 920, Station U, Toronto, Ontario M8Z 5P9
Queries regarding rights and permissions should be addressed to Carol Publishing Group, 600 Madison Avenue, New York, N.Y. 10022

Some of the contents have been adapted from *A Pictorial History of the Western Film* copyright © 1969 by William K. Everson. Most of the material is new.

Carol Publishing Group books are available at special discounts for bulk purchases, for sales promotions, fund raising, or educational purposes. Special editions can be created to specifications. For details, contact: Special Sales Department, Carol Publishing Group, 120 Enterprise Avenue, Secaucus, N.J. 07094

Manufactured in the United States of America

10 9 8 7 6 5 4 3 2 1

Designed by A. Christopher Simon

LIBRARY OF CONGRESS CATALOGING-IN-PUBLICATION DATA

Everson, William K.
    The Hollywood western / by William K. Everson—Rev. ed.
        p.   cm.
    Rev. ed. of: A pictorial history of the western film. 1969.
    ISBN 0-8065-1256-3
    1. Western films—History and criticism.   I. Title.   II. Series:
Everson, William K. Pictorial history of the western film.
PN1995.9.W4E85   1992
791.43′6278—dc20   92-18280

Contents

The Hollywood Western

ONE

An Introduction to Ninety Years of Westerns

As these notes are written, the Western film is more than ninety years old. During that time, it has undergone continual changes of emphasis to appeal to an adult audience in one era, a juvenile one in another, and a calculated combination of both still later. It has had to accept and learn to use technological changes in the art and mechanics of filmmaking, and to reshape itself to fight off the inflation of ever increasing production costs. It has apparently bitten the dust on the theater screen only to be reincarnated on television, and has seen itself produced en masse in Germany, Italy, Yugoslavia, and Spain. It also apparently and permanently "died" in the 1970s, when audiences seemed to abandon the genre, and, despite several sporadic attempts, widely varying in scope, style, and content, Hollywood was unable to bring it back to life. Yet *Dances With Wolves* swept the board of Academy Awards in 1990 (winning far more than any Western had *ever* won) and seemed to have brought the genre back into critical and public repute again.

The Europeans have always seen the Western as a major contribution to American art and culture, as integral a part of American folklore as the *Odyssey* is of the Greeks'. And to American audiences, at least until the mid-1970s, and hopefully now again, the Western, whatever its size—grand scale epic in color and wide screen, humble "B" feature, or half-hour television potboiler—has always been one of the enduring staples of movie entertainment. Regardless of superheroes transposed from the comic strips (*Dick Tracy, Batman*) and futuristic spacemen, there is a period in every child's life when a cowboy on a galloping horse is the most exciting vision imaginable. And as long as the disciples of John Ford, Henry King, and John Wayne are there to wrest poetry, beauty, and drama from a genre somewhat restricted in narrative content, the Western will work its magic on the adult too. For even the most sophisticated adult seems to retain loyalties to the movies of his youth, while his tastes in literature or music are usually subject to major change.

Perhaps the most remarkable aspect of the Western is not that Hollywood has been able to draw so much variety and inspiration from one geographic location and a fairly rigid and even clichéd set of basic plot lines, but that it has been able to do so to the tune of thousands of films for so long a period. Germany has made but intermittent use of its Wagnerian legends as film material; in Britain, the novel *Lorna Doone*, though partially based on fact, was its only real parallel to the outlawry of Jesse James, and it was filmed only three times between 1912 and 1934 (plus a Hollywood version in the fifties), never spawning a whole subgenre of outlaw films as the James exploits did. The legends of Robin Hood, eagerly exploited by both Britain and Hollywood, remained firmly in place in terms of incident and locale, rarely wandering far from the confines of Nottingham and Sherwood Forest. Every time the story was retold, it was essentially the same story, redesigned only to fit the medium (fragmented and expanded for a television series, for example) or to accommodate the star involved, from Fairbanks and Flynn to Connery and Costner. Even Britain's colorful Civil War (King Charles I versus Oliver Cromwell) has been almost totally ignored, though it contains the same potential for drama, action, spectacle, and sentiment as America's Civil War or the French Revolution. Yet for over ninety years now, the American movie has made box office hay out of the "Wild West"—a period surrounding and containing the rise of the great cattle empires, and in terms of actual duration, about a third of the time span already devoted to it by the movies.

Despite its long history, however, the Western as a genre has rarely been accorded the respect it really deserves. Apart from the justified praise heaped on *Stagecoach* (1939) because it *was* both a superb *film* and a fine *Western* (and came after many barren years of routine "shoot-'em-ups"), respect for the Western as a whole came much later, when the auteurist critics of the fifties discovered Curtiz, Hathaway, Walsh, King, Wellman, and Vidor, and, perhaps a little surprised to find so many of the genre among their filmographies, almost grudgingly began to admit (and sometimes to overstate) the artistic potential of the Western. Even then, it was the Westerns with "something to say"—or, in the parlance of the post-fifties, the Westerns that "made a statement"—that were singled out for praise. The great mass of remaining Westerns were still treated to the "if you've seen one, you've seen them all" brand of criticism, usually accompanied by a sneer, a downplaying of the acting contribution, and a snide summing up of alleged clichés. In the mid-sixties, a major television network doing a documentary on the Western thought it might be amusing to edit together a collage of scenes showing a character pointing offscreen and informing the hero, "They went thataway!" as being the epitome of clichéd storytelling. But while it's a good line with which to prove a point, it isn't a line that has been used *that* much. *Bar 20 Justice* and a couple of other Hopalong Cassidys used it, and it certainly turned up elsewhere, but only a devoted aficionado with a lifetime of Western viewing under his belt could have remembered them. After much frustrated screening by its producers, the television program had to get along without the line. If there *is* one key line that typifies the formularization of

the smaller Western, it is that classic and usually last-reel decision by the losing villains, "Let's get outta here!" But it doesn't have the same easy ring to it as "They went thataway!" and in any case its omnipresence in so many "B" Westerns would not be apparent to television "researchers" who rarely have time to look at anything but the obvious and usually already carefully researched.

In April of 1969, a New York *Sunday News* article on the changing styles in the Western commented that contemporary movie cowboys are "nonheroes and obsessed by sex," a statement ignoring the fact that, with the possible exception of John Wayne, there *were* no more movie cowboys as such, merely actors (Brando, Fonda, Holden) who occasionally appeared in individual Westerns. More than twenty years later, that still holds, with the added drawback that most of the actors newly recruited to the genre—Kevin Costner, Danny Glover, Brian Dennehy, Jeff Goldblum, even Britain's John Cleese, *all* of whom appeared in *Silverado* (1985)—look even less at home in the saddle. The same article, summing up the old-time cowboy hero in one convenient if inaccurate phrase, added that in earlier days, "the hero would kiss his faithful horse and ride off alone into the sunset." This again is a fallacy that has been repeated so many times that it has been accepted as part of the unwritten law ruling the making of Westerns, but it just isn't supported by the facts. William S. Hart, it is true, had a deep affection for his horses—partly because the affection came naturally to him, and partly because he recognized the very real comradeship and mutual dependency between a man and his horse in the early West—and tried to show it in his movies. However, he kissed his beloved pinto Fritz only in moments of such rare dramatic stress, when he had been rejected by humans, or when, as in *Pinto Ben*, the horse was dying, that such an excessively emotional gesture would be accepted. But Hart certainly never once kissed his horse before riding off alone into the sunset, or as a substitute for feminine caresses. Hart's leading ladies were always well and truly kissed, usually well before the fadeout. Furthermore, he was such a romanticist that the number of films in which he died or sacrificed his happiness at the end by renouncing the woman (as in *The Toll Gate*) were much in the minority, and he invariably wound up with the heroine as his bride.

This in fact applies to almost all of the cowboy heroes, since the heroine's love was the only concrete reward they could hope to gain for all of their Herculean labors and courage. Logic, admittedly, played little part in love in the rapidly paced smaller Western. Apart from comforting the heroine when her father had been murdered, or enjoying her home-cooked meal (really just a plot device by which she can outline all the problems he will then offer to solve), the hero spent precious little time in her company, and it often seemed presumptuous indeed for her to make a coy last-minute suggestion that they become "partners for life" when in fact he hardly knew her, had made no romantic overtures at all, and might well have *preferred* to ride off into the sunset. Quite certainly, romance was seldom stressed in the average Western, any more than it was in the equally innocent comedies of Harold Lloyd or Buster Keaton. But it was present, often a definite plot motivation. Oddly enough, while the villain frequently had a lecherous yen for the heroine, he was usually sufficiently conventional to want to marry her, despite her obvious distaste for him, and even rogues like Fred Kohler seemed to have a *certain* code of honor where the ladies were concerned. At least up until the standardized "B's" of the forties, most of the cowboy heroes kissed their heroines if not regularly, then at least occasionally. Stars like Buck Jones, who made fairly realistic and sensible Westerns and had an adult as well as a juvenile following, never had any qualms about a climactic kiss. Others, whose appeal was more to juveniles and who followed a very rigid code of conduct, tended to apologize for their lack of romantic ardor by joking about it—having the wise Wonder Horse nudge them into a kiss offscreen, or just before The End title arrived to cover up their passion.

Another cliché that has been much misunderstood, and its application exaggerated, is that of the white Stetsoned hero and the black-hatted villain. Admittedly, such visual distinctions are an easy way of symbolizing good and evil, but this line of reasoning doesn't hold much water when one realizes how relatively few heroes sported the stunningly white Stetson (Charles Starrett was an exception, but only in his earlier days) as opposed to those (William Boyd, Tim McCoy, Buck Jones) who favored wholly black outfits, or stars like Bill Elliott and Roy Rogers who confusingly opted for in-between grays!

Clothes in general, not just the hats, provided far greater nuances than just a straight division between good and bad. The *chief* villain's clothes were usually well tailored, often to a point of ostentation, implying an affluence which (since it was not shared by the regular townspeople, who dressed in standard Western garb) could only be supported by illicit activity. If the villain were a gambler, then the frock coat and ruffled sleeves underlined his separation from the working men. Too, it provided a mark of distinction between his culture, and the lack of it in the bulk of his gang—most of whom would tend to be dirty and unshaven and dressed in clothes that often looked dangerously close to falling apart. And as part of the economics of filmmaking, distinctive costuming cut down on the need for establishing shots and careful editing, making it easier to keep

tabs on who was who in the long shots and fast action scenes. It made it easier to use doubles without the deception becoming obvious; a wide-brimmed hat can hide an awful lot of face, though youngsters may often have wondered why Ken Maynard, Gene Autry, or William Boyd, leaping into the saddle and racing out of town, made such a point of keeping their heads *down* and averted as they (or more likely, standard double Cliff Lyons) rode past the camera position. Far from least, it made it possible to reuse footage in later films if the new actors wore matching clothes, a practice that became distressingly overexploited as cheap Westerns neared the end of the trail in the early 1950s.

There were other visual clues to character makeup. Despite the *appeal* of a mustache to heroes of swash-bucklers (Fairbanks, Flynn), romances (Colman, Gable, William Powell, George Brent), and half of the movie detectives ranging from Warner Oland's Charlie Chan to William Powell's Philo Vance and Nick Charles, the idea of a mustachioed Western *hero* never caught on. (It might be claimed that it would be unrealistic for a range rider to keep a mustache in trim—but since he managed to keep clean-shaven, that is a poor argument!) The various exponents of the Cisco Kid character, from Warner Baxter to (most successfully) Gilbert Roland, *did* sport a mustache, but their image was more of a romantic than an adventurous one; they were following in the footsteps of John Gilbert rather than Tom Mix.

Apart from the bigger stars, whose screen persona was well established (Jack Holt in the silent period, Errol Flynn in particular in the sound), and under certain special circumstances (Richard Dix's mustache in his Westerns of the forties was probably kept as a confirmation of maturity; without it he might have been accused of trying to look unconvincingly younger than he clearly was), the few attempts by only a very few Western stars (Buddy Roosevelt, Buck Jones, Bob Steele) to add a touch of novelty via a mustache were quickly rejected. Oddly enough, even in later years, when the acceptance of a greater realism in the Western also brought acceptance of the hero with a long-unshaven chin (Fonda, Eastwood, and, most extreme of all, Mark Stevens as *Jack Slade*, looking almost like a heavy from a silent comedy with his excessive chin makeup), the mustache still did not gain recognition. Perhaps as a subliminal echo of the mustache-twirling villains of old stage melo-drama, the mustache remained primarily the property of the villain: Brian Donlevy, Robert Preston, Harry Woods, Noah Beery, Robert McKim, Roy Barcroft, Walter Miller, Wheeler Oakman, Charles King, Karl Hackett, and scores of others. Before leaving the not exactly critical matter of the mustache, it is however worth mentioning that its overall *avoidance* made it a useful cliché-reversal device at times. In films dealing with an aging hero—John Wayne as the retiring cavalry officer in *She Wore a Yellow Ribbon*, Charlton Heston as the old-timer cowboy in *Will Penny*, and most of all Gregory Peck in *The Gunfighter*—the mustache was used as a kind of subliminal symbol of defeat. In fact, the subtle droop of Peck's mustache almost of itself heralded the film's inevitable tragic ending, while the conformist normalcy of the cut of the mustache (backed up by very plain clothing) emphasized the total lack of glamour of the character—legend notwithstanding. Seldom has a single item of prop makeup been so important to a film's mood!

Other uses of props as a "reading" of character often become obsolete with the passing years. In the twenties, curiously, it was considered effete—even effeminate—for a man to wear a wristwatch. If the script called for the villain to lose the respect of his own men, one of the ploys often utilized was for them to make fun of his wearing a watch. And in the Easterner-comes-West-to-make-a-man-of-himself plotlines, one of the first things he would do would be to divest himself of his watch. Too much was never made of such incidents; effeminacy and homosexuality were rarely dealt with on the silent screen except (and that frequently) in terms of very broad and often heavy-handed comedy. The wristwatch motif was usually brushed over slightly in the fairly sure knowledge that audiences then would get the jibe; today, of course, such isolated moments tend to mystify audiences. Other elements have remained more fashionable: the use of the woolly chaps to ridicule an Eastern "dude" trying too hard to look Western has been a standard ploy from the beginning, from Douglas Fairbanks, Sr., through to Jack Benny and Bob Hope, and into the nineties, Billy Crystal—or even William Boyd, when his Hopalong Cassidy decided to masquerade as a dude in *The Sunset Trail*.

Despite obvious concessions to the show biz flair of stars like Tom Mix, Gene Autry, and Roy Rogers, costuming generally has been far more consistent (and reasonably convincing if not accurate) for the males than for the ladies. Since women, particularly in "B" Westerns of the thirties and forties, had relatively little to do, it was not at all uncommon for them to wear their own contemporary clothes (including modern shoes) that looked decidedly anachronistic as they strolled through the studio Western towns peopled otherwise by extras in appropriate period garb. When the Westerns got slicker and more streamlined in the forties, the leading ladies' clothes got sexier—tighter satin blouses and shorter skirts. However, nothing quite matched the startling effect created by Ken Maynard (his own producer as well as star) in *Smoking Guns*, (1934) when he clad his amply upholstered leading lady, Gloria Shea, in an *extremely* low-cut wide-bodiced gown that seemed to be revealing more and more with every jolt of the wagon, which fortunately was heading for the traditional fade-out and End title logo!

Considering the basically standardized action content of the Western—the chase, the Indian attack, the gun duel and the fistfight, and a few more specialized elements such as the stampede, the dynamited canyon, the last-reel race to complete requirements for a deal (a stagecoach race with a mail contract as the prize, or an Army contract if wild horses are delivered by a specified time)—it is surprising how so few basic ingredients have been pressed into service to flesh out so many plot lines. Far from being "all the same," the Westerns have in fact managed to offer far more story variations than their Oriental counterpart, the Japanese samurai film.

The pioneering themes—the wagon trek or the great cattle drive or the building of a railroad—have of course occupied a large percentage of the plots. But despite inspiring themes of national progress and historic achievement, most of these story lines have still depended on villainy for their precise motivation, since the hero's activities have remained quite constant, and would indeed be largely passive were it not for his need to combat villainous intervention. The railroading epics are typical. While in John Ford's *The Iron Horse* (1924) the main obstacles were time, terrain, and Indian hostility, it was the hero's long search for the killer of his father, a man also tied in with opposition to the railroad, that supplied the sustaining story line. DeMille's unofficial remake, *Union Pacific* (1939), acknowledged but downplayed the physical difficulties of terrain and the antagonism of the Indians to stress a story line in which political and banking "influences" back East were seeking to delay the railroad so that the matching railroad from the West would get to a key position first and control the profits to be made from the completed line.

The railroading theme was extremely popular with producers of "B" Westerns too, since the films could in a sense coast on the reputations of the few epic Westerns on the same subject and imply a *sense* of epic without having to spend any extra money. One popular theme was for the villain to try to discourage (by raids and other destructive means, often blamed on the Indians) the use of a planned route so that it would be necessary to divert to another route—and another town—which he happened to control. Another variation on this theme had the villain obtaining advance information that a railroad was to be constructed and the route it was to take, whereupon he would launch a reign of terror to force all the landowners to sell out cheaply, enabling him to make a killing by owning the land that the railroad *had* to use.

The intellectual villain: Harry Worth in *Bar 20 Rides Again*

City clothes and a mustache identify the villain: Alfred Hollingsworth (left) with William S. Hart in *Hell's Hinges*

The same tradition more than two decades later: Brian Donlevy (about to get his comeuppance) in *Jesse James*

William S. Hart

William Boyd

The beauty of this plot line was that it didn't need any extra budget to create a sense of size: the importance of the railroad could be stressed by an opening montage of stock shots, and all that was necessary after that was a periodic return to shots of laborers clearing land and laying ties. At the end of the film, a rousing speech by a visiting politician could restress the epic quality, and another stock shot could imply that a train was actually on the location, or possibly an inexpensive mock-up might be achieved. (Stills show that trains in cheap Westerns were often no more than simple cardboard cutouts, yet cunning lighting, angles, brevity of shot, and the use of good sound effects usually created an aura of quite acceptable reality.)

Discounting the pioneering and epic themes, most Western plots fall into one of a dozen groups. First, there is the Sin Town masterminded by the villain from his gambling hall. Despite the enormous profits from his always crooked games, the bad guy can't resist such extralegal activities as robbing stages and rustling cattle.

Buck Jones

If he's lucky enough to have Evelyn Brent working for him as his saloon hostess, he can also get garrulous miners drunk and indulge in murder and claim-jumping. This kind of catchall plot allowed for either a straightforward action approach or a semihistorical foray which tried to parallel the activities of Wyatt Earp or Bat Masterson. Dodge City, Deadwood, Nevada City, Wichita, Tombstone, Waco, Brimstone, and a dozen other frontier hell towns were cleaned up scores of times, in virtually identical ways, by Hollywood heroes, from Richard Dix and George O'Brien to Roy Rogers, Bill Elliott, and Johnny Mack Brown.

Frequently, however, the villain was something of a specialist, with a very specific objective. Establishing a vast cattle empire was an idea better undertaken by the villains of bigger Westerns (Joseph Calleia in MGM's *Wyoming*) because they needed a certain panache to pull it off, and few among the "B" Western heavies had it. Occasionally an element of mystery might creep in to baffle even the hero with the reigns of terror designed to force ranchers off their apparently worthless land. Regular Western audiences, however, knew that the solution lay within two possibilities: either one section of land controlled the water for the entire area and the villain was after total acquisition of the water rights, or gold or other mineral deposits had been discovered on land other than his own.

His deliberate sabotaging of progress made the villain doubly despicable, unpatriotic as well as greedy. He might be destroying the telegraph lines (possibly stirring up racial unrest on the side, by contriving to blame it all on the Indians) to protect his own (news-carrying) stagecoach business, or he might be out to prevent the honest citizens from voting their territory into the Union, knowing that such a move would inevitably bring law and order and an end to his profitable virtual dictatorship. (This theme was quite popular during the war years in such Westerns as *Deep in the Heart of Texas*, and the word *dictator* was often used quite freely, if incongruously, to stress the contemporary parallel.)

The simplest plot device of all, of course, was for the Texas Ranger or U.S. marshal hero to pose as a badman, join the outlaws, gain their confidence, and work from the inside to bring about their downfall. (It worked just as well in the gangster genre, and since producer Thomas Ince used it as early as 1914 in *The Gangsters and the Girl*, it probably was first a big city plot ploy.) A subtheme was for the outlaws to have a hideout on the Mexican side of the border, do their plundering in Texas, and then scamper back to safety . . . all usually leading to a hell-for-leather climax in which the hero would somehow trick the gang into chasing him across the border, where a Ranger posse would be waiting. This ruse was used many times, but because of an exceptionally com-

"They went thataway"—an exaggerated cliché. (From *The Mexicali Kid* with Jack Randall)

15

plicated array of story threads and unusually rugged mountain exteriors, it rarely worked better than in *The Last of the Duanes* (1930), one in a fine series of high-calibre Westerns that George O'Brien was then making for Fox.

Republic Pictures made some of the slickest and best "B" Westerns, with a stress on action first and foremost. Republic didn't care too much about plot lines, but when the studio came across a good one, it tended to use it as often as the traffic would bear. Undoubtedly Republic's favorite—because it suggested, subliminally, a kind of historic spectacle, and also lent itself to stock-footage montages, always an effective money-saving device— was what might be termed the "Reconstruction" Western. These were stories set in the immediate post–Civil War period, with corrupt politicians and their guerrillas legally taking over defeated territories and plundering them via excessive taxes. Republic used—and reused— this story for all its Western stars, and for both "A" and "B" movies. It served John Wayne at least twice, as well as Roy Rogers, Bill Elliott, and others.

Stirring up the Indians was another tried-and-true favorite. The basic villainy usually was performed by a white trader or crooked Indian agent who plied the redmen with liquor and guns and assured them that the Great White Father in Washington spoke with a forked tongue (as indeed he did, much of the time). Thus it was easy to use the Indians and assorted stock footage for all kinds of mayhem, and then, at the end of reel six, send them on their way somewhat decimated with an understanding if condescending pat on the head, the white heavy having received his just desserts in the meantime. In fairness, while the Indians were used as a convenient mass villain (and target) and were certainly stereotyped, they were not usually treated with hostility. While Westerns like Tim McCoy's *The End of the Trail* (1932), a quite remarkable pro-Indian forerunner of Kevin Costner's *Dances With Wolves* (1990), were far from common, so fortunately were films like Gene Autry's *Ride Ranger Ride* (1936), in which the "The only good Indian is a dead Indian" motif was repeated ad nauseum by the two-pronged comic relief of Smiley Burnette and Max Terhune, and where Chief Thundercloud's attempt to collect a scalp in settlement of a bet is used as a running gag throughout. In fairness to Autry, he had insufficient clout at that very early stage in his career to object to the content of his scripts, but clearly this one embarrassed him. Later, when he had formed his own production company releasing through Columbia, he more than made amends with films like *The Last Roundup* and *The Cowboy and the Indians*, presenting a far more sensitive treatment of the American Indian.

Having the hero escaping from (or returning to) prison to prove his innocence was a plot device used mainly by the more serious Western stars like Buck Jones and George O'Brien. William Boyd, Gene Autry, and others with a more predominantly juvenile following were anxious to avoid having their heroes burdened, albeit innocently and briefly, with a jailbird stigma. In any case, such plots (George O'Brien's *Lawless Valley* of 1938 would be a prime example) usually required a little more serious acting (and writing) as the hero faced local ostracism, and that in turn might reduce the action potential.

There was a lot of mileage to be had from family feuds and range wars between cattlemen and sheepmen. Few Westerns had the sheer guts of *To the Last Man*, a Zane Grey story which made no bones about two clans seething with mutual hatred and ultimately wiping each other out. Usually the ploy was the simpler one of having the villain prodding the feud along for his own selfish ends. Rather surprisingly, this plot continued to be used in stories with *contemporary* settings, as in Roy Rogers's *The Man From Music Mountain*, where the old-time villainy sat a little anachronistically alongside the situation of the hero, a big radio star taking time out to settle the feud.

The problems of running freight lines or stagecoaches, or of getting a contract to supply horses to the army (flexibly adaptable to Teddy Roosevelt's campaign in Cuba, via *Texas Trail*, a superior Hopalong Cassidy of 1937, or to *Phantom Plainsmen* of 1942, in which the Nazis inexplicably needed horses for their European war effort), invariably led to a climactic race between competitive rolling stock or horses. (Equally invariably, the bad guys had a reliable backup brigade headed by Tom London, Edmund Cobb, Ernie Adams, and Yakima Canutt to try to sabotage the good guys!) Republic favored these story lines since their climactic races provided a field day for Yakima Canutt and his unique organization of stuntmen. And since the studio had done it before so many times, there was an impressive library of stock footage to be utilized.

And last but not least, there was another old faithful: the hero's relentless search for the murderer of his father. This theme became a popular one with Bob Steele, who in picture after picture grew to manhood doggedly tracking down the killer. In *The Man From Hell's Edges* (1932), it seemed that a note of novelty might have been struck, with the film seeming to follow an orthodox good-vs.-evil path, while in the final reel Steele captures the leading miscreant and bests him at fisticuffs. But seconds before the "End" title, Steele springs the bombshell: in addition to his other crimes, the villain was *also* the man who had killed his father, an element not even suggested in the preceding reels. Most

Union Pacific

of the films in which this stalwart-tracking-his-dad's-killer story line occurred were directed and sometimes written by one Robert N. Bradbury, who was Steele's father!

A related offshoot of this "quest" Western plot was that of the two brothers, separated when mere lads by an Indian attack or a bandit raid. The brothers grow to manhood quite separately, one of them frequently "going bad" in the process—only to save the other's life at the cost of his own just after they have rediscovered one another. Yet a further tangent of this theme was for a young boy to be separated from his outlaw father, and to grow up to be a lawman who tracks down the man he no longer knows to be his dad. Smaller Westerns like this were very much in the minority as they automatically required better directing, acting, and writing than most "B" Western producers thought was necessary. But because of that, when they *were* made, they invariably turned out to be minor classics, within the parameters of that overused term. Certainly *Thunder Trail* (1937) and *Courage of the West* (1938, and the first of the Bob Baker Westerns to be directed by a notable new talent, Joseph H. Lewis) fell into that category, and for reasons

The Man Who Shot Liberty Valance: John Wayne and James Stewart

in addition to those of plot, both are outstanding "B" Westerns. Even the independent *Toll of the Desert* (1935), one of a handful of starring Westerns made by Fred Kohler, Jr., much better as a villain, took on stature because of such a theme.

During the mid-thirties, there was a curious but extremely entertaining minor cycle of "B" Westerns about the *making* of Westerns. Charles Starrett as a pampered Western star who isn't allowed to ride a horse *(The Cowboy Star)*; Gene Autry and Buck Jones as stuntmen who ultimately take over from the conceited stars for whom they are doubling *(The Big Show* and *Hollywood Roundup,* respectively); Richard Dix as a washed-up silent cowboy star, patterned on Tom Mix, who makes a comeback (the rather charming and too little known *It Happened in Hollywood*); Tom Keene and George O'Brien as Western stars on location who get mixed up in local range wars *(Scarlet River* and *Hollywood Cowboy,* respectively, both RKO Radio films); and Gene Autry again as a double who rises to stardom in *Shooting High* and, on a more novel front, as a local rancher who suspects something is amiss when fellow cattlemen are conned into putting up the money for a John Wayne Western and then head for Mexico with the proceeds *(Down Mexico Way)*. There were others, most of them entertaining, and usually far more accurate in their depiction of working Hollywood than many much bigger productions. *(Hollywood Roundup* for example, though such was probably not its aim, has far fewer mistakes about *how* movies are made than MGM's far more ambitious *The Bad and the Beautiful)*.

In the mid-forties, there was a brief revival of this cycle, though on a less serious level: Republic made a number of Westerns, *Bells of Rosarita* being the most typical, in which all of the studio's currently active Western stars played themselves and left their employers in the lurch while they went out West to help Roy Rogers in his perennial battle against Grant Withers and Roy Barcroft! Probably the strangest of this whole cycle, and most charming in a Disneyesque way, was the Roy Rogers vehicle *Trail of Robin Hood,* one of a group made in Trucolor, and perhaps the first real Christmas Western. In this one, Roy goes to the aid of Jack Holt, who plays a retired silent Western star who raises Christmas trees that he sells at giveaway prices to orphans and poor children. Even though the couple of wagonloads that he sends to market can hardly make much of a dent in the national Christmas tree trade, it seems to arouse the ire of the villains, who make a huge seasonal profit out of *their* trees, so much so that they resort to arson and murder to drive Holt out of business. Nostalgically, the help coming from the studio includes not only some of their current Western stars, but also old-timers William

Farnum, Tom Tyler, Tom Keene, and George Chesebro, a stock villain, who in one of the best gags in the film, is regarded with suspicion until he explains that his motives are quite pure. Despite its patent absurdity, it was an engaging film and certainly different, slammed over with tremendous style by one of the best action directors of them all, William Witney, about whom *much* more later on.

While the plot lines herein described do belong primarily to the "B" Western, it must be remembered that it was these "B's" that made up the bulk of the overall Western product, and that these plot lines, refined and fitted out with stronger romantic elements, were still basically the same ones that the "A's" fell back on. (In *The Iron Horse* (1924), the hero's search for his father's killer provides the cohesive thread on which the epic story hangs, while in *The Big Trail* (1930), the only change is that the hero is searching for the murderer of his friend.)

Since the 1950s, and the mid-decade disappearance of the orthodox "B" Western, only two new themes have been added to the genre's storytelling arsenal. In truth, even they were not new, since they had certainly surfaced before, but they were new as a *genre.* One was of the transition from the Old West to the New, and with it the realization that the old-time gunman was becoming an anachronism. Films like *Butch Cassidy and the Sundance Kid, The Man Who Shot Liberty Valance, The Wild Bunch,* and, most of all, *Ride the High Country* represented this new cycle. Then there were the revenge Westerns, in which the hero—most often Randolph Scott, though occasionally a Gregory Peck—remorselessly tracked down the man who had betrayed, raped, or murdered his wife. Revenge had always been a theme forbidden by the Production Code, so when a "B" Western hero took the trail after the killer of his father, it was clearly stated that he was searching for *justice,* not vengeance. With the relaxing of the Code, cold-blooded vengeance became not only a permitted theme, but also a useful one for a veteran star like Scott, now getting along in years and looking for scripts with more plot and characterization than physical action. The revenge theme also had the advantage of acknowledging love and marriage, but putting it in the *past,* avoiding the possible embarrassment of an older man–younger girl liaison.

Within the framework of all of these plot lines, the action itself was often utilized in very specific ways. The runaway horse or stagecoach was a perfect way for boy to meet girl. The shoot-out in the dusty main street was a means of gaining some respect for a three-dimensional villain; at least he had the courage to engage in a fair fight rather than trying to shoot his opponent in the back. And initially, the big fight between hero and villain (preferably as a climax to a horseback pursuit, although an encounter in the saloon was almost as acceptable) was considered, by juvenile audiences at least, the only honorable way to conclude any Western. When a Western had its fight early in the proceedings, the rules seemed to have been broken, and the climax, no matter how exciting in a nonfistic manner, seemed to be lacking. If a Western was generous enough to have two fights, it was considered a classic; if it lacked fisticuffs entirely it often provoked loud boos. Considering how well known these basic requirements were, it is surprising how often the cheaper Hollywood Westerns made by companies like Puritan and Crescent flouted audience expectations by delivering Westerns with no action at all. (Yet the publicity stills and lobby cards frequently contained absurdly unlikely fight or stunt scenes, posed solely to lure audiences in).

Equally hard to accept was the basically good Western that fizzled out at the end, sometimes literally fading out (as a couple of Tim McCoy Columbias did) as a climactic fight was about to start. The kind of audience for these films had no way of knowing that budgets and shooting schedules *had* to be met, and that if the time—or the money—ran out before an expected action sequence was shot, then the film would somehow manage without it. If the audience *had* known, it would have (rightly) asked: "Then why not shoot the important stuff *first,* and leave the comedy padding or the odd romantic scene until the last?" However, these complaints belong primarily to the thirties. In the forties, as Westerns became more and more mass produced on a virtual assembly-line basis, while they may have possessed even less individuality, there was little for audiences to complain about in the action department. They became literally *all* fights, chases, and nonstop mayhem. Buster Crabbe had only to saunter into PRC's somewhat threadbare saloon and Charles King would remark, "Stranger, I don't like your face!"—instantly provoking a vigorous brawl.

It is these latter-day, Poverty-Row Westerns that perhaps justify the scornful appraisal of the "B" Westerns as merely a collection of clichés. The formularization of plot lines had been increasing throughout the thirties as more "B" films were produced, and as production costs soared, making it imperative that they be made even quicker and more economically, quality diminished via the route of longer takes, less dialogue, and greater use of stock footage wherever possible. This lessened concern for quality can also be discerned in the carelessness with which titles were selected—and in the near-fraudulent use of attractive titles with little in the films that related to them. In the silent period, most Western titles were in some way related to the film's plot content. With the thirties however, there was a marked increase

in the use of ambiguous titles: *Riders of the Rockies, Gunsmoke Trail, The Phantom Ranger, Riders of the Dawn.* None had any direct relationship to the films they graced, nor were those phrases even used within the body of the dialogue. On the other hand, they weren't shamefully unrelated either. The musical Westerns provided greater leeway: *Sunset in Eldorado, Sierra Sue, Ridin' Down the Canyon,* and *In Old Monterey* (which was entirely *modern* and localed nowhere near Monterey) were not backed up by any characters, action, or location in their respective movies, but those title tunes were sung somewhere along the way. True, occasionally the use of a current hit song did inspire the creation of a plot which supported it, Gene Autry's *South of the Border* being a prime illustration.

Since the studios sold *groups* of Westerns in advance of production, and via packages of six or eight that had to *sound* attractive to exhibitors, many Westerns of the forties had even more nebulous connections with their handles. *Covered Wagon Days* implied a historically oriented tale of pioneers, but in actuality dealt with gold mine claim jumpers with nary a covered wagon in view. *The Kansas Terrors* was set in an unnamed island republic, presumably Cuba from all the hints dropped. Zorro was neither seen nor referred to in *Zorro's Black Whip,* Billy was likewise invisible in *Captive of Billy the Kid,* and *The Phantom Plainsmen* was a classic case of pinning the titular tail on the donkey.

One rather spectacular cliché that was born with the "B" Westerns of the thirties stayed around until the demise of the species in the mid-fifties. The heroine was, almost without exception, a biological freak, the apparent offspring of but a single and male parent. Western leading ladies just never seemed to have mothers. Occasionally, in dire straits, a hard-pressed father might murmur "Oh, if only your mother were alive. . . ." but that cursory nod to maternity apart, the mother was literally obliterated from the West—or there by subliminal suggestion only, as one of the wives present at town meetings.

The reasons, of course, were economic, not genetic. A mother could perform no useful function. Father could be robbed or cheated, used as lever to coerce his daughter into marriage, or killed off, leaving the heroine conveniently and entirely dependent on the hero's protection. Even a small sister or brother could be of value: they could be kidnapped by an inheritance-seeking bad guy (as in *Moonlight on the Prairie*), or, better still, they might be lame (as in *Arizona Badman* and *Heart of the Rockies*) and subject to frequent beatings by an evil stepfather (who would delight in kicking their dog, too), thus paving the way for the hero's protective intervention. But the mother could perform no such creative

The Trail of Robin Hood: Jack Holt (left) with Roy Rogers and Foy Willing

Jack Slade: Barton MacLane (left), Mark Stevens, and Dorothy Malone

function. She couldn't have babies, since pregnancies were unheard of in the "B" Westerns. Any babies that were seen were either survivors of Indian or outlaw raids, or orphans suddenly dumped in the hero's lap—and usually productive of the kind of comedy mixed with sentiment that was not generally liked by the Saturday matinee crowd. Mothers couldn't be killed off, either, since that might be emotionally upsetting to the small fry. In other words, she was quite useless, eating up $200 of character actress money that could be put to better use paying a stuntman to fall off a horse. So the mother of the heroine remained a virtually nonexistent figure in the small-budget Westerns, rearing her unwanted head only on the rarest of occasions. She did appear rather prominently in Ken Maynard's *Heir to Trouble,* but then Maynard was an innovational Western practitioner who could always be counted on to come up with something unusual and usually bizarre.

It was television that restored Mother to her rightful prominence in the Western, and it did so with a vengeance. Realizing that it is the contemporary mom who has to select and pay for the cereals and other goodies with which the commercials bombard her offspring, television couldn't afford to ignore, let alone affront, her. Far from just reestablishing Mother within the classic family hierarchy as a figure with which TV-watching moms could identify, it put her on a pedestal, typified best by Barbara Stanwyck as an aggressive, athletic, entirely self-reliant matriarch of a pioneering family in the *Big Valley* series, or a Barbara Bel Geddes as Miss Ellie on *Dallas.*

Certainly the Western over its ninety-year history—and especially in the last sixty of those years—has clung rigorously to a well-tested group of characters, story lines, and situations. But perhaps this is an evolving tradition rather than casual cliché. After all, if we apply the same standards to the seasons of the year, spring is very definitely a cliché. It comes along unchallenged at the same time every year, always without change, the same old revitalized fresh air, the same old colors in the countryside, the same old flowers. We neither expect nor want change, and love it for the same reasons that most of us love the Western—for its beauty, simplicity, and invigorating qualities. The perennial (if not always continuous) popularity of the Western over and above specific cycles and box office fashions can perhaps be ascribed to the fact that it represents a way of life that has become a legend and perhaps a dream for some, but is still sufficiently close to our own time for us to know that, despite Hollywood's exaggerations and romanticisms, it *was* a reality. As time passes, our knowledge of the hardships of those days fades, but the good things stand out in greater contrast. We are hemmed in on all sides—increasing crime and violence, rising problems

with drugs and AIDS, involvement in wars, strikes, racial and social controversy, travel restrictions, taxes, bureaucracy, a countryside littered with beer cans and advertising billboards, city air polluted by chemicals and fog, and ever more revelations that government agencies and individuals whose integrity once would never have been questioned are in fact untrustworthy and corrupt. Thus, it is reassuring and revitalizing to look back a hundred years to a period when almost none of these problems existed, when a man could breathe free, clean air, go where he wanted, do as he pleased and—for a few years at least, and if he were strong enough—be the sole master of his own destiny. We know those days can never come again, but we can steal them back briefly, and as through no *other* kind of movie, via the Western.

TWO

The Beginnings—And Broncho Billy

The Western movie came into being by cashing in on and exploiting the huge popularity of the dime novel—which was indeed the *only* source that movies *could* draw on. It was the work of novelist Zane Grey that first created the kind of romantic Western adventure that would lend itself so admirably to location-filmed "Wild West" movies. But Grey's first orthodox Western novels, and certainly his first commercial hits, didn't arrive until 1910 and 1912, with *Heritage of the Desert* and *Riders of the Purple Sage*. Grey himself had been inspired and partially influenced by the Indian adventure novels of James Fenimore Cooper that he had read in his youth. Indeed, Cooper's novels exerted such an influence on early movies that the Indian hero predated the cowboy hero by many years. Despite the stereotypes created by the dime novels, the image of the Indian was essentially one of nobility, wisdom, and reliability: his impassive face was used to sell all manner of products, from fruit to tobacco, much as the mounted cowboy today is used to sell a specific brand of tobacco, implying that virility, courage, and self-reliance somehow go hand-in-glove with smoking!

In the pre–Zane Grey years, the most logical source for Western movie material would have been the stage. Such venerable plays as *The Squaw Man* (1904), *The*

Virginian (1904), *The Eagle's Nest* (1887), and *The Girl of the Golden West* (1905) would of course eventually be turned into movies, and all but *The Eagle's Nest* would become hardy perennials to be remade frequently. But when the movies began, they were clearly impractical. First, they were valuable commercial properties for which movie rights would have to be obtained—as the Kalem Company found to its cost with an early version of *Ben Hur* that it filmed without clearing such rights. And second, they did not lend themselves to even the simplest and most elementary kind of screen adaptation. They were vehicles for actors and stars, of which the movies had none. Nor were there directors capable of tackling such ambitious material.

In fact the Western images that were first caught by movie cameras could only reflect, not even copy, the influence of the dime novel—which itself glamorized and exaggerated the Western frontier life that was rapidly disappearing but was still far from being past history. And those images came into being before there were theater screens on which to show them. The first movies, often only a minute in length, were produced for exhibition in the Mutoscope parlors, on machines that permitted only one person at a time to view them, cranking a handle and peering through a peep-show aperture. From the beginning however, the essence of the Western was captured in images of action: buffalo moving across the plains, Indians performing ceremonial dances, rodeo performers riding and roping. The aeroplane and the automobile were still in their infancy, and it was the locomotive that was the prime example of speed and power, a piece of machinery ideally suited to the new moving pictures—as pioneers were discovering in France and England, too.

In 1896, the Edison Company filmed the famous Black Diamond Express roaring through rocky terrain in upstate New York. Despite their similarity of "theme," other trains were shown in subsequent films, many of them shot in genuine Western locations, which at that particular time could be reached *only* by railroads. Movies had come along just in time to record major mechanical and technological changes at the turn of the century, including the New York subway system, which opened in 1904. Although the word *documentary* had not yet been coined, many of these short vignettes were virtual documentaries of the changing American scene. Still others, while devoid of plots or acting, staged reconstructions of "typical" Western incidents: a stagecoach holdup, or Indians scalping a victim. (The commercial value of shock and violence was discovered very early, though more prominently in the big city "crime" films or the tableaulike reconstructions of battlefield action or of executions.) Buffalo Bill Cody was recorded on film, and in 1898, the Edison Company made what might technically be called the first Western, a brief little tableau entitled *Cripple Creek Bar Room.* There is no plot and no action: merely a top-hatted dandy (presumably a gambler, and interestingly already the *only* one in the group to be sporting a mustache) and several miners or cowhands in very nondescript working clothes lounging in a saloon presided over by an apparently Indian female barkeeper who actually looks like a male actor beneath the wig.

Despite the many Matthew Brady photographs of the Old West that must have been easily available for study, the scene has the artificial look of a dime novel illustration, and is devoid of any attempts at realistic details. The "set," probably redecorated after use in another vignette, has brickwork showing through the painted plaster, there is no sawdust on the floor, and the wall illustrations, when examined under a magnifying glass, do not seem of the type to encourage either drinking or gambling.

The same Edison Company also made a major contribution to the development of the Western just five years later with *The Great Train Robbery* (1903), directed by Edwin S. Porter in passable rural New Jersey locations. It was hardly, in view of all the vignettes that had preceded it, the "first Western" or, as has so often been claimed, the "first story film." But it undoubtedly was the first Western with a recognizable form: it established the essential pattern of crime, pursuit, showdown, and justice. Within its ten-minute running time, it included—in addition to the train robbery itself—fisticuffs, horseback pursuit, and gunplay, along with suggestions of small child appeal and almost certainly the first use of that cliché-to-be, the saloon bullies forcing the city dude into a dance by shooting into the floor around his feet. In later years, this was to be a useful plot contrivance with which to introduce the hero and provoke a saloon fracas between the villain and him as he came to the victim's assistance. *The Great Train Robbery* was a remarkably sophisticated film for 1903, keeping briskly on the move and using its locations intelligently, despite the too-Eastern look and the too-modern telegraph lines that paralleled the railroad track. There was interesting use of double exposure and a neat bit of tricky jump cutting when a dummy is substituted for one of the trainmen and thrown off the engine after a fight. Most of all, the film benefited from an effective form of film editing and a good sense of storytelling and suspense.

One might fault Porter for making the robbery itself the highlight: it occurs early in the film, and is the most spectacular scene of all due to the hordes of extras pressed into service to descend from the train to be robbed. But after all, that *was* the title of the film, and it was such a precedent-making film that there was no way of knowing that the sheer size and activity of that one scene would make the ultimate finale anticlimactic. In any case, the film was such a sensational success that it is doubtful that any more "showmanship" in terms of building to a bigger climax would have improved its commercial possibilities. Porter unfortunately didn't realize quite how effective his construction was in telling his story. Essentially a technician (and a brilliant one) with no experience in handling actors, he would come up with technical solutions to the solving of story problems without ever realizing that those same devices could be used, or reshaped, for other circumstances. *The Great Train Robbery* was put together the way it was because it seemed the logical way to tell that particular story.

While Porter's later films often had moments of great ingenuity, none of them approached the innate cinema-grammar sense that was displayed in *The Great Train Robbery.* Even some of his (very few) post-1913 full-length features, such as *The Count of Monte Cristo,* were, if anything, a retrogression from that early Western. But if he missed the opportunity to become the father of the *art* of cinema, he *did* create the first American movie milestone. The huge popularity of *The Great Train Robbery* prompted not so much sequels as

Cripple Creek Barroom, directed by W. K. L. Dickson for the Edison Company in 1898

extensions and outright imitations. In those days of loose copyright protection, when movies were still copyrighted as photographs rather than motion pictures, it was all too easy for film pirates to make duplicate negatives of completed films (which were always sold outright to exhibitors, making policing difficult) and sell them as their own, or to inject key copied scenes into their own films. Philadelphia's Lubin Company even went so far as to remake *The Great Train Robbery* virtually scene for scene, with only an occasional isolated detail—a different calendar for example—to show that it was not the identical film. Imitations and plagiarisms were legion, and a year or two later, the Edison Company itself made a charming little parody under the title *The Little Train Robbery*. The impact of the title was such that it was always to remain before the public eye; radio comics using gags about age would refer to it as one of their earlier films, while several other (non-Western) films were to use the title in later years.

Despite the enormous popularity of the train robbery

Edwin S. Porter's *The Great Train Robbery* (1903): the shootout

The Great Train Robbery

Lubin's 1904 scene-by-scene copy of *The Great Train Robbery*

films, one enhanced by topicality since such robberies were still not uncommon, the growth of the Western was slow. One reason was that, prior to the advent of D. W. Griffith, the art of "direction" was still virtually unknown, and the art of storytelling primitive. Early directors, like Porter, were often also the cameramen, and their main responsibility was to good images on screen. Initial scripts, especially at the Edison Company, were little more than two or three sheets of paper in which the story was broken down into a list of shots that gave virtually no information as to motivation, the desired length of a shot in order to give it added or reduced importance relative to the one that followed, or ways to concentrate audience attention on the character or piece of action that should dominate any given scene. Most directors, having read and understood the shot list, assumed that it would be a simple matter to transfer those images to the screen, and that audience understanding would be automatic. Given the simplicity of plots then, this was often the case. But it is also surprising how even these simple plots could be rendered incomprehensible without a modicum of film grammar. An unimportant early Western, *The Sheriff's Love,* is typical. The screen is so "busy" with movement, all in medium or long shot, that the audience never knows where or at whom to look, and the sparse titles are inserted arbitrarily, too often describing action that is

about to take place, rarely (due to inept editing) cut so that they refer to a specific action by a specific person.

While this was a problem common to all early narrative films, it was a *particular* problem with the Western since the stories involved so much physical movement. The key element missing, however, and this would not be apparent before several more years of trial and error, was the lack of a Western *hero* around whom the action would revolve, and with whom audiences could identify.

Slowly, formulas began to evolve, the characterless groups of good guys and bad guys giving way to individual heroes and villains. Typical of this transitional stage was *A Race for Millions* (1906). Despite the mixing of flat, studio-painted sets with genuine exteriors, it featured a solid little claim-jumping plot, a hero and a heroine, an exciting auto-vs.-train chase (already Westerns anticipated the Tom Mix–Roy Rogers streamlining by incorporating modern elements into the plot), and what may well have been the first use of the traditional *High Noon* man-to-man shootout in the deserted main street. Already too, the villain was black-hatted, wore a mustache—and *drank* before the duel, which was supposed not only to weaken his character in the eyes of the audience, but also to explain why an experienced gunman should be beaten to the draw by a comparatively innocent hero (and an Easterner, at that). This ploy worked just as unobtrusively and just as effectively thirty-three years later when killer Luke Plummer (played by Tom Tyler) downed whiskey in the bar before

26

A Race for Millions (Edison, 1906), climaxed by a *High Noon*-type shootout

stepping out into the street with his two brothers to confront the Ringo Kid (John Wayne).

All Westerns were still single-reelers, running for some eleven minutes or less and limited to simple story lines, and most of them were made in the East, in New York and New Jersey. There were still sufficiently rugged locations, particularly in upstate New York, for the exteriors to double reasonably well for the West, though directors were notably careless in angling their cameras to avoid highways or modern houses in the distance, and occasionally a placid New Jersey stream just did not live up to its subtitled description as "a raging torrent." Physical action was still limited to mild horseback cantering, always shot from a fixed position, and unconvincing bouts of wrestling. The art and profession of the stuntman had yet to be created, and nobody knew yet how to stage wagon crashes, horse falls, or all-out fistic battles, least of all the actors, many of them recruited from the stage or from the ranks of the director's family and friends. The acting—one might more accurately say "posing" in most instances—was stiff and unsubtle, devoid of close-ups and thus denied the possibility of subtle facial nuance even if the actor had been capable of it. Costuming was a weird mixture of the players' own Eastern clothing, complemented by nondescript semi-Western hats, sheriff's badges, sheep-wool chaps, and such other accoutrements as could be borrowed, rented, or made. The early Eastern Westerns had a far-from-authentic look to them, and, oddly enough, Westerns already being made in France (decidedly rugged, with more emphasis on violence, lynchings, and sudden death) had both more convincing flavor and costuming and, surprisingly, better selection of outdoor locales.

However, audiences were more gullible and less critical then, and since there was no evidence as yet that movies would develop into a serious art, they did not attract intelligent criticism. That authenticity of plot, costume, and locale was not in itself an open sesame to creating better Westerns and winning audience approval for them was proven by a most peculiar little film of 1908 entitled *The Bank Robbery.* It was filmed entirely on location in and around Cache, Oklahoma, by the Oklahoma Mutoscene Company, and its plot vaguely paralleled that of *The Great Train Robbery,* although it did attempt to win a little sympathy for the outlaws by showing their concern for a wounded comrade and putting their own escape in jeopardy by stopping to care for him. The dusty little Oklahoma "town" with the bank as its focal point was obviously the real thing, and at two reels the film was the longest Western yet made. Its "director" was famed frontier lawman William M. Tilghman (later a good friend and advisor to William S. Hart), and its "cast" included Al Jennings, the train robber who had only recently been released from jail. Tilghman was undoubtedly an efficient and courageous frontier marshal, but it is fortunate indeed that he never had to make his living as a movie director. The film is so inept that one wonders whether Tilghman had even *seen* a movie at that point. Not only did he lack knowledge of the most rudimentary techniques—some of the panning of the camera is so jerky and so appallingly performed that once, when the outlaws race out of town, the camera never does achieve anything more than a glimpse of the flying tail of the *last* horse—but he had not the faintest idea of showmanship either. (It was too early for high-grade publicity campaigns of course, but movies had to be *sold,* first to exhibitors and then to the public, and *most* films had some kind of element that could be pressed into service for advertising purposes.)

The movies had no stars of their own as yet, but "stars" from other walks of life—Buffalo Bill Cody, Lillian Russell, Queen Victoria, Annie Oakley, Sandow (Ziegfeld's strongman), Emile Zola—had been captured on what amounted to newsreel vignettes, and had been duly exploited. One would have thought that with a "celebrity" like Al Jennings in his film, Tilghman would have made some effort to spotlight him, either by making him the leader of the outlaws or by giving him a key scene. But there is not so much as a medium shot to give audiences the chance of recognizing Jennings, or even a title identifying him. He is merely one of the gang, photographed almost entirely in long shot throughout, and if not familiar with Jennings's face and slight stature from his later starring films, one wouldn't be able to pick him out of the crowd. A sadly missed opportunity, for locale and costuming *look* right, and if it weren't so totally disorganized, *The Bank Robbery* would be a valuable piece of near-documentary Americana.

Fortunately, something happened in 1908 to weld the plots of the Eastern Westerns like *The Sheriff's Love* with the geographic authenticity of *The Bank Robbery* and to add one new, vital ingredient. Gilbert M. Anderson, a beefy former photographer's model with aspirations to acting and direction, had played several small parts in *The Great Train Robbery* and in the years between had turned his hand to other Westerns, none of them markedly successful. Then, without any inkling of the impact it would have, he made a short Western entitled *Broncho Billy and the Baby,* playing the lead himself. The title and the story itself came from a published Peter B. Kyne story. Anderson neglected the niceties of acquiring legal rights to the story before he filmed it, and was soon visited by Peter B. Kyne himself. The author fortunately liked the film well enough to take no legal action, while making it plain that Anderson couldn't expect such generosity to apply in the future. (Kyne, like James Oliver Curwood, was such a prolific writer of virile action stories that not only were many of them adapted to the screen, but his name became so synonymous with action and outdoor melodrama that in time it became a kind of guarantee in itself, of more box office importance than the story. In the 1930s in particular, independent producers like Sam Katzman would buy the rights to a Kyne title and attach it to one of their own properties, which might not have the slightest resemblance to the original work!)

Broncho Billy and the Baby was a pleasing mixture of action and sentiment, with a "good badman" hero who sacrifices his chance for freedom in order to aid a stricken child—the kind of story that would later see much more ambitious service in the various versions of Peter B. Kyne's own 1913 enlargement of his original

Early French Westerns: *The Hanging at Jefferson City* (left) and *The Cowboy Kid*

story as *Three Godfathers*. (At least four major versions were made: two by John Ford, one by William Wyler, and one by Richard Boleslawsky.) It was an instant success, and the reasons were not difficult to discern, since its main departure from previous Westerns was in its concentration on a colorful hero—a man who was rugged and a law unto himself, but also possessed of the courage and nobility of Arthurian knights. The titular name of Broncho Billy stuck, and Anderson became Broncho Billy Anderson in hundreds of one- and two-reel westerns.

Until this point, Anderson had considered himself more of a director and an executive than a star, and was a partner with George Spoor in the Chicago-based Essanay company. Soon, working out of Niles in California (a little community some fifty miles from San Francisco), he would devote himself entirely to Broncho Billy Westerns. That he was not exactly young-looking *or* a handsome leading man hardly mattered. In fact, he looked more like villain Fred Kohler than he did standard leading-man types. But as he was the *first* Western star, he was creating precedents, not following or breaking them.

Anderson was a poor rider, and his bulk made him look uncomfortable on a horse, but he learned quickly and even managed a stunt or two as time went by. Big and brawny, he was well able to handle himself in the still not very demanding fight scenes. He became quite adept at rope twirling, and his large build, paw-like hands, and rough-hewn face quickly became advantages in his evolving characterization as he seemed to sense instinctively the qualities that would win laughs and

DANNY TO THE RESCUE

THE COWBOY KID

A Photo-play which appeals to every lover of Western Life, showing the exploits of the eight year old "Danny," the youngest cowboy in the world. He alone discovered the revengeful plot to entrap his sister's fiance and by means of torture force him to acknowledge himself a thief and oust him from the country. With his sister's aid he released the artist and by his splend'd riding brought the cowboys to the rescue whereby the gang of horse thieves who had so long terrorized the vicinity were finally tracked and all captured.

APPROX. 1000 FT.   G. MELIFS, 204 EAST 38th St., NEW YORK CITY   7-4-12

audience sympathy, especially his clumsiness and lack of self-confidence in dealing with the ladies. The sheepish grin and fumbling with the hat while confronting the heroine—a standard bit of business for every movie cowboy from William S. Hart to Ken Maynard to John

29

Wayne—was born in the Anderson Westerns. They were surefire audience pleasers, and while Anderson possessed none of the intense dedication to either art or a true depiction of the West that was to characterize William S. Hart's work, he was a good showman who tried the best he knew how, never just grinding out little actioners, but improving steadily as he went along.

Anderson's Westerns had strong little plots, and doubtless many of the standard "B" Western narratives were first introduced to the screen by him. His California locations gave his films a tremendous scenic advantage over the Westerns still being made in the East. While the main highway from Oakland (just across the bay from San Francisco) to Niles is now a non-ending eyesore of advertising billboards, gas stations, and used-car dealers, obscuring the pleasant hills and rural scenery behind them, the little community of Niles remains pretty much as it was. Presumably when movie production stopped there, nothing took its place. A (somewhat inaccurate) historical marker indicates where the studio once stood, and across from it is a little restaurant which looks old enough to have served the Anderson and Chaplin units. The streets are named after the stars who worked there—Chaplin, Ben Turpin, Anderson, Swanson. And the wooded canyons, conveniently right off the dusty main street, look much as they did when Anderson chased rustlers—or Chaplin skip-hopped into the iris fadeout of *The Tramp.*

Relatively few of Anderson's films survive today— *tragically* few in view of his importance—but the handful that do have a great deal of vitality, charm, and sometimes quite surprising production values. Even today, and with so little evidence, it's easy to understand his appeal.

Tom Mix came to movies with the Selig Company while Anderson was at the peak of his popularity, and made little initial impression, even though from the very beginning it was obvious that his riding and other cowboy skills were superior to Anderson's. Later, of course, Mix would become the biggest Western star of them all. Anderson's popularity waned in 1914 when William S. Hart came to the screen with a more dynamic personality, bigger budgets, and genuinely adult stories. Broncho Billy knew that he couldn't really compete, but he did go out with a flourish, making a transition to full-length features and also, near the climax of his career, producing some of his best and most polished shorts. One of these, *Shooting Mad,* is a kind of apotheosis of all the Broncho Billys, although its subtitles (as though spoken by an old-timer looking nostalgically

The Girl on the Triple X: Broncho Billy Anderson

backward) and its very last shot (a genial plagiarism from the last shot in Chaplin's *Easy Street*) suggests that its approach was partially tongue-in-cheek. Still in circulation, and frequently exhibited by film societies and film schools, it may mislead scholars into an exaggerated impression of Anderson's achievement since an archival error often causes it to be dated as 1912 instead of the correct 1918. Even for 1912, it wouldn't be as good as the best of Griffith and Ince at that date—but it *is* good, and the best of the surviving Andersons.

After 1920, Anderson returned briefly to producing with a series of Stan Laurel comedies satirizing current movie hits, and then he virtually vanished. Many assumed that he was dead. He resurfaced in the late fifties and was pressed into service as a guest star in a brace of television documentaries on the Western, and also filmed an hour-long interview. And in 1965 he joined other Western old-timers at the Paramount Studio to play a character cameo in his first and only sound, color, and wide-screen Western, *The Bounty Killer*, one of two that producer Alex Gordon made as a kind of last hurrah for veteran director Spencer Gordon Bennet and such venerable former Western stars as Tim McCoy, Johnny Mack Brown, Buster Crabbe, and Bob Steele. Exactly sixty-two years after his first appearance in a Western saloon, in *The Great Train Robbery*, Anderson was sitting in a saloon again—not spry enough to redo his

Typical examples of early Westerns that followed in the wake of Anderson, but were lacking in the star charisma: *The Final Settlement* (top) and *Thou Shalt Not Kill*

spirited dance, but with those eagle eyes as alert as ever, aware no doubt that he had pioneered everything that was taking place before the cameras. He has never been bitter at the relatively brief tenure of Broncho Billy's career, or at the sudden collapse of the Essanay Studio after its biggest star, Chaplin, left. After all, he had single-handedly established the premise of the Western star, and set up the basic formula for the series Western. The Broncho Billys were the bedrock on which D. W. Griffith, Thomas H. Ince, William S. Hart, Tom Mix, and John Ford would now build the art of the Western.

Broncho Billy Anderson

Broncho Billy's Oath (Essanay, 1913)

Broncho Billy filming an interview in New York in 1959

THREE

Pioneers of the Art: D. W. Griffith and Thomas H. Ince

Although their major contributions to the development of film as a whole far transcend the importance of the ones they made to the Western, the Western film in its early formative days nevertheless owed a huge debt to David Wark Griffith and Thomas H. Ince. Those pioneers, in their turn, learned a great deal from their work with the Western.

Both men—incidentally actors of competence but no great distinction—came to film at approximately the same time and made their most important contributions in the years from 1908 to 1913. Admittedly, Griffith's masterpieces came later, but they would not have been possible without the "language" and "grammar" of film that he evolved in those initial years, and which has been absorbed by every filmmaker since. Ince's importance was even more indisputably concentrated in those early years. The creative side of his career dwindled rapidly after 1916; he abandoned directing in 1912, although as a producer and supervisor he was to remain active and prolific until his death in the mid-twenties.

The two men (working separately at first, though from 1916 through 1919 working if not together, then side by side for the same companies, Triangle and then Paramount) complemented one another rather nicely. Griffith was wholly devoted to the art of film, to improving

the quality of screen acting, and to developing new and dynamic means of telling stories on film. He worked creatively, intuitively, and with enormous energy, but he had a poor head for business organization, and indeed little interest in that aspect of movie-making. His personal drive and magnetism would ultimately be put to good use in raising money for his increasingly ambitious productions, but once his films were made, his lack of experience in marketing prevented their making money for him, although other persons might derive huge profits from them. In any case, once a film was complete, his mind was already concerned with the next project.

Ince, though also (at first) a director, soon became much more valuable as a production supervisor, establishing methods by which productions could be organized economically in a virtual assembly-line process. He supervised his directors, rewrote scenarios, and insisted on super-detailed scripts that gave those directors every kind of assistance by outlining mood, describing sets or desired locations, suggesting how certain effects could be achieved at minimal cost, giving the cameramen tips as to the style of lighting and the color tints to be used. And, perhaps recalling the inadequacy of the "scripts" for the Westerns being made back in the East, he even provided extensive dialogue for all of the

33

David Wark Griffith

characters so that the actors would understand the motivations and nuances of their roles, even though the films were silent and such dialogue would ultimately be condensed into subtitles. Griffith, conversely, used no scripts at all—a method he followed even in his later multi-reel historical epics—working entirely by instinct and keeping not only complicated story lines but also the even more complicated editing patterns in his head.

Each method worked well for each pioneer; a Griffith film was always recognizably his, and an Ince film somehow always had his indelible stamp on it—often quite literally, since Ince was rather a vain man who loved to see his name on the credits as frequently as possible. (He was probably the only man who added his name to the leader of the film—footage at the beginning and end of each reel, never intended for projection, and seen only by the projectionist as he prepared each reel for exhibition!) This innate vanity of Ince's eventually tended to work against him, since he was not averse—when a film turned out *particularly* well—to adding his name in such a way as to suggest that he even directed it, the actual director being bypassed or given a lesser

34   Thomas H. Ince and his Indian star William Eagleshirt

credit. Since Ince was also not overly generous in the salary department, he ran out of creative people—actors and directors in particular—rather rapidly, unlike Griffith who retained the loyalty of his "family" until the very end.

If the Griffith and Ince methods presented two extremes, at least both approaches produced far better results than the compromise methods utilized by other studios. The Edison Company, continuing to produce well into the teens, seemingly never improved or updated its scripting methods of supplying the director with barely more than a list of shots which offered no help to an unimaginative director and no stimulus to a creative one. It's significant that while the rosters at Griffith and Ince teemed with names (often actors like Francis Ford, Frank Borzage, Raoul Walsh, and Donald Crisp) who quickly became major directors, at Edison, apart from Edwin S. Porter, only Alan Crosland and John Collins emerged as important directorial talents. The thespic roster, on the other hand, did little more than create Viola Dana and some useful character actors and lesser leads: Frank McGlynn, Sr., Robert Walker, Arthur Housman, Edward Earle. Apart from the early pioneering work of Porter and the later and sophisticated work of John Collins, almost everything that came out of Edison seemed stodgy and at least five years behind the times in terms of technique.

Both Griffith and Ince made a great number of one- and two-reel Westerns. Ince made them because he was showman enough to realize that they had a market, and because he had standing sets of Western towns, ranches, and saloons, and maintained a permanent company of cowboys, Indians (including some who had the potential for stardom), and trick riders, with accompanying wagons, horses, buffalo, and other livestock. To Ince's credit, he was the first to try to create stars of some of his Indian players, such as William Eagleshirt. But (although other producers, including DeMille, attempted the same ploy) it was an attempt doomed to failure. Apart from ceremonials and dances, Indians had no acting tradition, and make-believe came hard to them. Moreover, while they played "themselves" well, their value lay in their classic Indian features, making it difficult for them to play other roles. Although William Eagleshirt and other genuine Indian players made a real contribution to the Ince Westerns, the bigger Indian roles were usually played by actors as diverse as the Japanese Sessue Hayakawa or the Caucasians Francis Ford and Ann Little, all of whom of course, as part of the Ince stock company, could play non-Indian roles as well.

Griffith was attracted to Westerns (though they occupied a relatively small percentage of his output) because they provided him with an ideal framework on which to

Griffith's *Ramona* (Biograph, 1910)

hang stories of action and suspense, and to exploit space and landscape. On the one hand, even within the limitations of one- and two-reelers, he was making films that had something to say culturally or socially: commentary on current political or social attitudes, or adaptations of literary classics. On the other, he was honing and extending his revolutionary editing patterns with films that could loosely be described as "chase and rescue" films, whether they were Civil War stories, crime thrillers, train melodramas, or Westerns. Most of these had simple story lines: a few deft scenes established period and milieu, and then right away would jump into one basic situation which would be milked for suspense and action. While the plots themselves were simple, there was often considerable subtlety in characterization, which added depth to essentially one-dimensional stories. The Western, with its already established premise of "good" guys besieged by villains or Indians, and a climactic race to the rescue, provided Griffith with the perfect background for his experiments with film grammar, and the still wild and rugged hills and canyons of Hollywood enabled them to be made on the spot, without time-consuming location jaunts. Griffith clearly loved the chase and the excitement it created; he continued to use it throughout his career, constantly expanding, developing, polishing, so that in later epics like *Orphans of the Storm* (1921) and *America* (1924) it would consume literally the final third of the whole film. However, in these early Westerns, he used the chase not just for its own automatic thrill, but also as a way by which audiences could become emotionally involved, making them participants in the action rather than mere spectators to it. Just how advanced Griffith was in his filmmaking ideas and how little they were understood by his contemporaries (until their validity was proven in dollars and cents terms by the fantastic success in 1915 of *The Birth of a Nation*) can be demonstrated by a comparison of two Westerns almost identical in structure but poles apart in style, excitement, and cinematic sophistication: the Edison Company's *The Corporal's Daughter* (1915) and Griffith's *Fighting Blood* of four years *earlier*.

The Corporal's Daughter, utilizing East Coast scenery tolerably well, was considered an average, acceptable product in its day (partly because what astute "criticism" there was seemed to be limited largely to the trade publications catering to exhibitors; criticism aimed at the buying public was more concerned with the full-length features, and the shorts, apart from the Keystone comedies, warranted little attention). The film is almost an object lesson in how to take seemingly foolproof material and even in the brief running time of ten minutes make it seem dull and overlong. The characters seem to be literally flung on to the screen without any kind of establishing scenes, relying entirely on inter titles to tell us who the characters are and of their relationships to others. There are no close-ups of their faces to indicate their emotions, no seemingly extraneous "bits of business" to humanize them and get the audience to care. What little suspense the story has (a cavalry troop cut off by Indians; the hero preparing to sacrifice himself, mistakenly believing that the girl he loves is in love with another) is undercut constantly by titles that tell us what is *going* to happen. Threatening Indians ride into static camera setups and halt just in front of the lens to perform their essential bit of action. We can't always believe in what the titles *tell* us; one such informs us that the outnumbered cavalry are gallantly fighting back against overwhelming odds, and we *then* see *several* cavalrymen strategically placed behind rocks high on a hill, shooting down at considerably fewer Indians! When the relieving troop races to the rescue from its fort, just the slightest shift of camera position would have hidden the fact that the fort was built adjacent to a modern concrete highway with a storm drain distressingly obvious. And the rescue itself is accomplished without any excitement-building crosscutting. The troop suddenly appears on the scene, hero and heroine embrace, and the film cuts to "The End" without any neat little comic or romantic touch to round it all off.

Viewing *The Corporal's Daughter* today (the title is quite meaningless and has no bearing on the story line), it is hard to believe that audiences could have found it acceptable in the light of a film like Griffith's *Fighting Blood* and the even bigger and better Griffith Westerns—to say nothing of those from Ince—that immediately followed it. In *Fighting Blood* (in which the inter titles never anticipate the action, but do constantly provide additional information and interest-arousing

dialogue), Griffith wins audience sympathy instantly by showing us a likable family of pioneers with a large contingent of children eking out a hard existence. The father is a Civil War veteran and something of a martinet; he even drills his youngsters military fashion. In a few deft scenes, Griffith sketches in their warmth as a family unit and their innate patriotism, while establishing one child as mischievous and the eldest son (played by Robert Harron) as being in love with a neighbor across the hills, and as something of a rebel against parental authority. Well within the first third of this one-reel film, separate subplots have evolved. The Sioux are on the warpath. The son, having fallen out with his father (Mother takes *his* side, creating another level of subliminal conflict), has gone to visit his girl, has become involved in some skirmishing with the Indians, and has decided to get help from a cavalry post.

At one point, as he tries to mount his horse to ride for help, it shies away, probably scared by all the shooting and noise. Griffith, possibly having no time (or excess footage) to reshoot the scene, just uses as much of it as he can, cuts away to a different angle of the fighting, and then comes back to find the hero safely on his horse—a bit of instinctive editing that probably never even occurred to the Edison director confronted with that highway drain! From here *Fighting Blood* builds constantly in both excitement and size of action, cutting from Harron as he races for help (and engages three Indians in a running horseback duel) to the settlers fighting off the Indians. And even in these extremely well-staged action scenes, Griffith never forgets to *continue* to engage audience sympathy: two of the children cower under the bed, as excited as they are frightened—a foreshadowing of a similar scene of Mae Marsh and Miriam Cooper reacting to a guerrilla raid in *The Birth of a Nation*—while an older girl pantomimes that she can't shoot a gun because the noise hurts her ears, but that she'll help out by loading the rifle for Pa. The cabin is set afire; water to fight it is getting low.

The hero meanwhile has encountered a cavalry troop, which races to the rescue. Imaginative camera placement by Griffith and his superb cinematographer Billy Bitzer here manages to suggest that the troop of possibly fifty men is actually hundreds of riders by having the audience first see a long line of riders racing to the right on the screen from a great distance away, and then a few moments later the apparent front rank of that line gallops into the forefront of the frame. This was a shot that Griffith repeated in his 1924 epic, *America*, and in an identical context. Now Griffith cuts back more and more between the battle and the rescue troop, and when the cavalry finally races on to the scene, he has his camera high atop a nearby hill, creating a vast panorama which takes in the cabin, the encircling Indians, and the onrushing cavalry in extreme yet crystal-clear long shots. To round off his story, Griffith stages an emotional reunion between father and son and, for a final, audience-pleasing fillip, has the now relieved and beaming children emerge from under the bed onto a cabin floor realistically covered with spent cartridges. *Fighting Blood* may well have been the best-directed and best-edited film of 1911, although with so much early material permanently lost, *positive* claims such as that would be a little foolhardy.

Even though prior to 1913 Griffith divided his time between New York and Hollywood, he kept the Western themes for his wintertime West Coast sojourn. From simple little dramas like *Friends, Broken Ways,* and *The Goddess of Sagebrush Gulch,* he progressed to spectacular films on epic themes: *The Last Drop of Water* (1911), a precursor of *The Covered Wagon; The Battle of Elderbush Gulch,* a superb action film that was almost a dry run for *The Birth of a Nation,* featuring many of the same players (including Lillian Gish, Mae Marsh, Bobby Harron, and Henry B. Walthall) and notable also for the remarkable savagery of its Indian fighting scenes; and perhaps best of all, *The Massacre,* a stark yet poetic film loosely based on the Custer massacre. It was decidedly sympathetic to the Indian point of view, and as were many of the later Griffith films, it was also a parable on the tragedy and futility of war. The massacre of the title is not total. One by one the white settlers fall, gambler and priest dying side by side. When the rescuing cavalry finally arrives on the scene of carnage, it finds everyone seemingly dead—until a hand waves feebly from beneath a pile of bodies. The heroine (Blanche Sweet) and the baby that she clutches to her breast are the only survivors. Although Griffith and Ince both made Westerns in which the Indians were the standard, mass villains, they also made a great many that were sympathetic to the Indian and critical of the whites' actual if indirect policy of extermination. Interestingly too, there was a middle ground, in which Indians were shown to engage in savagery and torture but could be understandable human beings at the same time, a realization that Indian characteristics and culture could be entirely separate from and incompatible with white standards, a gray area that more recent villains, as in *Dances With Wolves,* seem unwilling to acknowledge.

Ince's films in particular were meticulous not only in documenting the Indian way of life but also in establishing him (and *her,* since Indian *women* were very present in the Ince films) as an individual with recognizable emotions. *The Indian Massacre* (known in Europe as *The Heart of an Indian*), a little masterpiece of 1912 directed by and starring Francis Ford, was one of the very best of these films, stressing the courage and tenacity of the white settlers, but emphasizing most of all the relentless extermination of the Indian. Its closing scene—the silhouette of an Indian woman praying and mourning beneath the wood-frame burial pyre of her dead child—was as beautifully composed and photographed as anything in later John Ford films. Even allowing for the input of Ince himself, the importance of Francis Ford to these early Westerns cannot be underestimated, though conversely it is difficult to sustain or analyze, since relatively little of his large output from this period still exists. As an actor, Ford had an ability to underplay; as a director, he was expert in staging action and had a fine eye for pictorial composition and use of landscape. His career was an enigma. Possibly like Michael Curtiz, who seemed to work well only within the Warner Bros. system, Francis Ford might have needed the crew, the short film format, and the production methods employed at Ince to function well. Away from Ince, he became both a lackluster actor and director, sometimes in the latter capacity showing flashes of inspiration but no more. By the early twenties, just as brother John was carving a name for himself, Francis was already reduced to working on second-rate independent Westerns and serials. Some of his films, such as *Blazing the Trail* (1912), contained scenes that were (on a bigger scale) repeated almost verbatim in such later John Ford works as *She Wore a Yellow Ribbon* (1949). They *must* have had considerable influence on John Ford, who was just then about to begin a Hollywood career as an actor, yet he never acknowledged such an influence, gave no help to Francis's sagging career in the twenties, and from the thirties on, offered his brother considerable and effective employment in character and comedy roles in his films, but again witheld the kind of major help that could have restored some of Francis's reputation. (He did have bigger roles in non-Ford films, and continued as an actor until his death in 1953.) However, John Ford was known for unexplained feuds, and his later neglect of former stars Harry Carey and Hoot Gibson was equally bizarre and inexplicable.

Influenced by the novels of James Fenimore Cooper, stories of the American Indian were extremely popular in the early days of Westerns, and indeed throughout the entire silent period. Many eschewed Indian-white conflict entirely to deal with stories of wholly Indian content—simple romances like *Little Dove's Romance* or Griffith's 1912 *A Squaw's Love,* in which comedienne-to-be Mabel Normand engaged in some stunt leaps and underwater swimming in a story of intertribal rivalry. Many of the non-Griffith and non-Ince Indian films had a sameness to them, the Pocahontas story being updated on more than one occasion, but since many of them were

Griffith's *Goddess of Sagebrush Gulch* (Biograph, 1912) with Blanche Sweet

photographed by Arthur Miller (who would later become one of Ford's top cameramen in his later sound period at 20th Century-Fox), they were visually quite pleasing.

Direct adaptations of Fenimore Cooper stories (*Leatherstocking, Deerslayer*) were naturally popular, although since they were set along the Eastern seaboard and often shot there, not strictly speaking Westerns in a geographic sense. Already in this period, the movies were exploiting the theme (popular in novels and in such stage plays as *Braveheart*) of the "college" Indian returning to his people hoping to bring them the benefits of the white man's education, but being rejected by them—and at the same time being unable to return to the white man's cities. The impossibility of a Indian-white romantic alliance was also a key plot element in these films.

Thomas Ince certainly ran a definite second to Griffith in terms of technique and directorial finesse, but his stories were strong, running to a multiplicity of characters and presenting themes of moral regeneration and self-sacrifice, these "heavy" elements being more than offset by the skill of the spaciously staged action sequences. Movies were still not considered "respectable" in many quarters and constantly sought to win approval by teaching valuable "moral lessons" along with their entertainment. Ince's Westerns were especially functional in this respect, being full of missionary ministers or evangelical badmen who reformed and conquered the lawless elements, or cowards and moral weaklings who

Kate Bruce and Lillian Gish in Griffith's *The Battle of Elderbush Gulch* (Biograph, 1913)

"found themselves" out West. The obvious distinction between good and evil was achieved by pitting church against saloon in such early Ince Westerns as *Past Redemption* or such later William S. Hart features as *Hell's Hinges* and *The Return of Draw Egan*, both of 1916. Moral retribution in Ince Westerns was surprisingly severe. The heroine of *The Woman* marries bigamously only to raise money for her desperately ill husband, this after having taken a bad spill in a creditably staged land rush in an effort to win land in a warm climate where his tuberculosis might be cured. When he dies soon afterward, she feels that she has betrayed both him and her illegal gambler husband, and her only solution is suicide. The heroine of *Past Redemption* had sold firewater to the Indians (led astray by love for a no-good father) and had shot down a cavalryman or two. She was thoroughly "saved" by the Church, but when the minister fell in love with her and wanted to marry her, she felt so thoroughly unworthy of him that the only way out was to leave him and trek across the desert, dying of thirst. (The mortality rate in Ince's Civil War films was even higher, including a likeable little drummer boy whose death seemed totally gratuitous!)

The stress on unhappy endings to many of the Ince Westerns was certainly unconventional, but was perhaps hardly as daring as it might seem today. When seen individually, they indeed seem starkly dramatic and even uncommercial, but as a group, the tragic denouements of so many of them seem a rather pointless contrivance. Ince in fact was treating tragedy as a gimmick, using it for a shock ending much as Griffith used the chase for an action ending. Too, the star system was still in its relative infancy. Prior to William S. Hart and Charles Ray, Ince had no players of major importance. Audiences were not sufficiently familiar with the likes of Tom Chatterton and Francis Ford to regard them as favorites or to care too much when they were unexpectedly killed off.

The majority of Ince's Westerns were either cowboy-Indian or cavalry-Indian stories, though occasionally, as in *In the Tennessee Hills*, a Western-type plot but minus Indians, would be transported to a differing locale. They were often surprisingly elaborate in the scale of their action and the number of extras and horses employed, and often, as in the case of *The Invaders*, running to three reels instead of the customary two. Ince's canny business sense told him that it was worth spending extra money on big action or battle scenes and to shoot them from a variety of angles, since these could then be cut into other films with similar themes and players. He became the first producer to economize deliberately via the use of stock footage, something that became a fine art in the last days of the "B" Western in the mid 1950s, when some 75 percent of the action material would be

War on the Plains (Ince, 1912)

stock lifted from other pictures. The impressive size of Ince's films also made it feasible for entrepreneurs of the 1920s to reissue them, cashing in on Ince's then more famous name, and expand them by cutting in related footage from other Ince films, or creating simple new subplots with new players, shooting additional scenes to pad the overall footage. By this means, two 1912 Ince two-reelers, *War on the Plains* and *Custer's Last Stand*, mysteriously reappeared on the independent market in 1925 as the five-reel feature *Custer's Last Fight*, credited to Ince as supervisor even though he was now dead. Like ingenuity was employed in reediting quite disparate Tom Mix shorts for the Selig Company to reintroduce them as "new" features once Mix had achieved major stardom at Fox. The polish and scope of Ince's original action footage can be attested to by the fact that it was *still* being used as stock to pad out new "B" Westerns (*Roll Wagons Roll, Buffalo Bill in Tomahawk Territory*) in the forties and fifties. The graininess of the much duplicated stock and the differing speeds gave the game away of course, but stylistically it was so much superior to the cheaply staged "matching" new footage that few complained.

Ethel Grandin in scenes from *Blazing the Trail* (Ince, 1912)

In 1913—the year of his biggest short Western, *The Battle of Elderbush Gulch*—Griffith left Biograph and New York to move to Hollywood and the less-restricting Reliance company, taking with him most of his big stars and cameraman Bitzer. He had big plans, and for him the Western had served its purpose. Indeed, for the rest of his career, he would personally direct only one more bona fide Western, *Scarlet Days* (1919), one of his least successful features. It was hardly more than a standard Biograph two-reel plot expanded to four times its length and climaxed by a traditional last-reel fight and race to the rescue. But his 1924 *America* (dealing with the Revolutionary War on the Eastern seaboard, and containing some magnificently staged Indian fighting and battle scenes) owed much to his early apprenticeship to the Western, while his protégé directors Christy Cabanne and Chester and Sidney Franklin made several Westerns in the post–*Birth of a Nation* period, carefully retaining the structural and editing techniques perfected by their mentor. Cabanne's *Martyrs of the Alamo* (telling of the fall of the Alamo and Sam Houston's

The Invaders (Ince, 1912)

The Deserter (Ince, 1912) with Francis Ford (John's brother)

subsequent routing of Santa Anna) and the Franklins' beautifully-made *Let Katy Do It* are typical of 1915 Westerns that acknowledge and benefit from Griffith's influence throughout.

At the same time, Ince, though no longer a personal director, was on the threshold of unwittingly making one of the greatest contributions of all to the future well-

being of the Western. In 1914, he would introduce to movie audiences a veteran stage actor, William S. Hart. Hart had been associated with classic theatre for so long that to this day the legend persists that the S in his name stood for Shakespeare. (Actually Hart's middle name was Surrey, a name deriving from an idiom, not from the

The Indian Massacre (Ince, 1912) with Ann Little and Francis Ford

The Battle of the Redmen (Ince, 1912)

high-toned little horse-drawn carts or from the British county. The phrase "on the Surrey side" indicated a certain obstinacy, and it provided a most apt middle name for Hart!)

Most stage players brought to the screen in the early days of full-length silent features failed badly. Usually they were too old—and looked even older on screen—or they were unable to adapt to the looser, more under-played style demanded by the screen. Once their initial novelty wore off, they returned to the boards or contented themselves with character roles rather than leads. The three most notable exceptions to this generalization in the 1914 to 1916 years were John Barrymore, Douglas Fairbanks, Sr., and William S. Hart. Hart was the first of the three to make movies and to establish an international reputation through them. The French were especially enthusiastic about him, and dubbed him "Rio Jim." As the Westerns moved out of the one- and two-reel time-killing category and moved into full-length fea-

Desert Gold (Ince, 1914) with Clara Williams, Frank Borzage, Bob Kortman

A typical Ince saloon set; William S. Hart in foreground

44

A much-later reissue poster for Ince's 1912 special

Griffith's only feature-length Western: *Scarlet Days* (Paramount, 1919) with Richard Barthelmess and Carol Dempster

tures, they needed a guiding hand desperately—not just a gifted director or a colorful star, but also someone who loved the West, understood it, and could mould its screen interpretation with sympathy and affection. Bill Hart was a perfect example of exactly the right man being in the right place at precisely the right time.

Scarlet Days: Barthelmess and George Fawcett (center)

The Return of Draw Egan (1916): William S. Hart with perennial saloon vamp, Louise Glaum

FOUR

William S. Hart

In 1914, thanks primarily to Mary Pickford and, by the end of the year, Charlie Chaplin, the star system was just beginning to evolve systematically. Prior to William S. Hart's arrival on the scene, only Tom Mix and Broncho Billy Anderson could be said to represent the Western hero on screen: Anderson in short Westerns that were essentially of Eastern conception, and Tom Mix in fairly crudely made films for Selig, many of them pure comedy, that did nothing to harness, let alone exploit, his unique personality. Despite the high quality of his now abandoned short Westerns, Griffith had never tried to develop a single Western player with recognizable characteristics and costume that carried over from picture to picture. Rather he used his regular roster of players— Bobby Harron, Lionel Barrymore, Charles West, Henry B. Walthall, Joseph Graybill, Walter Miller, Alfred Paget, and others—to enact Easterners, Northerners, Southerners, and Westerners with fine impartiality. Only Harry Carey, in Biograph shorts like *The Wanderer* and *Broken Ways*, seemed to fall naturally into Western roles, and of course as soon as he left Biograph and joined Universal, he would specialize in them.

To many, William S. Hart, who so quickly filled the Western star void, is still the embodiment of the "strong, silent," often self-sacrificing cowboy hero on screen, a powerful if nostalgic stereotype, and no more. Admittedly, one's first introduction to Hart (depending, of course, on the film one sees) often does tend to confirm that impression. But how inaccurate it is, and what an injustice it does to a man who was not just a star but, together with John Ford, a major force in the shaping and development of the Western genre.

Hart was already a mature man, with a substantial theatrical experience behind him, when he came to the movies, a medium he had very little respect for, thanks largely to the unrealistic and juvenile depictions of the West that he had seen in them. His first movie—a supporting role only—was done largely as a favor to old friend Ince, and with no thought of its launching a new career for him. But his impact on both critics and audiences was such that it was clear to Ince that Hart had a big future in Western movies. Although Hart had left Hollywood to return to the theatre, Ince called him back—and Hart, glad of the opportunity to put the "Real West" on the screen (or at least, his conception of it) accepted with alacrity.

Not quite the authentic Man of the West that he, in later years, loved to pose as (through a sheer admiration for that pose, not out of a desire to deceive), Hart had done much of his growing up in the West, accompanying his father on business trips. He had seen the last days of frontier gunfighting firsthand, had a baby brother buried on the plains, and knew and loved the West and its way of life, even if as an observer rather than a participant he tended to romanticize it.

With producer Ince's backing, Hart's dream of putting the poetry and austerity of the West on screen was quickly realized, to a critical acclaim and popular success that neither of them had expected to arrive so rapidly. Hart was somewhat of an opportunist. At one point (later in his career, when he was able to exert a little more clout on his own behalf) such hostility existed between Ince and him that he refused to let his pinto pony Fritz (the first of many movie horses whose own "fan" following contributed to the success of his master) appear in any of the movies from which Ince would profit. Hart even took out big trade paper advertisements to advise exhibitors of Fritz's "retirement." But regardless of the business and personal differences between the two men (differences that Hart noted with satisfaction later on were resolved or at least lessened before Ince died), Ince deserves a great deal of credit for giving Hart his first opportunity and for having the foresight to recognize his potential and his individuality, giving him a free hand with his films. Since Hart was a novice as both a screen actor and a director, and all of his films, even from the beginning, seem assured and disciplined, one must also assume that Ince gave him a great deal of useful advice and practical help while he (Hart) was still getting his feet wet as a filmmaker.

Rapidly graduating from two-reelers to features, Hart surrounded himself with a stock company of players (Robert McKim, Louise Glaum, Robert Kortman, and crowd "extras" such as John Gilbert and Jean Hersholt, who would soon find stardom on their own), writers (C. Gardner Sullivan was the best, ideal for the gritty, lean stories in which Hart excelled and he remained a major screenwriter for many years), directors (Lambert Hillyer, Reginald Barker, Cliff Smith) and cameramen (especially the brilliant Joseph August). But Hart was the guiding spirit behind all of his films, a collaborator on the scripts, and frequently the actual, not just the nominal, director. Because his films were so dominated by his personality as an actor, Hart's skill as a director has often been either underrated or ignored entirely. By 1915, the art of direction was still relatively new, partly because film was seen as an alternative to and imitator of theatre, and telling a story coherently was seen as more important than devising effective new means of pictorializing a story. D. W. Griffith was still considered supreme, and there were only a handful of really accomplished directors to rival him, often on quite different levels: Maurice Tourneur, Cecil B. DeMille, Herbert Brenon, Raoul Walsh, and Charles Chaplin.

It's interesting that Chaplin and Hart made the most rapid progress of the newer directors, perhaps because they were looking at film from three angles: as theatre, as a vehicle for their performing talents, *and* as a way of breaking *away* from theatrical conventions. Chaplin's progress was undoubtedly the more remarkable: each subsequent series—first Keystone, then Essanay, and then Mutual—between 1914 and 1916 literally doubled the sophistication and comic effectiveness of the series that it was replacing. Hart (an older man) reached his peak by 1916; after that there was continued skill, but little further development. On the other hand, he made the transference from shorts to features in only two years; Chaplin, working more cautiously and advancing through three- and four-reelers, took six years.

Even though Hart's range was narrower, he certainly belongs in that illustrious group of the half-dozen directors who in one way or another could be said to rival Griffith in the 1914–16 period. Hart's use of landscape was unique, his control and organization of mob and mass action scenes often superb, and he managed to extract extremely subtle underplaying from the best of his leading ladies. While he was never one for showy technique—especially technique that would seem to throw a conceited spotlight on to the star—he understood the tools of film and when best to use them. Though he frequently panned his camera to make the most of panoramic locations, he rarely used a *mobile* camera. But when he did, it was for a purpose—as in *The Return of Draw Egan* when, after a long period of enforced delay and indecision, he finally strides from his sheriff's office for a showdown with the villain, and, briefly, the camera tracks back in front of him to underline his resolution. His costumes and livery trappings were accurate, the ramshackle Western towns and their inhabitants like unretouched Matthew Brady photographs, the sense of dry heat ever present (an effect that was softened and glamorized with the introduction of panchromatic film in the twenties), and clouds of dust everywhere. When Hart rode into town from the desert, he was often literally grimed with it. Directors less concerned with authenticity soon devised the trick of wetting down the ground so that riding scenes would be cleaner and crisper and the dust wouldn't rise.

Hart was almost certainly the first director of Westerns to use landscape symbolically. He didn't reserve the most rugged scenery for a spectacular action climax—a device used to good effect in some of Fox's early sound Westerns—but instead he made the land itself the dominant motif in his films. His skylines were always *very* high in the frame; little of the sky was shown, and rugged plains and mountains filled some 80 percent of the frame. Man—good and bad—was dominated by the land, in keeping with Hart's belief that the West would

Hell's Hinges (Triangle, 1916): Hart prevents the town rowdies from disrupting the church service

bring out the best in strong men, and the worst in the weak. His chase scenes were invariably shown in extreme long shots, pursued and pursuers looking almost puny as they followed their destinies against the awesome space of the West. John Ford, in contrast, took a more optimistic approach. To him, the West was there to be conquered and civilized by man; his horizon lines were usually *low* in the frame. The land was dominated by expanses of sky, and man linked the two by being silhouetted against the skyline—especially when man was represented by the cavalry, banners flying, rousing military music emphasising the themes of a westward march of conquest, and Technicolor (in such later films as *She Wore a Yellow Ribbon* and *The Horse Soldiers*) completing the wholly romanticized image.

Hart's films were the first "adult" Westerns in the truest sense of that much abused term. His zeal did, admittedly, occasionally lead him astray; his sentimentality began to intrude too much into his later films, and even basic honesty can become a cliché when presented via situations, characters, and a style of subtitling that are repeated in almost every film. (It's a pity that sound films hadn't arrived two decades earlier; Hart's rich theatrical voice would have counterbalanced his sometimes mannered acting style, while the natural sounds of the West—the creaking of harnesses and wagons, the hurly-burly of saloon and campfire camaraderie, the documentarian sounds of wagon treks or trail drives—would have

Hell's Hinges: A typical C. Gardner Sullivan inter title expressing a typical Hart emotion

minimized the often pantomimic quality of physical action.)

However, Hart's clichés—and pet themes—were such personal ones that they never became absorbed into the mainstream of Western film clichés except in terms of contemporary satire. (Hart's almost evangelical Westerner was so intense that he was an easy target for

Hell's Hinges: Hart, a gentleman with the leading ladies, has no compunction about throttling vamp Louise Glaum after, on the villain's orders, she has seduced the minister

Hell's Hinges: Hart leaps into the saddle near the film's climax

comedy; producers Mack Sennett and Hal Roach, and stars Mack Swain, Will Rogers, and Buster Keaton were among the many who satirized Hart with wit and often telling accuracy.) He loved his sister dearly, and a recurring theme in several of his films called on him to avenge the seduction, death, or other betrayal of a sister. To Hart, every woman was a lady, to be revered and protected with the chivalry of old. But woe betide the saloon girl to whom Hart gave the benefit of the doubt and who then betrayed him; her status as a woman wouldn't save her from a vigorous manhandling!

To modern eyes, one of the more fragile of the Hart clichés was the way his "good badman" reformed almost from the first glimpse of his leading lady. "One who is evil looking for the first time on that which is good" is how an inter title in *Hell's Hinges* put it, to be followed shortly thereafter by "I reckon God ain't wantin' me much, ma'am, but when I look at you, I feel I've been ridin' the wrong trail." Sometimes the reformation could be mutual: in *The Narrow Trail* Hart is smitten by his first glance at the girl in the stagecoach he is holding up, not knowing that she is a "fancy lady" from the East, albeit one forced into a life of unspecified vice by an exploitive uncle. In turn, she too reforms, insisting on abandoning life in San Francisco for "the clean, honest mountains" of the West. Hart, a supreme sentimentalist, not only identified with his screen image, but cherished his leading ladies offscreen as well as on, to the extent of proposing marriage to all of them who weren't already hitched. Only one of them, Winifred Westover, liked the idea. A horrified Hart tried to back out, but she pursued him with grim determination. The wedding took place, but the marriage was not a happy one and ended in divorce. It also produced a son who failed to live up to Hart's rather rigid requirements and expectations.

Since Hart had an unerring eye for beauty and aristocratic bearing in his leading ladies (Bessie Love, Jane Novak, Eva Novak, Anna Q. Nilsson), his instantaneous conversations were often quite convincing in individual films, but became rather amusing when the situation was repeated verbatim in too many films. The ploy also fell down sometimes when rather plain heroines like Sylvia Bremer and Clara Williams were his nemesis. "A different kind of smile, sweet, honest, and trustful, and seeming to say, 'How do you do, friend?' " was the masterly inter title that C. Gardner Sullivan created to mask the bland expression, excessive eye makeup, and hesitant twitch of the lips with which Miss Williams confronted Hart, and whose smile frankly seemed to be saying no such thing. Hart's gallantry did have some curious tangents, however.

As a change of pace (as for example in *The Testing Block*, in which Hart played the leader of a band of outlaws "collected by the broom that swept out Hell"), he'd get roaring drunk or totally disillusioned with women (or both) and force the virginal heroine into marriage with him at the point of a gun. However, such behavior always took place at the beginning of the film, providing ample time for remorse and self-sacrifice on the part of Hart, and allowing the girl equally ample time to fall genuinely in love with him and present him with a child.

Hart's batting average was high. His early features were the best and tightest. He would spend roughly a month shooting a five-reel feature on a budget of approximately $14,000, with his own salary as producer/ star/director/writer, or any combination thereof, never more than and often considerably less than $2,000. No wonder that Ince made a small fortune, and that Hart felt himself ill used. Nevertheless, his resentment never reflected itself in his films, nor did he ever make any attempt to skimp on production values to steer more of the budget in his direction. He kept turning out Westerns—and an occasional non-Western—of quality and excitement, with titles like *The Desert Man, The Apostle of Vengeance, The Aryan, The Cradle of Courage,* and *The Square Deal Man,* in which he played characters with such colorful names as "Ice" Harding, "Blaze" Tracey, "Square Deal" Sanderson, "Truthful" Tulliver, and Three Word Brand—the last almost a Damon Runyon persona with his trademark of biting out terse

The Testing Block (Paramount, 1920): Hart (at his peak) with Eva Novak and Richard Headrick

A fight scene from *Three Word Brand* (Paramount, 1921)

answers in only three words! Sometimes, as in *Hell's Hinges*, a kind of Western *Sadie Thompson*, he included plot elements (the systematic seduction and destruction of a weak minister by the town trollop) that even today would be considered daring in a Western. Action was not necessarily a prime requirement in the Hart Westerns (as a genre it was still sufficiently new for the locale and the colorful characterizations to be appealing enough in themselves) though he was a good rider and a rugged athlete who rarely used doubles in his fight scenes. The much vaunted "classic" fight in *The Spoilers* (1914) between William Farnum and Tom Santschi actually pales beside some of the brawls that Hart staged, particularly one in *The Narrow Trail* (1917) in which, disillusioned by the discovery that the girl he has followed to San Francisco is "no good," mad at the world in general, and particularly irked at Bob Kortman who has him marked as a shanghai victim, he cleans out an entire waterfront dive of assorted thugs. One of the toughest scraps seen on the screen to that date, it moved France's Jean Cocteau to describe it:

> A little masterpiece . . . in the center of a half-blinded and horrified crowd, the two figures circle . . . the camera draws back, moves nearer, rises higher. The naked bodies, slippery with blood, take

Hart as *Wild Bill Hickok* (Paramount, 1923)

on a sort of phosphorescence. Two mad creatures are at grips, trying to kill each other. They look as though they were made of metal. Are they kingfishers or seals, or men from the moon, or Jacob with the angel? Is it not some Buddha, this great naked figure which falls to its knees and dies there like a thousand little fishes in a lake of mercury? M. Ince may be proud of himself, for a spectacle such as this seems to equal the world's greatest literature.

Whatever Cocteau was smoking at the time may well have contributed to this floridly enthusiastic description. Hart did not shoot additional footage for foreign versions, and in the excellent prints of this film that survive there are no "naked bodies slippery with blood." But in a very general sense, the scene *does* justify Cocteau's rhapsodic response. *The Narrow Trail* was Hart's first film for his own company under a new deal with Paramount, and though Ince was still marginally and contractually involved, Hart was enjoying total autonomy and clearly wanted to show *just* what he could do in this film. Apart from being a virtual apotheosis of all the Hart "good badman" movies, it had more physical action than usual, including a splendidly done climactic horse race. But many of the Hart films, and not to their

Tumbleweeds (United Artists, 1925): Hart's final film, and his first use of a comic partner, Lucien Littlefield

disadvantage, often tended to be stronger on plot and characterization than on fast action. This hardly mattered up to 1918, when his formula was still fresh, and his films had such strong plots and tight construction that interest never flagged. But from 1920 on, the repetition began to show and the pace slackened. Hart, after all, was in his late forties when he made his *first* film; now his age began to be emphasized in plots that contained romantic liaisons with girls at least twenty years his junior. As if to stress Hart's he-man virility, these were never May-December romances but always boy-girl love stories. (While this was acceptable in the fifties and sixties, when long-popular stars like Clark Gable, Cary Grant, and John Wayne were aging and audiences were reluctant to let them go, it was a very different matter in the twenties. Women stars especially were considered "over the hill" when they reached thirty; male stars of exceptional popularity might hold out until they were fifty. These were not just standards applied to Holly-

wood *stars;* they were standards considered to apply to life in general, and movie plots of the silent period reflected those criteria of age.)

Hart's films slowed down—at the precise time that Tom Mix's popularity was in its ascendancy backed by a formula of nonstop action, circuslike stunts and fun, and virtually no sentiment or romance. Hart had never liked action purely for its own sake, and apart from isolated highlight moments—a horseback leap from a high cliff or through a plate-glass window—his films were extremely sparing in their stuntwork. If there was a spectacular horse fall, the chances are that it was a genuine accident, and having captured it on film, Hart would keep it in. (This supposition is more than borne out by horse falls in films like *Hell's Hinges*, where the camera was not placed to advantage to catch the action, and the fall had to be "built" by sometimes awkwardly cut-in reaction shots.) In his last film, *Tumbleweeds* (1925), one shot of a covered wagon approaching a rocky gully was

Wild Bill Hickok: Hickok visits General Custer and announces he is coming out of retirement—to clean up Dodge City

Detail shot from the land rush sequence of *Tumbleweeds*

faked via a trick glass-shot, while a wagon crash was done in two separate shots. Neither scene benefited from the services of a stuntman, and neither scene was particularly exciting. Hart felt that elaborate stunt work smelled of trickery; he'd settle for a lesser thrill but greater conviction (although the latter did not necessarily follow automatically). But in the wake of Tom Mix's Westerns for Fox, Hart's films seemed increasingly turgid and old-fashioned. Now that he was making fewer but bigger films for Paramount release, the studio felt that it had a right to ask him to move with the times, to "modernize" the style of his films and arrest their diminishing box office returns. Hart refused. Grimly sticking to his guns and his convictions, he insisted on making Westerns his way or not at all. To his credit, while he may have misjudged public support for his brand of film, he faltered badly only once. *Singer Jim McKee* had a rambling, near incoherent story line, a plethora of overdone sentiment, and a total disregard for time and logic. Hart, already a veteran outlaw when the story gets under way, reforms, raises to womanhood the baby of a fallen comrade, ultimately marries her, serves time in jail, and returns to her and their child in what must conservatively have been his 110th year!

Hart's other later films of the early twenties were, however, slow-paced or not, good movies that carried the mark of his own integrity. His *Wild Bill Hickok*—prefaced by a title in which the star apologized to his audience for looking more like Bill Hart than Bill Hickok!—had two very well staged gunfight highlights and a reasonable if romanticized respect for the historical facts, even bringing in an ignored (by Hollywood) period in Hickok's life when he was losing his eyesight and for obvious reasons of self-preservation had to conceal the fact.

Hart's last film, in 1925, was his only genuine epic, *Tumbleweeds* (although the success of the earlier, smaller-scale *Wagon Tracks* had spurred Paramount to produce *The Covered Wagon*). Despite one minor concession to popular appeal—the addition of a comic sidekick in Lucien Littlefield—and some too protracted comic and romantic interludes with the heroine (Barbara Bedford) in which Hart's coyness was a little too forced, it was a fine film, worthy of being ranked with *The Covered Wagon,* though admittedly inferior to *The Iron Horse.* Directed by Hart and King Baggott, *Tumbleweeds* had as its highlight a massively spectacular reconstruction of the Cherokee Strip land rush, which was not only splendidly staged and photographed, but also edited with a mathematical precision and rhythm

In 1932, Paramount used Hart to publicize—and Americanize—Maurice Chevalier

worthy of Eisenstein. Later land rush sequences, and specifically those in the two versions of *Cimarron*, borrowed a great deal from this, and while they were slicker and *looked* bigger because of their utilization of panoramic long shots taken from high camera cranes, they also looked like what they were: Hollywood reconstructions. Hart's version had the look of a contemporary newsreel, even to its retention of one or two awkward panning shots where the camera temporarily lost the rider it was following. Although Hart was now fifty-nine, he did all of his own riding and one could easily have forgiven him if he had indulged in vanity to a certain extent and included some running inserts, riding close-ups taken from a camera truck running parallel to or in front of the galloping horse. But Hart had always been reluctant to use such a device, feeling that it would too readily suggest the omnipresence of a camera crew, although he had used such inserts to excellent effect in the climactic horse race of *The Narrow Trail*, not to stress his own riding skills but to emphasize the grace and speed of his beloved pinto Fritz.

Hart quite certainly knew what he was doing in the

William S. Hart, with Robert Taylor (then starring in the 1941 remake of *Billy the Kid*), by the grave of Fritz, Hart's pinto pony, at his ranch in Newhall.

staging of the land rush sequence, and if perhaps the individual thrill was sacrificed due to the minimizing of stunt work and camera fluidity, then the cumulative thrill more than made up for it. The sequence comes to its close on a scene of sheer poetry: Hart, a late starter in the race, gradually overtakes the other riders and, in a sustained burst of speed, is finally out in front. He gallops his horse over the crest of a hill and the camera, angled slightly above ground level, picks out for a few seconds one of the loveliest images any Western has ever given us: horse and rider, free of restraint and contact with the earth, apparently galloping through space.

Tumbleweeds was mishandled by its distributor, United Artists, who wanted to cut it severely. Hart was able to prevent this, and the film, though not reaching anywhere near its full commercial potential at a time when epic Westerns were temporarily in vogue, was nevertheless both a critical and a popular success and seemed to have vindicated Hart's stubborn sticking to his own methods. Wisely, he didn't try to top it. Prophetically, he had included a scene early in the film where he and a group of riders rest their horses atop a hill. Hart removes his hat and looks off to the great cattle herds winding their way across the plains that are soon to be evacuated and the land thrown open to homesteaders. "Boys," he says via inter title, "it's the last of the West." *Tumbleweeds* was the last of the West for Bill Hart, too. He had no wish—or need—to continue making Westerns in the style that the studios demanded and that he despised. He retired to his Newhall Ranch (now a museum open to the public) to write his autobiography, *My Life East and West,* a vivid if romanticized work, and books of equally vivid Western fiction and poetry. (The latter was awkward and sometimes rhymed badly, but Hart's blazing sincerity was in every word of it.) He never cut himself off from Hollywood entirely, playing himself in King Vidor's *Show People,* a satire of Hollywood life, and also returning to coach Johnny Mack Brown and lend technical advice in Vidor's early talkie *Billy the Kid.* He allowed one of his silent hits, *O'Malley of the Mounted,* to be remade as a sound Western with George O'Brien. While it was a good enough Western, not enough of Hart remained in it for him to be wholly satisfied, and the experiment was not repeated.

From the beginning, Hart's influence on others was readily apparent and not too surprising, since his initial dominance of the Western field was so complete that there were no others to emulate. Buck Jones and Harry Carey, both serious actors rather than rodeo showmen, were among the first great Western stars to adopt Hart's style and stance. And, of course, there were the lazy imitators seeking a quick route to fame—Neal Hart, no relation but with a similar, somber countenance, made

films in the Hart manner, no doubt hoping that the name would suggest a relationship. (Art Mix and William Fairbanks tried to pull the same stunt). And for reasons of economy and sheer feasibility, the copying of Hart extended well into the twenties. To emulate Tom Mix one needed a budget that would allow for outstanding natural locations and the staging of expensive, large-scale action sequences. One also needed to be a star having Mix's daredevil riding skills, qualities possessed by Ken Maynard and Fred Thomson, but by few others. To copy Hart, it helped to be a good actor, but one didn't need a big budget, so that most of the small independent Westerns and hopeful potential Western stars found it expedient to travel the Hart route.

Typical of the rock-bottom Poverty Row Western quickies that tried to cash in on the Hart persona was *Fangs of Fate* (1925), directed by Horace Carpenter, a former DeMille actor who would achieve greater if more dubious fame for his exploitation/horror/sex curiosity *Maniac* (1934). *Fangs of Fate*—which contained no fangs of any kind, fateful or otherwise—is listed in the American Film Institute's catalogue of twenties films only via the entry "No information available." It is an incredibly cheap little film which spends its opening reel just getting off the ground; for a while it looks as though it will consist of nothing but close-ups of uninteresting townspeople and neighbors who presumably contributed a few dollars to a meager budget on the off chance of finding fame and fortune. But once it gets under way, it isn't all that bad, and director Carpenter comes up with some interesting pictorial compositions. Moreover, it has one plot gimmick that might be entirely unique in the history of Western movies: the mysterious unknown leader of a band of outlaws is revealed at the very end to be the hero! While leading man Bill Patton had an unfortunate tendency to resemble comedian Larry Semon, when photographed carefully he could pass as a Bill Hart type, and his "good badman" act (his basically good qualities allow for him to be pardoned in the climactic and very threadbare courtroom scene) was clearly derived from a careful study of Hart's movies.

Far more successful Hart derivatives appeared in the sound era, particularly from Joel McCrea, a close friend of Hart's, and Bill Elliott, the Western star who most resembled Hart in looks, acting style, and—when he had any kind of input into his films—story content. Elliott's *Topeka,* a well above average Western of 1953, was a fairly careful reshuffling of Hart's *The Return of Draw Egan.*

When *Tumbleweeds* was reissued in 1939 to cash in on the great new Western cycle launched by the success of *Stagecoach,* Hart faced the cameras once more, dressed in the kind of authentic costume that had long disappeared from Hollywood Westerns, and from his Horse-shoe Ranch in Newhall, filmed a memorable ten-minute introduction to it. First as a storyteller, relating the historic facts leading up to the opening of the Cherokee Strip, then as a moviemaker proud of his record, recalling the past with deep emotion and honest sentiment, paying tribute in passing to his beloved Fritz, and finally as a man literally delivering his own obituary as he bids farewell to his audience for the last time, Hart brought

all of his long theatrical experience to bear. His voice, rich and beautifully modulated, occasionally dangerously close to a sob, not only made this speech one of the most poignant ever put on film, but also made many of his admirers realize for the first time what a magnificent contribution Hart could have made to the sound film, had he been younger, or as a character actor, had he been so inclined.

Whether Hart's influence on the Western was as far

reaching as John Ford's or Tom Mix's is both arguable and unimportant. But certainly, in the context of his time (and Hart's career spanned a mere eleven years, as opposed to twenty-five for Mix and fifty for Ford), he made a major contribution, rescuing the Western from obscurity and scorn, gaining for it both artistic respect and commercial value and, in Europe (and France especially), establishing the legend and myth of the American West on an effective level superior to that of the novel or of the art of painting, the latter being the media by which many European intellectuals were first made aware of the West.

White Oak (1921)

John Ford

FIVE

John Ford: A Half Century of Horse Operas

In the long run, director John Ford probably contributed more to both the popularity of and artistic respect for the Western than any other individual. Certainly he made more of them than any other major director, and over the years maintained a substantially higher standard than Howard Hawks, Henry Hathaway, King Vidor, Henry King, and Raoul Walsh. Admittedly, these directors never *specialized* in the Western, but they did return to it frequently as a kind of aesthetic and commercial haven. Although Ford made close to sixty Westerns (a misleadingly large figure perhaps, since many of them were early silents of relatively brief footage), in his later years he tended to downplay any great affection for the genre or even a special talent for making them. In 1968, in the only long interview with Ford on film—almost two hours of it, done for British television—he stated that "none of my so-called better pictures were Westerns" and maintained that his principal reason for doing them was the sheer pleasure of getting away from Hollywood, producers, and accountants and relaxing in the open with crew and players that were old friends. However, Ford always had been notorious for disliking interviewers and—a trait that increased with old age, poorer health, and crotchety irascibility—for his tendency never to give a straight answer. (He gave the BBC-TV interviewer a particularly hard time; for every question about black, Indian, or racial problems in the United States, he would counter with a barbed thrust about British-Irish relationships and antagonisms!)

Opinions and "facts" given to one interviewer were often directly contradicted by those given to another. Like Hawks and Walsh, he was both irritated and amused by the pretentious analyses of his work—he disliked the theory-oriented highbrow critics who offered such an approach often in virtually undecipherable language, and he was equally contemptuous of the self-important directors who took it seriously. But in his dislike of sham and artifice, he often went to the other extreme of denying *any* qualities of art or importance in his work: "It's just a job of work, that's all . . . you do the best you can. It's like the man digging the ditch who says, 'I hope the ground is soft so that my pick digs deeper.'"

Stars and particularly cameramen who have worked with Ford confirm that this easygoing attitude was genuine, and that he never consciously strove for "art." (One or two obvious exceptions, like *Mary of Scotland* and *The Fugitive*, merely confirm the accuracy of that generalization.) Yet Ford's films themselves are the best rebuttal of his dismissal of them. As with no other American director, they all bear his recognizable signature, and whether they were photographed by Joseph August, Arthur Miller, or Gregg Toland, or art directed by William Darling or James Basevi, they all looked like Ford pictures. And they were full of images where obviously great pains had been taken to create an evocative set for perhaps just a few seconds of screen time, or where clearly a great deal of time and patience had been spent to achieve the right combination of natural light, art direction, and cinematographer's lighting for shots that (in a purely narrative sense) could have been made quicker and more economically or dispensed with altogether, and undoubtedly would have been with a less caring director at the helm.

Familiar faces are scattered through all of Ford's films, a stock company built and nurtured at least from his very first feature, *Straight Shooting* (1917). John Wayne made his first appearance in a Ford film with a large (and extremely enthusiastic) bit role in *Hangman's House* (1928). The musical scores, with their perennial recourse to "Red River Valley" whether the film is a Western or not, were always recognizable Ford scores. No matter how skillful the players, composers, and cinematographers were at anticipating and delivering the mood or nuance or look that Ford wanted, the consistency of the finished movies had to come from Ford himself. Although he was known to very occasionally reshoot scenes he deemed unsatisfactory after a picture was officially completed, this rarely happened. He worked quickly, energetically, and efficiently, and when the film was finished, he was usually immediately immersed in the next project instead of staying around to fuss over the mechanical laboratory polishing and processing of the completed work.

Cunningly, however, he left the studio technicians little option other than to present his film literally as he had shot it. Ford turned in little excess footage—no alternate takes of tricky sequences, and particularly no optional close-ups to boost the ego of a star. He had even been known to discard elements of the script that he felt were extraneous, or too time-consuming. In a sense, he edited his films in the camera. His virtues—a strong pictorial sense, vigorous action, honest sentiment, the ability to get away with a plot cliché and make it seem fresh, the outstanding performances he got from players (John Wayne, Victor McLaglen, Wallace Ford) who were often merely adequate under other directors— were as consistent and clear-cut as his weaknesses. These included too great a fondness for slapstick comedy, the professional Irishman's dislike of the British (conveyed through many barbed and overdrawn British stereotypes, even in so basically pro-British a film as *The Long Voyage Home* [1940]), and a sloppiness in filming what he considered to be merely necessary but not important sequences.

The use of back-projection. nonmatching locales and cut-in close-ups (as in John Wayne's first scene in *Stagecoach*) and obvious studio interior "exteriors" marred several Ford Westerns. But he never "cheated" in the big dramatic scenes or action highlights. *Stagecoach* certainly has its share of mismatched locales (the grandeur of Monument Valley locations intercut with scenes filmed in drab Chatsworth, just a few miles outside Hollywood), but once Ford sweeps into the magnificent chase across the salt flats, or follows Wayne and Claire Trevor through the well and consistently designed studio sets of Lordsburg, there is never any suggestion of economy or "hurry-up" production short-cuts. Nor does Ford ever mind "breaking the rules" of traditional filmmaking if the pictorial results justify it. Several times in the *Stagecoach* chase there are abrupt changes in rhythm as Ford suddenly alters screen direction—the coach going from right to left at one moment, and left to right the next—but the sequence is so superbly built in terms of both drama and excitement that one hardly notices. One such particularly abrupt cut was made solely so that Ford could shoot directly into the sun and achieve a marvelous, smooth tracking shot of the coach racing along through the dust and early twilight.

On other occasions, Ford could be almost perverse in his deliberate flouting of traditional methods. *Fort Apache* contains an excellent sequence of a band of Indians pursuing a much smaller group of cavalry. In camera angling, fluidity of running inserts, and expertise in stunt work it is flawless—yet Ford insists on shooting the Indians racing across the screen from left to right, and the cavalry making their flight from right to left. It looks not like a chase, but two groups of horsemen charging headlong into one another! Even if the sequence had been shot that way accidentally, which is unlikely, its absurdity must have been revealed when the rough cut was assembled, and it would have been a simple matter to remedy the problem by flipping the negative of one of the groups of riders so that all were heading in the same direction. But Ford left it as it was in the release prints, to the eternal chagrin of film students but, it must be added, to the probable unconcern of the average audience, too wrapped up in the expertly staged action to know what a blunder had been made.

Ford's films, put together, provide—far more than the bodies of work even of such directors as King, Griffith, and Vidor—a remarkably comprehensive panorama of Americana and American history, ranging through the War of Independence, the Civil War and its aftermath, the opening up of the West and its attendant decimation of the Indian, immigration at the turn of the century, World War One, Prohibition and the gangster era, World War Two, Korea, and, in between, forays into

Straight Shooting (Universal, 1917) with Harry Carey and
Hoot Gibson

the development of the locomotive and the aeroplane and the submarine. All this material was covered in his regular Hollywood output and supplemented by his outstanding contribution to the documentary film in World War Two. There were also occasional side trips (not surprisingly, often quite critical!) into British history. Reasonably accurate historically, in some cases remarkably so, these visions of America's past have been somewhat colored by Ford's own viewpoint, attitudes, and politics.

Ford's career began in 1914 as an actor and stuntman for his brother Francis, but really took off in 1917 when he signed with Universal to direct two-reel Westerns, starring in one or two of them and still calling himself Jack. Placing much greater stress on action than acting ability (though the plots were often quite strong), director Ford used as his initial stars at Universal ex-rodeo rider Hoot Gibson and Harry Carey; within a few years, having moved to Fox, he would be directing Buck Jones, Tom Mix, and George O'Brien.

Because he served his apprenticeship on bread-and-butter actioners, made for a studio that still called itself, without any frills, the Universal Film Manufacturing Company, Ford never forgot the basics that audiences wanted from a Western—a lack of pretention and a maximum of action. Most of his later epics, when his name carried prestige with it, steadfastly refused to be

overawed by their size and importance and continued to deliver the ingredients audiences expected. Even when occasionally shot out of the saddle by an overly talkative and actionless script (*Two Rode Together* [1961]), Ford still kept his film visually on the move, playing out the long conversational scenes on horseback or against pleasing natural riverbank and other exteriors.

Of the twenty-eight films Ford made for Universal between 1917 and 1921, only three—*Straight Shooting, The Last Outlaw,* and *Hell Bent*—are known to have survived, and those largely due to the vigilance of European film archives. Obviously this was an extremely important group of Westerns, for not only was Ford laying the foundations for his own later and more imposing work, but he was also setting new standards in a style quite unlike that of William S. Hart, the only other filmmaker devoting himself almost exclusively to the Western. While Ford's plots were frequently strong, they were at the same time uncomplicated, and action and superior photography of striking locations were their common denominators. Reviewers who usually bypassed the non-Hart Westerns watched for each new Ford, noting the steady improvement of Harry Carey as an actor under Ford's direction, and the magnificent visuals. *Photoplay,* in reviewing *The Outcasts of Poker Flat* (1919), commented: ". . . absolutely incomparable photography . . . the film is an optic symphony." (Interestingly, two sound remakes of this Bret Harte tale were stodgy, studio-bound versions, heavy on dialogue and weak on visuals.)

Very fortuitously, the small cross section of Ford's earliest silent work that *does* still exist includes his first feature, *Straight Shooting* (1917). The others that have

Straight Shooting: A favorite location

The Outcasts of Poker Flat
(Universal, 1919) with Gloria Hope
and Cullen Landis

survived are *Hell Bent* (1918), a feature starring Harry
Carey, a sturdy, decidedly unconventional Western unfortunately marred by bad patches of decomposition in
the surviving print material, and *The Last Outlaw,* the
last of the two-reel Westerns that Ford continued to
make for Universal even though well established in
full-length features. Apart from the film's intrinsic merit,
it's especially interesting in that Ford, who wrote the
original story, always hoped to remake it on a larger
scale. That was done at RKO Radio in 1936 as an
above-average programmer, cofeaturing Ford's two
Universal stars, Harry Carey and Hoot Gibson, but, alas,
with lackluster director Christy Cabanne missing far too
many marvelous opportunities. Ford, deprived of the
opportunity to remake it *then*—RKO Radio was making
few big Westerns in the 1930s, and Ford was by then far
too big a director to be assigned a program Western—
still hoped to remake it later, and at one time was
planning a new version at Fox to star Tyrone Power.
Unfortunately nothing came of this.

 Ford's own recollections of the *merits* of *Straight
Shooting* were vague, although this may have been
because the film had been lost for years (eventually it
was rediscovered in the Czech Film Archive), and with
all of the early Universals of such a uniformly high
standard, Ford would have had no reason to recall the
specifics of this particular one—other than that it was
planned as another of his series of two-reelers, and that
he expanded it to a full five reels, delighting his studio

George O'Brien, a new star created by Ford in *The Iron Horse*
(Fox, 1924)

bosses, enhancing his own prestige, and giving a much-needed shot in the arm to Harry Carey's somewhat stagnating career. Clearly Ford had a greater affection for *Marked Men* (1919), an early version of *Three Godfathers,* the Peter B. Kyne story that saw two other notable remakes before Ford's own in 1948 with John Wayne. In the original story, all three of the titular godfathers—outlaws who stumble across an orphaned baby in the desert—sacrifice their lives in order to save the child, an ending followed in the two interim versions. But in *Marked Men* Ford had transformed the lead bad guy into Cheyenne Harry, the sometime outlaw but essentially "good guy" hero that had become a very popular figure in Harry Carey's hands, both in two-reelers and in many of the features following *Straight*

Shooting. Ford certainly wasn't going to kill off a character that had such a huge following, so Cheyenne Harry survived, his outlawry pardoned. John Wayne enjoyed the same reprieve in his version, partly because he was approaching a new peak in popularity, but mainly because *Three Godfathers* was slow and rather heavy going, and a totally tragic ending in a largely actionless film would have been bad showmanship. But critics who repeat the cliché of Wayne's "indestructible" image, claiming that he only died on screen at the very end of his career, forget that he chalked up a total of nine screen deaths, four of them between 1943 and 1949.

Although long unavailable and almost certainly lost, *Marked Men* was one of the few films before *The Iron Horse* that Ford would even deign to talk about in

Stagecoach (United Artists, 1939): Ford's first use of Monument Valley as a location

Ahead for Ford:
Stagecoach

Rio Grande (Republic, 1950): J. Carrol Naish and
John Wayne

interviews. Yet good as it undoubtedly was, it can hardly have been as much of a milestone film as *Straight Shooting*. Quite apart from being Ford's first feature, it was also very close to the beginning of his career. For a film made by a man with literally only six months' directorial experience behind him, it is in many ways a remarkable piece of work, although curiously, not at all what one would expect of an early Ford. His later fondness for roistering comic action, plus the fact that he had been working in two-reelers where the action was fast and straightforward and the heroes rowdy (one of them even frequented a bordello!) would lead one to expect a rough and tumble actioner for his first feature and probably a somewhat untidy one, due to the unofficial expansion from two reels to five. Yet its *Shane*-like plot, of a range war between cattlemen and homesteaders, and the intervention on behalf of the underdog homesteaders of a professional gunman, has a surprising depth of characterization and a rather slow, methodical structure, punctuated by a burst of violent action at midpoint, and then culminating in a large-scale and traditional finale: the shoot-out in the dusty main street, the besieged homesteaders, and a ride to the rescue. There is a certain amount of influence from William S. Hart, but this was inevitable since Hart's were the only major Westerns then being made, and Harry Carey's persona certainly overlapped Hart's, even though it preceded it.

Tom Mix's first film for Fox, and Ford's *Straight Shooting* were made virtually simultaneously and copyrighted only a week apart, so obviously there was little likelihood of a Mix influence. The limited Hart influence can be seen in the general austerity of the production (with the word used to indicate a lean style rather than economy) and in the characters—good and bad intermingled in both the heroes and the villains. The sheriff (the only character too Hollywoodian in his garb) is a nebulous, ineffectual figure, and it is a gang of "good" outlaws who make up the rescuing posse for the film's climax. One of them is even "human" enough to steal a pot of jam from the heroine's kitchen. But if its plot and characters and a deliberate striving for realism represent echoes of Hart, then there is also a production polish and a showmanship that is far more typical of the later Ford. It builds both its plot and its excitement steadily and in a methodically rising tempo, in a calculated manner that Hart usually avoided, and it is exceptionally smooth in terms of composition, locations, and lighting, looking far more like a production of the early twenties than one of 1917.

Economies are creative as well as budget-conscious; for example, all of the cabin interiors are photographed on an outdoor stage with just a flat or two, but ingenious lighting emphasizing the darkness "inside" and the sunlight outside, suggested by the framing device of doors and windows, makes them work extremely well. The Devil's Canyon hideout of the outlaw band (a narrow trail through a deep gorge, actually created artificially for a planned but subsequently abandoned railroad right of way) proved to be a valuable location for Ford. He returned to it periodically in such films as *The Iron Horse* and *Stagecoach*. Keaton used it too (in *Seven Chances*) but Ford was quite probably the first director to recognize and exploit its pictorial values. The whole chase and rescue climax of the film suggests quite strongly that Ford had learned a lot from watching Griffith stage the protracted climax to *The Birth of a Nation* in which Ford had ridden as a Klan extra, and then observing how superbly that staging (and editing) worked in the finished film. Not only in its construction but also in the interrelation of certain shots and in their pictorial composition, Ford's climax is plainly an immediate descendant of Griffith's. The rounding up of the posse, the ride to the rescue, specific shots inside the besieged cabin (a gun barrel being pushed through the weakening door), all of this is heightened by heroine Molly Malone's slight resemblance to Mae Marsh being played up by Ford, easing her into as many Marsh/Griffith postures as possible (although, of course, Marsh did not figure in the climactic sequence of *The Birth of a Nation*).

Even that early in his career, Ford was astute enough to realize not only *how* Griffith achieved certain effects, but also *why*. In the sequence of the cattlemen assembling their forces, acknowledging their leader, and riding into ranks, he copies *exactly*, if on a smaller scale, the parallel sequence of the Klan assembling in Griffith's film. A vast open field is "framed" by foliage and trees; not only is the composition pleasing in itself, but a few riders concentrated into the center screen area are able to suggest a much larger assemblage in the unseen off-screen space. A measure of the expertise of the climactic action scenes is that many of them were still being used as stock shots in "B" Westerns of the thirties and forties.

Though it is easier for us to appreciate the value of *Straight Shooting* in retrospect, since we can recognize in it so many of the roots of later Westerns, including of course many of Ford's, its merits *were* appreciated at the time by certain discerning critics. A reviewer for *The Moving Picture World* called it ". . . a clean-cut, straightforward tale. Both the author and the director are to be congratulated for having selected compelling scenes and situations for the production. The Western panorama is set forth in clear, attractive photography and the riding and fighting episodes are enacted with dash and enthusiasm. So successful is the offering that it deserves to rank with *The Virginian* and *Whispering Smith.*"

Straight Shooting is also full of moments that antici-pate Ford's celebrated ability to create highlights out of improvisation—or misfortune. The former is illustrated by a brief and beautifully underplayed moment in which the heroine is setting the places for the evening meal and, without thinking, automatically lays a place for the brother who has only just been slain, then, suddenly realizing, removes the plate. And while the improvisa-tion has nothing to match the sudden electric storm which added such dramatic beauty to *She Wore a Yellow Ribbon,* it does reaffirm that Ford could always recog-nize the value of a genuine accident if it added excite-ment to the film. In one sequence, Hoot Gibson is racing across a river, and midway his horse stumbles and falls. Clearly the fall was not planned—if it had been, it would have taken place nearer the camera—and Gibson merely remounts and continues his ride. Probably he expected the scene to be reshot, as he is grinning broadly as he races past the camera, fortunately far enough away for his amusement not to be disturbingly apparent. But Ford uses the entire shot as is, and if it lessens (slightly) one's respect for the horsemanship of the hero, at the same time one believes in him a little more as a real person. And Ford's main street shoot-out—in a small, dusty street, with only a building or two to offer minimal cover, and but a handful of scared onlookers—remains far more convincing, if admittedly less cinematic, than the far more elaborately composed climactic ones in *Stagecoach* and *My Darling Clementine.* It also conveys a real sense of *pain;* Carey's opponent is shot in the belly, and looks surprised as well as agonized as he slides down the shack wall to die, with a slight kick, in the dust.

There are signs in *Straight Shooting* and *Hell Bent* that Ford had already evolved a style of his own, and undoubtedly, if more films of his were available from that early period, one would not merely have to assume that. But certainly from 1920 on, when his new Fox contract overlapped with the ending of his Universal one, enough of his material survives for the rapid development of that style to be apparent. Ford would always be open to influence from outside when that influence would help a specific film, though signifi-cantly, apart from a return to the Hart manner in *Three Bad Men,* a recognizable influence of others on Ford films was essentially in the non-Westerns. In the late twenties, Ford was briefly, impressively, but unchar-acteristically influenced by the Germanic visual style of F. W. Murnau, a contemporary at Fox over the years 1927–29, and from 1933 to 1936 (when Ford made no Westerns at all) there was a rather spectacular renais-sance of both thematics and stylistics of D. W. Griffith. Ford neither boasted of these "homages" nor did he try to conceal them, although he made no secret of his intense admiration for Griffith.

Between 1920 and his first major hit, *The Iron Horse* (1924), Ford wrapped up his Universal contract by making another half-dozen Westerns with either Harry Carey or Hoot Gibson, while his prolific early Fox period included two Westerns each with Buck Jones and Tom Mix. Indeed, his first film at Fox, *Just Pals* (1920), was a Buck Jones vehicle that was hardly a typical Western except by geographic location, but certainly contained enough Western elements, especially in its climax, for Buck Jones to remember it well and to remake it as *The Cowboy and the Kid* in 1936, when he had his own producing unit at Universal.

The Iron Horse not only was Ford's biggest film to date, but also remains one of the biggest Western epics from any period. Slightly marred by a subsidiary plot line (the hero's long search for the man who killed his father) which occasionally took attention away from the empire-building theme, it was nevertheless superb recon-structed history and splendidly staged and edited action entertainment, a huge organizational undertaking for a director still in his twenties. James Cruze's *The Covered Wagon,* produced in 1923, was the first entry (unwitt-ingly so, since its success and influence were not antici-pated) in the cycle of epic Westerns, but it was a primitive film by comparison, inferior to Ford's in every way except cinematographically. Yet even *The Iron Horse* has to yield pride of place to *Three Bad Men* (1926), Ford's last and best silent Western. Originally planned as a vehicle to costar Fox's three big action stars, George O'Brien, Tom Mix, and Buck Jones, that idea was eventually dropped, probably because the story called for the titular badmen to be killed off, *Three Musketeers* style, in the film's climax, leaving the West-ern equivalent of a D'Artagnan to win the girl and settle down. It finally emerged with George O'Brien as the nominal hero, and the character actors Tom Santschi, Frank Campeau, and J. Farrell MacDonald in the larger title roles. A little slow in getting under way, it built (like *Stagecoach*) to its major action sequence (a beautifully staged land rush sequence) which it placed at the three-quarters point, leaving the last couple of reels for a settling of personal scores with the villains.

Three Bad Men (actually based on *Over the Border,* a novel by Herman Whitaker, though often erroneously confused with *Three Godfathers,* by Peter B. Kyne) was one of Ford's most unpredictable Westerns, a unique blending of the austere and the traditional with the romanticized and the streamlined. Its heavily sentimen-tal plot, and particularly the subtheme of Tom Santschi out to exact revenge on the man who seduced and discarded his sister, was pure William S. Hart at the very

The Searchers (Warner Bros., 1956): John Wayne and Ward Bond

expect is the occasional order for an individual print or two for an archive or perhaps for specialized television usage. As a result, they feel that if they have done *adequate* work (and if you can *see* the film, they regard it as adequate!), they have done their job. When the big preservation and restoration push was in the works some twenty years ago, too much material had to be handed over to too few laboratories willing to do the work, and almost none of the results did anything like justice to the rich pictorial values of the originals. Fortunately, from the 1980s on, smaller, specialized laboratories on both coasts, began to devote themselves more and more to meticulous preservation work, and the results have been infinitely superior. (Laser-disc and videocassette technology has also made it possible to transfer 35-mm material to tape at the right speed with no loss of quality, an enormous step forward, though the screening material thus produced is of course reference rather than preservation footage.)

These advances in both technique and human special-

time that Hart, deemed too old-fashioned, was making his farewell from the screen. Its strong, evangelical fervor was also closer to Hart than anything that subsequently appeared in a Ford Western.

Even now rarely seen, for years it was considered lost, until a somewhat battered and incomplete print turned up at the Czech Film Archive. Then, happily, Western producer turned archivist Alex Gordon found a superbly preserved 35-mm nitrate print in the Fox vaults. Unfortunately, the very richness of the print, its pictorial nuances, and its usage of toned stock defeated the efforts of the laboratory in making a fully representative duplicate negative. Or perhaps one should say that the loving care necessary for such a preservation undertaking *discouraged* the laboratory from working on it as carefully as it should have. Major film laboratories today *hate* the idea of preservation work; it is time-consuming, requires special equipment in many cases, and when the work is done, there is little likelihood of mass print orders to bring revenue into their coffers. The most they can

The Horse Soldiers (United Artists, 1959): Ford with Hoot Gibson on the set

69

ization came too late, however, to save the beauty of films such as *Three Bad Men*. A Hollywood laboratory working on a restored negative produced a succession of prints which showed only a slight improvement in timing each time; when finally it looked as though progress was being made, the laboratory gave up in disgust, proclaimed that what it had was the best it could do, and refused to work on it any longer. As a result, a negative which was only one generation away from a superb original print looks as though it was at least four generations away—and it is this material that future scholars will have to fall back on to assess the value of Ford's silent work. Typical of the loss is a magnificent scene near the opening of a lone pioneer chopping down a tree (following introductory material of immigrants arriving on the West Coast by boat). The scene is presented within an iris, concentrating attention on his single action. But as the tree prepares to fall, the iris suddenly opens up to full screen size, and behind the falling tree we see a spectacular vista of the West—lake, forest, an Indian encampment, and behind the trees, mountain peaks towering almost to the top of the frame—virgin territory awaiting exploration and development by those same immigrants. In the original print, it is an image full of rich detail; in the preservation copies, it is so bleached out that one cannot even *see* the crest of the mountain range, with a thin line of covered wagons crossing it, until just before the fadeout when the timing of the scene changes, and for about a second one can see the image as it *should* be. All the information is there, but shoddy laboratory work has managed to hide it.

Despite the inadequate print quality now available, and with perhaps a shade too much boisterous comedy for a film of such epic stature and possessing such real poetry, *Three Bad Men* remains one of Ford's major works. Surprisingly, it was remade only once—in 1931 as *Not Exactly Gentleman* (in Europe, *Three Rogues*), and then probably only to ride on the coattails of the success of the same year's *Cimarron*. The big land rush sequence was of course lifted bodily from Ford, and the film as a whole was little more than a vehicle for Victor McLaglen, much watered down from the powerful original.

Despite the popularity of *Three Bad Men,* it was Ford's last Western for thirteen years. He was kept (successfully) busy in other areas—Americana, war adventure, crime and gangsterism, and the apparent decline of the Western's popularity when sound came in kept him away from the genre for the balance of his first contract with Fox. The studio's "B" Westerns with George O'Brien in the early thirties, though of an exceptionally high standard, were not important enough to warrant a director of his stature. Apart from Raoul

Walsh's *The Big Trail* in 1930, Fox virtually abandoned the super-Western between the advent of talkies and *Jesse James* in 1939. Not until his classic *Stagecoach*, produced independently by Walter Wanger, also in 1939, did Ford return to the Western. Despite the acclaim it won for him and the new respect that it achieved for the sound Western (oddly enough, it was not a *big* commercial success initially, winning much of its audiences and its receipts over the long haul, including reissues and television), Ford seemed to show no signs of wanting to make a follow-up. In post-*Stagecoach* 1939 and 1940–41, he was riding the crest of an unbroken series of films that were both critical successes and box office hits; moreover, with America's involvement in World War Two, Ford was anxious to contribute his filmmaking skills to the war effort and the making of valuable documentaries.

Only after his second sound Western, *My Darling Clementine* (1946), best of all the Wyatt Earp movies and certainly one of Ford's loveliest, finest, and most disciplined films—did he embrace the horse opera wholeheartedly again. The group that followed, many of them in color, included two permanent classics of the genre—*She Wore a Yellow Ribbon* (1949) and *Wagon-Master* (1950)—while the others—*Fort Apache* (1948), *Three Godfathers* (1948), *Rio Grande* (1950), *The Searchers* (1956), *The Horse Soldiers* (1959), *Sergeant Rutledge* (1960), *Two Rode Together* (1961), *The Man Who Shot Liberty Valance* (1962), *How the West Was Won* (1962), and *Cheyenne Autumn* (1964)—comprise a remarkable and closely interrelated series of essays on the American Civil War and its aftermath, the cavalry and its traditions, and the Indian wars and racial problems arising therefrom. Indeed, it seems almost heresy not to include *The Searchers* and (in a very different way) *The Man Who Shot Liberty Valance* from this period as also being among his masterworks. While somewhat studied and self-conscious, unusual traits in a Ford Western, *The Searchers* is usually (though arguably, and especially in this corner) regarded not only as his peak film, if it is possible to find a single peak in such a prolific and varied output, but as one of the finest Westerns from any period and any director.

Many American directors, and King Vidor and Orson Welles are names that come most readily to mind, have made individual films superior to Ford's best, but no director, not even Griffith, maintained such a *consistently* high standard over such an extended period of time—more than a half century of active filmmaking. Ford had always been taken for granted, rarely honored as he should have been. In some ways, this may have been a blessing in disguise, since it enabled Ford to go on making films the way *he* felt they should be made instead of, consciously or otherwise, catering to the demands of critics and the interpretations of cultists. His work remains both a credit to the industry and an acknowledged inspiration to other directors. Quite certainly, in the specific realm of the Western, it is impossible to overemphasize the contribution Ford made to the genre as a whole, or the beauty, poetry, and excitement he brought to his own Westerns.

Fortunately, before he died, appropriate recognition *did* come: a tribute by the American Film Institute (at which even the President of the United States added his own accolade); an elaborate documentary, *Directed by John Ford,* which summed up his work; and several in-depth books and biographies, both American and European, analyzing his films in ways that would have aroused his scorn in public, even assuming he would admit to having read them, but that privately would probably have delighted him.

The Man Who Shot Liberty Valance (Paramount, 1962): James Stewart and John Wayne with Ford

Tom Mix

SIX

The Pre-Twenties—and Tom Mix

From 1970 on, a number of important rediscoveries of films from the 1914–18 years have allowed us to revise and reevaluate our long-held conception of film history in the pre-1920 period. Raoul Walsh's first film, *Regeneration* (1915), not only in some ways anticipated Stroheim and even Fellini, but also showed that a director who had learned his craft under Griffith could in some ways surpass him. These years can now be seen to contain Cecil B. DeMille's best work. There is remarkable sophistication and charm, as well as a determined attempt to weld theatre and film, in the early features of Maurice Tourneur. The previously unknown John Collins, virtually the only director of stature to emerge from the Edison Studios, is now appreciated and mourned—for his death in the influenza epidemic of 1919 robbed us of a major innovative filmmaker. Even a basically poor (dramatically) film like *Second in Command* (1914) shakes up a lot of our generalizations with its evidence that it seems to have been designed largely to exploit and explore the possibilities of the mobile camera, coming up with tracking shots that almost rival Max Ophuls in their complexity.

But apart from the rediscovery of John Ford's *Straight Shooting*, which, after all, merely confirmed what we had suspected from the always adulatory trade press

reviews of Ford Westerns of that period, there have been no major surprises in the Western film arising out of preservation work. Lost Westerns *have* been rediscovered, but for the most part they have merely served to expand our knowledge of a given director or star. Nor is this necessarily bad or disappointing; while major discoveries like Walsh's *Regeneration* or the Ince film, *The Italian*, are stimulating, at the same time (especially when there is increasingly less chance of old film surviving if it is secreted away awaiting rediscovery) a confirmation of the status quo can also be reassuring.

The one potentially major archival discovery unfortunately proved to be just that, a discovery of archival value only—but because of its significance if not its merit, it should be noted for the record, since the film is now available for study at the UCLA archive in Hollywood.

Its title is *The Argonauts of California*, and its producer was Edward L. Grafton, a Los Angeles publisher whose books had included a history of California written by John Steven McGroaty, the eighth chapter of which was to provide the basis for the film. Elizabeth Baker Bohan, a novelist, was employed to add what was presumably intended as a showmanlike romantic plot to link the historical data. And finally, Henry Kabierske was signed to direct, having formerly been associated with author McGroaty in a pageant-like theatrical venture, *Mission Play*. Therein lies the not-so-mysterious reason for the film's failure: *none* of the people involved knew *anything* about movies.

Its production began in September of 1915, and was concluded the following summer. Its significance lies in the fact that the success of *The Birth of a Nation* suggested that the same formula could be applied to an epic about the West. The surprising thing is that the idea came to non-industry people, and, of course, the sad thing is that they didn't succeed, thus delaying another parallel experiment until 1923 and *The Covered Wagon*.

Incidentally, published material on the film in the trade press of the time—actually cunningly disguised publicity puffs from friends and "disinterested" observers—avoided quoting the cost of the film, stating that the producers wanted the film to impress on its own merits, not those of budget. But one of those invaluable "close friends" of the producer leaked the information that it certainly cost in excess of $100,000. This seems extremely unlikely, since *The Birth of a Nation* had cost only about $65,000 in actual production costs. Judging by what appears on the screen, one must assume that it cost no more than $30,000—and that figure encompassing a more than average amount of money wasted, or possibly cheated out of the producers, through their inexperience.

For 1916, it is a primitive film, far below the standards of most full-length features from 1914 on. However, at ten reels it is almost certainly the very first Western epic, and perhaps the only film of its kind until the twenties. The phrase "almost certainly" is essential these days, however, because it is no longer safe, nor should it be, to claim a "first" for anything. Until its rediscovery in 1980, none of us knew anything about *The Argonauts of California*, and might well have made such claims for the Griffith-supervised *Martyrs of the Alamo*, which did come first in terms of release (late 1915) but also was decidedly less of an epic.

What is especially fascinating about *Argonauts* is its recognition of the success of Griffith's methods, its blatant copying of them, and its total inability to do so successfully because none of the participants seemed to have any understanding of film. Interestingly though, the writers *anticipate* a number of subthemes (lovers kept apart because of a differing social status, the kept apart because of a differing social status, the heroine's betrayal and social ostracizing when her illegitimate child is born) that Griffith himself would not use until later. *The Birth of a Nation* was quite obviously the catalyst for this film which, while dealing with an earlier epoch, copies Griffith's structure and individual incidents, and even purloins inter titles which it rewords

only slightly. The plot substitutes the discovery of gold at Sutter's Mill in 1848 for the Civil War and deals with the wagon treks west and the lawlessness in San Francisco that is put down by ruthless vigilante counterattack. An attempt is made to interweave history and fiction into one tapestry, but director Kabierske seemed unable to cope with this, handling it all like one of his stage pageants so that it moves in stops and lurches, suddenly switching to documentarian reconstructions of actual events and then reverting back to the separate fictional narrative. It does not help that there are no known actors in the leads, despite original promotional notes that every player was handpicked for his or her role. There are only two recognizable faces in the entire film, Vera Lewis and Harry Cording, and those in smaller roles and in crowd scenes, and most of the players were probably locals or performers from the director's pageants. (Actor and John Ford associate Frank Baker, who was able to see the film shortly before dying, knew that his wife was in it, but was unable to recognize her.) Almost everybody seems stiff, ill at ease, and devoid of personality, so it is difficult to become involved with their characters or even to know much about them. Griffith always gave his principal players little "bits of business" so that the audience was given an instant insight into both their characters and their persona. Nor are clarity or dramatic values helped by very awkward titling. Before we are introduced to the heroine, an inter title refers ambiguously to "the unfortunate daughter of . . ." whereupon she is shown cradling a baby. And in virtually the next title, she is protesting that her father has thrown her out because of "a little error." Coincidentally, the little error remains steadfastly the same size throughout the whole wagon trek and then through the first year of life in California. Conveniently, the baby eventually dies, thus abolishing the woman's "shame" and permitting marriage to the man who has always loved her.

The camera rarely moves intentionally; once, placed inside a wagon, probably because it was the simplest way to shoot a scene sustained for some length, it enables the film to come to life so startlingly, to move from pageant to vivid reality, that one wonders why the director didn't use the device more often. Yet there are odd moments of imagination. After an early skirmish, an Indian's body floats downstream—both an interesting shot in itself and a useful narrative linkage, since it is apparent that discovery of the body will arouse his tribe to attack the pioneers, and for once the film creates suspense and exposition entirely via images.

Following the structuring pattern of *The Birth of a Nation*, there is a big action sequence (the Indian attack) as the climax to the first half, then a respite and a buildup to a second, larger climax which is two-pronged, dealing

DeMille's *The Squaw Man* (Famous Players, 1913) with Dustin Farnum and Red Wing

The Spoilers (Selig, 1914) with William Farnum, Wheeler Oakman, and Kathlyn Williams

Douglas Fairbanks, Sr., star of *Wild and Woolly, Man From Painted Post,* and other lighthearted Westerns of the pre-1920s

in a general sense with the mob scenes, vigilante action, and summary executions to restore law and order, and in a more specific sense with a traditional ride to the rescue. The villainous betrayer of the heroine has also come West. An out-and-out rotter, he has abducted

A *Romance of the Redwoods*
(Artcraft, 1917): Cecil B.
DeMille directs Elliott
Dexter and Mary Pickford

another girl and sold her to a lustful Mexican, who is trying to rape her while the vigilantes ride to her rescue. These climactic episodes do have some inherent excitement, as the mob scenes are genuinely spectacular and the vigilantes' ride very lively, though performed mainly in long shots and deprived of the camera mobility, crosscutting, and use of extreme close-ups that made the parallel ride of the Klan in Griffith's film so dynamic. Too, the vigilante-justice scenes do have considerable power, possibly because many of them are based on old engravings and photographs, and thus a subliminal kind of realism shows through. Perhaps cautious after reactions to Griffith's Klan, the film is somewhat vague about pinpointing the actual status of the vigilantes. Quite frequently, *background* information aligns them with the "Seeing Eye" group, a Klan-like organization that was featured in several post-*Birth* films, including Mae Murray's *A Mormon Maid,* a bizarre semi-Western in which the heroine's virginity, or possible lack of it, is the focal point of the film! But the inter titles are at great pains to establish the vigilantes' totally objective and nonracial modus operandi.

The Argonauts of California is probably the first film after *The Birth of a Nation* to demonstrate so clearly the influence of the latter, and from a purely academic and teaching tool, would be an invaluable companion piece to John Ford's *Straight Shooting,* one of the first to show

the same influence but with a *full understanding* of it. Artistically, even in terms of undemanding entertainment, it is a minor find. In terms of film history, however, it is a fascinating if essentially archaeological rediscovery. Yet it is sad that in the decade since its preservation, it has been shown publicly only once, at a Santa Fe Film Festival (devoted to the Western) in April of 1981, where local critics were somewhat puzzled by its inclusion along with the best of Ford and Peckinpah, and many did not bother to stay to see more than a fragment of it.

One of the tragedies of (increasingly expensive) film preservation is that, with the more primitive films, once they are saved, nobody seems to want to utilize them. Such an attitude obviously discourages the expenditure of money on more of the same. Yet two hundred years hence, *The Argonauts of California* may prove to be of much greater value to social, Western, and movie historians than the overpreserved and overprotected *Casablanca.* The most elaborate of a handful of films produced in and around Monrovia, California, it apparently made but little impact at the time however. By mid-1916, its sheer length and the scope of its content just were not enough, in view of the films in release from Griffith, DeMille, Brenon, and others, to compensate for the general amateurishness of its presentation.

Even allowing for the dominant influence of William

76

Two scenes from *Deuce Duncan*, a 1917 Triangle Western starring the very popular William Desmond; Luella Maxim is his leading lady

S. Hart, there was considerable variety in the Westerns that were produced in the years prior to 1920. Apart from the occasional D. W. Griffith or Herbert Brenon twelve-reel spectacular, this was still well before the period of the "super" film—while the period of the double bill was even further into the future. The average movie program was headed by a feature of approximately six reels in length and supported by a short or two, usually a slapstick comedy or a serial episode. The Western feature thus had to be capable of holding its own in direct competition with romantic, dramatic, or adventure movies and had not yet become a staple programmer "filler" of reduced importance. Many popular players such as Roy Stewart and William Desmond, while really not Western stars, certainly made many of them, while romantic leading men like William Farnum often proved to be so popular in Westerns that they returned to them frequently.

The popular serials of Pearl White and others often overlapped into Western territory. White's Eastern-filmed *Perils of Pauline* contained some Western episodes cashing in on the literally cliff-hanging possibilities of the Palisades over the Hudson River, but its geographic locales throughout the serial ranged further afield. The mystery story, the jungle adventure, and (in wartime) the spy theme dominated the serials far more than did Westerns. It wasn't until the 1920s that Westerns formed a major part of the serial output. Helen Holmes's popular railroading adventures, and especially her early *Hazards of Helen* one-reelers were usually done in the framework and setting of the Western, although most of the key action revolved around locomotives.

Furthermore, the Western could call on the well-loved novels and stories of Rex Beach, Owen Wister, Peter B. Kyne, and increasingly (since he was a new and popular writer), Zane Grey—stories that were both fresh and exciting, and were being brought to the screen for the first time. Some of the best of the early features, even those without the persona of a star like Bill Hart, were good just *because* they were Westerns, telling stories in terms of visuals and action, and presenting fewer difficulties to fledgling screenwriters, who still tended to construct scenarios in terms of tableaux and lists of shots.

Rex Beach's *The Spoilers* (technically a "Northern," although it contained most of the stock Western characters and actions), shot in 1914 by the Selig Company, and remade four times since, was an exceptional film for that comparatively early date. Running for close to ninety minutes, it managed cohesion despite a multiplicity of characters, created a very creditably realistic milieu of a muddy, brawling, gold-mine boomtown, and was the first Western to build deliberately to a grand scale climactic fistfight between good guy and bad. Without doubles (and admittedly without some of the spectacular if unlikely thrills that stuntmen—aided by slicker editing, breakaway furniture, and the punctuation of a musical score—brought to later versions), William Farnum and Tom Santschi put on a rousing fight that looked real all the way, and was climaxed by Farnum's victory and his classic (inter title) line "I broke him—with my hands!" as the cavalry arrived to arrest the defeated villain. Although the fight seems a little tame and stiff by contemporary standards, it served as a yardstick for many years. Farnum and Santschi, probably only for publicity purposes, were shown visiting the set of the 1930 sound remake allegedly to coach Gary Cooper and William (Stage) Boyd in the staging of their fight scene, and shortly thereafter staged another scrap of their own in the temperance melodrama *Ten Nights in a Bar Room.*

So successful was *The Spoilers* that, two years later, Selig shot additional footage (including some of author Rex Beach) to expand the film to twelve reels, and rereleased it to cash in on the public's interest in long superproductions as created by Griffith, and by Herbert Brenon in his Annette Kellerman vehicles. Only in its intertitling did *The Spoilers* reveal any kind of hesitancy

about how to translate written material into film. Every line of dialogue first identified the speaker and his or her character name on the left side of the screen with the matching line of dialogue printed to the right. Sometimes when two-way conversations were recorded on a single title card, there were two or three such identifications per title. Thus, momentarily, one was taken entirely "out" of the movie and given, in essence, a page of play-script to read. However, this kind of literary echo was of brief duration: from Griffith, directors soon learned how to edit so that audiences knew exactly *who* was saying *what* without having it spelled out.

Griffith himself, having spent so much time on Westerns in his Biograph days and now having much more ambitious plans, had little interest in them, although under his overall supervision, fledgling directors working in his Fine Arts producing wedge of the Triangle Company (the other members of the Triangle being Ince and Sennett) did make a number of Westerns in the Griffith manner. The most interesting of these was *Martyrs of the Alamo,* the first feature to deal with the Sam Houston–Santa Anna conflict. Lacking the kind of glamorous star personas that surrounded John Wayne's *The Alamo,* the film was cast entirely with Griffith's character players (Walter Long as Santa Anna, and rather surprisingly, Tom Wilson, primarily a blackface comedian, as Houston) giving it, especially today, a kind of documentarian look.

Ostensibly planned as a much bigger production, and originally subtitled *The Birth of Texas,* it was presumably intended as a follow-up to *The Birth of a Nation,* aims that were reduced when the Mutual Company was transformed into Triangle, and when Griffith diverted most of his energies to the upcoming *Intolerance.* Nevertheless, it *was* put into release with the prestige of a musical score arranged by Joseph Carl Breil, who had performed the musical chores for *The Birth of a Nation.* It was efficiently directed by Christy Cabanne—who would remain a competent, reliable hack director right through the 1940s—but it did not create a sense of size or spectacle. Presumably Griffith realized this and beefed up the film after its completion by adding color and information to the intertitles—including the rather astonishing and oft-repeated assertions that Santa Anna spent all of his off-duty time on drugs and sex orgies, which, if true, would be quite remarkable considering the ruthless efficiency with which he handled his military campaigning.

If Griffith avoided the Western in this period, so in a sense did Cecil B. DeMille, although he did produce a handful, primarily stage-derived properties as vehicles for stars like Mary Pickford. Henry King made Westerns for the American Film Company. Starring William Rus-

Keith of the Border (Triangle, 1917) with Roy Stewart (checkered shirt), another star hoping to duplicate the success of the studio's top-liner, Bill Hart

sell, they were curious in their anticipation of King's best later Westerns, like *The Gunfighter,* in that they stressed such qualities as mood, tension, and naturalism far more than action. Other directors like Frank Borzage, whose later work rarely ventured into even the fringes of the Western, made surprisingly *good* Westerns in this period.

Even without many stars in whom to center their appeal, the enormous popularity of the Westerns as a genre at this time is pinpointed by the number of films that were *not* traditional Westerns but that aimed, by their titles, to attract a Western audience. *The Sunset Trail* (1917; the title was later used for a number of traditional Westerns) was not a Western at all, but a rather pleasing though decidedly noneventful backwoods romance in which an explanation for the title had to be dragged in by the heels. *The Ranger,* an independent film of 1918, *did* have a Western locale, but was essentially a story of World War One, the smuggling of German propaganda across the American border, and an involved plot that includes the good badman's discovery that the hero is his own son. *The Sundown Trail* (1919) is set during the California gold rush, but is essentially an emotional drama of mother love and the importing of Eastern brides for the isolated miners.

The Heart of Wetona (1918), a Norma Talmadge vehicle, was one of many films that utilized the location-

Last of the Duanes (Fox, 1918) with William Farnum

M'liss (Paramount, 1918) with Mary Pickford and Thomas Meighan

The Roundup (Paramount, 1920): Wallace Beery held at bay by Fatty Arbuckle in only a semi-comic role

filmed *space* of the West to tell an emotional story of Indian-white race problems. Or, in this case, problems created purely by social convention. The half-caste Indian girl, seduced and betrayed by the white villain, Gladden James (always an expert at playing spineless weaklings), causes problems when she confesses that she is no longer "fit" to be a vestal virgin in a harvest ceremonial. Her father assumes the Indian agent (played by Thomas Meighan) to be the culprit, but ultimately, and rather surprisingly, after the seducer (also revealed to be a coward) is killed off, Indian girl and government agent marry. Stories like this were popular with producers because their basic expense (and in those days it was not a major one) was that of location shooting; the films capitalized on the public interest in the West, but did not require spectacular staging or an action star to pull them off successfully.

Because appearing in a Western was a surefire way to build popularity and was far from the "slumming" it came to be regarded as later, many of the stars of the pre-twenties era were ready and willing to appear in horse operas. Dustin Farnum had set the pattern in DeMille's *The Squaw Man,* and in his wake came J. Warren Kerrigan, Robert Edeson, House Peters, Charles Ray, Elliott Dexter, Jack Holt, Harold Lockwood, and Wallace Reid . . . some of them of course being already too mature to achieve lasting stature as stars of Westerns and moving into character roles, or in other cases just proving unsuitable over the long haul. But Westerns were good to them and for them at that stage of their careers. Mae Marsh made *The Wild Girl of the Sierras,* while another Griffith heroine, lovely and lively Dorothy Gish, kidded the genre in *Nugget Nell.*

Next to Charlie Chaplin (who never got closer to a Western than *The Gold Rush,* and thus was perhaps the only major comedian, silent or sound, never to do a Western spoof), the biggest stars of those years were Mary Pickford and Douglas Fairbanks, both of whom numbered Westerns among their bigger successes. (In fact, Mary's last film, *Secrets* (1933), was basically a Western, albeit an emotional one.) Pickford is too often shunted aside as a dated, stereotyped, sentimental figure. But while sentiment and pathos were certainly ingredients of her films, so were horror, stark drama, and melodramatic action. Her DeMille Western, *A Romance of the Redwoods,* though a little old-fashioned in its theatrical plotting, was still quite strong stuff, while in *M'liss,* Mary rushes to save an innocent man from a lynch

A production shot from the early twenties; Mix's top cameraman, Dan Clark, at extreme left

mob, points out the actual miscreant, and looks on approvingly as he is taken away and strung up from the nearest tree!

The Douglas Fairbanks Westerns were unique, and are still as fresh, delightful, and full of surprises as they ever were. Initially at Triangle, and then later at Paramount, Fairbanks was working on the same lot as William S. Hart. Hart, of course, took his Westerns very seriously, but occasionally when he wanted to let his hair down—just a little—he would do a story about the strong, silent Westerner who comes East (or further West, to San Francisco) and whose strength and integrity confound the city crooks. *Branding Broadway,* one of the more lighthearted of these, had him chasing the villain on horseback through Central Park. Doug, on the other hand, never took his films seriously and found in the West a perfect outlet for a modern tongue-in-cheek D'Artagnan, and also for the little boy or Peter Pan imprisoned within, needing only the freedom of the West for his personal optimism to win through. Thus his scripts, usually written by Anita Loos and John Emerson, often found him as the cowboy-crazy Easterner, chained to a dull desk, working for a tyrannical employer (usually an uncle or relative, making escape more difficult), wishing that he had been born in an earlier age and then going out West where he proves to be a rougher buckaroo than any of them. Such films as *Wild and Woolly* (still one of the fastest ever made, and cut with the mathematical precision of an Eisenstein, the average shot lasting only a few seconds), *Manhattan Madness,* and *Knickerbocker Buckaroo* enabled Doug to engage in acrobatics, kid modern foibles, expound his optimistic philosophy (practical only if one had the unlimited funds necessary to follow one's dreams instead of earning a living), and satirize Western clichés and traditions all at once. Yet Fairbanks's exuberant love of the West in its own way matched Hart's more emotional dedication. An early scene in *Wild and Woolly* shows Fairbanks admiring Frederic Remington's superb 1903 painting, *His First Lesson,* the original of which is a keynote illustration in the many magnificent displays of Western art at the Amon Carter Museum in Fort Worth, Texas. It shows a somewhat cautious cowboy reaching for the pommel of a fractious horse in a small corral with an adobe hut in the background. (It's interesting that Fairbanks would be honest enough to associate himself with a novice, rather than daydreaming of Hickok, Cody, Custer, or other legendary figures). The scene then dissolves into a meticulous reconstruction of the painting, as Fairbanks mounts the horse and gallops around the corral.

Doug's films moved like lightning, were as funny as they were thrilling, and had a grace, charm, and zip that his later, much longer swashbucklers largely lacked. And while they espoused the accepted sportsmanship clichés of the West, at the same time they were punctuated by sudden moments of realism or black humor. Having captured the villain in *Wild and Woolly,* Fairbanks needs to ride off to rescue the heroine, but also wants the now unarmed villain to stay put. His sensible solution is to shoot him in the leg so that he *can't* run away!

Mack Sennett (a contemporary of Hart and Fairbanks at the same studio) had been satirizing Westerns for years, and would continue to do so throughout the twenties. *His Bitter Pill* (1916), with bulky Mack Swain (a sheriff with a mother fixation) lampooning Bill Hart, was a classic of its kind; Swain himself later remade it (even funnier, with some very spectacular action) as *Cowboy Ambrose.* Even D. W. Griffith, in his rural romance, *Hoodoo Ann,* the same year, has Mae Marsh and Bobby Harron go to a small-town movie house, where they see a Western in which Carl Stockdale burlesques Hart. The movie-within-a-movie also kidded what had already become clichés of carelessness and lack of continuity, such as the hero falling to a bullet so badly aimed that it couldn't have passed within six feet of him.

This kind of satire grew both in number and subtlety as the Westerns themselves grew in popularity, reaching a peak in the early twenties with Sennett's *A Small Town Idol,* starring Ben Turpin as a Western star returning to his Western hometown (a feature now unfortunately lost, save for a two-reel version reissued with sound and gag narration in the forties). There also were such Hal Roach takeoffs as *The Uncovered Wagon* and two Will Rogers lampoons, *Two Wagons Both Covered* and *Uncensored Movies,* in which the star does devastatingly accurate sendups of Hart and Mix. The Mix spoofs were especially funny, since there *was* a slight facial resemblance and Rogers was able to include nuances of expression as well. In addition, his own riding skills enlarged the scope of the satire.

Still, it is probably the Fairbanksian spoofs that hold up best, probably because they work on two levels—as satires *and* as enjoyable examples of the genre that is being kidded. If Fairbanks loved the West as much as Hart, he loved it for what it stood for rather than for what it was; he never romanticized it and was shrewd enough to include a scene near the end of his films where he admitted he had been somewhat of a fool, whereupon the level-headed Westerners—and the heroine—accepted him for what he was.

Even the great (and sadly underrated) Fatty Arbuckle made a Western feature during this period, following such typical Sennett knockabout slapstick two-reelers as *Fatty and Minnie Ha Ha. The Roundup,* based on a 1907

Hello Cheyenne (Fox, 1928): Tom Mix's last film for Fox

play, was far from being a comedy. Actually, Irving Cummings (who became a director) and Tom Forman had the leads, but because of his popularity and the fact that this was his first feature, Arbuckle got top billing. The role was a key one, but, in terms of footage, a supporting one; he played a genial sheriff, much in the manner of Eugene Pallette. When the film was remade by Paramount in 1940, Richard Dix and Preston Foster had the leads, the Arbuckle role being taken by the rotund Don Wilson, Jack Benny's announcer and stooge.

As the teen years moved on to the twenties, the star system had taken hold with a vengeance, and it became apparent that certain stars would always enjoy their greatest popularity in Westerns. Universal had developed Harry Carey and Hoot Gibson; Roy Stewart at Triangle, intended as a second-string Hart, had none of Hart's creativity or powerful acting style, but still built quite a following. Franklyn Farnum, in two-reelers, seemed to be another star to watch, but his career never really took off, and it was a supporting player in those shorts—Buck Jones—who frequently "stole" them and who ultimately acquired much greater fame.

Fans were irked by stars who, on their own or at studio prodding, gave themselves names that suggested kinship with established stars: Neal Hart, William Fairbanks, Al

The Circus Ace (Fox, 1927): Mix with Stanley Blystone

Hoxie, Art Mix. Even though some of them were reasonably accomplished performers, the ingrained resentment against them remained, and their careers were brief and limited to cheap independent productions. Nevertheless, their presence helped to begin a roster of players who would devote themselves exclusively to Westerns, a roster, and a genre, given new impetus by the advent of the most popular Western star of them all, Tom Mix.

When Mix ultimately became a big star at Fox, publicity created a "biography" for him far more colorful than any of his movie roles. But it was exaggerated only in that no one man could have crammed so much into so few years and over such a widespread geographic area. Mix, being a showman and himself a teller of tall tales, did nothing to minimize the creation of his offscreen image. But if exaggerated in the sheer profusion of incident, it was not too far from truth in its basic elements; there is no doubt that he did have a rugged and adventurous life prior to his movie days, seeing action with the army, breaking horses for the British for their use in the Boer War, and serving for a period as a deputy United States marshal in Oklahoma. He had also been a rodeo rider and performer with the Miller Brothers 101 Ranch Show. So with all this material to build from, it is not surprising that Fox's publicity department, after creating a whole new and totally artificial exotic background for the studio's vamp star Theda Bara, built for him an image that was a composite of D'Artagnan and Wild Bill Hickok!

With all that activity and three of his five wives behind him, Mix was on the verge of settling down to ranch life when he became associated with the Selig Company. Selig was about to shoot a semidocumentary short entitled *Ranch Life in the Great South West* and arranged with Mix to use his ranch, livestock, and advisory services. The project finished and apparently forgotten, Mix had no thought of pursuing a career in movies. Later, however, the Selig people contacted him again and offered him a vague but all-purpose job in which he would handle livestock, double for actors in tricky action scenes, and generally advise in the production of a series of Westerns. Mix accepted, and was assigned to the company's California studio. Although active and for a while prosperous, Selig was a minor company in terms of creativity or concrete contributions (*The Spoilers* excepted) to the development of film. It specialized in Westerns, jungle pictures (above average if only because Selig maintained its own wild animal zoo), serials, and contemporary crime stories.

Selig, unlike Biograph, Ince, and Vitagraph, nurtured but few embryonic talents, and Mix was the only really big name to result from an apprenticeship there. However, between 1911 and 1917, the period of Broncho Billy Anderson's rise and decline, and William S. Hart's ascendancy, Mix made almost a hundred films for Selig, ranging from one- and two-reelers to, ultimately, features. Initially they were artless, off-the-cuff affairs, loosely strung together, many of them looking as though they were filmed without scripts and concerned as much with folksy humor in the Will Rogers tradition as with action. Mix had been a friend of Rogers and may well have intentionally aimed at cultivating a Rogers image, since Rogers had as yet shown no inclination to try for a movie career himself. On many of the films, Mix was author, star, and director, an ambitious undertaking for one with so little business and creative experience in his background. If for nothing else, Mix deserves credit for turning out so much product so regularly. Too, the films did improve as they went along. Mix gradually dropped the stress on comedy *(Why the Sheriff Is a Bachelor)* in favor of stories which allowed him to exploit his riding and stunting prowess: *The Stagecoach Driver and the Lady, Pony Express Rider,* and *In the Days of the Thundering Herd.*

Many of Mix's early Selig films were comedies or simple dramas about the making of Westerns, a cunning way of making movies with even less set dressing than usual. Some of them, like *Mr. Haywood Producer* and *Sagebrush Tom* (in which the cowboys decide to stage a Western version of *Quo Vadis?*), have added historic interest today in that they have thus preserved detail of the working methods of the Selig company, shots of camera equipment, and even close-ups of studio note paper with instructions to the crew. But as a group the Tom Mix Westerns, even the better features, were mild and inferior to such Selig "specials" as *The Spoilers* or a 1913 William Duncan vehicle, *The Range Law.* Later, with Mix a big star at Fox, "new" Mix features were created by taking the shorts and with considerable ingenuity reediting and retitling them into five-reel features. *Twisted Trails* was a typical example. After devoting some footage to Bessie Eyton from a non-Mix film, they finally meet and, with a title announcing that "Thus were the twisted trails of the boy and girl joined together," the way was paved for the use of shorts in which they appeared together and which could be linked to a fairly cohesive story line. With the exception of *Chip of the Flying U* (1914), which had a good original story by Peter B. Kyne and also had Selig's top director, Colin Campbell, at the helm, none of Mix's Selig films made a very strong impression. On the other hand, considering how many were made, a relatively minute proportion survives for reappraisal today. Too, Selig had relatively few marketable stars and carried less and less clout as competition from other producers grew. The company,

The Fourth Horseman: Mix with Fred Kohler in one of the best of his early talkies for Universal

however, did gain a strong foothold in Europe and had particularly strong representation in, for example, Austria—where Tom Mix became an established and popular name well *before* Chaplin.

Mix's rugged qualities, though, had attracted the attention of Fox, which offered him a contract in 1917. Although he made his debut there with a trial balloon two-reeler, *Six Cylinder Love,* that he wrote and directed himself, he immediately thereafter switched to features and left the direction to veterans better qualified: Chester and Sidney Franklin, John Ford, Lynn Reynolds, John Blystone, and Lewis Seiler. Although there was a certain understandable overlapping into William S. Hart territory at the beginning—the first Mix films tended to be the most serious, dealing with heavy themes of revenge, for example—it was not long before Mix's unique quality was recognized and exploited, and a deliberate attempt was made to differentiate his style from that of Hart, who was now beginning to slip at the box office.

Mix's films came to include liberal doses of comedy and small-child appeal. (Youngsters undoubtedly adored Hart for a while, but he made no attempt to cultivate their sustained favor by including elements expressly designed to please them). Furthermore, they were action-packed yet essentially nonviolent. Gradually a kind of "circus" approach was formulated; his films were full of fights, chases, and stunts, often clearly showing Mix doing his own tricks, realistic in such detail as costuming and location, but emphatically escapist in dramatic terms. No serious issues were raised, and nobody was expected to take them too seriously; youngsters loved them for their fun and action, adults enjoyed them because in a sense they were continuing the Fairbanksian sense of fun and exuberance when Doug transferred in 1920 to the bigger costume adventures.

While Fox was wise enough not to tamper too often with a successful formula, at the same time the Mix films continued to provide variety. At the peak of his popularity in the mid-twenties, Mix made *Riders of the Purple*

Sage and its immediate sequel, *The Rainbow Trail*. These two close adaptations of Zane Grey were a little heavy for Mix and not among his best pictures, though they were so well made that fans had no cause for complaint. The complicated story line left too little room for action, and Mix's role as a revenge-obsessed wanderer was at odds with the lighthearted image that had been created. Basically, as the popularity of the Mix films increased, so did their story lines tend to become more contemporary and less realistic. His plots provided him with sojourns in Arabia and Ruritania, and in *The Good Bad Man* (which closed with an absolute marathon of action), he had flapper Clara Bow as his sparring partner. Essentially up to the minute, his films concentrated on modern speed—locomotives, racing cars, ocean liners, and planes were incorporated into his stories as props on which even more action could be hung. Only once did Fox really miscalculate, and that was when it tried to emphasize his kinship to Fairbanks by starring him in *Dick Turpin* and stressing its "special" qualities by adding a couple of extra reels. Fans just did not accept him out of Western costume or, even sympathetically, on the wrong side of the law as the notorious British highwayman—although the script juggled history so that Dick gave up his life of crime to settle down to a happy marriage! Actually *Dick Turpin* was and is a most enjoyable film, but Tom seemed almost as hemmed in by frills and laces as Douglas Fairbanks. But (commercial) mistakes like *Dick Turpin* were few, and the bulk of Mix's films concentrated on action and excitement rather than logic. Mix went out of his way to devise and perform elaborate stunt sequences.

Despite horrendous threats by the villains, the mortality rate in the later Mix films was practically nil. He would subdue his opponents with fists or some fancy lasso work, often by humiliating them, rarely by shooting them. His unlikely but likeable hero, clean living to a fault, possessed of no vices (certainly not smoking or drinking, habits that Hart emphasized rather than suppressed) and all of the virtues, was not absurd in his own make-believe world. Often Mix's introductory segment would stress the basic unreality of his character. He is first seen in *The Great K and A Train Robbery* hanging on to a rope, one end of which is attached to the top of a high cliff, the other to the pommel of the saddle on wonder horse Tony far below. An introductory title tells us only that he is a stranger . . . out of nowhere, asking no questions. How he had the foresight to set up his precarious perch *just* to hear the villains outlining their plans on this particular occasion is never explained. When the heavies catch sight of him from above, Tom immediately adjusts a mask over his eyes (although from their vantage point they could hardly see his face any-

way) and slides down the rope on to Tony—and into a full reel of nonstop action involving trick riding, transfers to and from a train, and sundry stunts. Such an unreal opening immediately disarms any potential criticism of the story, which has a contemporary (1926) setting, yet has a train-robbing theme which harks back to the days of Jesse James and the Daltons!

Mix's impossibly virtuous heroes set the pattern for a long time to come, though it was a pattern that seemed a little ridiculous in Westerns that took themselves more seriously than those of Mix. Since he always delivered the entertainment goods in terms of interesting stories and extremely lively action, nobody quibbled at his radical departure from the traditions previously laid down by Hart. Moreover, Mix's films were always good to look at. He used the best cameramen available, and the great Dan Clark whenever possible, and made a point of shooting many of his films amid the awe-inspiring scenery of the national parks. *Sky High*, for example, was shot almost entirely in and around the Grand Canyon, its action ranging from a rugged fight on the banks of the churning Colorado River to exciting and precarious chases along the narrow trails lining the chasm walls and aerial stunting in a plane just skimming the canyon. *The Great K and A Train Robbery*, one of Mix's very best and most typical films, used the Denver and the Rio Grande railroad, and apart from a short sequence inside the train's coaches and a nocturnal visit to the heroine's home, was shot entirely out of doors, primarily in the Colorado Gorge. Although not all of the Fox Mix films survive, enough of them do to provide a reliable cross section of his career there, from the early and more serious ones to the later all-action shows like *The Last Trail*. Fox filmed this Zane Grey story three times; each version was totally different from the other and had no connection whatsoever with Grey's original tale, which dealt with a family feud. Mix's version, the liveliest, started with an Indian attack and concluded with a large-scale and stunt-jammed stagecoach race. The final version, a George O'Brien Western of the early thirties, was a thoroughly contemporary thriller, one of several that took modern city gangsters to the West.

By the mid-twenties, Mix was earning a salary of $17,000 a week and living it up accordingly. However, he more than earned it. Fox, no longer as successful as it had been in earlier years, needed the huge profits from the Mix films. Without them, such classic films as F. W. Murnau's *Sunrise*—the kind of film that every studio wanted for "prestige" purposes even though individually they rarely showed a profit—could not have been made. Similarly, at Warners, the Rin Tin Tin action adventures were underwriting the big John Barrymore prestige films.

Despite its huge success, Fox was smart enough not to deviate from the popular formula of the Mix films. Even at his peak, and apart from the atypical *Dick Turpin,* Mix—who had his own unit and was very much the guiding force behind his movies—limited himself to five- and six-reel features that *really* moved and gave audiences just what they wanted. No pretention ever crept into his films although, their success assured, they were sometimes favored with better directors and supporting casts than would normally have been allotted to a Western. But not a nickel was spent in weighing down the star with "art" in the form of decor, sets, or literary scenarios. This was a lesson that Republic Studios, number-one makers of Westerns in the talkie era, several times failed to heed. Having built Bill Elliott into a top draw via a series of expert and fast-moving "B" films, they changed Bill to William, promoted him to nine-reel historical Western—"Specials" in which he was hamstrung by frock coats, silk shirts, reels of dialogue (once even a tragic ending), studio "exteriors," back projection, prominent non-Western character actors like Joseph Schildkraut in support, and far too little fresh air, horses, and wagons. Expensive films of the forties like *In Old Sacramento* and *The Plainsman and the Lady* contained not a quarter of the action or appeal of his six-reelers, and he lost much of his popularity until he reverted to his former style—and scale—with a good "B" series at Monogram. To a degree, Republic made the same mistake with Gene Autry and Roy Rogers, overloading their musical Westerns with protracted song and dance at the expense of action, though the studio remedied it before much permanent damage was done.

The result of not letting Mix step out of his class—and away from his audience—was the most consistently satisfying and profitable series of Westerns in the history of the movies. They sounded the death knell for William S. Hart, rapidly overtaking him in popularity and mass appeal. He neither could nor would compete, and eased himself into retirement, with distinction and honor, to be replaced not only by Mix but also by the new breed of cowboy he had brought to the screen. Two of the best of them, Buck Jones and George O'Brien, came from the ranks of Mix's own unit, while by the early twenties many others—Hoot Gibson, Fred Thomson, Ken Maynard, Tim McCoy, Yakima Canutt—were ready to cash in on and expand the streamlined format that Mix had pioneered. The austerity of Hart and his "strong, silent" image were too firmly entrenched to be dismissed entirely, and his breed of Westerner still had its loyal following. Hart himself remained in the saddle until 1925, and Harry Carey, Jack Holt, Art Acord, and a handful of others continued to play in the Hart manner. But for the most part, Mix had established a formula both for the series Western and for the Western hero that would remain unchanged until the small Western itself bit the dust in the mid-fifties, scalped by the impossible odds of rising production costs and driven off their ranges by the inroads of television, just as surely as the American Indian had been decimated by the coming of the Iron Horse and the slaughter of the buffalo herds.

Karl Brown shooting the main title for *The Covered Wagon* (Paramount, 1923)

The Covered Wagon

SEVEN

The First Epics

Although the popularity of the Tom Mix films certainly increased the box office value of the Western and stimulated additional production in the area of the two-reeler, it did not materially alter the number of feature-length Westerns being made. That catharsis was provided by Paramount's 1923 production of *The Covered Wagon.* So successful was it that the number of Westerns filmed in the year of its production—approximately fifty—was tripled in the year following its release.

Based on Emerson Hough's novel, *The Covered Wagon* was put into production as a result of the success of William S. Hart's *Wagon Tracks,* which while not a particularly ambitious production in itself, suggested that the larger-scale Western had possibilities. Actually, Hart realized the possibilities first. *Wagon Tracks* was a 1919 film; he followed through with the bigger but similar *White Oak* in 1921. While neither was among Hart's best, each was different from his usual run of Westerns, and the wagon trek theme common to both made each stand out. Shot very largely on location with lesser names (its biggest star, Mary Miles Minter, had been replaced by Lois Wilson), *The Covered Wagon* almost unwittingly grew into epic proportions. Word of its unusual qualities got back to Hollywood, causing Paramount to invest more money in it. When it was

finished, Jesse Lasky apparently tampered with it to its benefit, inserting additional scenes and bits of business that gave it greater stature and humanity. As the first real super Western, its success with both critics and public was instantaneous. *The Covered Wagon* does not survive the years well; today it seems both disappointing and unexciting, and its hero (J. Warren Kerrigan) too virtuous, too theatrical—especially when surrounded by the likes of Tully Marshall and Ernest Torrence—and too neatly garbed, much in the manner of Alan Ladd's costuming in *Shane.* Yet it *is* one of the key Western films, one of perhaps a half dozen that have made a definite contribution to the development of the genre, whether it be artistically, thematically or commercially. *The Covered Wagon* is a milestone film, important because it it introduced the epic tradition to the Western, giving it scale and poetic and documentary values. Thanks mainly to the grandeur and panoramic vistas captured by Karl Brown's superb camerawork, it is easy to understand why the film so captured the imagination of audiences in 1923. Ford's *The Iron Horse,* made the following year, is unquestionably far more exciting as entertainment and more creative as film, but it undoubtedly owes its existence to the success of *The Covered Wagon.*

The major shortcoming of *The Covered Wagon* lies with James Cruze, who would soon become one of the best-paid directors of silent films. At that time, his simple, uncomplicated style found a certain favor. Both audiences and critics were beginning to resist what they considered "arty" trends in European imports. In retrospect, one can recognize that in almost all of Cruze's silents theme and content were far superior to execution; they were generally plodding, unimaginative works. This is especially true of his big epics of American history (including *Old Ironsides* and the talkie *Sutter's Gold*). Curiously enough, some of his less-ambitious silents and lesser-known talkies revealed real flair and talent, and the lethargic pacing of his bigger silents was so at odds with the crackling tempo of some of his Depression-era movies—especially *I Cover the Waterfront* and *Washington Merry-Go-Round*—that it's hard to believe they were all the work of the same man.

In *The Covered Wagon*, Cruze used little of the basic grammar of film language, and it seems an especially dull movie when compared with Griffith's *Orphans of the Storm* of the previous year. Cruze seldom moved his camera, and even the usually foolproof runaway horse sequence—always useful as a piece of short punctuating action, and as a way of introducing or cementing boy-girl relations—is handled in one single long shot, as though it was an obligatory episode that the director just wanted to get out of the way as soon as possible. Even Edwin S. Porter, shooting a similar sequence in *Life of an American Policeman* in 1905, had at least broken it up into three or four shots. Cruze likewise seemed to care nothing for the cumulative effect of editing, and the cavalry's ride to rescue the besieged wagon train from Indian massacre is almost as lackluster as the similar ride in *The Corporal's Daughter* (discussed earlier), though sheer size, enhanced by Brown's cinematography, was something of a saving grace. However, a basic lack of excitement in this sequence was underlined by the kind of dime-novel melodramatics that had a small, determined youngster ride to get the rescuing troops because "no *man* could get through," according to one of the inter titles. And despite almost automatically recreating the conditions of an old wagon trek, Cruze seemed indifferent to the cause of realism. Paramount's publicity trumpeted that there wasn't a phony whisker in the entire cast, which may have been true, but if Cruze couldn't shoot genuine riding close-ups on location, then better none at all than the patently fake ones (a "rider" bobbing up and down on a barrel against a moving cycloramic background) that marred the buffalo hunt sequence. As Bill Hart observed somewhat contemptuously, no wagonmaster worth his salt would camp his train in a box canyon in the heart of Indian country!

Even allowing for the fact that the film was started as a normal "A" production and enlarged in scope as it progressed, it contains some very barren writing. There is no vital, dramatic sense of opening up new frontiers. Even the period is a bit hazy, and the titles constantly fall back on dates and gratuitous references to Brigham Young and Abraham Lincoln as a means of documenting what is going on. Nor is the reconstruction of the period helped by the imbalance between events; a conventional fight between hero and villain is given far more prominence and footage than the discovery of gold in California, which is treated in a totally offhand manner.

But much of the scope and richness of the film's visual tapestry does still have power, as does the superb teamwork of Ernest Torrence and Tully Marshall as two old scouts. It is probably their work in this film that laid the groundwork for the constant reuse of such characters in related Western epics *(The Big Trail, Fighting Caravans, Union Pacific)*. Not only do they *belong,* and create a kind of realism often denied by the costuming and persona of the star, but they can also contribute naturalistic comedy without slowing up the narrative. The "buddy" comics who appeared in "B" Westerns and who derived from the Torrence/Marshall characters—George Hayes and Raymond Hatton in particular—

Director James Cruze, technical advisor Tim McCoy, and one of the Indian chiefs used in *The Covered Wagon*

Lois Wilson, leading lady of *The Covered Wagon* and its sequel, *North of '36*

The Iron Horse (Fox, 1924): It's almost difficult to tell whether this is a production shot from the film or a photograph taken during construction of the railroad originally

The Covered Wagon: Awaiting the Indian attack in a box canyon

were always far more effective (and funnier too) than the in-disguise clowns like Smiley Burnette, Dub Taylor, and Fuzzy Knight.

The panoramic scenes of the wagon train snaking its way across the plains, the near-documentary footage of campfire singing, a burial on the trail, the crossing of a swollen river, and the hazards of snow and mud, are still stirring and pictorially very beautiful. (A prairie fire sequence was cut after the original road show exhibitions, probably because it was so brief and prosaic as to be merely frustrating within the framework of an epic.) All of this, of course, proved invaluable as establishing stock footage right through the thirties and forties, primarily by Paramount (which made many economic Westerns seem much bigger by the use of such impressive old footage). It was also sold away, though, to other companies, and its usefulness ceased only when color became too widespread for black-and-white footage to be incorporated easily into new films.

The Covered Wagon was never officially remade, probably because its bare-bones plot was plagiarized many times, and eventually all it really had to offer was a title. Paramount however, often *talked* about a remake. Its *California* (1946) had all the earmarks of having been *planned* as a remake. Ray Milland, never too much at home in Westerns, especially in this, his first, was literally replaying the J. Warren Kerrigan role from the original. The film opens with a impressively created prologue of wagons crossing mountains, plains, and rivers, none of it stock footage, and all of it too elaborate to have been made just for an opening montage. It looked as though Paramount had planned a bona fide remake, shot much second-unit material on location, and then shifted gears as the script was developed. Possibly Barbara Stanwyck's omnipresence as a shady lady gambler who has to be reformed ruled out the possibility of its being anything but a vehicle for the two stars. *California* was lively but not very good, and suggests that a remake at that time would not have been very impressive. A decade later, after the surprise success of *Shane,* Paramount thought so seriously of *The Covered Wagon* as a follow-up vehicle for Alan Ladd that it took aggressive steps to stop so-called illicit showings of the silent original on the grounds that it could materially hurt the studio's investment in a new version. But, again, the plans never materialized. However, in 1991 Paramount did release the original *Covered Wagon* to the videocassette market in a version of length and quality unseen for a great many years.

Apart from the Mix and Hart films, most of the

Westerns in release immediately prior to *The Covered Wagon* were the relatively unimportant programmers with the likes of Francis Ford (now losing much of his individuality as a director/star, and leaning toward imitating Hart) and Roy Stewart. Even so charming and well made a Western as King Vidor's much underrated *The Sky Pilot* created little excitement. The following year, however, the Western land rush was on with a vengeance!

The biggest and most successful of all the follow-ups was *The Iron Horse*, made by Ford for Fox. It succeeded in nurturing a sense of urgency and pride in the joint contribution to national progress that had been largely missing from Cruze's film. More important in terms of film history, it was to be of considerable influence on such later films as the Russian silent *Turksib*, the British *The Great Barrier* (about the building of the Canadian Pacific Railroad), and DeMille's *Union Pacific*, while the many lesser and more standardized railroad Westerns of the fifties—*Santa Fe, Kansas Pacific, The Denver and the Rio Grande*—inevitably if not intentionally derived much from it.

While *The Iron Horse* was Ford's first spectacular, most of his output till then had been Westerns, and he knew and loved the genre. It was an epic in every sense of the word, yet he was clearly not overawed either by

the importance of the film or by his responsibility for handling such a major undertaking. *The Iron Horse* is big and sprawling, but unlike so many historical super Westerns (especially Frank Lloyd's *Wells Fargo*), it doesn't allow itself to slow down into stiff tableaux.

Shooting *The Covered Wagon* in Snake Valley, Nevada

Although the script and especially William Fox's insistence that the project also be conceived and presented as a kind of homage to Abraham Lincoln make the film somewhat slow in getting under way, the action is rugged and vigorous. The climax—with its massed Indian fighting, the locomotive racing men to the rescue, and hero and villain settling personal scores with a particularly convincing fistic bout—is one of the most exciting such sequences ever committed to film. If its epic theme is occasionally minimized, it is usually for the right reasons, and because Ford's fondness for the entertainment values of the smaller Western lead him to insert raucous Irish stereotyping and to milk slapstick scenes for more than they are really worth.

Ford emulated *The Covered Wagon* by shooting almost all of the film on location and under great hardship, especially insofar as the comforts of accommodation were concerned. Much of it too was shot in temperatures of extreme cold. There is a minimum of studio work, and the film was put together in much the same manner as the original Union Pacific railroad was constructed, the unit building itself little work and lodging towns as it moved along, and using a train of fifty-six coaches for transportation of cast, crew, and equipment. The film's publicity made much of the many historic artifacts actually or allegedly employed, including Hickok's derringer, a stagecoach supposedly used by Horace Greeley, and, for the climactic linking of the rails, the two original locomotives. The film's air of realism, though, was actually created by the fact that it was dealing with events only some fifty years in the past, and that many of the participants in them were still alive and able to act as consultants. It is sobering to realize that there is a substantially greater period of time between us today and the making of *The Iron Horse* than there was between that film and the event that inspired it.

But apart from the stress on location shooting, Ford's film was the very antithesis of Cruze's, which so deliberately underplayed its few action highlights. Cruze's big Indian battle had been staged on a large canvas, but was almost casually thrown away, with no attempt to build suspense. He would utilize one shot of a charging horde of Indians and then forget them. Ford on the other hand, shot his riders from all angles, intercut them, pointed out that Indian cavalry fought for and with the railroad men against their own people, built excitement steadily, cut away to the rescue party in the nearby town, created further delays and tension by showing some of the railroaders as reluctant to take up arms and having them shamed into action when the women of the saloon board the train in their stead, cut back to the scene of battle, thence again to the rescue train, constantly changing the vantage point of his cameras.

Despite its superior qualities, *The Iron Horse* did not duplicate the huge critical acclaim of *The Covered Wagon*, but it did get a most enthusiastic critical reaction, followed by great popular success. It ran for a full year in its New York premiere at the Lyric Theater and won praise and endorsements from governmental and educational bodies. One critic dubbed it "An American Odyssey," a description that would remain peculiarly appropriate to so many of Ford's later films. It also made a major star of its husky and likeable hero, George O'Brien, an appealing combination of brawn, good looks, a sprightly sense of humor, and an acting ability which certainly improved through the years as long as the demands placed on him were not too great. At a time when most Hollywood male stars fell into one of three camps, the exotics (Valentino, Novarro, Cortez), the low-key if pleasant and gentlemanly boys-next-door (Barthelmess, Neil Hamilton), and most of all, the bread-winning dependables (Lewis Stone, Thomas Meighan, Conrad Nagel, Milton Sills) whose main function in cinematic life was *not* to outshine the glamorous Bow, Moore, Swanson, Negri, and later Garbo, opposite whom they played, O'Brien was unique and could appeal to both men and women. Fox, in fact, pushed this quality in its ad campaigns for *The Iron Horse,* claiming as a fait accompli a popularity that could not follow until after the film had circulated to the hinterlands. "He's not a Sheik or a lounge-lizard, but a man's man and the idol of millions!" claimed one ad that concentrated more on George O'Brien than on *The Iron Horse* itself. While never a superstar, O'Brien was a *major* star in the twenties, working again for Ford and also for Curtiz, Murnau, Hawks, and other key directors. In sound films, he was universally accepted as one of the best stars of smaller Westerns, and he worked for Ford a number of times in later Westerns, beginning with *Fort Apache.*

Oddly enough, while the success of these two initial epics created a spectacular demand for more big-scale Westerns, it did not spur a whole cycle of similar follow-ups (in the way that *Broken Arrow* in 1950 launched an immediate series of pro-Indian films), and the documenting of Wells Fargo and Western Union and the taming of Dodge City, Wichita, and other frontier towns all had to await the coming of the sound film. To be truly successful in a commercial sense, the epic needs to feed off an audience feeling of pride and patriotism. It, in return, can perform morale-boosting and propagandist services as well as entertain. It is no coincidence that the best and most effective of the Western epics were made in periods when America most needed a sense of national pride in achievements of the past, and a rekindling of the pioneer spirit—during the early days of the Depression, and at the beginning of World War Two. It can be argued that America certainly

John Ford directs Iron Eyes Cody (right) in *The Iron Horse*

needed that sense of pride and unity in the twenties, but the film can only reflect it, not create it. The twenties were an era of moral and legal upheaval, when it was deemed fashionable to drink liquor merely because it was against the law, and when divorce and Freud were sophisticated subjects of conversation. In such a milieu, and against a background of fun and prosperity, appeals to national pride seemed old-fashioned and Victorian. After the war, the movies had firmly rejected the Victorian morality that had guided the plot lines of so many pre-twenties films. Films which adopted a patriotic stance were somehow deemed quaint and out of date. (Ironically, most films with those values have survived rather well, and it is the modern "sophisticated" films of the era, like Valentino's *Blood and Sand,* that tend to date most of all.) Griffith's Revolutionary War spectacle, *America* (made the same year as *The Iron Horse*), was a noted casualty of this atmosphere, and the consensus was that *The Covered Wagon* had scored because it was new and different, *The Iron Horse* because of the sheer expertise of its action, not because of their themes or attitudes.

This seemed to be confirmed when James Cruze

The Iron Horse: George O'Brien and Madge Bellamy

95

The Iron Horse: George O'Brien
and J. Farrell MacDonald (right
foreground)

attempted to duplicate the success of *The Covered
Wagon* with *The Pony Express.* Alas, the two films were
related not only by thematic titles but also by their
virtues and shortcomings. Again, the best things about
The Pony Express were the superb photography of Karl
Brown and the colorful supporting performances as
old-timers and outlaws by George Bancroft, Ernest
Torrence, and Wallace Beery. Apart from these, it was a
stiff and disjointed film, slow-paced, with too many
characters and too much interweaving of a stereotyped
story with involved political scheming. Ricardo Cortez
was as out of place in the West as J. Warren Kerrigan had
been. The big-scale action climax of an Indian raid on
the town of Julesburg was a little more effective and
certainly more realistic than the parallel sequence in *The
Covered Wagon,* but it was still relatively unimpressive.
The most interesting aspect of *The Pony Express* was the
surprisingly accurate use of Jack Slade (played by
George Bancroft) as the villain. An interesting and
unorthodox character, Slade was employed as a trouble-
shooter by the stage lines and given a free hand in
combatting lawlessness. Unfortunately, he became a law
unto himself and an even greater menace than the
element he was fighting. Ultimately he was hanged by
the vigilantes. Written up somewhat admiringly by Mark
Twain in *Roughing It,* Slade later became the subject of
a reasonably honest if somewhat neurotic biography in

the fifties with Mark Stevens both playing the lead and
unofficially codirecting. George Bancroft played him as
an ostensibly lovable rogue, but with a hidden streak of
sadism and ruthlessness. Not only did Slade manage to
turn most situations to his advantage, emerging prosperous, triumphant, and totally unpunished at the end, but
he even contrived to have a hapless (and always loyal)
Indian henchman hauled off and lynched by the populace to cover his own crimes!

However, the failure of *The Pony Express* in 1925
can't altogether be blamed on its shortcomings as a film.
Although bogged down in plot complications and lacking
the sustained visual sweep of *The Covered Wagon*—
much of it takes place in the towns at either end of the
pony express run—it wasn't so markedly inferior to it.
The public obviously was not sympathetic to the epic as
a genre. But *The Covered Wagon* had established a
market for the big-scale Western, and Hollywood exploited it to the full, but giving the public what it
apparently wanted—mass action, size, name stars—
without the emotional involvement that the epic (at its
best) demanded and needed.

Paramount filmed other Emerson Hough novels, one
of the more interesting being *North of '36,* a direct
sequel to *The Covered Wagon.* Considerably shorter
than its two predecessors, and with a first-rate director
(Irvin Willat) at the helm, it benefited from the presence

of a hero (Jack Holt) who looked as though he *belonged* in the saddle. Fortuitously, Paramount was able to send a production crew along with a genuine cattle drive—one of the last big ones. But while the real thing was in front of them, Hollywood no longer put much faith in accuracy, and insisted on changing all the details to meet audience expectations. Thus while the wagons that were part of the drive were hauled by oxen, they were replaced with horses for all scenes that would appear in the film. Star Lois Wilson, an amateur photographer, filmed much of the proceedings with her 16-mm camera. Fortunately both *her* record of the drive proper and the slick if unrealistic film translation of it still exist. Seen side by side, they provide a fascinating illustration of actuality and myth. (*North of '36* was remade by Paramount in the mid-thirties as *The Texans*, a lively but generally undistinguished pocket epic that incorporated much action footage from the silent version.)

Paramount probably made more big Westerns in the twenties than any other company, and this paved the way for the studio doing the same thing in the thirties, when it had directors like Cecil B. DeMille, King Vidor, Henry Hathaway, and Frank Lloyd under contract—and a great deal of large-scale action footage from the twenties that could be reemployed as stock.

One of Paramount's most ambitious yet ultimately most disappointing films was *The Vanishing American* (1926), based on the Zane Grey novel published only the year before. It had every opportunity to be the definitive statement on the American Indian, but something went sadly awry. It started out with a long quasi-poetic prologue ostensibly about the history of the American Indian, but in actuality covering the history and culture of the *South* American Indian, and the Aztecs' misfortunes at the hand of the Spanish invaders. No real link with the Navajo Indians, whose story formed the basis of the film proper, was ever made. George B. Seitz, who directed, was an old serial maestro and a first-rate action director, but he was not given (at least at this stage in his career) to subtlety or to handling emotional material. The powerful story material—dealing with the poverty of the Indian in America in the recent past, his valor in serving in World War One, and the renewed exploitation and broken promises after the war—was both needed and topical. It was to Paramount's credit that it handled the subject at all, and certainly set up a climate where other serious protest films on the American Indian could and would follow. But unfortunately Seitz played it purely for melodrama and action, a quality stressed by having Noah Beery play the corrupt and lecherous Indian agent villain with all the stops out. Beery was the stock villain in Paramount's series of Zane Grey Westerns, and he was fine in them. However, his unsubtle

James Cruze's *The Pony Express* (Paramount, 1923): Ernest Torrence, Ricardo Cortez, and George Bancroft

William K. Howard's *The Thundering Herd* (Paramount, 1925): Raymond Hatton, Jack Holt, and Lois Wilson

Tumbleweeds (United Artists, 1925): the opening of the Cherokee Strip

playing of the badly overwritten role was the last straw in turning *The Vanishing American* into sheer melodrama, though the sincere playing of Richard Dix as a Navajo and Lois Wilson as the white schoolteacher he loves (and who loves him in return, despite the hopelessness of their situation) was able to restore some of the poignancy that was obviously intended, when their scenes did not also involve Beery. As with *The Covered Wagon*, the film's importance lay in the fact that it was made at all. Incidentally, it was at least partially shot in Monument Valley, a full thirteen years before that magnificent location was "officially" discovered by John Ford!

The Vanishing American was certainly successful enough for Paramount to offer a follow-up—*Redskin* (1928), also starring Richard Dix—and on this occasion the second film was infinitely superior. Perhaps it succeeded so well because it was content to be an honest (but not overdone) melodrama, offering no social protest undertones other than those that came naturally out of its story line. Technical advances, surprisingly little exploited by Westerns, had a great deal to do with the film's success. It was a story that started back east with Dix as yet another college-educated Indian and followed him west, where white renegades try to cheat him out of a fortune in oil discovered on Navajo land. The college sequences were printed in sepia and all of the Western ones in the new and very pleasing (especially in its usage in this particular film) two-color Technicolor. Moreover, the suspenseful and unusual climax, in which Dix runs overland to beat the claim jumpers to the registry office, was designed to be shown on the expanding Magnascope screen. Finally, the film, actually released in early 1929, benefited from a musical score and sound effects. So color, wide screen, and a form of sound helped to enhance what was already a much better film than its inspiration, although, smaller in scope, it cannot truly be termed an epic.

Nor can Paramount's many Zane Grey adaptations, including one of the best—*Wild Horse Mesa* (1925)—which is more appropriately described in the next chapter. But the late twenties were full of Westerns that might be termed aborted epics: films in which the epic potential was deliberately played down not only for economy's sake, but because the less pretentious Westerns did better at the box office. MGM had two such Westerns: *The White Desert* (a 1925 film, brief at only six-and-a-half reels, directed by Reginald Barker), an interesting yarn of railroading and the construction of a tunnel through a Colorado mountain, highlighted by near-Stroheim savagery as the villain goes mad with lust and hunger in the climax and attacks the heroine. She resourcefully throws boiling water in his face (without slowing him down to any noticeable degree). *Tides of*

Empire (1929) was a large-scale entry by Allan Dwan, but again with a short running time, a *very* melodramatic story line, and an (as yet) unimposing hero in George Duryea, although later as Tom Keene he would make an interesting lesser Western star. But the story by Peter B. Kyne had too much happening too fast, and the title—and the careful and elaborate reconstruction of a frontier town—were its only real relationships to the world of the epic.

One of the few follow-up epics that did click was Henry King's *The Winning of Barbara Worth* (1926), a success perhaps because it told a modern, near contemporary story, had a duo of very popular stars in Ronald Colman and Vilma Banky, and a dynamic, attention-grabbing newcomer in Gary Cooper. Why the myth persists that Cooper was turned into a star overnight by his brief (if admittedly very good) scene in *Wings* is a mystery. Cooper had the third lead in *The Winning of Barbara Worth*, the most interesting role, and certainly the one that won the greatest audience sympathy.

Producer Sam Goldwyn was obviously aware of the performance that Cooper was giving and the excitement it would cause, because he had some of Cooper's footage reshot and extended and deleted his death scene, allowing him to survive even though he lost the girl to Colman—an act that won him even more sympathy! *The Winning of Barbara Worth* was in release a full eight months before *Wings* was premiered. Both the critics and the public embraced Cooper as a new find, and *Variety* went so far as to say that he virtually stole the picture from Colman and had a big future in store. In light of this acclaim (though possibly because the picture itself was not well remembered in later years), it's hard to understand why Paramount *still* propagates the myth that Cooper was discovered in *Wings*; harder still to understand why the studio failed to capitalize on him immediately but decided to "build" him via bits in *It* and *Wings*.

The Winning of Barbara Worth was based on a novel by Harold Bell Wright, a mediocre writer who has been singularly well served by Hollywood, which rewrote most of his stories substantially and, as in *The Shepherd of the Hills*, presented them with Technicolor, John Wayne starring, and Henry Hathaway directing. Audiences discovering Wright for the first time via the movies, and going back to the source, must inevitably be disappointed. Based on fact, *The Winning of Barbara Worth* had as its highlight and climax the bursting of a dam, part of an irrigation project to reclaim barren land, and the ensuing flood which sweeps away a whole township. Even in the twenties, when cataclysmic sequences such as this—floods, fires, earthquakes, even the end of the world in *Noah's Ark*—were relatively commonplace, the expertise of this sequence, so superbly photographed by George Barnes and Gregg Toland, and convincingly blending miniatures with full-scale reconstruction, was quite breathtaking, and it has dated not one iota today.

But for the most part, after *The Iron Horse* and Ford's own follow-up *Three Bad Men,* audiences wanted the big SHOW, not the big THEME. Universal's *Flaming Frontiers,* released in 1926, had as its highlight an elaborate scale reconstruction of Custer's Last Stand, but the events and personal stories leading up to that climax were as far-flung and basically unrelated as those in *The Charge of the Light Brigade* (1936). It was sold on its basic action and its stars, Hoot Gibson and Dustin Farnum (who played Custer), certainly not as a saga of the West.

A new high-water mark was set in 1925 in the number of Westerns, big and small, that Hollywood had produced. New stars were emerging to meet the demand, while prominent directors-to-be (William Wyler,

John Ford's *Three Badmen* (Fox, 1926): Tom Santschi, J. Farrell MacDonald, and Frank Campeau

Henry King's *The Winning of Barbara Worth* (Goldwyn-United Artists, 1926): Vilma Banky, Ed Brady, and Gary Cooper

William K. Howard, W. S. Van Dyke) were learning their trade in the best school of all—making Westerns that *moved,* making them fast, and making them cheaply. The quickie producers were coming in, like sooners in a land rush, capitalizing on a great and newly popular genre, cheapening it, hastening the arrival of the double bill. Typical of these fly-by-night operators was one Anthony J. Xydias, who specialized in Westerns made very much on the cheap, but gave them cheater titles that promised a great deal more than they delivered: *With General Custer at the Little Big Horn, Buffalo Bill on the U.P. Trail, With Sitting Bull at the Spirit Lake Massacre* (a singular fraud in that the massacre takes place offscreen and is merely referred to in an inter title), and *With Kit Carson Over the Great Divide.*

The titular characters usually had very little to do in the films, and production values were of the cheapest. However, photography was always good, and the films kept out of doors most of the time in pleasing locations. Because of the need to, in some ways, tie in with the great events promised by the titles, the plots were sometimes a little out of the ordinary, and names that had slipped a little—but were still recognized by loyal fans—and could be hired cheaply, were brought in for a day or two's work, and their scenes scattered throughout the films. Typical is *With Kit Carson Over the Great Divide* in which the lead was once-popular Roy Stewart,

(Here, and on facing page) The land rush in Ford's *Three Badmen*

and the rest of the cast included Jack Mower (only a few years earlier playing in DeMille films) and two of Griffith's old reliables, Henry B. Walthall and Sheldon Lewis. The film starts with an imposing foreword, and then the information that Captain Fremont's expedition is unexpectedly halted by the swollen Platte River. The "expedition" turns out to be a single wagon accompanied by a quartet of riders, and the flooded river seems perfectly placid and fordable! Throughout the film, whenever a title leads us to expect a pitched battle with impressive troops of cavalry and hundreds of Indians, we get mild skirmishings with a decided paucity of extras. However, so many cheap Westerns were made in the late twenties, most of them finding appropriate slots in small towns on Saturday afternoons, costing so little to make that they could hardly lose money, creating so little enthusiasm even among the small fry that each series had a short life and a quick death, that by comparison the Xydias epics weren't so bad. Presumably their exposure was not extensive; in the thirties they were sold to the home movie market, and flawless new 16-mm prints were made from virtually unblemished and spotless original 35-mm negatives, implying that those negatives had had *very* little use at the time of original release. But out of these Poverty Row Westerns, and out of the higher-class Westerns made by the major studios, a whole host of new Western stars were born to join Tom Mix in the stampede to the nation's box offices.

Universal Studios in the early twenties: home for Hoot Gibson, Harry Carey, Art Acord, Jack Hoxie, and many others

102

EIGHT

Stars of the Twenties

Almost anything can be "proven" by statistics. Every so often we are regaled with the information that such and such a film is one of the most popular of all time because its grosses, in the millions, have reached astronomical heights. Overlooked is the salient factor that a major contribution to those grosses is the ever-escalating admission price, which in the nineties averaged seven dollars per ticket in first-run houses. The only reliable guide to a picture's real popularity is the *number* of admissions, and in that respect *The Birth of a Nation* will probably always remain the number-one box office champion, even though the low admission prices of that day, often only twenty-five cents, would give it an overall gross easily outdistanced by contemporary films. Similarly, back in the sixties, television rating specialists loved to demonstrate that on a given night x-million viewers saw a specific television Western, and since that exceeded the number that saw any given theatrical Western with Tom Mix, then that television star was automatically the most popular Western star of all time.

Forgotten are such intangibles as the fact that the show in question might have been the best of several mediocrities available that night, that 90 percent of those tuned in might have tuned out again five minutes later, that television was free, that viewers didn't have to exert

or inconvenience themselves in any way, and that once the ratings started to fall and the series was cancelled, that fantastically popular Western star might never be heard of again. The relative failure in theatrical Westerns of such TV cowboys as Hugh O'Brian and James Arness (to say nothing of lesser ones like Wayne Maunder) is proof that genuine popularity has to be earned.

Stars of the twenties had to earn their stardom and then their popularity—but that popularity, once earned, was never lost. Moviegoers of the silent days offered genuine love and admiration to their favorites, not merely manufactured overnight idolatry. They picked the star whose personality or type of Western most appealed to them and they remained loyal through the bad pictures as well as the good. Children who grew up on Ken Maynard or Hoot Gibson in the twenties may have seen fewer Westerns as those children matured, but they would always remember their particular idols with affection and spring to their defense when some new cowboy hero was hailed as a pretender to their throne. Elderly gentlemen in their eighties can grow nostalgic today when a Jack Hoxie or a Tom Tyler is mentioned, and often have an amazing recall of plot details or specific stunts. How many television watchers, five decades hence, can be expected to demonstrate such erudite devotion to the careers of Will Hutchins or Chuck Connors?

The innate good judgment of the moviegoing public has always been underrated. That public discovered Fairbanks, Chaplin, Pickford, and Laurel and Hardy well before the critics did, and made deserved stars of Tom Mix, Fred Thomson, and Buck Jones, while rejecting those who had nothing to offer—Al Hoxie, Fred Church, Fred Humes, Don Coleman, Dick Hatton.

While the mediocrities deservedly fell by the wayside, the lineup of Western stars in the twenties was so rich and varied that many who should have been successful but just lacked that extra individual something likewise failed to make the grade. Wally Wales (in the later sound era rechristening himself Hal Taliaferro), Jay C. Wilsey (often billed as Buffalo Bill, Jr.), and Edmund Cobb were athletic, likeable and able performers whose pictures were usually enjoyable, but who never reached even the second echelon of stars. They became better known as character actors and villains in the sound period, Wales in particular developing a distinctive makeup, costuming, and speaking style that made him instantly recognizable. Small wonder that the likes of these and Bob Custer, Bill Cody, Jack Perrin, Guinn Williams, and Tex (later Kermit) Maynard made little headway in the face of such an onslaught of stars from the early twenties on. Others, like Leo Maloney, *did* achieve considerable second-level popularity, and their surviving films leave one wondering just *why*. Maloney in particular seemed to have little personality, and his films had nothing out of the ordinary to offer. Perhaps his unassuming quality and his friendly manner were sufficient and a striking enough contrast to the many more dynamic stars to make his very normalcy seem appealing. In any event, he was very well liked, and Ford Beebe, who wrote and directed many of his films (and who went on to work with many of the top sound Western stars), had nothing but praise for him.

In all fairness, Western stars in the silent period had much more chance of catching the public's fancy than they did in talkies. Many of them were poor actors, one or two even semiliterate and unable to read scripts or remember lines. And in the cheap Poverty Row Westerns, the scripts were often the weakest elements, lacking original plots or even smartly written inter titles. But in silent Westerns, even the cheapest could fall back on good locations and photography, and backed up by those elements, even the most inept of actors could make a go of it if he could sit a horse well and handle himself in a scrap. The twenties were awash with silent Westerns made by such companies as Aywon, Goodwill, Ellbee Pictures, Anchor Films, Fred McConnell Productions, Iroquois Productions, and scores of others. Some held their own for quite a few years, turning out unremarkable but serviceable productions, while others folded after just a picture of two.

But most silent Westerns, no matter how lacking in drama, production values, or magnetic stars, were at least good to look at. Even the cheapest of them would use toned stock—ambers, blue for night scenes, red for fires—and on the rich old nitrate film, it was like looking through a window into life, and the great outdoors seemed within arm's reach. With all of the technical improvements in film, nothing has ever come along to replace the vivid, crystal-clear sharpness of the nitrate film, which was finally abandoned and even outlawed in the late forties because of its dangerous, combustible qualities. How many film scholars, let alone Western devotees, have ever heard of a small 1926 Western called *Code of the Northwest,* made by the long forgotten Van Pelt Brothers, written and directed by the equally obscure Frank Mattison, and released by Chesterfield? Its simple plot was little more than the shuffling around of a group of characters. Mountie Tom London (in one of his few starring roles) is sent to "get his man," a murderer who happens to be his own brother. He is also a wife-deserter, and his wife has had his child. Her father has thrown her out, but is now blind and unaware that she has returned. These characters, and a wonder dog known as Sandow—billed without much substantiating proof as America's smartest police dog—all converge in a picturesque little backwoods community. The length of the film is only 3,965 feet—yet in the mere forty minutes that it takes to unreel, the distraught mother tries to commit suicide by jumping from a high cliff (she is forestalled by Sandow), her sister is rescued from a raft adrift in the rapids, and there are some mild chases and fights, and much snarling help from the wonder dog. Almost everything takes place out of doors, and there are stunningly beautiful vistas of mountain ranges, waterfalls, and so forth, as well as cunning utilization of a local railroad. None of it is exactly overwhelming, but it is all photographed by Elmer Dyer—later a specialist in aerial photography, with *Lost Horizon* (1937) among his credits—and seen recently in a surviving amber-toned print, it was a joy to behold.

An equivalent sound quickie (*The Timber Terror,* for example, also with Tom London as one of the villains) would have betrayed its cheapness by hackneyed writing and poor acting of mediocre dialogue. *Code of the Northwest* is certainly neither a notable nor even a particularly good film, but its rich pictorial beauty typifies one of the major assets of this kind of silent movie, and explains why so many of them were made and found a ready market—especially as they were cheap to produce and didn't need major exhibition outlets to turn a small but satisfying profit.

Fred Thomson was the closest rival to Tom Mix. His

Buck Jones

Fred Thomson

Harry Carey

Jack Hoxie

Tom Mix

Tim McCoy

initial Western series, made for FBO (a compact little company presided over by Joseph P. Kennedy, and the forerunner of RKO Radio) was carefully patterned after the Mix formula: lighthearted, filled with stunt action (Thomson was a splendid athlete and used relatively few doubles), handsome films made by experienced directors like Al Rogell and photographed by top cameramen. Thomson was a good-looking fellow who had studied for the priesthood, and because of this he stressed strong moral values, avoided sex (even in the limited way that some Westerns at least acknowledged it) and undue violence, and intended his films to be a good influence on youth as well as entertaining them. To that end he often worked in subplots (one involving Boy Scouts for example) that he felt would be meaningful to youngsters. At times he quite rivaled Mix in his action sequences, emulating Fairbanks by bringing in (as in *Thundering Hoofs* [1924]) comedy or action stunt sequences that were basically extraneous to the plot. And while Mix dressed fairly realistically in his movies, reserving his elaborate uniform-costumes for personal appearances and premieres, Thomson frequently wore costumes that smacked more of the rodeo than the range. His career, which had begun with straight dramatic roles (including one opposite Mary Pickford in *The Love Light*), was tragically brief. After the expiration of his FBO contract, he moved to Paramount to star in Western specials as a replacement for William S. Hart. Best remembered of his Paramount films was *Jesse James,* a nine-reeler that whitewashed the outlaw considerably and concluded with a highly fictionalized version of Jesse's marriage, cutting off before a tragic ending. Sadly, Thomson died at the peak of his popularity.

Art Acord is a prime example of the star whose reputation has been sustained almost solely by word of mouth from his fans. Practically nothing is left of his work today. We can see him playing two different bit roles (an Indian and a white settler) in the early Ince film *The Indian Massacre,* and we can watch one or two of his last cheap independent films like *Fighters of the Saddle.* A man of short stature, with a weatherbeaten face in the Harry Carey tradition, he shows little real star quality in these films from the extreme ends of his career. Yet in his big Universal serials and Western specials in the intervening years, he proved to be another major rival to Mix. (The mysterious circumstances of Acord's death—some sources cite suicide, others hint at a border skirmish with the law—have helped to keep his memory alive in the absence of his best films).

Jack Hoxie was a player of restricted talent and variable pictures, and his huge popularity must be attributed to the fact that he made more good pictures than bad ones, and that when they were good, they were *very* good). Evidence unearthed as recently as 1990 indicates that he left home at an early age to dodge a murder charge (though apparently a "justifiable homicide") that was hanging over him, started out in straight dramatic (though supporting) roles as Hart Hoxie, made an interesting if not very actionful series of independent Westerns in the early twenties (offbeat to say the least, one of them even had a dream sequence with pixies!) and then joined Universal in 1924. Hoxie was a curious *looking* man for a Western star, sporting a very strange hairstyle, and looking very much like the Lon Chaney, Jr., of the 1940s. He was a big, amiable man whose large frame made him seem clumsy afoot, and his expression always unfortunately suggested that his mind was a complete blank except when the director instructed him to pantomime a specific emotion. But on a horse, he was something else again. His first for Universal, *Don Quickshot of the Rio Grande,* fortunately kept him in the saddle most of the time and provided him with some elaborate stunts, leaps, and a transfer from galloping horse to moving train. Hoxie's film never took itself seriously, but it *moved* from the first scene to the last, and was beautifully photographed against majestic exteriors. It opened with an elaborate dream sequence lampooning the days of King Arthur's knights. If nothing else, the film seems to have impressed Ken Maynard a great deal, since he obviously based *The Grey Vulture* (1925) on it, even to copying that dream/knighthood prologue.

But Hoxie needed constant speed and motion, anything to prevent his getting off a horse and having to confront dramatic situations. When he was given a more serious Western, such as *The Back Trail* (directed by Cliff Smith, Bill Hart's old crony), a slow-moving, somewhat sentimental story of post–World War One regeneration that would have been much better suited to Hart, Hoxie fell down badly, being unable to suggest any kind of motivation or emotion that would snare audience interest in his character. Since he was one of the biggest Western money-makers of the twenties, obviously Universal handed him few assignments like *The Back Trail.* Hoxie was not an educated man, but he was a good sport about accepting some rather cruel inside jokes in his films about his illiteracy. However, the inability to read, remember, or deliver a line eventually defeated him when sound came in. Fewer stars can ever have had fewer, or simpler, words to speak than he was assigned in independent Westerns like *Outlaw Justice.* He drifted out of movies and, a fairly wealthy man, devoted himself to ranching for the rest of his life.

After appearing though not officially starring in John Ford features, Hoot Gibson found himself "promoted" downstairs into a series of highly popular two-reelers in

William Desmond

Hoot Gibson

Bob Steele

Ken Maynard

the early twenties. Western two-reelers were plentiful then, and Universal had a strange policy with them: the studio wanted them fast and actionful, but it wanted them to avoid killing or undue gunplay. Thus—and a William Wyler two-reeler starring Edmund Cobb and titled *The Two-Fister* is particularly typical—they tended to be overgenerous with prolonged chases and fistfights. Gibson decided to be different and to develop a slow, bantering comedy style, with little physical action of any kind. To emphasize this he never wore a gun belt and holster, and if he ever needed to use a pistol, he'd usually borrow one and stick it in his boot. Because of their novelty, Gibson's ingratiating style, and the fact that he was an ex-rodeo champ who could deliver action when needed, these shorts were extremely popular, although seen in isolation today, not juxtaposed with the many all-action shorts that surrounded them at the time, they seem rather pointlessly slow in their deliberate avoidance of real thrills. Gibson was soon returned to features, but retained his emphasis on comedy. His initial features were extremely good, slow-moving openings amply compensated for by dynamic endings, as in *The Phantom Bullet* with its last-reel fight, chase, and spectacular stunt of an auto diving from a high cliff into a lake. (Curious how such straightforward films often, years later, find themselves in august company. In the eighties the Cinemathèque in Paris did a complex series, with Antonioni's *Blowup* as its centerpiece, dealing with films in which the act of taking a photograph accidentally captured and revealed some aspect of life, usually, movies being what they are, a criminal aspect. *The Phantom Bullet* was one of the first features to use such a plot element, and thus—too late for them to be aware of it—Hoot Gibson and director Cliff Smith found themselves sharing an academic investigation cobilled with Antonioni!)

Many of the Gibson Westerns had pleasing novelty elements—in *Hit and Run,* he was an amateur cowboy baseball player who finds big city success and runs afoul of crooked gamblers—but his series deteriorated badly toward the end of the twenties. Action content got even less, the comedy was padded and extended by bantering inter titles, and the slim plots got even leaner. *Chip of the Flying U* was virtually *all* comedy, and *King of the Rodeo* was a bland bore except for an enjoyable last-reel sequence of Gibson racing through the streets of Chicago on a motorcycle. Comedy was now less of a novelty in the Western—Tom Mix, for instance, donned spectacles and did a delightful Harold Lloyd takeoff in *Soft Boiled.* Gibson fans remained loyal, but the trade press began to complain about the increasing paucity of action in his features. The situation got even worse with Gibson's first talkies, also for Universal—which were literally *all* talk, dominated by romantic byplay and comedy, and with action hardly getting a look-in. Fortunately, Gibson was to revert to more typical Western fare, without in any way abandoning his happy-go-lucky character, in independently made Westerns of the early and mid-thirties. They may have had less production values than his Universals, but they gave Western audiences far more of what they wanted.

One of the most likeable Western stars of the period was Ken Maynard. He came to the screen via a bit in one of Buck Jones's Fox westerns, attracted notice playing Paul Revere in *Janice Meredith,* made some cheap independent films which were short on logical plots but long on displays of Maynard's riding skill, and finally landed a series of eighteen Westerns at First National. They stressed action and streamlined production values before all else. In terms of action and sheer size, they were some of the best program Westerns ever made. Exhibitors and audiences alike were well pleased with them, as well they might be. Their plots may sometimes have been skimpy, especially for the seven-reel lengths that they sometimes ran to, but they had the production mountings of a *Stagecoach:* extensive location shooting and no stinting on extras, horses, or wagon power. When the script called for a mad stampede of fifty covered wagons, it got them, not just a half dozen carefully intercut with stock footage. Al Rogell, who had worked on *Thundering Hoofs* and some of the best Fred Thomsons at FBO, directed the best of them, and their superior camerawork utilized several camera trucks to the fullest, providing continuous speed and variety of angle in all of the exceptionally smooth running inserts. Maynard was slim, good-looking, and, at his physical peak, an incredible trick and stunt rider. Most of his riding and stuntwork was shot in full close-up, precluding the possibility of doubles, and frequently even within a given action sequence the script would provide an extra and unexpected thrill. In one lively chase sequence, for example, one of Maynard's cronies falls out of the saddle and is dragged by the stirrup. Maynard races alongside, leans backward out of the saddle and helps him back into position. The whole stunt is somewhat unlikely and perhaps even impossible, but the camerawork is fragmented, and in the key rescue scene the camera is right down to the level of the dirt road picking up the detail of Maynard's maneuver.

When talkies came, Maynard proved to be a rather clumsy and self-conscious actor with dialogue, often given to ad libs and seldom able to achieve the subtlety of underplaying a dramatic or comic line. He was to have his own production unit at Universal, and with that sense of power turned out some of the most unusual, one might even say grotesque, Western stories ever, some-

Wally Wales (later Hal Taliaferro)

Leo Maloney

Edmund Cobb

times even rivaling von Stroheim in their bizarre quality. But for those few years at First National in the late twenties, he was in his prime, and the equal of Tom Mix. The care that went into films like *Red Raiders* and *Señor Daredevil* more than paid off in an unexpected way. For years, First National was able to build its talkie "B" Westerns around the Maynards, using the same basic plots and most of the spectacular action sequences. It did this first in a John Wayne series, and later in another with Dick Foran; since the Forans were made in the middle of the thirties, the use of stock footage was now becoming a little obvious because grain and photographic quality didn't always match. In films like *Prairie Thunder*, Maynard himself could easily be spotted in the old shots, although since the Forans—more than most "B" Westerns—were designed primarily for youngsters, there were few complaints or cries of recognition. When Warner–First National abandoned "B" Westerns later in the decade, it continued to sell this footage to Columbia, Republic, and other companies.

Some measure of the remarkable quality of these films can be gleaned from the fact that *Red Raiders*, one of the best of the group, with magnificent climactic battle scenes and intercutting in the very best Griffith tradition, was also one of the *last* in the series. Normally, as a series winds down, corners are cut and costs reduced, but *Red Raiders* was as good and as carefully made as the first in the series. One of the few to survive, it is also the program Western to have been most consistently included in retrospectives staged by such cultural bodies as Lincoln Center in Manhattan, the George Eastman House archive in Rochester, Cinematheque Canadienne in Montreal, and the Venice Film Festival. While *Red Raiders* never purports to be a serious Western, its treatment of the Indians is at the same time rather interesting. Inter titles frequently explain Indian lore and phrases, while an Indian named White Man Runs Him, a survivor of Custer's Last Stand, is given a small part and identified. While the Indians take to the warpath perhaps a little too readily at the instigation of the sole evil Indian in the movie (a young chief played by Chief Yowlachie), it is not without a good deal of antiwar counseling on the part of the older chiefs. And when *he* is removed by being conveniently killed in the final battle, all of the pillaging and slaughter he brought about is suddenly forgotten as "White Man and Red Are Friends Once More."

Almost as elaborate (though surprisingly, much shorter) were the historical Westerns that Tim McCoy made at the same time for MGM, the only time in fact that the lordly studio ever stooped to making a Western series! Technically, it was an action adventure series, but of the sixteen produced between late 1926 and mid-1929, only three were unquestionably non-Westerns: *Foreign Devils*, dealing with the Boxer Rebellion in China; *The Adventurer*, a Latin American-localed melodrama; and most peculiar of all, *The Bushranger* which began in England and concluded in Australia more than a decade later, its plot combining elements of *Beau Geste* and one of Australia's own literary favorites, *For the Term of His Natural Life.* Four others, semi-Western in plot if traditional Western in action, dealt with the war against the British on the Eastern seaboard (there were two of those), the Civil War, and the California-Mexico conflict. These seven were slotted in between the regular Western titles—*Law of the Range, Spoilers of the West*, etc.—so that for sales purposes MGM could keep its prestige intact and not admit to the production of a Western series, for which it could not ask as much in rentals.

McCoy was a handsome, smiling Irishman, a military man, and an authority on Indian lore and history. He was introduced to the movies via *The Covered Wagon*, where his function had been to represent and work with the many Indians employed in the film, ease them into the ways of Hollywood showmanship when they appeared at the Los Angeles premiere, and then take them to England for its London debut. (McCoy's autobiography has some hilarious stories of their initial clash with British culture and their problems in settling in to snooty London hotels.) Reputedly he also did some of the trick riding in the film, although there is precious little of it and none that couldn't have been performed by any competent wrangler. With his military bearing and good looks, he would have seemed to be a natural for Westerns, but Paramount already had a similar type—Jack Holt—and was only now just beginning to utilize him as a Western star. McCoy was given a good supporting role, possibly as a kind of extended screen test, in *The Thundering Herd*, made in 1924 after McCoy's Indian-chaperoning chores were completed, and released in 1925. But it *starred* Jack Holt, in his best Western role to date, and possibly the juxtaposition of the two good-looking he-men in the one film caused Paramount to wonder about the usefulness of McCoy. In any event, no further offers were forthcoming from them, and MGM's bid to him was probably made as much in recognition of what his Indian knowledge and connections could bring to the studio's planned economy-size *Covered Wagons* as his as yet unproven star capabilities and box office value.

The purpose of these films was manifold. They provided useful second features for Metro's own "A" features in the slowly growing double-bill market, and they were big enough in size to play single bill in the action houses. They also were useful training grounds for new directors, and at times they could even be used to discipline temperamental stars whom the front office accused of getting delusions of grandeur. Joan Crawford was taken down a peg or two by being cast as McCoy's leading lady in *Law of the Range* and *Winners of the Wilderness* in 1927 and 1928 respectively.

The McCoy unit boasted some prestige names behind the cameras, but there wasn't the same consistency that had been present in the Bill Hart films when the same three or four creative personnel were present throughout. Scripts and original stories came in from all sides, with Peter B. Kyne's name well to the fore. Photographically the films were superb, and most of them were shot by Clyde de Vinna, an outstanding cinematographer for location work. He soon proved his mettle by leaping straight from the McCoy films into the classic *White Shadows in the South Seas*. The best of the series' directors was W. S. Van Dyke, who likewise made his reputation with *White Shadows in the South Seas*. Assigned as an assistant to Robert Flaherty on that film, he took over when Flaherty withdrew. Van Dyke remained one of MGM's top directors until his death in the 1940s, turning his films out with the speed and efficiency of a grade "B" director, but entirely unique in that he was able to combine lightning shooting schedules with top-flight artistry. He was the envy of every director on the MGM lot; the only ones reluctant to work with him were the temperamental leading ladies who liked to be coddled with deferential treatment and flattered with time-consuming close-ups and fancy lighting. Incidentally, W. S. Van Dyke's assistant at this time was Lesley Selander, who in the thirties and forties became one of the ablest directors of the Buck Jones and Hopalong Cassidy Westerns (among many others) before moving on to bigger-scale horse operas.

The other directors on the McCoy films were either less talented or less suited to the demands of that kind of film; they included the Russian Tourjansky, William Nigh, Nick Grindé, and the curious John Waters, who had directed eight of Paramount's Zane Greys as well as two of the McCoys. Since so many of the Paramount films are lost, it is unfair to generalize about Waters's capabilities as a director, but on the evidence of his surviving *Nevada* from Paramount and McCoy's *The Overland Telegraph*, he was a flat and plodding director unable to instill much excitement even into promising material. Asked about him in the early 1970s, McCoy remembered him well and summed him up succinctly as "Good enlisted man, but not commanding officer material."

McCoy was a good actor and a striking figure of a man who wore both cowboy costumes and military uniforms with distinction and flair. While he was in excellent

Buffalo Bill, Jr. (J. C. Wilsey)

Fred Humes

Buddy Roosevelt

physical condition (and remained so throughout his life, still slim and in possession of that erect bearing until the end), he always believed that the story—and where possible, an adherence to the facts—mattered more than action. In any case, he exuded a natural dignity which somehow made it seem inappropriate for him to engage in fistfights or flying leaps into the saddle, although he was capable of both. Except for McCoy's brief period in Columbia's earlier sound Westerns, his films on the whole contained less physical action than those of other major Western stars, and he used doubles far more liberally. However, nobody was his equal at entering a saloon, letting the swinging doors flap behind him, and then cowing the entire room by flashing his steely eyes!

Despite their often spectacular action climaxes and their brief running times (in actual footage, they often ran less than five reels, although the appropriate projection speed usually brought them up to about an hour), the McCoy Westerns were not markedly popular with the youngsters. Historical data was often documented at some length, the romantic elements were more important than usual, and in the Indian-oriented stories, McCoy often played the role of peacemaker, trying (successfully) to avoid a spectacular conflict between Indians and whites. Certainly, in their "class" production values, the films were not tailored to the juvenile market, and as a footnote without further comment, the MGM product of the late twenties displayed a rather surprising fondness for male nudity in situations of bondage and torture, ranging from the trussed-up galley slave in *Ben Hur* to a writhing victim burning at the stake in *Winners of the Wilderness.* Admittedly, such scenes were discreetly photographed from the rear, but whatever segment of the moviegoing public they were aimed at, it was definitely not the kiddie trade!

McCoy recalled the first of the series, *War Paint,* as being the best, most likely because MGM would undoubtedly have been generous with the budget to impress both exhibitors and the public. Unfortunately, it does not appear to have survived, although footage of Indians at the Wind River reservation, and especially pleasing long shots of the Indians leaving their camp to ford the adjacent river have been reused many times since, at least twice by McCoy himself before they made their way into basic stock footage libraries available to all. Of the handful of McCoy Westerns from this series that do survive, the most impressive is probably *Winners of the Wilderness,* technically an "Eastern" in that it deals with the Indian alliance with the French. One of the Van Dyke/de Vinna entries, it was, at seven reels, longer than most and even boasted some Technicolor scenes. Although historical figures such as George

Washington were brought into the narrative, and some of the Indian torture scenes were quite grim, it was essentially a larger-than-life swashbuckling adventure, very much in the Fairbanks manner, an approach stressed by McCoy acrobatic escapades and trick riding, and by the full-blown, smirking villainy of Roy D'Arcy, almost surpassing the villainous excesses he displayed in von Stroheim's *The Merry Widow.*

One of the most durable—and likable—of the new Western heroes was Buck Jones, who starred for Fox in a series secondary both in importance to the studio's Mix films and in the care with which they were made. Jones struck a neat balance between the conviction of Hart and the excitement of Mix. His films had sensible stories and good if not flamboyant action. There was one added ingredient, an unstressed but pleasing element of folksy Will Rogers humor. This may well have been a quality that Jones devised himself; gestures and bits of comedy business that he used in such early films as John Ford's *Just Pals* (1920) and Frank Borzage's (non-Western) *Lazy Bones* (1925) he retained and developed through the years. When, in the thirties at Universal, he was in charge of his own productions (and even directed), he often overdid these comedy elements. This was primarily because he was a serious actor, one of the best in the Western roster, and his comic byplay did not always come naturally to him, occasionally seeming forced when it should have been totally relaxed. Over his twenty years of stardom, Jones maintained a remarkably high standard and held the distinction of being, with Tom Mix, a rare silent Western star to make the transition into talkies without once having to descend to Poverty Row quickies.

Another star who, like Jones, retained a certain allegiance to the Hart image was Harry Carey. His always mature features and the fact that he was an actor first and an athlete second, probably made that allegiance unavoidable. In his plots, too, he followed the Hart tradition, although of course they were always mixed with an unofficial acknowledgment of his "Cheyenne Harry," the character he had created in his first John Ford Westerns. In *The Prairie Pirate,* a smoothly done Hunt Stromberg-produced Western, he turned good badman to track down the murderer of his sister, while *Satan Town* was a vigorous reworking of one of Hart's best pictures, *Hell's Hinges.* Even as a young man in his Biograph films for Griffith, Carey looked far older than he really was, and while his maturity—and his appearance hardly changed throughout his long career—didn't rule out a romantic element in his films, he frequently played the older, wiser man who solves all the problems and leaves the girl to a younger love interest. None of the Westerns that he made after leaving John Ford were outstanding, but they were enjoyable, intelligent, and well above average. Even while enjoying a career as a cowboy hero, he made a wonderful villain, vicious yet possessed of an endearing sense of humor, in Clarence Brown's little-seen and much underrated *The Trail of '98* (1928). In one of his best scenes, Carey returns from a long trek through the wilderness, lines up all the cans of beans that he can find, and then tells them to watch while he enjoys a nice juicy steak! Carey also continued well into the talkies, first as a star of serials and independent Westerns, and then as a character actor. (Hitchcock had wanted to use him as the Western-based Nazi-sympathizing villain in *Saboteur,* but was overruled on the basis of the defeatist morale-lowering that would result if such a beloved American icon was revealed as a wartime villain. A more traditional heavy was used in the person of Otto Kruger).

Of the lesser silent Western stars, Yakima Canutt and the earlier-referred-to Leo Maloney were among the most interesting. Maloney's loyal following could have built him into a top-ranking star had he knuckled down to it. But he was never very serious about movies and would go off on spur-of-the-moment sprees during shooting, a serious problem for the economy-conscious two-reelers and features that he made. Anticipating such difficulties, his writer-director, Ford Beebe, would construct the plots so that the hero was absent a great deal of the time. With an offscreen leading man, the action content of the films was never pronounced and hurried rewriting sessions sometimes resulted in the desperate pilfering of plots and situations from other stars' movies. The entire climax of Bill Hart's *Square Deal Sanderson*—an unusual and easily recognized sequence—was borrowed in this way, its plagiarism all the more apparent because Francis Ford had done exactly the same thing in *Another Man's Boots.*

Ex-rodeo champ Yakima Canutt likewise never realized his full potential in silents, but for different reasons. Probably the finest all-around stuntman the screen has ever had, he tried to make Westerns in the Mix manner, but unfortunately was limited to the cheaper independent companies like Goodwill Productions, which could never provide the budgets necessary for sustained, elaborate stunt sequences, and whose directors were second-rate. Canutt Westerns like *Hell Hounds of the Plains* and *The Iron Rider* had colorful titles that promised more than they delivered, but they did offer a good stunt or two, often photographed from multiple angles (such as a dive from a high cliff in *Hell Hounds*) to maximize their effect. Occasionally the climactic chases would be prolonged far beyond their true worth in order to provide a solid reel of stunt action, but it was obvious, repetitive stuff. Canutt's only really first-rate silent

Ted Wells

King Vidor directing John Bowers and Colleen Moore at Truckee locations for *The Sky Pilot* (First National, 1927)

Western was *The Devil Horse,* one of several of Hal Roach's vehicles for Rex, a handsome but surly and difficult to handle "wonder" horse. Directed by Fred Jackman, it was a large-scale programmer with excellent mass-action sequences as well as impressive individual stunts, and superior photography (George Stevens was the film's second cameraman) of breathtakingly beautiful locations. Even as a young man, however, Canutt had a slightly sinister look that suggested he'd be more at home playing villains.

Although *The Devil Horse* survives in some good original prints which do full justice to its fine pictorial values, and it *used* to be shown at film festivals, it tends to be unofficially suppressed today because of its condescending and even hostile attitude toward the Indian. Certainly not conceived as anything but a straightforward action show, its unintended racism tends to offend contemporary audiences who seem unable to view it in the context of its time. Canutt came into his own in the talkie period as a stuntman, villain, and character player in scores of independent Westerns, and particularly at Monogram (where he doubled for and coached John Wayne in the art of creating realistic fisticuffs) and at Republic, where he eventually created a unique organization of stuntmen specializing in mass horse action. Ultimately, he became one of the best-known second-unit directors for films like *Ivanhoe, Ben Hur,* and *Mogambo* that feature large-scale and tricky action sequences with horses and other animals.

FBO (Film Booking Offices), which, next to the Ken Maynards at First National, made the best Westerns of the later twenties, was an enterprising independent company devoted almost exclusively to the shooting of expert action pictures. These included the stunt thrillers of Richard Talmadge and some railroading melodramas, but Westerns predominated. Tom Mix was with FBO briefly, after he had left Fox, replacing Fred Thomson who had gone to Paramount. FBO's other Western stars were Bob Custer, enjoying a brief popularity not sustained in the sound period, where his poor acting ability reduced his status; Tom Tyler, teamed with a diminutive Frankie Darro; Buzz Barton, the boy stunt rider (who continued in sound films too, but as a second stringer to stars like Rex Bell); and Bob Steele.

Slick, well-photographed, and action-packed—the FBO series—each with its own distinctive style—provided the consistently good quality that was to characterize the Republic Westerns of the thirties and early forties. Very few examples survive in the United States, but fortunately a number of good 35-mm prints were found in France, where they had been used as attractions at fairgrounds. They are now housed in the Cinemathèque Royale de Belgique in Brussels, not easily accessible, it's true, but at least available to those who need to see them. In this country, some of the Bob Custer negatives were found in the sixties, chopped up, gagged up, doctored with sound effects and an obnoxious small boy voice-over narration, edited down to five-minute segments, and under the overall title of "Billy Bang Bang," rented to television for inclusion as fillers in kiddie programs. Somehow their innate qualities still managed to make themselves felt.

Unfortunately, all too few of the independent Westerns of the twenties matched the quality of the FBOs. The market for double bills was expanding, Westerns were popular, and they were still the cheapest kind of film to make. Since all the Westerns really had to worry about was fast action and good photography, it's amazing how often they failed to deliver the goods. Indian uprisings could consist of a few scraggly extras emerging from two or three tepees, fights were badly staged, the simple plots were prolonged, and expensive footage was eliminated through the excessively detailed dialogue titles. The rule of thumb for these titles was to allow a reading time of one second per word, and then to add five seconds to the total. Thus if a film turned up short of the required running time, it was an easy (and boring) matter to create length merely by extending conversations within the film. With so many good Westerns on the market, it is a wonder that cheaters like Dick Hatton's *Pioneer Days* or Al Hoxie's *The Ace of Clubs* could survive. Why should anyone book a nonaction Western with a nonentity as star when for a few dollars more he could get a crowd-pleasing Tom Tyler film, or for a slightly higher price, a Tom Mix that would undoubtedly outgross John Barrymore's *When a Man Loves?* The answer of course is that these kind of Westerns didn't survive for long, and they didn't have to. They got only nominal bookings, but their production costs were so low that they needed relatively few bookings to show a profit.

Exhibitors, on the other hand, *did* find them useful. There were so many theaters then that, even in the small towns, a Tom Mix could expect a first-run followed by secondary exposure at lesser houses. That still left others specializing in action material that would prefer a minor Western *first*-run than a Tom Mix in its third or fourth exhibition. Then of course there were the *very* small towns that might have only one movie house, and where the bill of fare might be changed three or four times a week in order to provide maximum entertainment variety for a relatively small populace. After all, this was well before television, and even though radio was a competitive factor from 1925 on, the one thing it couldn't provide was physical action. Dyed-in-the-wool movie fans would come back for every program change, so while a Tom Mix or a Fred Thomson would get the playdates with the most potential, these stars didn't make *that* many films, and there was still ample room for a Buddy Roosevelt or a Bill Cody on other occasions.

Once exhibitors found that their audiences were vocal in their dislike for a certain star or series (and audience-exhibitor relationships, especially in small towns, were much closer then), they'd bypass that particular line of product when the next booking season came around. By

Durand of the Badlands (Fox, 1925): Buck Jones (standing)

Range Buzzards (Vitagraph, 1925): a primitive-looking Western starring Pete Morrison

Bela Lugosi's dignified presence as Uncas (center) was the only distinguishing feature of a dull, primitive German version of *Last of the Mohicans* in the early twenties

The Prairie Pirate (PDC, 1925): Robert Edeson, Trilby Clark, and Harry Carey that time another fly-by-night outfit would have ambled over the horizon, and it too would be given a chance to fill unimportant, one-day, bottom-of-the-bill bookings. The producers came and went through ever-revolving doors, and the lesser stars devoid of ability and often not even the possessors of a likeable personality or a pleasant face, came and went with them. The independent silent film field contained many writers who couldn't write, actors who couldn't act, comedians who couldn't raise a laugh no matter how energetically they fell down, and Western stars without any get up and go. (Interestingly, while there were obviously cinematographers who were better and more creative than others, there don't seem to have been any *bad* ones. If there were, their short-comings were doubtless brought to light while they were serving as assistants, and they were never promoted to positions where they could do any damage.)

Before passing on from the independent field, one might also mention a kind of parallel to the small Western much more common in the silent period than it would prove to be in the sound—the Northern melo-drama of the snows. These provided less opportunity for traditional action than the standard Western, so they were never mass-produced, but at the right time of the year, when certain California locations and especially the High Sierras provided plenty of snow, they could still be made fairly economically, and the majestic snow-scapes made for a spectacular change of pace from Western ranges. While MGM made its big-scale *The Trail of '98* and Universal did its medium budget *The Michigan Kid* (with a wonderful forest fire climax, and intriguing subjective footage when a camera was sent down a miniature cataract and over a miniature water-fall, all most convincingly), the smaller independent companies were making impressive little films like *The Snowshoe Trail, The Test of Donald Norton,* and *The Call of the Klondike,* which, even when seen today, hold surprises in terms of their pictorial values, offbeat plots and often quite powerful action sequences.

One of *the* most enterprising of the snow and wilderness filmmakers was a remarkable lady—Nell Shipman, a producer-writer-star of her own films, whose career has been brought to light in recent years mainly through the efforts of Tom Trusky of Boise State University who has been uncovering some of her lost films and getting them shown around the world. Shipman started out as a scenarist at Vitagraph and by 1920 had become virtually her own boss. At a time when women producers and directors were still rare (they were never common), she had her own studio in Idaho. Hers was a fascinating if short-lived career—full of melodrama that sounded like publicity material for the rugged adventure movies she filmed, yet virtually all of it was true: the mysterious

killing of one of her favorite dogs by a vengeful trapper, a romantic liaison with her director who ultimately went mad, the death of one of her stars through the rigors of location work. Like Francis Ford Coppola, she was a maverick. She tried to buck Hollywood and failed, though in her case it was the mishandling of her finest film by an inept (or dishonest) distributor that ruined her, forcing her to curtail her activities drastically, and most heartbreaking of all (to her), having to shut down the zoo that she maintained to care for the wild animals, often wounded, that she rescued, cared for, and used in her films.

In a sense—though certainly not politically—she was a kind of Leni Riefenstahl of the West and Far North, working primarily in Idaho and Canada, and for a time, collaborating with James Oliver Curwood. In the silent period, several authors—Zane Grey, Edgar Rice Bur-roughs, and Gene Stratton Porter among them—tried to form their own production units or team up with existing ones like Miss Shipman's so that their works could be brought to the screen faithfully. Whatever the literary or artistic virtues involved, these ventures always seemed doomed to failure commercially. At times Curwood was most enthusiastic about their work together, while at others he was bitterly critical. Certainly he never had a more devoted ally than Shipman, and his complaints seem almost pointless when one looks at the huge body of work allegedly adapted from the Curwood stories, much of it using his name and a title and little else.

Nell Shipman was an attractive woman, though a difficult one to photograph in that she often looked far different in profile than in head-on close-up. A show-woman, too, she didn't mind using her body in discreetly handled nude bathing scenes that were well played up in the advertising. A woman of determination and skill, Shipman was an "auteur" long before that term fell into overusage. Personal foibles and convictions recur fre-quently in her movies. A love of animals and a recogni-tion of the need to protect and conserve them was something that she practiced personally and a theme that she often brought into her films. Strong and inde-pendent, she usually cast herself in that light, frequently having to protect a weak and ailing husband from the rigors of the North. Somewhat like William S. Hart in his attitude to the West, she loved the Northern wilderness for its own sake and great beauty, but also saw it as a massive character-testing background which brought out the best and worst in men.

Two of the Shipman films are of especial interest. *Something New,* a Western that she wrote and codi-rected with Bert Van Tuyle, her costar in it, stresses her quite coincidental relationship to the working methods of von Stroheim, of which more in a moment. It's a real

Douglas Fairbanks in action in *The Mark of Zorro* (1920), a blend of the Westerns in his past and the big swashbucklers in his future

Open Range (Paramount, 1927): Betty Compson with Lane Chandler, a bigger star then than Gary Cooper but would wind up playing bit roles in later Cooper talkies

Sunset Sprague (1920): one of the earlier Buck Jones films for Fox, with Henry Hebert

curio, "starring" the Maxwell auto, a vehicle that probably owes its enduring fame to its much later use as a running gag by Jack Benny. Shipman was given the assignment of making a short commercial for the automobile, stressing its strength, adaptability, and durability when subjected to hazards and terrain it could hardly expect to encounter during its normal working lifetime. A one-reel short was probably all that was anticipated. Shipman and her small crew managed to expand it to a feature-length Western which is virtually all action and chase. After a bantering comedy introduction, Miss Shipman is kidnapped by a murderous bunch of Mexicans who carry her off to their hideaway in the hills. Fiancé Bert Van Tuyle arrives on the scene to find no horses available, and the only means of pursuit a Maxwell jalopy. This is pressed into action to race over rocky scrubland, through rivers, up hills and down valleys, and over and around boulders. Sometimes the rate of progress is so tortuous, slow, and dangerous that he'd probably have made better time afoot! The first half of the film is taken up with the chase to the bandits' lair, the arrival arranged fortuitously to circumvent the time-honored fate worse than death. The second half is an even wilder and more perilous flight *from* the bandits. Just as they are about to close in for the kill, the bandits are done in, *Riders of the Purple Sage* style, by a Shipman-contrived avalanche which wipes them all out.

Despite the emphasis on almost constant action, Shipman is a good enough writer to pause occasionally for interludes of comedy and even genuine, quite intense, emotion. But she's also smart enough to realize that nobody is going to take this farrago too seriously, so she wraps it all up by presenting it as a story that she, as a writer, is making up, smiling cheerfully at the audience for the fadeout when we leave her sitting at her typewriter finalizing her creation.

The basic appeal of *Something New* may well be to the auto buff who gets an entire film dedicated to the Maxwell. Western fans may be a trifle less excited. While it is *all* action, it is somewhat repetitive action. Nevertheless, it's a fascinating novelty and certainly an amazing tribute to the Maxwell, which, even in those far-off days when cars were built to last, has incredible energy and recuperative powers. Not surprisingly, it has become somewhat battered by the film's end. But remarkably, the same car *was* used throughout, the only "cheating" being that a single backup vehicle was taken along so that parts could be cannibalized if serious damage was done. Since the car hurls itself over rocks and actually climbs cliffs, this minimal poetic license seems justified. The ravaged remains of the heroic car went on tour with the film and were displayed at key engagements. Incidentally, if the Mexican villains seem even more swarthy, lecherous, and generally stereotyped than was the norm

Hell's Hole (Fox, 1924): Buck Jones, Ruth Clifford, "Lefty" Flynn, and Eugene Pallette as a Mexican—a curious Western with an actionful plot that turns out to be a dream!

The frame-up.

HOOT GIBSON
IN THE UNIVERSAL PRODUCTION
"HIT AND RUN"

COUNTRY OF ORIGIN AND PRODUCTION U.S.A.

A lobby card for a 1924 Gibson Western

at this time, it's probably because cameraman Joseph Walker (later Frank Capra's number one cinematographer, and an important member of Shipman's team) had once been kidnapped by Pancho Villa's men. While he had survived intact, he doubtless saw this film as a means of getting some personal revenge.

Shipman's films—her run of success began with *Back to God's Country* (1919)—were not markedly original in their plotting and were often derivative in their technique. What gives them their strength is their drive and Shipman's dedication to putting a way of life on the screen. Nowhere is this more apparent than in her last and best film, *The Grub Stake,* released in 1923. Produced for only $180,000—certainly not a cheapie, but still a remarkably low budget for a film requiring such difficult and protracted location work—it had an original scenario by Shipman and was an impressive film to have been made outside the Hollywood studio system.

Though lacking the spectacular highlights and MGM production gloss of *The Trail of '98, The Grub Stake* is not at all unworthy of comparison with it. *The Grub Stake* betrays its economy mainly through the occasionally bland and too-new look of some of the interior sets and the lack of recognizable names in the supporting cast. Alfred Allen is an appropriately despicable but unimpressive heavy, a role crying out for the likes of Noah Beery, Sr., or Montagu Love, while Walt Whitman and Lillian Leighton are the only representatives of Hollywood. But once it gets into the outdoors—and after a slightly delayed start it remains in the wilderness most of the time—it more than rates comparison with the bigger-budgeted Hollywood films made closer to home.

Like Erich von Stroheim, Nell Shipman was always in a somewhat precarious situation. She seemed to approach each film, this one especially, as though it might

119

William K. Howard, director of some of the best of Paramount's Zane Grey Westerns of the twenties

Trick riding that characterized Ken Maynard's excellent new series for First National (1926–29)

Ken Maynard on the set of his *Red Raiders* (First National, 1927)

Señor Daredevil (1926): first of the Maynards for First National

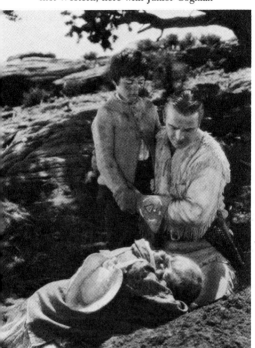

The Last Frontier (Pathe, 1926): William Boyd's first Western, here with Junior Coghlan

Nevada (Paramount, 1927): Gary Cooper (mounted) and William Powell

be her last, cramming in a little too much plot and incident. Typical are her marital travails in this film. She is tricked into a marriage with the villain, a launchpad for her trek north. *He* thinks it's a mock marriage, since he already has a wife, and when Nell finds out, as she's about to be passed around in his bordello, she leaves him. Later, it is revealed that his real wife had died *before* he wed Nell, so the marriage is in fact quite legal. By the time Nell discovers *that,* she's genuinely in love, and of course she has to repudiate her new beau. The ultimate death of the villain clears up the confusion, but it is a subplot that has consumed far too much footage. Then, midway through the film, the story comes to a veritable halt when Shipman's heroine discovers a Disneyesque hidden valley, shares a cave with a bear, and communes with nature for a reel or so. And the end backtracks into the movie to such an extent that the whole last quarter of the nine-reel film is virtually *all* climax, milking suspense and crosscutting last-minute rescues and literal cliff-hanging to the nth degree. Strictly speaking, the film *is* too long, but as it happened, Shipman never did get a chance to make such an ambitious one again, and had she not poured so much into it, many great sequences might never have made it to the screen at all.

Young Buzz Barton, star of his own series at FBO, in *The Young Whirlwind* (1928), laying down the law to Frank Rice

121

The Grey Devil (Rayart, 1927): White-hatted Jack Perrin

Arizona Bound (Paramount, 1927): Gary Cooper and Jack Daugherty

Interesting, too, is the influence on the film from classic directors. Joseph Walker recalled that location shooting was deliberately delayed so that he could see the opening of a new Griffith film first. Certainly Griffithian editing patterns and compositions abound, with *Broken Blossoms* particularly omnipresent, and elements in the climax suggest that *somebody* associated with the film got a good look at Abel Gance's *La Roue* as well. The decline of Miss Shipman's career after *The Grub Stake*, which was mishandled by its distributor and later drastically cut for reissue, is sad, particularly as she was at her peak. One wonders why she didn't try to make a deal with Pathé, then an expanding company, and one shy of the sort of product she made so expertly. But second-guessing more than sixty years after the event is pointless; possibly Pathé felt that its Hal Roach outdoor films and its serials provided all the action fare it needed. However, as a writer Nell Shipman stayed in the industry until the mid-thirties, and also penned an excellent autobiography. Her son, Barry Shipman (who appeared in many of her nature shorts), later became a notable screenwriter of both "B" Westerns and more serious Westerns of real quality, such as *Stranger at My Door* (1956). The space herein devoted to Nell Shipman shouldn't indicate that her importance was equal to that of Ford or Hart. But their work is familiar and well documented; hers isn't—yet. She was unique, made a

William K. Howard's *White Gold* (Pathé, 1927): George Bancroft, Jetta Goudal, and Kenneth Thomson major and sincere contribution, and should be acknowledged and honored.

By 1925 the movies had had a foretaste of what was in store for them when television began to offer such major competition in the late forties and early fifties. Attendance had fallen off due to the competition of "free" home entertainment—radio. Briefly, Hollywood panicked—and then hit back in the best and only way possible, with good, even outstanding pictures (though most notably in the non-Western field). However, there was a distinct tendency to upgrade even the so-called ordinary films, and this was pleasingly apparent in one of the best of Paramount's Zane Grey Westerns, *Wild Horse Mesa* (1925).

The long-running Grey series had begun in the early twenties as "specials" and concluded in 1940, by which time they had changed into extremely high quality "B" pictures. For years, it was frustrating that there was an almost total absence of any of the silents, which had received both popular and critical acclaim, and had been the means of building the careers of several major directors and stars. Adding to the frustration was the large-scale use of stock footage from the silents in Paramount's sound remakes of the mid-thirties: *The Thundering Herd, Man of the Forest, Desert Gold.* This footage, albeit nonmatching and often speeded up, seemed to confirm that the silents were as good and as spectacular as they were supposed to be. Ironically, the two or three films that did finally emerge were largely unrepresentative: *Wanderer of the Wasteland,* notable mainly as a showcase for the early two-color Technicolor system, the weak *Nevada* (dull, despite having Gary Cooper and William Powell in the cast), and *The Vanishing American* (already discussed). Then, in the mid 1970s, *Wild Horse Mesa* (directed by George B. Seitz) reappeared to whet appetites anew and to confirm what a good and carefully produced series Paramount had created in its Grey adaptations.

True, it is not overly actionful, and it so takes its time getting under way that neither hero nor villain appear until two reels into the eight-reel film. (One is more conscious of this today perhaps, when most films start with a precredit teaser sequence, designed to rivet attention immediately and establish momentum, so that when the film eventually hits the television market it is going to grab viewer interest immediately.) But if nothing else, this is indicative of an unusual fidelity to the original Grey story. (It is also one of the first movies to deal with the potential dangers of using barbed wire to fence off ranch boundaries from open range, a theme that was to return in several Westerns of the fifties.) Very few "adaptations" had done more than pay lip service to

The Golden Princess (Paramount, 1925), from a Bret Harte story: Betty Bronson and Neil Hamilton

the Grey originals. The same story was remade often, each time with a *totally* different plot. Some of the Grey "original stories" just do not exist at all, and Grey was paid merely for the use of his name, or perhaps a scribbled plot outline that might in some cases be borrowed from another source. Fox's *Smoke Lightning*, for example, owed far more to Booth Tarkington's play, *Cameo Kirby* (which Fox owned and filmed twice), than to Grey.

Wild Horse Mesa, however, is about the most faithful of all Grey adaptations and encompasses most of his emotional feelings about the West as well as some of his less admirable moral and racial quirks. He was on location for much of its shooting in the four-corners locale of the novel, though primarily in Arizona. At the time, he announced himself well pleased with the treatment it was getting. The film makes up for its leisurely pacing with a story that is both solid and complex and action sequences that are *well* done. Virtually all exteriors, it was photographed by Bert Glennon, later a John Ford regular, with *Stagecoach* among his credits. Jack Holt (once described by director William K. Howard as the finest rider in Hollywood) is such a manly and virile hero that there's no need to underline his heroics, and opportunities to spotlight him via such devices as riding

Vivid action scenes from *California Mail* (First National, 1929), seventeenth in the Maynard series, with no lessening of quality

125

close-ups seem almost deliberately ignored. Noah Beery, as always, makes a marvelous villain, obviously having the time of his life hatching schemes that are usually as lecherously motivated as they are illegal. So jovially expressive is his face that inter titles seem to disappear when he makes his entrance, and his mobile features alone tell us what is going on. Douglas Fairbanks, Jr., in his third film, and Billie Dove provide youth and beauty, and Bernard Siegel plays one of the first of his "stoic, faithful Indian" roles, the most colorful of which was slotted into Frank Lloyd's mid-thirties *Wells Fargo.* Odd jazz-age details place the film in a contemporary (1925) setting, rendering it a trifle anachronistic, but that was a fairly regular trait with Grey. Sadly, no other silent Paramount Greys have been rediscovered in the nearly two decades since *Wild Horse Mesa* came to light.

The sudden popularity of German films, created primarily by *The Last Laugh* and *Metropolis,* and the growth of the "art house" exhibition outlet, made it fashionable for Hollywood to import German directors and stars—and for Hollywood filmmakers to inject German "technique" into their own movies. Unexpectedly, even the Western managed to absorb some of this style. A humble Jack Perrin Western for Universal, *Wild Blood,* was made in 1928—perhaps not too coincidentally, the year after German import Paul Leni had directed the very Germanically designed thriller, *The Cat and the Canary. Wild Blood* started off as traditional as apple pie, with horses conversing with each other via titles, and commenting on human frailties. But by the end of the film, the heroine nearly went mad and the hallucination and trick effect scenes were right out of *Warning Shadows* (1922). Far more notable, though less surprising in its absorption of Germanic style, was *White Gold* (1927), one of the near-forgotten classics of the silent period. It was directed by William K. Howard, a man always notable for pace and dazzling technique (especially in the sound period) and certainly more of a specialist in action and melodrama than psychology. He had directed *The Border Legion* and others in Paramount's Zane Grey series. Yet *White Gold* was a slow-moving, deliberately claustrophobic story with only two settings, five characters, and no physical action at all. Pacing was created by subtle intercutting and a remarkable sequence in which the hero—if one can term him that—plays cards with himself via multiple exposures while he argues with his conscience. The film dealt in intangibles such as jealousy, envy, and frustration and handed the audience at least two big shocks. One was the killing off of the "hero" (George Bancroft) quite casually and unexpectedly; the other was a deliberately ambiguous climax in which the audience had to decide for itself just what *had* happened and what was *going* to happen to the heroine, who was *probably* a murderess. Audiences in those pre-Godard and Resnais days were not used to being forced into thinking out problems and solutions which the film did not see fit to spell out for them. (Howard's use of German stylistics was not merely a lazy way of being fashionable; he had a genuine admiration for the work of German directors, and for a while was working alongside F. W. Murnau at Fox. He was one of Murnau's pallbearers when the director died in 1931 in a traffic accident, and German references continued to mark Howard's work in the thirties.)

White Gold was a big critical success, being compared favorably with *The Last Laugh,* but was considered a box office failure—although it must have been economical to make, and losses, if any, could not have been great. *White Gold,* not easily available for screening today, was overlooked and largely forgotten when, just a year later, MGM made a similar film, *The Wind,* with Lillian Gish starring and Sweden's Victor Sjostrom directing. The theme of a woman battling inner turmoil and the physical hardships of the wilds or the frontier was one that appealed to a number of directors at the end of the silent era, perhaps because of the simplicity and austerity of theme and the opportunities afforded for both virtuoso performances and direction. Murnau's *City Girl* and William Beaudine's *The Canadian* were two other related films from this period. But *White Gold* (its title refers to wool, the story taking place on a sheep ranch) was arguably the best of the group, and may well have been the inspiration for *The Wind,* just as *that* film may have spurred Murnau to make *City Girl.* In any event, it was the most notable psychological Western until the arrival two decades later of Wellman's *The Ox Bow Incident* and King's *The Gunfighter.*

By the end of the twenties, the important Western was at its lowest ebb since Hart and Ford had put it on the map in the teen years. The arrival of talkies brought both technical problems (especially where location shooting was involved) and the commercial need to exploit dialogue for its own sake. A further, if less expected, handicap to the Western was Lindbergh's epochal flight across the Atlantic, which seemed to stress that this was also a period of exploration. Overnight, the nation, and especially the Western's biggest audience, the *youth* of the nation, became aviation conscious.

Photoplay magazine editorialized in April of 1929:

> Lindbergh has put the cowboy into the discard. . . . The Western novel and motion picture have slunk away into the brush, never to return. The cow ponies are retired to the pasture with the old fire horses. Tom Mix, Hoot Gibson, and Ken Maynard must swap horses for airplanes or go to the old actors' home.

NINE

The Coming of Sound

One would have thought that the Western—telling its story in terms of visual action and needing perhaps only the simplest form of dialogue—would have had no trouble in making the transition from one medium to another; that like Laurel and Hardy in their comedies, it would not have needed to alter its format or content one iota other than to add sounds and speech that emerged naturally and without specific effort.

Actually, while some *styles* of filmmaking suffered from the coming of sound, most *genres* benefited in the long run. The Western, however, encountered more problems than most. First, there was, as *Photoplay* indicated, the threatened obsolescence of the cowboy hero. It was, of course, an exaggerated threat, especially as there was no reason why the cowboy could *not* keep himself up to date with planes and cars—as, in fact, Tom Mix had been doing for years. But the Lindbergh flight, coupled with the spotlight being thrown on Admiral Byrd's exploratory expeditions, shifted the emphasis, particularly for America's youth, to a new hero—that of the aviator-explorer. War films like *Hell's Angels* and *The Dawn Patrol* (and many follow-ups) and aviation films such as Frank Capra's *Dirigible* and *Flight*—all of which made excellent use of sound effects as well as dialogue— helped launch a whole new series of exploration adven-

tures. These ranged from such documentaries as the Martin Johnson travel films and *Rango* through such superficially realistic films as the German–U.S. coproduction *S.O.S. Iceberg* (far more exciting and uninhibited in its German version) to the extremes of fictional adventure in *Tarzan the Ape Man, King of the Jungle,* and ultimately *King Kong,*—all of this in the first four years of sound.

Furthermore, these films were all set in the present, representing a justifiable form of escapism. That word "justifiable" is important, for with the coming of sound, Hollywood (at least temporarily) felt that it had to abandon its old ideas of romanticism and, to an astonishing degree, laughter. If films now talked, they were inescapably realistic—and if they were to be realistic, that meant they had to take themes largely from the present. That, unfortunately, meant the Depression— which coincided with the coming of sound—and stories about unemployment, gangsterism, just staying alive. If the Lindbergh and Byrd names hadn't been so much in the news, it is doubtful that the explorer cycle would have taken off when it did. And it was a prolific cycle, spawning such films as *Eskimo, Igloo, Trader Horn,* and *Nagana,* in addition to the key titles already mentioned. Since they *were* inspired by current events and headlines, there could be no arguing against them as "unrealistic," and they provided a much needed morale-boosting escape from Depression problems. Certainly for a while the aviator's helmet and the explorer's pith helmet did replace the cowboy's stetson, and by the time these films had run their course, a new American hero, more easily placed in the Depression and the needs of the people, had arrived to take his place—the doctor. Whether a small-town physician (Will Rogers as *Dr. Bull*), an experimenting scientist (Errol Flynn in *The Green Light*), or one who was both (Ronald Colman in *Arrowsmith*), the kindly and idealistic doctor had many of the characteristics of the helpful cowboy hero, and in addition had the advantage of usually coming from the bestselling novels of Lloyd C. Douglas, A. J. Cronin, and Sinclair Lewis, offering a presold quality against which the cowboy hero could not compete.

Quite apart from these temporary setbacks to the character of the cowboy hero, the Western movie faced technical problems as well. Among other genres, the mystery film and the sophisticated comedy were forced to tell their stories via dialogue, and in order not to seem aggressively stagey and static, they *needed* camera mobility and as much of the filmic grammar of the silents as could be salvaged. For the most part they didn't get it, not least because audiences seemed quite happy with the pedestrian quality of the new sound films just so long as they talked; the big hits at the box office were those films that most resembled the stage play, like George Arliss's *Disraeli*. Because of many actual though in some cases only assumed problems, including the recording of their own operational sound, the cameras became rooted to the ground, housed in literal "sweat boxes." For at least two years, the cinema duplicated the theater as it had done in 1912, when full-length features were introduced; dialogue was king, style and grammar nothing. Of course, the good directors—Vidor, Mamoulian, Milestone—insisted on trying for the blending of sound and image. There was enough genuine experimentation, especially in 1929, and enough thoroughly cinematic films resulting in the period immediately following, to confound the smug claims by many later historians that the art of cinema came to an absolute standstill in those days. But achieving this artistry, and repudiating the claims by technical "experts" that such and such just couldn't be done, took time, sweat, and mechanical know-how, and in the first years of sound, the Western didn't seem important enough to justify this kind of effort. Like the elaborate swashbuckling adventure or the period romance, it was considered a relic of the silents and of little commercial value.

MGM scrapped its elaborate Tim McCoy films entirely. FBO, undergoing corporate and policy changes that transformed it first into RKO-Pathé and later RKO Radio, became virtually a new company dedicated to the exploitation of sound via adaptations of stage plays and novels and small-scale musicals that would eventually escalate into the Astaire and Rogers films. In the meantime, RKO scrapped its many series of program Westerns, although in a year or two it would resume with a Tom Keene series and thereafter maintain a regular Western series until the early fifties. Warner Bros., also in doubt about the commercial value of Westerns, likewise jettisoned them, resuming in 1932 with its John Wayne series.

Of all the major companies, only Universal, geared to smaller films and rural audiences, carried its silent cowboy heroes over into talkies. Nothing if not prolific, Hoot Gibson had eight Westerns in release in 1929 and six in 1930. While his amiable, folksy character was well suited to sound, and there was a relaxed, unselfconscious quality to his voice, still the almost total lack of action in his final films worked against him. Even experienced action directors like Reaves Eason and Arthur Rosson could do little with scripts which talked their way out of melodramatic confrontations, and were far more concerned with comedy—as in *The Concentratin' Kid*, concerning Hoot's infatuation with a radio singer who conveniently comes to his part of the West.

Even more frustrating were the Westerns with the titles that promised much action, like *Roaring Ranch* and *Trigger Tricks*, and delivered none. *Trigger Tricks* may well have set a record as the most talkative talkie Western ever made. Once Gibson's Universal contract ran out, he turned to the independent market. There his films improved somewhat in content, but of course lacked production values. At the very end of his career in a Monogram series of the forties, Gibson (with many doubles) did return in Westerns which deliberately stressed action and in fact, according to the advertising, were made to cater to the nostalgic Western devotees of old, who were not getting their quota of fights and chases in the currently popular musical Westerns.

With its Maynards, Universal had something of a problem. He was not a good enough actor, nor did he have enough of a flair for comedy, to emulate the Gibsons, which Universal wouldn't have wanted anyway. Yet the studio realized it *had* to offer talkie Westerns or lose out on the new market; at the same time it had to serve the slowly dying remnants of the silent market, but was reluctant to spend extra money on what it felt was still an unimportant product. The Gibsons had provided one (unsatisfying) solution: all talk and comedy, no money diverted to action sequences. For the Maynards, another and more workable compromise was reached. Once or twice in each film, the plot would stop dead in

Warner Baxter won an Academy Award for his Cisco Kid role in *In Old Arizona* (Fox, 1929) and repeated the characterization and variations of it for ten years

The eight Ken Maynard productions for Universal over 1929–30 are a fascinating group. They give a kind of sneak prevue of Maynard as an "auteur," a position in which he would exert more clout when he returned to Universal in 1933 as a replacement for Tom Mix, having worked in between on above-average Westerns for independent companies. Since the most interesting Maynards come from that second group, detailed comment will be reserved until then, but suffice it to say that Maynard, as his own producer, knew what the fans expected but also knew the *different* kinds of Westerns he wanted to promote. Even in that first series, where he was his own producer, he came up with some bizarre entries. *Mountain Justice* seemed strange enough, but since it had a whirlwind of action for its climax, there was no cause for complaint. But *Song of the Caballero*, which followed two movies later, was something else again. With Maynard's *Smoking Guns* (1934) it must rank as about the most bizarre Western ever made. It looks for all the world like an imitation-Fairbanks swashbuckling script, a silent that Universal had never been able to make because it was too expensive and for which, with the possible exception of Norman Kerry, it had no suitable star.

Maynard, it would seem, latched on to it and turned it into a Western with no changes other than that of transposing a (presumably) European locale into California. The most curious aspect of it all, perhaps indicative of haste, is that all of the dialogue was taut and stilted, as though the players were limited to mouthing

its tracks for a long dialogue sequence, perhaps with music thrown in; that would satisfy those demanding sound, and the film could easily be shortened and titled for the silent version. (In *Lucky Larkin*, a prolonged expository dialogue sequence took place in an oblong boxlike saloon). Universal's ten-episode Tim McCoy serial *The Indians Are Coming* (1930) was full of elaborate moving camerawork and was basically well paced, but likewise contained a static dialogue exchange in each chapter. The last chapter, as a kind of bonus, disposed of its wrap-up action very quickly (incidentally, most of it was stock from the Last Stand highlight of *Flaming Frontiers*, giving us a tantalizing glimpse of a film that seems otherwise not to have survived), and then devoted the bulk of its footage to a long conversation between the hero and the heroine (Allene Ray) in which she sorrowfully describes his best friend's apparent death, only to have the friend (Edmund Cobb) turn up alive and kicking as a rationale for more all-talking explanations and rejoicings!

Victor Fleming's *The Virginian* (Paramount, 1929): Gary Cooper being stalked by Walter Huston

the original subtitles. There was an endearing quality to the bemused heroine (Doris Hill) listening to Maynard's declarations of love, couched in phrases better suited to Valentino or Fairbanks, and which Maynard delivered as though reading them for the first and only time, which he probably was. Even casual expressions retained the flavor of a different locale and period; Maynard constantly refers to his pals as "Comrades," and the dusty trail is always "the King's Highway." Fisticuffs are jettisoned in favor of rapiers, and in the climactic set-to, Maynard is leaping over balconies and dueling with a half dozen of the villain's cronies. Since the chief villain is Gino Corrado (who had played Aramis to Fairbanks's D'Artagnan in *The Iron Mask* just the year before), who could clearly have finished Ken (or Juan, as the script has it) in one thrust had he been allowed to, Maynard's distinctly clumsy swordplay is far from convincing.

However, the film moves, it is lively, and it is *fun;* audiences doubtless enjoyed it infinitely more than they had the current Hoot Gibson releases. A further innovative aspect of the early sound Maynards was his use of Western songs. Technically, Maynard can be considered the first "Singing Cowboy," although he made no move to exploit that fact and used songs naturally and casually rather than as set pieces. Sometimes he sang himself; on other occasions he was said to use a voice double, and he usually accompanied himself with no great virtuosity on the violin. The results were interesting and at least nonabrasive, but whether the voice was Maynard's or that of another, the films weren't sufficiently revolutionary to bring about a cycle of musical Westerns. That had to await 1934 and Gene Autry, who coincidentally was introduced via a Ken Maynard feature.

Fortunately, the stalemate of the over-talkie or the hybrid part-talkie Western was solved very quickly, and particularly by two big-budget Westerns made in 1929. Raoul Walsh began directing *In Old Arizona* as well as playing one of the two leads. He was injured during production (and blinded in one eye) and had to relinquish his acting role to Edmund Lowe and his directorial chores to Irving Cummings. Possibly it might have been a much better film had Walsh finished it, although his films were a little uneven at this point, his other big 1929 one, *The Cockeyed World,* being overlong and certainly far too noisy and talkative. *In Old Arizona,* the first of many sound Cisco Kid adventures, is credited with having alerted audiences to the exciting use of sound in the outdoor films. Microphones were hidden under sagebrush or behind rocks to pick up on-location dialogue and the sounds of hoofbeats and gunshots. However, as in many cases, the legend isn't really borne out by the facts. There are few exteriors in the film, and many of those take place at night, so they could as easily have been shot in the studio, and probably were. There's

The Virginian: Walter Huston in black outfit and mustache

6-SHEET A

12-SHEET A

6-SHEET B

48-SHEET

TRAILERS

for all Paramount
Pictures can be
obtained from the

NATIONAL
SCREEN
SERVICE
LIMITED

25 Denmark Street
London, W.C.2

6-SHEET C

The above slip is
available free of
charge for all sizes
of Posters when a
Silent design is
used for Talking
version.

12-SHEET B

Posters for Paramount's hot new Western

THE NEW
Paramount
SHOW WORLD
Pictures

TALKING ★

A PARAMOUNT
TALKING
PICTURE

B. P. SCHULBERG,
GENERAL MANAGER,
WEST COAST PRODUCTIONS

ADOLPH ZUKOR AND JESSE L. LASKY PRESENT

"THE
VIRGINIAN"

WITH
GARY COOPER AND
WALTER HUSTON
RICHARD ARLEN AND MARY BRIAN

A VICTOR FLEMING PRODUCTION
BASED UPON THE NOVEL BY OWEN WISTER
AND THE PLAY BY OWEN WISTER AND
KIRK LA SHELLE

ADAPTED BY GROVER JONES AND
KEENE THOMPSON
SCREEN PLAY BY HOWARD ESTABROOK
DIALOGUE BY EDWARD E. PARAMORE, JR.

THE NEW
Paramount
SHOW WORLD
Pictures

SYNOPSIS, AD.-AIDS
AND PRICE LIST

The Virginian: talk was more important than star names, Western tradition, or classic novel

Billy the Kid: Johnny Mack Brown (left) being coached by William S. Hart who also loaned one of Billy's six-shooters; director King Vidor is in the center

very little action, and so much talk that the film seems far longer than it is. And its most quoted use of naturalistic sound, the hiss and crackle of frying bacon isn't there at all. There is a mild scene (with muted sound) of ham and eggs—but the famous bacon-frying scene comes in a later and better movie, King Vidor's *Billy the Kid.* What probably caused the excitement attached to *In Old Arizona* was the fact that Warner Baxter, a very staid and unexciting player in silents, here had a colorful role with a Mexican accent. That in itself probably provided the novelty that won Baxter the Academy Award for Best Performance that year, though it was a routine piece of acting at best. The Western also had a vocal theme song, *My Tonia,* played before the credits (since Tonia turns out to be a far from romantic leading lady, and in fact is rather cold-bloodedly killed off in a morally dubious deception created by the Cisco Kid for the film's climax). If *In Old Arizona* disappoints today, as it almost inevitably must, it should be remembered that it was produced in 1928 and released in January 1929, and in that early epoch, its use of sound was indeed novel. Another 1929 release, *The Virginian,* was *far* more effective in its creative and naturalistic use of sound, but it was released at the *end* of 1929, with almost a whole year passing between the two films.

In its first reel, *The Virginian* showed just how much the Western could benefit from natural sound. The opening scenes show a cattle herd and a locomotive arriving in town at the same time; the creaking of harnesses, the whinnying of horses, the peaceful mooing of the cattle changing to a more urgent sound as they are alarmed by the steam and the whistle of the train, all with the camera constantly mobile, tracking along with the cattle, picking up casual greetings and pleasantries from the trail herders. If the overexuberant colloquialisms as old friends Gary Cooper and Richard Arlen meet ("You ornery old horse thief," etc.) are too protracted and fulsome, it was understandable at the time, and in any case worked far more convincingly than had the same kind of dialogue in the subtitle of silents. Within minutes, the film moves into the saloon for casual horseplay, the sound of floorboards and scraping chairs, guns shooting coins out of the air, and finally the time-honored initial meeting between the Virginian and the villain Trampas ("When you call me that, *smile!*") and the opportunity for two very different kinds of actor (Gary Cooper and the stage-trained Walter Huston) to create very different characters through accent, tone of voice, and the style of dialogue itself, eliminating the kind of pantomime that accompanied even the best of similar confrontations in the silent films of William S. Hart. *The Virginian* has always been a slow and somewhat stereotyped story; earlier silent versions had been unexciting, as was a later sound and Technicolor remake with Joel McCrea. But the sheer novelty of sound, the skill with which it was used, and the way it enabled the concentration to be placed on characters rather than on action made this version (which was basically no more exciting than any other) the best and definitive adaptation of the Owen Wister novel.

Follow-ups to *In Old Arizona* were modest. In 1930, Fox made a sequel, only to find out at the last minute that studio rights in the character extended to only the one feature. While rights were being renegotiated, the studio hurriedly rewrote its second film, now calling it *The Arizona Kid,* although the Baxter characterization was exactly the same. Considering that there was well over a year between the two productions, it was a humdrum production that showed no marked sign of improvement, the utilization of Carole Lombard as a villainess being its only element of surprise. However, with rights reclaimed and adjusted, a third film, titled simply *The Cisco Kid,* was made in 1931. Less ambitious, running only an hour, it was easily the best of the three. It was exceptionally well photographed (especially in a nighttime chase at the beginning) and featuring a lively musical score. Fox however, did little more with the character until the late thirties and early forties, when a sprightly if rather slow-on-action "B" series was produced. Thereafter, Fox lost interest, and Cisco, along with Fox's Honolulu detective, Charlie Chan, suffered the indignity of being sold to Monogram, although, as it happened, as acted by Gilbert Roland, the Monogram Cisco Kids were extremely good.

In this period of transition to sound, the studios were again experimenting with the oft-tried and oft-abandoned idea of wide-screen projection—a curiously ill-timed experiment, since two different sound systems (sound on film, the better and surviving system, and sound on disc) were battling one another and the expense of installing either or both systems in a Depression economy was a major one, especially for smaller exhibitors. Wide-screen presentations would seem to be an unnecessary complication at that time, particularly with new color processes, and especially an improved Technicolor, likewise competing for attention.

Obviously, though, the Western was an ideal testing ground for the giant-screen movie, and two major ones were produced in 65 mm; however, after a few showcase runs, they were distributed in the standard 35-mm format. The first of these was *The Big Trail,* directed by Raoul Walsh for Fox. It gave John Wayne his first starring role, and indeed his first role of any kind other than extras and bit parts. In its full form, it ran well over two hours. In terms of size and action, it was, and is, a classic, everything that *The Covered Wagon* should have been and wasn't, certainly the closest any Western epic

King Vidor's *Billy the Kid* (MGM, 1930): Wallace Beery and Johnny Mack Brown

had yet come to documentary realism. (Its German version, with a totally different cast, was still playing commercially in German cinemas immediately after World War II, at a time when the original was thought to have been lost.) Its big Indian battle scenes and panoramic long shots of the wagon train were used throughout the thirties and forties to pad out cheaper Westerns, especially such Republic titles as *The Painted Stallion* and *Pioneers of the West*, while its impressive and almost agonizingly convincing shots of the wagons being winched over and down steep cliffs were reused by Henry Hathaway in *Brigham Young*.

However, it wasn't just the spectacular action that made *The Big Trail* stand out; it was also the use of extensive locations, the bustling detail of the arrival of immigrants by riverboat, the assembly and departure of the wagon train, the detail of tree-felling to create a path for the wagons through virgin forests, the battle against sand and snow, desert heat, and winter cold, the fording of a swollen river, a buffalo hunt, scenes that established the Indian as a potential friend. All of it was enhanced by naturalistic sound and dialogue that was sometimes stiff and unpolished—as it should be with hardy pioneers who are unprepared, in moments of sudden crisis, to make decisions in situations that are forced on them, or who face situations that demand leadership and who lack the experience of oratory to back it up. This all was slammed over with Walsh's reclaimed virility and pace (the uncertain pacing of his 1929 movies was gone) as well as his traditional black humor. Rather surprisingly, for such an early talkie, there was an excellent musical score, too, though one reserved primarily for punctuation, highlights, and as backups to the inter titles that were still used as segues between sequences.

At the end of its fourteen reels, audiences really felt that they had been on a wagon trek that had lasted for months, as opposed, for example, to a similar later film, *The Way West* (1967), where, despite extensive location shooting, there was no sense of hardship and one was constantly reminded of an omnipresent Hollywood. So authentic did all of *The Big Trail* look (even to women's clothing and lack of makeup) that when, in the mid-sixties, a Kansas City historical institution came across some glass negatives of the wagon train assembly and departure sequence, it excitedly waxed long and enthusiastic about its discovery of rare original photographic records of the actual event! If ever a Western deserved to be a financial success, it was *The Big Trail,* but circumstances were against it. Most of all, it was an unprecedented undertaking. Walsh was shooting widescreen and standard screen versions, and French and German versions were being shot at the same time. Complicated scenes had to be restaged with different actors, and the work consumed a great deal of time. No extensive location work had ever been done before with so much sound and camera equipment in tow, to say nothing of American and European casts, technical crew, and much rolling stock. The sheer logistics of accommodation and preplanning were enormous, added to which were such unexpected setbacks as discovering that many of the Indians employed as extras no longer rode horses. When they found that they had to, they came through—but also suffered painful sores on their legs.

When the film was completed, it shared with Vidor's *Billy the Kid* the virtue of seeming real and authentic almost to a point of crudity. Probably both Walsh and Vidor wanted that effect, but in any case it arose naturally out of the conditions under which the films were made. Too, audiences were now used to the

Raoul Walsh's *The Big Trail* (Fox, 1930)

all-talkies—and the all-singing, all-dancing musicals—which, though they can be seen·to have many rough edges today, seemed to exude studio gloss and glamour in 1930. Editorials like the one in *Photoplay* had also told them that Westerns were old hat. Moreover, they were at the beginning of a depression that promised to be a long and bitter one. Hardship and survival itself were everyday concerns, and a Western that showed the same things was hardly escapism. And although it showed that sacrifice was worthwhile and that there were rewards at the end of the trail, it was dealing with the past, not the present, and audiences were hard pressed to find either allegories or parallels. The extreme cost of production due to all the technical problems involved, coupled with the apathy of the public, made the film (for its day) something of a cause-célèbre as a box office disaster. By the time Wayne was a big enough star for his earlier films

The Big Trail: John Wayne helps fend off an Indian attack

The Big Trail: John Wayne, Charlie Stevens, Tyrone Power, Sr., and Ian Keith

to be reissued to exploit his new fame, *The Big Trail* was considered too long, unwieldy, and primitive to be so handled.

Through the years, *The Big Trail* became something of a joke, perpetrated largely by those who had never seen it, who assumed that anything that lost so much money *had* to be a bad film. Wayne himself, in later years, certainly didn't help matters by denigrating the film or his performance in it. Admittedly, while it may

Illustrierter Film-Kurier Nr. 221

DIE GROSSE FAHRT

Die Grosse Fahrt: German version of *The Big Trail*, with Theo Shall and Marion Lessing in the John Wayne and Marguerite Churchill roles

their quality steadily improving throughout the thirties until capped by *Stagecoach.* (Ironically, his success in that film was almost accidental; producer Walter Wanger had wanted but could not get Gary Cooper, then committed to Sam Goldwyn and Paramount.)

Fortunately for the cause of film history, *The Big Trail* was rescued, after a fashion, in the mid-sixties, and prints from rather well-worn American and French sources were available, though surprisingly little utilized for commercial exhibition except in Europe. Then in 1990, New York's Museum of Modern Art—which had often exercised bad judgment in determining the priorities of preservation projects—more than made up for past mistakes by producing a superb wide-screen reconstruction of *The Big Trail.* Printed via the CinemaScope process, but not entirely filling that frame because of its faithful adherence to the shape of the original 65-mm format, it derived from the virtually unused original 65-mm negative, which had miraculously been discovered by archivist Alex Gordon in the 20th Century-Fox vaults (where its existence had long been denied). Not only did the wide-screen version contain a reel or so of footage trimmed from the regular release version, but the pictorial quality was absolutely stunning. Because the original negative had not been used, it was free of scratches and splices; it literally looked as though it had been photographed that very year. If only more audiences could have seen it that way in 1930, it might well have prevented the apathy which so rapidly overtook the big-scale Westerns and it might have hastened the cause of the wide screen, which was about to be abandoned for another twenty years. Shown to a packed audience on the huge screen at the National Gallery of Art in Washington in January 1992, *The Big Trail* literally took their breath away. And this of course was an audience used to all the wide-screen processes up to Cinerama and Imex, and to seeing them in color. How much greater that impact would have been in 1930. Its compositions and *use* of the wide screen were, incidentally, far more inventive and sophisticated than in the stunt and novelty uses to be dreamed up for it in Cinerama's *How the West Was Won.*

King Vidor's *Billy the Kid,* made for MGM in 1930, was an equally worthwhile and interesting film, but slower and on a smaller scale. Photographed largely on the actual locations of the famous Lincoln County wars, it was again carefully composed with the giant screen in mind. There were superb panoramic shots (though sometimes wasted on a story that did not deal in spectacle) and intricate use of terrain and natural lighting, as in a sequence where Billy is besieged in a cave among colorful rock formations, while Sheriff Pat Garrett below entices the starving outlaw into surrender by frying

not have been intentional, the very ingenuousness of his performance is partly what makes it work so well today. Surrounded by veteran players, cast as old-timers or experienced confidence men from the East (Tully Marshall, Tyrone Power, Sr., Ian Keith), Wayne, as a mountain man more at home with trappers and Indians, gives a needed innocence to the role that in many ways predates qualities in his Ringo Kid performance in *Stagecoach* almost a decade later. Clearly however, stardom was thrust on him too quickly: he reverted to supporting roles and leads in "B" Westerns, his work and

The Great Meadow (MGM, 1931): Eleanor Boardman in a domestic scene with Johnny Mack Brown (above) and attempting to hold off a savage (below)

bacon. In fact, the whole film was so meticulously composed for wide-screen projection that, encountering the same problems as the early CinemaScope films of the fifties, it avoided close-ups entirely. When seen on a normal screen—which is the way most 1930 audiences did see it—the film and its concentration on long and medium shots gave it an aloof, impersonal quality. One somehow felt too detached physically from Billy to be involved emotionally in his problems. Already rather an old-fashioned film, it (unlike *The Big Trail*) also had no musical score at all, and it sorely needed one, if only for punctuation in transitional scenes. In lieu of music, silent style inter titles were employed to bridge gaps in time, locale, and dramatic change. Moreover, Vidor deliberately tried to avoid the traditional MGM gloss; the photography is good but always naturalistic, the characters drab in their dress, the buildings ramshackle, the streets dusty. It is a long film, with its main action sequence placed in the middle, so that it doesn't even build to a climax as most Westerns do. Its script is frankly untidy, yet despite many flaws, the film is certainly the best of the many screen interpretations of Billy the Kid, certainly far superior to MGM's own Technicolor remake a decade later with Robert Taylor.

Wesley Ruggles's *Cimarron* (RKO Radio, 1931): the Cherokee Strip land rush

Johnny Mack Brown, very soon to be one of the most pleasing stars of "B" Westerns for twenty-odd years, was, prior to this film—and primarily in silents—a clothes-horse leading man to Joan Crawford, Greta Garbo, and Mary Pickford. As a former football player, he brought a husky athleticism to the role of Billy, although it was Wallace Beery as Pat Garrett who gave the best performance, a surprisingly underplayed piece of acting for one well-known for his extroverted, blustering playing.

In *Billy the Kid,* Vidor created the first of only two early sound Westerns (the second was *Law and Order* in 1932) to really recapture the rugged austerity of the silent William S. Hart films. No doubt some of the film's authenticity of appearance can be attributed to the fact that Hart worked on it as an advisor, coached Brown, and even loaned him Billy's six-guns. Even if this move to employ Hart was prompted primarily for publicity, it certainly paid off, if only subliminally. Hart must have been dismayed however, by the tacked-on happy ending in which the suddenly benign Garrett, instead of shooting Billy down, sends him over the border to safety and a peaceful life with his sweetheart. A still romanticized but closer-to-the-facts ending in which Billy is shot by Garrett and dies in his arms was filmed, but retained only for the European release. Since Billy's various killings are shown as being decidedly cold-blooded, even

The Painted Desert (Pathe, 1931): Helen Twelvetrees, J. Farrell
MacDonald, and Clark Gable

when partially justified by circumstance, this sudden
ending is a little hard to accept. It is also at odds with the
grim and realistic tenor of the rest of the film. In its
midway battle scene, there is a real sense of pain, fear,
and desperation; when men die from gunshot wounds, it
is not in stylized peaceful pantomime, but writhing in
pain from a bullet to the stomach.

Despite Brown's success in *Billy the Kid,* MGM did
not have much more use for him. His musical, pronounced Southern accent was considered a liability in
talkies, and MGM had much more interest in building
up newcomer Clark Gable. While its faith in Gable was
certainly justified, one would have thought that a studio
as awash in star names as MGM could have found a place
for Brown as well. The studio did, however, put him into
a semi-follow-up, *The Great Meadow* (1931, directed by
Charles Brabin), which was actually a kind of Southern
equivalent to *The Big Trail,* dealing with an earlier
pioneering period and a 1775 trek from Virginia to
Kentucky. It had all of the virtues of *The Big Trail* and
inevitably suffered the same fate. If anything it was a
stronger film emotionally, stressing the breakup of families which might never be reunited. It was also extremely savage and even unpleasant in its Indian fighting
scenes. The romantic alliance between Brown and wife
Eleanor Boardman, a superb actress in one of her final

Cimarron: William Collier, Jr., and Richard Dix

roles before retirement, had unusual depth, poignancy,
and complexity. *The Great Meadow* was a minor classic
that, unlike *The Big Trail*, was totally forgotten and not
even joked about, probably because it was not as spectacular a financial loss.

139

Hell's Heroes (Universal, 1930), William Wyler's version of *Three Godfathers:* Fritzie Ridgeway, Charles Bickford, Walter James

The Spoilers (Paramount, 1930): William Farnum and Tom Santschi, stars of the first version, returned (for publicity purposes) allegedly to coach Gary Cooper and William Boyd for the fight scene, as Mary Brian watches

in any way be said to justify big-screen treatment. However, movie houses that had installed a Magnascope screen—one that could be expanded at will to accommodate either individual sequences or entire films—frequently, though depending on the showmanship qualities of the theater manager, brought them back into play for highlight action sequences. As recently as 1950, and before CinemaScope arrived, New York's Rivoli Theater used its old Magnascope screen for the big cavalry charge sequence in Robert Wise's *Two Flags West.*

Strangely, the much improved Technicolor system, then enjoying a big vogue, was not harnessed to the big-scale Western. Commercially it might well have saved it. But the two-color system in use then was of essentially pastel shades; it was pleasing and often dramatic, but it was considered unrealistic, and thus inappropriate to the extended location shooting of Westerns. It was used primarily for musicals and a brace of horror films at Warners, where it was done stylistically and most effectively. It was used in the West only when the film in question—*Whoopee* and *Rio Rita* come most readily to mind—was essentially a studio-based musical, with perhaps one or two establishing or linking shots of the authentic outdoors. Universal did use the cheaper Cinecolor process to experiment with a smaller-scale Western, *The Phantom of Santa Fe,* but apparently was unhappy with the results. It was shelved, and some six years later sold to the independent Burroughs-Tarzan Enterprises, whence it emerged with most of the key roles curiously redubbed by other actors. Technicolor, even when improved to the new three-color system,

Although the wide screen was well utilized in *The Big Trail* and *Billy the Kid,* enthusiasm for it did not last. Before its quick demise, it was already being used only as a gimmick to prop up weak pictures, as, for example, *The Lash,* a pedestrian Richard Barthelmess Western in which only a fairly large cattle stampede sequence could

would be applied to *outdoor* films of the later thirties (*Trail of the Lonesome Pine, God's Country and the Woman, Valley of the Giants*), but would not become a staple of the bona fide Western until *Jesse James* in 1939.

Cimarron (1931), the third big Western epic of the sound era, was commercially the "safest" of the three in that it was based on a best-selling novel by Edna Ferber, and had two popular stars in Richard Dix and newcomer Irene Dunne. A long film (well over two hours, though that was fairly standard for Ferber's rambling narratives) and an expensive one at $1.5 million, it quickly achieved an inflated reputation as a box office winner due to its "Best Picture" Academy Award for that year, backed by a couple of lesser Oscars. Like director Wesley Ruggles's later *Arizona,* it tended to bog down in character studies and too much plot, and had the structural flaw of presenting its highlight—the famous land-rush sequence—at the beginning of the film, with the rest of the footage devoted to the building and development of Oklahoma as an oil-rich state and the hero's widespread interests and activities, which included representing the underdog Indians. Nevertheless the opening reels were so strong, not just in the physical action of the land rush, but also in the convincing depiction of the building of the frontier town, that their impetus carried the film through its later, more pedestrian segments. However, *Cimarron* has dated badly: the rough-hewn quality that makes *The Big Trail* seem better than ever works *against* the talk-dominated story line of *Cimarron.*

In 1931, it was not immediately known that *Cimarron* would show a loss in excess of a half million dollars, and its apparent success and certainly the prestige it acquired prompted not so much a series of further Western epics as a number of outright imitations using the formula best demonstrated in Noël Coward's *Caval-cade,* but reversing the emphasis: dealing optimistically with the birth of a young nation rather than, sadly, with the (possible) last years of a great empire. The Mary Pickford–Leslie Howard *Secrets,* directed by Frank Borzage, was an interesting film in this small group, stronger on emotional and romantic qualities than on action, and rather surprisingly for such an expensive production, lifting a few stock shots from *The Covered Wagon.* Rather better, and preceding it by a year, was *The Conquerors,* an obvious attempt (but a good one) by RKO Radio to repeat *Cimarron* even to starring Richard Dix again, with Ann Harding taking over from Irene Dunne. Directed by William Wellman, it contained some unusually powerful sequences, including the death of the family's son in a buggy accident as crowds are lined

Law and Order (Universal, 1932): Neal Hart (left) turns accidental killer Andy Devine over to lawman Walter Huston

141

up to welcome the arrival of the township's first locomotive, and a grim mass lynching episode so starkly designed and lit and so casually underplayed that it quite outshines the more carefully and lengthily constructed lynching scenes in Wellman's much later *The Ox Bow Incident* (1943). Like many films of the Depression, *The Conquerors* almost deifies the banking profession. Hollywood needed the banks for its own financing and thus carefully nurtured the impression that, despite the occasional scoundrel, the banks were run by men of integrity and ideals. *The Conquerors* has Dix's bank literally building the West, and follows it through earlier times of economic recession, World War I, and the twenties and up to the current depression, when an excessively made-up octogenarian Dix watches with pride as a younger member of his family (also played by Dix) takes over, new blood and a faith in the country promising deliverance from contemporary woes.

Additionally, 1932 saw the production of another of the sound era's most overlooked Westerns (and one of the finest), *Law and Order*. Although based on a novel by W. R. Burnett and using fictional names, it was clearly built around Wyatt Earp (renamed Saint Johnson, and played by Walter Huston) and Doc Holliday (reincarnated via Harry Carey). Perhaps not too coincidentally the film paralleled an MGM release of the same year, *Beast of the City*, a gangster film also written by Burnett and starring Huston as a police chief who finally takes the law into his own hands and with a vigilante posse wipes out a nest of gangsters that corrupt politicians and crooked lawyers have kept safe from retribution. With gangsterism rampant, a surprising number of Hollywood films of this period were found to be taking a similar, almost Fascist attitude. The most outspoken advocate of vigilante law to combat gangsterism was MGM's *Gabriel Over the White House,* in which the American president himself (Walter Huston again!) sets up a goon squad to eradicate the gangsters—most of them foreigners, the script is careful to emphasize—who have placed themselves above the law. Although Huston had played as many villains as heroes at this stage in his career (his film career didn't begin until 1929, after many years on the stage, but once under way it was immediately prolific and varied) and was an especially effective Western villain, as *The Virginian* had shown, still the image that most immediately came to mind was as that of the martyred president in Griffith's *Abraham Lincoln.* In these first years of his career on film, Huston had also played the idealistic bank president in *American Madness* and the crusading district attorney in *The Star Witness;* he immediately conjured up an image of integrity, incorruptibility, and physical courage. Universal didn't make many gangster films, but had made a major

contribution to the cycle by espousing vigilante law in *Okay America* (1932), and *Law and Order* can be seen as being as much a part of that cycle as it is a Western.

The director of *Law and Order* was Edward Cahn, who had just completed an apprenticeship under a prestige "art" director, Paul Fejos, and was anxious to show what he could do. His directorial debut was also his artistic zenith; he never again made a film nearly as good, although he was given few opportunities to do so. He had a major talent in being able to work efficiently and at great speed, and was much in demand for the production of classy-*looking* "B" movies.

Law and Order, partially scripted by Walter Huston's son, John, had a great deal of tension but little physical action until the last reel, when it literally exploded into what is still the best reconstruction of the famous (though historically often disputed) gunfight at the O.K. Corral. Influenced no doubt by Fejos, who had always been an advocate of the elaborately fluid use of the mobile camera, Cahn (also a former editor) made his camera a literal participant in the short, tightly edited battle, darting from side to side in subjective viewpoints, catching the sudden terror of a frightened horse or the quick spurts of water when bullets missed their mark and hissed into a horse trough instead. Perhaps the real distinction of *Law and Order* lay in its formal yet unforced style. At the end, the marshal, sole survivor of the battle, rides out of town alone, weary of killing, yet knowing that more such towns await him and his guns. The composition and placement of the camera stresses his feeling of isolation; the church bell tolls ambiguously, either in celebration or mourning; the citizens are glad to have the job done but had been unwilling to involve themselves in that job—all of these visual and textual elements combine to achieve a sense of Greek tragedy without consciously striving for it, as *High Noon* was to do with such heavy-handed underlining.

Law and Order was remade in the forties, as a formula but above average Johnny Mack Brown "B" under the same title, and a few years later yet again as *Rustlers' Roundup,* a totally undistinguished "B" with Kirby Grant that borrowed all of its action footage from the Brown film. In the fifties, Universal made it once more, reverting to the original title but filming in Technicolor. This version, packed with violent and even brutal action, starred Ronald Reagan. The original film had no women at all, other than a saloon trollop who appeared briefly; the Reagan version had *two* leading ladies and a great deal of sex and bedroom suggestiveness. In one of the most touching and memorable episodes of the original, the lawmen are forced to hang a simpleminded, goodhearted farm lad (played by Andy Devine) who has become an accidental murderer, a subplot that effectively introduced problems of morality and conscience, considerations that could deter and confuse the decent early lawmen just as much as a confrontation with outnumbering enemy forces. In the remake, this outstanding sequence was distorted into a stereotyped lynching by the villains.

In 1930, it was mainly the content of films like *The Big Trail* that made them, to an audience, seem less sophisticated than a successful studio-bound all-talkie like MGM's *The Divorcee*. But by 1932, when movies had really solved all of their technical problems and were entering their lushest period of smooth-as-velvet cinematic gloss, it was theme plus style that made *Law and Order* seem to be so stark when directly juxtaposed against Lubitsch's silken *Trouble in Paradise* or Mamoulian's *Love Me Tonight,* two films that even today represent a high-water mark in sophisticated elegance. Far from matching their escapist qualities (apart from their wit and musical gaiety, those films were also set in faraway Europe, emphasizing that they were turning their backs on domestic depression), *Law and Order* showed more graphically than most later Westerns that life in the West could be lonely and harsh, and that dying from a shotgun blast was as much a part of the "glory" of the West as leading a cavalry charge against the Apaches.

Most of the other Westerns of the period—not that there were many of them—tended to maintain this downbeat attitude. Or, like *The Painted Desert* (1931), they remembered that they were "talkies" and told too much of their story in words rather than deeds. *The Painted Desert* was partially redeemed, however, by the dynamic presence of Clark Gable, playing his first major role—a villain—with such force and animal magnetism that he easily stole the film away from the placid and straightforward heroics of William Boyd.

But for the real excitement and action of the Western, audiences turned to the "B" movie. By 1932, most of the big silent Western stars were reestablished in series of their own: Tom Mix, Buck Jones, Tim McCoy, Ken Maynard. The independent producers, cashing in on a greatly expanded double-bill market (giving audiences *more* than they had been accustomed to was considered a useful way of keeping their patronage in the Depression years), embarked on the prolific mass production of scores of cheap Westerns, employing not only the lesser stars of the silents (Bob Custer, Bill Cody, Jack Perrin, Buddy Roosevelt) but also those bigger names (Hoot Gibson, Harry Carey, Bob Steele, Lane Chandler, Tom Tyler, Jack Hoxie) who were unable to find more imposing berths in the now restricted Western output of the bigger studios. Some of them, like Buddy Roosevelt, just didn't have what it took to meet the competition and faded away into bit roles. But for every one who did, there was a Rex Lease, a Fred Kohler, Jr., or a Reb Russell to take his place. And to the imposing list of veterans, interesting new stars were added: John Wayne at Warners, Tom Keene at RKO Radio, Randolph Scott at Paramount. When Gene Autry established the musical Western in 1935, he also established whole new careers for singing cowboys: Fred Scott, Roy Rogers, Dick Foran, Tex Ritter, Jack Randall. Studios like Republic and Monogram that honed the production of slick "B's" to a fine art would regularly introduce new Western stars. It was the beginning of the movies' biggest boom in profitable grade "B" horse operas, a boom that would sustain itself at peak level for some fifteen years and then slowly decline in quantity and quality for another ten. It was a veritable paradise for the Western fans who cared little for the poetry of Ford or the dedicated realism of Hart, but loved and could never get enough of nonstop galloping hooves, crackling six-guns, and the unique sound of the impact of fist on chin.

Universal Studios has one of the best Western streets in Hollywood, and one that has undergone few changes. It has served at least four versions of *Destry Rides Again*—this scene is from the most famous, the 1939 edition

Republic's Western street: Here Gene Autry's double removes Ann Miller's double from the path of a crashing stagecoach in *Melody Ranch* (1940) from which Yakima Canutt is leaping

Intermission

When expensive location jaunts aren't needed or can't be afforded, Hollywood has its own West right in its backyard, as these stills show.

On Columbia's Western street, the saloon has been given a false front in this shot, probably in preparation for a cattle stampede which will partially wreck it

The old Monogram street, here used in *Panhandle* (1948). Shortly
afterward, it was sold to Gene Autry

RKO Radio's Western street was wider than most,
allowing plenty of room for George O'Brien to stare
down the badmen in *Marshal of Mesa City* (1939)

Fox had an excellent Western street, and didn't
waste it. Cunning lighting and camera angling
uses just a portion of it in this 1930 George
O'Brien version of *Last of the Duanes*

Literally only a mile or two from Hollywood Boulevard, in the heart of Griffith Park, is rugged Bronson Canyon—used from the thirties on, and still very much in use today for Westerns (as here in 1933's *Honor of the Range*), serials, horror films, war movies, outer space adventures, and even a classic or two

Warner Bros. enlarged and reshaped its Burbank Western street as the occasion demanded; here James Cagney beats a retreat from it in *The Oklahoma Kid* (1939)

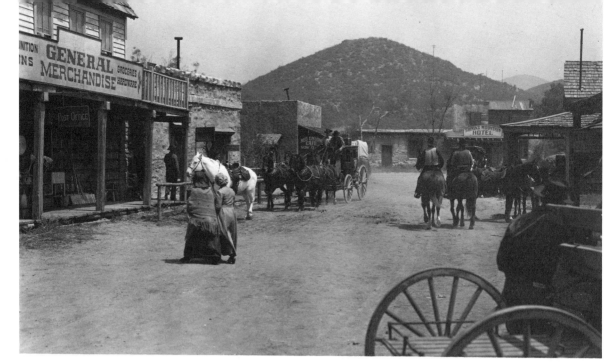

The Iverson Ranch at Chatsworth, a movie location rented out to all the studios, included this dusty Western town, seen in all its glory from both directions: Monogram used it extensively, but when dressed up in Technicolor by RKO for Fritz Lang's *Rancho Notorious* (1952), it could look more impressive than it really was

An even more ramshackle town, also in the Chatsworth area—some thirty miles outside of Hollywood—used primarily by PRC, here for the studio's Texas Rangers series with Tex (Dave) O'Brien and Tex Ritter

Included for the record since it is such a familiar street to Western fans, but somewhat further afield, is Kerneville, which had the advantage of a trail coming over the crest of a hill outside the town and right into Main Street—ideal for those last reel rides to a climactic roundup. This scene is from *Bar 20 Justice* (1938) with Hopalong Cassidy riding into town

An example of the cramped and much-in-need-of-repair street used for the cheapest of independent Westerns in the early thirties. In this scene from *The Way of the West* (1935), Wally Wales, Bill Desmond, Bobby Nelson, and others have to tread carefully to avoid many piles of horse manure

Two further views of the Chatsworth
landscape: up close it was drab and dusty,
but there were vantage points from which
good long shots could be taken

One of several ranch houses of various sizes that dotted the Chatsworth landscape. Iverson's Ranch, as such, is no more, the area having been subdivided and no longer used as a movie location

Dan Clark lines up his camera on the rim of the Grand Canyon for a George O'Brien Western

TEN

The "B" Boom

The new medium of talkies proved to be a great leveler, and the "B" Westerns of independents and major companies alike started out on a relatively even basis. Westerns could still be made cheaply, and the smaller companies as yet had no need to practice the extremes in economy that eventually would separate them from their big studio counterparts. The independents could still afford to hire enough extras so that crowd scenes didn't appear too skimpy, and a camera car was not yet a production luxury, so even the smallest budget Westerns could indulge in that ultimate finesse, the running insert or riding close-up. Shooting two or three Westerns at the same time justified the expense of going to a worthwhile location, but this was an economy that Paramount and Universal used, too. (When two Westerns were shot back-to-back using the same director and casts, it usually wasn't difficult, however, to spot which one was considered of greater importance and which one "fitted in" to whatever time was left).

The bigger studios of course had advantages in better cinematographers and better contract writers, although these qualities weren't of major importance to the audiences for which the smaller Westerns were intended. The one big drawback of all early "B" Westerns was the lack of a musical score. Agitato themes were an absolute essential to the genre, often literally making the difference between a gripping Western and a dull one. And while there were some excellent Westerns made without musical scores, especially if they had good scripts and production values, there wasn't one of them that wouldn't have been *better* for the addition of music. At the beginning of the sound period, however, musical scores generally were suspect and regarded as artificial in the new "realistic" medium. Not surprisingly, the best original scores were created for films which were not meant to be regarded in a realistic light—films as widely apart as *King Kong* and *Trouble in Paradise*. By 1932, scores came to be accepted again as an essential aspect of the movie—and they were an additional and considerable expense. The economy-minded independents were reluctant at that time to pay for what seemed a luxury, and this, probably more than any other single factor (except for the stature of the individual star) is what gave "class" to the major studios' small Westerns and denied it to the independents.

Prior to this distinction, both brands of Westerns shared the same physical "look" and the same shortcomings. Action sequences in the early talkies were often shot silent, and even filmed at the old silent speed. In the silent days, of course, if a director or cameraman made a mistake in deliberately shooting a scene too fast for its action effect, it could always be straightened out when the film was finally shown in a theater, merely by altering the speed of projection. This was not always done, but at least the music cue sheets for the theater's orchestra or pianist would invariably give the *correct* projection speed, which frequently varied throughout any given film. But in the sound film, when the action footage, no matter what its speed, was married to the sound track, it had to stay at a standard projection speed, and frequently had a frenzied look that was so unrealistic as to be absurd. This, of course, was a problem that was licked fairly quickly, although the device of speeding-up was often resorted to with a "hero" who couldn't ride or fight too convincingly and who, if nothing else, could be made to appear more energetic with an undercranked camera. While the major studios had their own standing sets and Western streets on the lot, and usually a ranch or township location up in the hills, the independents, generally with no studio facilities of their own, had to rent their ranch and street locales or go to locations where relics of the real thing still existed. (Even today, the main street in Santa Fe, New Mexico, or Jackson, California, could do service as Western locales if all the automobiles, TV antennas, and other signs of modernity could be obliterated. The streets themselves are remarkably unchanged, though in certain towns, like Virginia City, Nevada, or Sonora, California, they have been so preserved as tourist bait that they now *look* like studio sets!) These small, often shabby concentrations of wooden shacks and stores, huddled together on opposite sides of narrow streets, sometimes looked more convincing than the studio reconstructions and injected a certain amount of unsolicited realism.

In one other sense, too, the independents had a striking if unsought advantage over the majors. Anxious to turn out Westerns that *looked* expensive but were still cheap to make, the major companies frequently built whole series around the plots and stock footage lifted initially from silents, and in the forties and fifties, footage from the thirties. Big films (*Geronimo,* for example, of which more later) as well as small followed this practice right through the fifties, and while the results were sometimes exciting and often amusing or fascinating, they were rarely smooth or convincing. The independents, on the other hand, had little such footage to fall back on. They could buy basic establishing scenes from the stock-shot libraries—cattle drives or stampedes, stage or bank holdups, covered wagon trains—but these were used mainly as montages or to set the scene at the opening of the film. Without complete series around which to build new ones, the independents had to concentrate on story as much as action, and because of

this many of their unassuming little Westerns had plot lines superior to the more orthodox actioners offered by the majors. An early World Wide production, *Riders of the Desert,* a Bob Steele vehicle, boasted not only superior photography of unusual locations and good action sequences, but also a really strong plot line as well. *Law of the .45's,* one of the "Big Boy" Williams Westerns made for Beacon Pictures, was based on one of William Colt MacDonald's *Three Mesquiteers* novels and stressed mystery more than action, with appropriate atmospheric lighting to back it up. In *Arizona Badman,* Edmund Cobb's sympathetic good badman characterization in the old Hart tradition was actually given far more prominence than the standard heroics of nominal star Reb Russell. And *Toll of the Desert* came to a climax worthy of Zane Grey, wherein the apparently orphaned hero (played by Fred Kohler, Jr.) grows to manhood and a sheriff's post, and unknowingly executes his own outlaw father on the gallows!

Few independent series of the thirties matched the relative but consistent quality of a Kermit Maynard series produced by Maurice Conn for Ambassador Films. Half of them were regulation Westerns (*Valley of Terror, Whistling Bullets, Wild Horse Roundup*) and the other half were Canadian Mountie adventures, using many pleasing snowscape exteriors (*The Wildcat Trooper, Wilderness Mail, Red Badge of Courage*). A popular and long-running series, they were simple but adequate in their plots, but offered a certain polish in their utilization of musical scores, camera trucks for running inserts, elaborate opticals and trick dissolves, and other technical niceties usually denied the cheaper "B." A number of interesting leading ladies—Andrea Leeds and Ann Sheridan among them—used them as handy lower rungs on the ladder to success while some of the better ones were directed by John English, prior to his emergence as a major Western and serial director at Republic. They were generously supplied with action, but their biggest asset was star Kermit Maynard, who possessed a breezy, naturalistic acting style not unlike George O'Brien's, and was an accomplished stuntman and rider. Some of his leaps into the saddle were most spectacular, even if not always necessary. Lean and always in top physical condition, even at the end of his career when he was playing bit roles, he was actually a far better actor than brother Ken, but never had the opportunity to match his box office popularity.

But the "quality" independents grew less as the thirties progressed. Such films were sold to exhibitors in groups of six or eight per year and brought in a fairly fixed income regardless of quality, so there was little incentive to make a better product. The Westerns that aimed at a modicum of quality via either strong stories or

Buck Jones

Ken Maynard

an above-average star (Conway Tearle, a slipped matinee idol from the twenties, starred in one such series that included *Desert Guns, Judgment Book, Señor Jim*) spent their money in that direction and had little left over for location work or action. Usually such series were not markedly popular with audiences and disappeared after a single season, although a Harry Carey series, short on action but strong on plot and good locations *(Without Honor, Cavalier of the West)*, did prove saleable and stayed around for more than the customary one year. Tim McCoy's popularity enabled another series from Puritan to survive, although the best of them *(The Man From Guntown, Border Caballero)* were only routine, and most of them *(The Lion's Den, The Traitor, Aces and Eights, The Ghost Patrol)* so pedestrian and lacking in even rudimentary action that they bored their small-fry audiences to tears.

If action was the desired quality, usually the case in the cheapies from Resolute, Majestic, Freuler, and other small companies, then a maximum of poorly staged fights and chases, a constant use of stock footage and obvious miniatures (an oft-used shot of a burning ranch house must have been a model of no more than six inches in height, judging from the matchstick size and intensity of the flames), and a total lack of finesse were the overall

George O'Brien (with Maureen O'Sullivan in *Robbers' Roost*, 1933)

Further offbeat O'Brien roles: as an Indian in *The Golden West* (1932).

. . . and as a misleadingly dapper peace officer in *Frontier Marshal* (1934)

William Boyd as Hopalong Cassidy astride Topper

modus operandi. Usually these were salvaged at least for one season by the presence of an able star—Rex Bell (teamed with Ruth Mix and Buzz Barton) in the Resolute series, Tom Tyler at Freuler, and usually one good film, invariably the first, came out of each series. *Gun Fire* from Resolute and *When a Man Rides Alone* from Freuler weren't at all bad. But others in the series made them very much the exceptions.

These really cheap independent Westerns were usually shot in five days, though three wasn't unheard of, for a total negative cost of about $10,000, and every dollar that wasn't spent showed up on the screen. Retakes were rarely permitted, and if an actor fluffed a line or missed the stirrup when he raced to his horse, then the flaws were left in. Often one could pick up the background voice of the director giving instructions, and *Lightning Bill,* a quickie with Buffalo Bill, Jr., offered several illustrations of this kind of slapdash production. The camera was frequently so carelessly positioned as to show the ill-concealed mattresses on to which riders made their falls from the saddle, and in one gunfight sequence, a production assistant, thinking that the scene has been completed ambles out from behind a tree. Seeing that the cameras are still grinding, he makes for cover again—and then, some seconds later, makes a further foray into the open, only to retreat a second time.

The most popular of the Three Mesquiteers trio: Max Terhune, Robert Livingston, and Ray Corrigan, posing on location for *Heart of the Rockies* (1937)

Gene Autry and Champion

A later Three Mesquiteers reshuffling: John Wayne takes over from Livingston, while Terhune and Corrigan remain; with them in this posed portrait from *Overland Stage Raiders* (1938) is Louise Brooks, making her last film appearance

A popular starring trio: Bob Baker, Johnny Mack Brown, and Fuzzy Knight

157

Since he is dressed not too conspicuously in modern clothes, it was probably reasoned that he could pass as a nervous participant in the battle. However, the crowning indignity of this particular film was that even its main title was misspelled! (Not that *some* mistakes like this don't appear in major productions, but the most common one is for modern autos to be revealed on a highway at the very back of the frame—usually on key location shots that can't be dropped or duplicated. Such flaws are only revealed when rushes are screened back at the studio, and sometimes not even then. The hidden auto was a particular menace in the fifties in films designed for wide-screen release, with little attention paid to information at the very top and bottom of the frame. Then when the film went into regular or nontheatrical release with the old aspect ratio, this previously hidden anachronism became all too apparent.)

The quality of the independent Westerns picked up considerably, however, with the formation of two "in between" companies, Monogram and Republic. Both aimed at "bread and butter" product, but they had their own studios, contract writers, producers, and directors and used good veteran stars as well as developing new ones. Republic was at its peak in the late thirties and early forties, and turned the production of Westerns into a slick, streamlined art. Monogram, while never reaching Republic standards, especially technically, nevertheless turned out many excellent Westerns, particularly at the beginning of new series. Monogram did have one rather spectacular flaw: it would assign a top producer (often Scott R. Dunlap, veteran director of some of Fox's silent Buck Jones films) to guide the first couple of entries in a new series and allot a generous budget. Then, with the series under way and both exhibitors and audiences hooked, the specific producer would be withdrawn and the budget sliced, making it difficult for the series' momentum to be maintained, and relying very largely on the popularity of its star to keep it going. At their peak, both Monogram and Republic performed well, producing some of the best Westerns on the market, at all times well above the quickie level, and able to compete favorably with the concurrent product from the major companies.

As the thirties began, the best "B" Westerns, rather surprisingly, were those being made by the still young company, Columbia. It had two of the best Western stars of all, Buck Jones and Tim McCoy, making simultaneous series and, an unexpected bonus when the films were released to television many years later, a young John Wayne playing key supporting roles in several of them.

Both Jones and McCoy took their Westerns seriously and gave them such care and variance in plotting that none of them had an assembly-line look. Both stars

Buster Crabbe, Tom Keene, and Monte Blue in *Desert Gold* (1936)

Yakima Canutt, silent Western star, now put to far better use as a villain, character actor, stuntman, and double

alternated straightforward action Westerns with those in which the story played the dominant role. *The Riding Tornado* was, unusually for McCoy, all action stuff that lived up to its title, while conversely his *The End of the Trail* was a sort of pocket *Broken Arrow* nearly two

Kermit Maynard (left) and Gordon (Bill) Elliott in a scene from the 1938 serial, *Wild Bill Hickok*

Man of the Forest (Paramount, 1933): Randolph Scott, Noah Beery, Sr., and Harry Carey

Charles Starrett

Robbers' Roost (Fox, 1933), with George O'Brien

decades in advance of it, a slower, obviously sincere, and sometimes genuinely poetic study of the white man's betrayal of the Indian. There was no villain in the normal sense, other than government policy, and a surprising element of tragedy. McCoy's young son is killed by the cavalry, and in the original version, McCoy himself died,

Honor of the Range (Universal, 1933): Ken Maynard

Shooting a riding close-up from a camera car

The onscreen image: William Boyd in *Renegade Trail* (Paramount, 1939)

though Columbia hastily shot an alternate happy ending and tacked it on just before the film went into release.

Films like *The End of the Trail* were remarkable achievements, given the costs and intended market of the "B" movie, and it is sad that contemporary audiences don't understand those limits and cannot appreciate the love and dedication that was often poured into a five-reel Western. The very brevity demanded a kind of shorthand dialogue, which conveyed information instantly, and typecasting was necessary so that audiences could identify a character's motivations immediately and without wasted time. The major drawback of the "B" was that it *had* to sacrifice subtlety both in writing and acting in order to tell its story at all. As the record shows, the major companies had no interest in socially critical studies of the Indian at that time. Apart from Warners' startling and still little-known programmer, *Massacre* (1934), films making any mildly social protest statements about the Indian were usually camouflaged under the romantic melodrama of the likes of *Ramona* and *Laughing Boy*. If McCoy had not made *The End of the Trail* in 1932, and incidentally punctuated it with some unusually powerful speeches about the injustices heaped on the Indian, that story would not have been told until 1950 and *Broken Arrow*.

Yet at a 1976 conference on the Western film in Sun Valley, Idaho, a largely academic audience seeing both in the same day gave *Broken Arrow* the respect it deserved, but reacted with laughter to the more simplistic approach of *The End of the Trail*, unable to separate the two in terms of period, budget, and other significant factors. Clearly Tim McCoy, in attendance, was both hurt and bewildered by the reaction. To his credit, Clint Eastwood, also in attendance, was impressed by the film, and his brief and respectful association with McCoy during that nearly week-long event was reflected in his later *Broncho Billy*, somewhat of an homage to McCoy even though its quite endearing plot was pure fiction. Many of the other McCoys were essentially detective stories, the Western settings almost incidental, and because he still looked so good in any kind of uniform, Columbia put him into other actioners where he played a policeman or a fireman. They made for an interesting change of pace, but as with Buck Jones, who also did non-Westerns, McCoy was too much *of* the West to regard these forays as anything but momentary diversions.

Both the McCoy and the Jones Westerns at Columbia benefited from solid production values, good cinematographers like Ted McCord and Ted Tetzlaff, both of whom went on to distinguished "A" careers, and top-flight directors. Some of the films, such as Jones's *White Eagle*, directed by Lambert Hillyer, turned out so well that in later years they would certainly have been isolated from their series format and sold as specials. After a few seasons, however—and faced with the competition of top new Western stars like Gene Autry and William Boyd—the inevitable lessening of enthusiasm and budget cutting began to set in, and both series lost some of their luster. Jones actually left Columbia to go to Universal, where the process was repeated, and then returned to Columbia later in a "split" series that offered both conventional Westerns (*Overland Express, Law of the Texan*) and offbeat "modern" ones (as a lettuce farmer in *Headin' East*, and an arrogant Western star's double in *Hollywood Roundup*). However, at their best, McCoy and Jones both made some of the industry's best small Westerns at Columbia, films that could be enjoyed by adults as much as by youngsters. Indeed, some of them were obviously aimed primarily at an adult audience. Jones's *The Avenger*, in which he played Mexican bandit Joaquin Murietta, was a grim little film played for tension rather than action and had superb lighting and camera work from Charles Stumar, a cinematographer not normally associated with smaller Westerns. It was later remade in the forties, with Bill Elliott assuming the Murietta role.

Taking over as Columbia's new Western star was Charles Starrett. He was an ex-footballer, like Johnny Mack Brown and Reb Russell, and handsome and athletic. But his white Stetson and impeccable dress immediately proclaimed him as one of the new breed of streamlined stars, a far cry from the veterans he was replacing. Although he was not a singer himself, his films reflected the public's new interest in musical Westerns, usually by featuring a singing group such as the Sons of the Pioneers. (Finding something for Starrett to do while the group sang became a minor problem; after a period of having him rock rhythmically as he watched, Columbia eventually resorted to cutaways of him tending to his horse or shaving!) The initial Starretts were good, if a tad slow, and they soon got better, reaching their peak in the late thirties. Thereafter they rapidly became formularized, the same casts in picture after picture—Iris Meredith as leading lady, Edward Le Saint as her father (usually killed off by excessively villainous Dick Curtis), Jack Rockwell as the sheriff, and the same basic stories and situations recycled endlessly, a plethora of action, but a dearth of originality. However, thanks to Starrett's assured popularity, they retained a certain level of quality, declining only in the final years of the "B" Western in the early fifties. Starrett was unique in staying with Columbia as its number one Western star for almost two decades, making Westerns for no other studio. "Twenty years with the same brand" was the way he listed himself in trade paper ads of the later years.

Roll, Wagons, Roll (Monogram, 1940): Tex Ritter and Kenneth Duncan

A youthful Roy Rogers riding Trigger; biggest new Western star of the late thirties

Ghost City (Monogram, 1932): Bill Cody in white stetson, an interesting holdover from the silents

The Fugitive (Monogram, 1933): Rex Bell (left) and Bob Kortman

Tim McCoy

End of the Trail (Columbia, 1932): Tim McCoy, in his finest "B" Western, with Wade Boteler and Luana Walters

McCoy in one of his favorite poses: the Mexican bandit, here with Lane Chandler and John Merton at extreme left, in *Two-Gun Justice* (Monogram, 1938)

William Boyd in uncharacteristic garb in *Bar 20 Rides Again* (Paramount, 1935), the film in which George Hayes joined the series. Paul Fix is at right

Mulford's characters were well re-created in the early Hopalong Cassidy films; here, in *Bar 20 Rides Again*, Howard Lang plays Buck Peters, Frank McGlynn, Jr., is Red Connors, and James Ellison is particularly effective as Johnny Nelson

Russell Hayden (right) takes over from Ellison, playing Lucky Jenkins; in this scene from *Hopalong Rides Again* (1937), Ernie Adams is playing the corpse

Hayden (white shirt), Boyd, and George Hayes in one of the best of the series, *Texas Trail* (1937)

The studio also produced a Ken Maynard series, and used two straight if undistinguished actors, Jack Luden and Robert Allen, in short-lived series of the mid- to late thirties.

Far more successful was Gordon (later Bill) Elliott, a minor star in movies in the twenties, suddenly relegated to bit parts in the early thirties, slowly working his way up to near stardom again. He then was introduced by Columbia as a new Western star in the late thirties via the serial *The Great Adventures of Wild Bill Hickok.* For an actor who had been essentially a modern drawing-room type, he took to the West with surprising assurance. He played in a sober, restrained fashion, clearly modeling his characterization after William S. Hart. At one time he was under consideration to play Hart in a movie biography, but Elliott wasn't big enough, and Hart too forgotten, for the project ever to materialize. The initial Columbia Elliotts, especially *Frontiers of '49* and *In Early Arizona,* another unofficial adaptation of the Wyatt Earp story, were exceptionally good. (Inciden tally, the Earp adaptations were always "unofficial" because Fox owned the rights to Stuart Lake's biography of Earp. The studio filmed it a number of times, sometimes with a change of name for Earp, but the two best versions were *Frontier Marshal* (1939), directed by Allan Dwan with Randolph Scott as Earp, and of course John Ford's later *My Darling Clementine.* While the incidents involved were fairly common to all Westerns, linking those incidents to Earp's name could invariably produce charges of plagiarism from the copyrighted books, hence Universal's and Columbia's care in avoid-

Heart of the Rockies (Republic, 1937): The Three Mesquiteers protect children and wildlife but never let those worthy aims stand in the way of outstanding action content

163

ing his actual name, and those of Doc Holliday and the Clantons, in their thinly disguised versions.)

Elliott also made three serials for Columbia, superior in production values, but almost totally devoid of story quality, degenerating into a repetitious series of unmotivated fights and chases within the first couple of episodes of their fifteen-chapter length. After a promising start, the Elliott features declined in quality too, not even matching the more formularized but at least vigorous Charles Starrett series. However, Elliott was to regain lost ground in good later series at Republic and Monogram.

Fox, having lost Buck Jones and Tom Mix at the end of the silents, turned to George O'Brien as its Western star in the early thirties. No longer as big as he had been in the twenties (though through no fault of his own; with better handling, and perhaps more loyalty from John Ford, there is no reason why he couldn't have remained a prestige star), he had a large following in the action market that made his Western series at Fox probably the best around. Though short in running time, they were not "B's" in the sense that the Jones and McCoy films were at Columbia, and many opened at the top of the bill—or as solo attraction at Fox's New York showcase, the Roxy. With his excellent sense of humor and deftness in "Taming of the Shrew" situations, O'Brien starred in a unique series of Westerns, some based on novels by Zane Grey, Max Brand, and others, many of them originals designed to exploit his personality. Production values were often outstanding, and frequently awe-inspiring in their dramatic use of the Grand Canyon and other locations. They also served as useful training grounds for new players that Fox was grooming: Myrna Loy, Maureen O'Sullivan, Claire Trevor, George Brent, Humphrey Bogart.

Among the better ones were *Riders of the Purple Sage* and its sequel, *The Rainbow Trail, The Lone Star Ranger* and its related (but not really a sequel) *Last of the Duanes,* and a fifth Zane Grey adaptation, *Robbers' Roost.* Best of all was *Mystery Ranch* (1932), which partially overlapped into the currently popular horror film cycle, being based on a novel, *The Killer,* and bearing at least a casual resemblance to the same year's classic, *The Most Dangerous Game.* The moody, evocative camera work by Joseph August and George Schneidermann, both Ford veterans, contained echoes of the stylized Germanic visuals introduced to Fox by Murnau in 1927. Packed with action, *Mystery Ranch* was also quite brutal and even grisly at times; the only surefire O'Brien element missing was humor, and there was just no time or room for it. Like most of the O'Briens of this early period, it held back its most spectacular scenery for the climax, in which big-scale action sequences were

played out against and atop mountain crags, with background music introduced suddenly and effectively as the varied factions squared off for the climactic battles. These were strong, gutsy films—those based on Grey novels often having a pronounced element of sex—and were certainly not intended just for the kiddie market.

There are signs that Fox, pleased with the reception of these films, may have thought about upgrading them to "A" pictures. The last of the 1932 productions, *The Golden West,* was an unusually elaborate one, for billing purposes "based" on a Zane Grey story, though none such existed, and it was really a mosaic of Grey themes with enough plot for *three* movies. The opening section dealt with a family feud in the South; unjustly accused of murder, the hero joins a wagon train West, leaving behind his sweetheart, and rather surprisingly finding a new love on the trail, whom he marries and by whom he has a son. This middle portion of the film has some unusual ingredients, including a subordinate character (Bert Hanlon) used to establish the importance of the itinerant Jewish peddler in opening up avenues of trade in the young West, and a truly astonishing sequence of the girl's rescue from a maddened buffalo stampede. Some of this footage (and the locations) seem to be outtakes from *The Big Trail,* but the basic situation of the girl (Marion Burns—or her double), afoot amid a sea of buffalo, and being swept up on to O'Brien's horse, is a spellbinder. There are a number of ways it *could* have been shot and certain safety measures that *might* have been applied, but it's still a tricky and literally breathtaking sequence.

Abruptly, as this middle section is proceeding nicely, an Indian raid unexpectedly kills off the characters we thought were hero and heroine, and their young son is abducted. After a time lapse, he grows up to be a husky, loincloth-garbed George O'Brien, leading raids against the encroaching railroad which, in typical Grey/coincidence fashion, is bossed by his father's old enemy from the South—whose daughter (Janet Chandler) is abducted by O'Brien for (another Grey reliable) a forced marriage. The very complicated plot comes to its close with a reel or so of spectacular Indian fighting footage (from *The Iron Horse*) and, of course, the revelation of O'Brien's true identity. Stills from the film of scenes that no longer appear suggest that it was quite heavily edited down to a standard programmer length. Possibly its somewhat incoherent plot and the too obvious use of stock footage in such a large dose automatically removed it from the upper-bracket category, although it was certainly a bonus offering as a programmer. In any event, it failed to elevate the series to a higher status, and the 1933 entries, while still good, were less imposing than those of 1932.

Undoubtedly very expensive to produce, they were

abandoned after a few years because of the ever-expanding number of competing Westerns on the market. O'Brien was shifted into an independent series of lower quality, produced by Sol Lesser and merely released through Fox. On the whole, these were much slower and generally disappointing, though they had their own particular charm and O'Brien showed no sign of lessening his enthusiasm because of their downgrading. *O'Malley of the Mounted* was a pleasing remake of the William S. Hart silent, and *The Cowboy Millionaire* offered the novelty and luxury of George O'Brien on location in London. At least one of this series, *When a Man's a Man* (1935), based on the Harold Bell Wright novel, which had also been filmed as a silent, turned out to be a genuine sleeper. Intelligently played, with a particularly strong, honest, and likeable performance from Dorothy Wilson as the heroine, and with a logical, even literate script, it built up to an extremely exciting climax and had the wit to let its rather reasonable villain (Harry Woods) get away scot-free, except for a minor trouncing. Among its greatest assets was the beautifully lit camera work of one of the best and most underrated of all cinematographers, Frank Good. The closing scenes, shot in silhouette on a hillside at twilight, remind one of, but anticipate, the Ford of *Tobacco Road* and *She Wore a Yellow Ribbon*. *When a Man's a Man* is one of the best "little" Westerns ever made.

Right through the thirties Paramount continued to make (and remake) its highly popular Zane Grey series. At the beginning of the sound period, they were still almost "specials"—*Fighting Caravans* with Gary Cooper ran for nine reels. The early ones, though, too often succumbed to the notion of sound films being an alternate to theater, and Paramount's first sound version of *Light of Western Stars* was told entirely via dialogue, even its climactic fight between hero and villain only being *heard* from outside a cabin. Through the early thirties, they decreased in length—many running barely an hour—while increasing in quality, but by the end of the decade, there was a tendency for them to creep up to seven and eight reels again. Coincidentally, it was another *Light of the Western Stars* that went overboard on dialogue and in remaining faithful to Grey's original novel, though the presence of Alan Ladd in a supporting role made it a useful item for later reissue. Others, like *Man of the Forest* and *The Thundering Herd*, were built around footage from the silent versions, a deception made more feasible by the rehiring of many of the same players to repeat their original roles. Thus in the climax of *Man of the Forest* there are cut-in close-ups of Tom Kennedy reacting to, and expressing fright at, a fight he had with a mountain lion in the silent version. Randolph Scott's slim build and pencil mustache made it easy for him, especially when similarly garbed, to replace Jack

Holt from the silent originals, though Holt's ramrod-straight riding style did give the game away occasionally.

On the whole, it was an extremely good series, covering most of the Grey properties except those either never filmed or owned by Fox, making excellent use of such contract directors as Henry Hathaway and players like Randolph Scott, Buster Crabbe, Harry Carey, Tom Keene, Monte Blue, Noah Beery (a marvelous, fruity villain in many of them), and Russell Hayden. The series also provided initial or early opportunities for Shirley Temple, John Wayne, Gail Patrick, little Billy Lee, Ann Sheridan, and, rather regrettably, for his obtrusive comedy material got in the way of plot and action far too often, Robert Cummings.

Among a uniformly good series, four stood out. *To the Last Man* was almost a model of its kind, an exceptionally strong story of feuding families in the post–Civil War era, with a cast worthy of an "A" feature, excellent direction by Henry Hathaway, and an unusual climactic fight between the villain (Jack LaRue) and the *heroine* (Esther Ralston, in an especially appealing performance). *The Mysterious Rider*, several times filmed, was never done better than in the late thirties, when Harry Sherman took over production of the series while continuing to handle the Hopalong Cassidy Westerns. *The Mysterious Rider* was another eight-reeler, long for a "B" but good enough in story and production to warrant "A" time. Reasonably close to the Grey original, it offered Douglass Dumbrille, always such a good heavy, a rare good guy role. *Sunset Pass*, an early Hathaway Western, was not only one of the best but also one of the most surprising in presenting Randolph Scott and Harry Carey as *heavies*. This entry, and several others from Paramount in the early to mid-thirties—including *Nevada* and *Wanderer of the Wasteland*, both first-rate—unfortunately have never been reissued or made available to television or the video market, because the rights to those stories are now held by RKO Radio, which filmed its own remakes in the forties.

Perhaps best of all was *Thunder Trail* (1937), based on Grey's *Arizona Ames*, and the only time this story was filmed. A solid story of brothers separated as children following a bandit raid and brought up on opposite sides of the law to confront one another some fifteen years later, it ran a mere fifty-six minutes, yet despite almost constant action, it found time for good writing, subtle characterizations, a modicum of romance and comedy, some superb locations, an excellently staged runaway ore wagon sequence, and a well-sustained action climax. Since there was no earlier version to fall back on, there was no stock footage, and it was given additional freshness and depth by players not then associated with Westerns: Gilbert Roland, Charles Bickford, J. Carrol Naish, Marsha Hunt, and James Craig, plus some old

Overland Stage Raiders (Republic, 1938): One of the early highlights from this Mesquiteers entry is this fight scene with John Wayne in the cab of a locomotive

Ray Corrigan in a hefty fight scene from the Mesquiteers' *Night Riders* (1939)

Red River Valley (Republic, 1936): One of the earlier and better Autrys, featuring this fight scene with George Chesebro

reliables that were, including Monte Blue. In addition, it was photographed by the great Karl Struss and the extra care showed in every foot of film.

Despite some mistakes—too much talk in the 1930 period, a commendable but often misapplied attempt at novelty via the casting of players like Stuart Erwin in *leads,* and certainly too much unfunny comedy with Robert Cummings in the several entries in which he appeared—Paramount's Zane Grey series maintained a remarkably high standard over its more than twenty years of continued production. Those years obviously produced the occasional disappointment or misfire, but never a systematic and deliberate lessening of quality as usually happens with long-running series, Westerns or otherwise.

In 1935, Paramount introduced a new series, based on Clarence E. Mulford's "Hopalong Cassidy" books. Uncertain at first that the character would prove popular enough to justify more than one or two follow-ups, Paramount certainly had no idea that it would develop into one of the most successful Western series ever, sustaining itself (though latterly not through Paramount) until the end of the forties, and then enjoying a new lease of life on television. A major key to its success was the personality of its star, William Boyd, a former DeMille leading man from the silent period who could command the following of adults as well as youngsters. While there was some concession to Mulford's creation in the matter of age—initially, at least, the screen Hopalong would acknowledge his age and defer to his young sidekick in matters of romance or strenuous action—the character in Boyd's hands immediately became something of a cavalier and certainly a gentleman, a far cry from the scruffy old-timer that held sway in Mulford's books. The role was at one time considered for James Gleason, who would indeed have fitted Mulford's description, but presumably the thought of the series catching on prevented such casting. Gleason might have been fine for one or two isolated entries, but presumably would have been too unorthodox a piece of casting to expect to sustain a whole series.

The early cavalier quality of the Cassidy character was gradually extended and polished to a point where it eventually went overboard in establishing him as a role model of excessive nobility, placing him mawkishly on a pedestal for small boys, hard-pressed widows, and ill-treated dogs. Only the controlled underplaying of Boyd prevented the self-sacrificial leanings of the Cassidy character, especially in films like *Borderland* and *Renegade Trail,* from seeming ludicrous. Nevertheless, the Boyd characterization proved so popular that when the Mulford novels were later reissued, they were partially rewritten to conform to the "new" Cassidy image. Author Mulford was initially reasonably satisfied with the way his novels were translated to the screen—apart from the change in Cassidy himself; the early ones tried to stick to his story lines and characters and to the depiction of Western and ranch life that he prided himself on having researched so carefully. Thereafter he was increasingly critical, even angry, about the way that producer Harry Sherman was streamlining and standardizing his work.

The first Cassidy Westerns were some of the series' best. They lacked polish and were weak on action, but had good scripts and casts and created a realistic view of the boisterous horseplay and humdrum activity of much of ranch life. Action was played down at first, not least because Boyd, who had made only a couple of minor "A" Westerns before, was not yet an accomplished action performer, and had to be "doubled" in riding and fight scenes. The first dozen films, however, made up for their somewhat slow pacing by climaxes of remarkable vigor and scope. The buildup would be methodical, audience anticipation being created early on, and then these large-scale action climaxes—usually an assembly of one or more posses, a massed ride to the rescue, and a climactic gunfight—would hit the screen accompanied by the equally sudden introduction of background music (usually "Dance of the Furies" by Gluck) which had been withheld during earlier, smaller scale action incidents. The format was an interesting one, copied by many other Western producers, but it was also a highly restrictive one. Wisely it was abandoned just as it was becoming a cliché.

Because of their popularity, the Cassidy Westerns frequently extended their lengths, permitting them to play better houses and in many cases top of the bill, and it was not uncommon for them to run to eighty minutes. However, their scripts became somewhat simplistic, and the action content, even after Boyd had learned to ride well, remained mild, so that in most cases the added footage was something of a liability. The good Cassidy Westerns of this middle period, films like *Bar 20 Justice* and *Texas Trail* remained superior products, and in Lesley Selander the series had an efficient and innovative director to offset the heavy-handed approach of earlier directors like Howard Bretherton. Too many of the Cassidys were overly bland, however, going out of their way to avoid rough, realistic, or spectacular excitement. Other liabilities included a string of weak leading ladies (some of them tryouts for careers that understandably never materialized, others transients presumably being cast only to keep promises made for favors rendered) and a tendency to uninteresting villains. However, the initial Boyd-James Ellison-George Hayes combination, and then the Boyd-Russell Hayden-George

Hayes trio were both winning and appealing teams, and the entire series benefited from first-rate photography (usually Russell Harlan) and outstandingly beautiful locations. Even a dull Cassidy like *Cassidy of Bar 20* was consistently good to look at. In the forties however, the overall standard of the Cassidys was to improve considerably, the scripts were strengthened and the action content upgraded. Later Cassidys like *Wide Open Town, Doomed Caravan, Hoppy Serves a Writ,* and *Texas Masquerade* were first rate in every department, even the occasional considerably added length (as in *Wide Open Town*) being justified by a more in-depth script.

Warner Bros. produced only two Western series in the thirties. First there was the John Wayne series, of which *The Telegraph Trail* and especially *Haunted Gold* were probably the best. It was a curious and uneven group, some being built almost entirely around the same studio's silent Ken Maynard series, using the same plots and much of the footage, while others like *The Man From Monterey* were essentially "new," a little more polished, but singularly lacking in action. A later series with Dick Foran, billed as "The Singing Cowboy," was considerably better. Although, like the Waynes, they were at least partially constructed from Ken Maynard stock, they were slicker and more polished and generally produced on a bigger scale. If anything, they were *over*-produced, Warners trying to cram into an hour too much plot, too much production value, and too much background music; it was sometimes difficult to relax with them just because they moved too fast, and too noisily. Foran had an athletic build and sang well—no casual crooner, but a rich baritone—but in an effort to really sell him to the small fry, he tended to indulge in too much small boy sentiment and the dialogue was often artificial, dime novel stuff. But the method worked: the films *were* popular with children, and their solid production values enable them to stand up well today, although the first, *Moonlight on the Prairie,* was to remain the best. Warners used the series to try out new players—Wayne Morris and Jane Bryan among them—while Gordon (Bill) Elliott played both villain and secondary hero roles. Foran's popularity caused him to be promoted to dramatic features, and then Warners gave up series Westerns entirely, except for a group of two-reelers in the forties, no longer built around Ken Maynard stock, but rather more recognizably turned into pocket versions of much bigger films like *Gold Is Where You Find It* and *The Oklahoma Kid.* During the '40s, Warners also greatly expanded its schedule of "A" and programmer-level Westerns.

Universal was the one major company that maintained a full schedule of "B" Westerns without even a pause for stocktaking when the talkies arrived. The initial Hoot

Gibsons were discussed earlier. In Tom Mix and Ken Maynard (Maynard not running concurrently with Mix, but preceding and then replacing him), the studio had two top names for its Western series, and afforded them uncommonly good budgets. The Mix series, though off to a weak start (*Destry Rides Again* had to soft-pedal its action content because Mix was recuperating from an operation), tried hard to duplicate the successful formula of his Fox films, going in for both good rugged stories and the all-out circus approach. Typifying the latter was one of the best of the series, *My Pal the King*, a Ruritanian adventure in the *Prisoner of Zenda* manner. Mix played a Wild West show star touring Europe, who befriends little Mickey Rooney, not knowing at first that he is the Boy King of the small country. Fairbanksian in tone, even if some of the castle sets built on the Universal back lot had an ersatz look to them, it had much stunt action and built to a lively climax with Rooney trapped in a dungeon slowly filling with water. At one point early in the film, Mix came "out" of the movie to address the audience directly, asking them to put themselves in the mind of the Boy King seeing his first Wild West show. This simple (and in the thirties especially), totally unexpected device was rather charming and served to make the following exaggerated melodramatics far more acceptable.

Mix's speech was bad, unfortunately. He slurred his words, and read many of his lines with apparent disinterest. But he carried his years well, was still an expert rider, and managed his action with a modicum of doubles. The Mix series was a mixed bag, however, some of them being extremely niggardly on action, while *Hidden Gold* was at least 50 percent a city thriller, only opening and closing in the West. But, at least three entries in the series were up to Mix's old standards, the aforementioned *My Pal the King*, the rugged and gutsy *The Fourth Horseman*, and a surprising foray into extended length, the nearly eight reels long *Rider of Death Valley*, with grim closing ones somewhat reminiscent of the climax of von Stroheim's *Greed*. Mix's series for Universal was his final one, although in 1935, he made a kind of last stand with the Mascot serial *The Miracle Rider*, carefully constructed to keep him off the screen a great deal of the time and to minimize the action he had to do personally. Not a good serial by any standard, it was also hardly a felicitous farewell to the screen from its foremost cowboy star, although it certainly carried more prestige than the Poverty Row quickies and bit roles via which so many Western greats would eventually make their swan songs.

The Mix films at Universal were followed by a series with Ken Maynard, moving up the ladder again after some well above average independent Westerns, and by Buck Jones, coming over from Columbia. Both stars had their own units, and were largely responsible for the content and style of their films, selection of cast and directors, and so forth. Both in a sense were their own producers; Maynard wrote many of his own stories, and Jones even directed on one occasion.

Maynard, who throughout the sound era was to fluctuate between independents and bigger studios, was no longer in his prime and did not take well to dialogue. Either he had trouble remembering his scripts or he favored an improvisational approach. In any case, his films from the thirties on were full of ad libs, many of them clearly improvised as the cameras rolled and designed to replace dialogue he had forgotten or felt uncomfortable with. In his romantic scenes with the leading ladies, this sometimes created a pleasing, naturalistic quality. Although he still cut a fine figure in this second Universal series, there *were* signs of an approaching weight problem that would plague him throughout his career. (*Variety* was rather unkind in reviewing a fight scene with the always large Richard Alexander in a quickie of not too many years later as "five hundred pounds of excess weight thrashing around on the saloon floor.") Maynard also had a fondness for the bottle which would also be a big problem in later years, not only adding on the poundage but also making him somewhat unreliable as a star/producer, and thus accounting for the switches back and forth among Universal, Columbia, Grand National, Colony, and Monogram. From all accounts, Maynard was also surly, unpleasant, and difficult to deal with; if nothing else, his offscreen persona was so much at odds with his onscreen image that he must at least be given credit for being a good enough actor to be so convincingly amiable and easygoing in his movies.

While Maynard had a lesser budget to work with than Mix, his films at Universal were equally interesting and certainly gave audiences their money's worth. Had Maynard been a little more disciplined, they might have been outstanding in their particular field and enabled him to stay on top much longer than he did. If nothing else, there was nothing of the formula "B" about this series. *Strawberry Roan* (retitled *Flying Fury* in Great Britain and Europe, because of a well-loved rural novel, *Strawberry Roan*, which the British remade periodically) was a simple and straightforward little film built around the Western song. Others were far more bizarre and complicated, and in some cases unbelievable when normal logic was applied. *Smoking Guns* was a weird mélange of spooky "old house" thrills, crocodiles in South American jungles, and enough plot twists to rival von Stroheim's *Queen Kelly*. It started in the middle of a sequence framing Ken for murder, and among its wilder plot premises was that of having Texas Ranger Walter Miller

Public Cowboy No. 1 (Republic, 1937): Gene helps old-time sheriff William Farnum defeat modern city racketeer Arthur Loft

Public Cowboy No. 1 comes to the expected Autry climax: the baddies are rounded up and taken back to town, and on the way, Gene serenades leading lady Ann Rutherford

Colorado Sunset (Republic, 1939): Gene and Smiley Burnette (left) give Ethan Laidlaw a literal pasting as he tries to fix an election

Gene flanked by Barbara Pepper (left) and one of his pertest leading ladies, June Storey

When a Man's a Man (Fox, 1935), a classic among "B" Westerns: George O'Brien with Dorothy Wilson and Paul Kelly (left)

Wall Street Cowboy (Republic, 1939), a film with an undeserved bad reputation: Craig Reynolds and Fred Burns with Roy Rogers in one of his better and more action-filled earlier entries

Stunning use of Monument Valley as a location in the 1930 *Lone Star Ranger*

die in the jungle of fever (and the aftereffects of a leg amputation performed by Maynard!) after he has caught up with and arrested Maynard. Although there isn't the slightest resemblance between the two, Maynard is able to return to his (and Miller's) hometown, posing as Miller so effectively that even his fiancée doesn't spot the deception!

In *Honor of the Range,* Ken played a dual role as twin brothers, one strong and noble, the other weak, cowardly, and under the domination of the villains. Among its side delights were a sequence where Maynard poses (and performs) as a vaudeville song-and-dance man, and a remarkable climax in the villain's cave hideaway. The heavy, Fred Kohler, is musically minded and has had an organ installed in the cave. The heroine plays it furiously to drown out the sounds of battle when Ken arrives to save her from dishonor at Fred's hands. In contrast, *Wheels of Destiny* was planned as an elaborate special along the lines of *The Covered Wagon,* but something went wrong, probably with Maynard's fiscal organization, and it wound up relying far too heavily on stock footage. Nevertheless, Maynard's Universal series was enterprising and certainly unpredictable.

By contrast, the Buck Jones films for Universal were generally more orthodox, and on the whole more disciplined. The earlier ones, such as *Border Brigands, Rocky Rhodes, When a Man Sees Red,* and *The Crimson Trail* had good solid scripts and in the case of the last-named in particular, led to climaxes that were often marathons of well-staged action. In the middle of the series (*Sunset of Power),* there was a marked shift from action to plot as the inevitable budget cuts came in, and the last ones in the series (*Black Aces, Left Handed Law, Smoke Tree Range)* were noticeably smaller in the size and amount of action, in the number of extras circulating in the street and saloon scenes, and the increasing amount of scenes staged at night, cutting down on the need to see action clearly and to recognize obvious economies. Nevertheless, the Jones personality made up for many shortcomings, most films had at least one well done action highlight, and some of the plots were commendably out of the rut.

Lesley Selander directed many of them in the easygoing but satisfying style that would become his trademark, and *Empty Saddles,* a strange but somehow charming 1936 entry, started off with a ghost (that is never returned to or explained) and also offered Louise Brooks (in her penultimate film) as Buck's leading lady. They worked together well and seemed to respect one another's achievements and intelligence, and their scenes together had more depth than one usually finds in standard cowboy hero and helpless heroine relationships in small Westerns. While at Universal, Jones also made four serials. *The Roaring West* was all action and no plot, while *The Phantom Rider* reversed the priorities. *Gordon of Ghost City* struck a happier medium, and *The Red Rider* was best of all. Its dialogue was naturalistic, the action somewhat more inventive than the framework of the serial usually allowed, and several unusual plot twists included the villain, Walter Miller, leaving unwitting clues to his identity via discarded marijuana cigarettes. No critical issue was made of this vice, which in no way impaired Miller's ability to conceive inspired criminal schemes on the spur of the moment and put them into efficient execution. *The Red Rider* also had two ingredients notable for their almost total exclusion in the average Western serial, namely serious romance and some likable bantering comedy, from the villains as well as the heroes.

In the later thirties, in line with both a new economic structure for the company and changing audience tastes, Universal sought to alter its overall image and aim more at the family trade. Directors such as William Wyler, Frank Borzage, and John Ford disappeared, to be replaced by Henry Koster, Arthur Lubin, and George Marshall, with only James Whale remaining to link the old Universal with the new. In keeping with this kind of thinking, Karloff and Lugosi were replaced by Deanna Durbin; the rugged old Buck Jones Westerns were out (Buck went back to Columbia) and a new, streamlined series of musical Westerns with Bob Baker was in. The Bakers were pleasant, easygoing Westerns with mild villains (often a single old-timer like Jack Rockwell, or a led-astray youngster, Carlyle Moore, who would redeem himself in the last reel) and pretty, modern misses (Constance Moore, Marjorie Reynolds) filling the heroine spot and sometimes joining in the warbling. Often featuring unusual if not exactly strong stories, and filmed in beautiful locations, the best of them were the earlier ones, many directed by a former editor, Joseph H. Lewis.

The first of the series, *Courage of the West* (1937), was also Lewis's first film as a director. and showed unusual care and skill in camera placement and mobility, photographic composition, and editing tricks. A particularly involved circular tracking shot around a table didn't quite come off because it was the kind of shot that there was never really time for (needing both preparation and rehearsal before actual shooting) in the humble "B"; but it was the kind of extra finesse that would distinguish all of Lewis's films. Chase scenes would be staged on different levels of ground to provide a sense of added speed, and he would often change focus dramatically within a confrontation scene. (Once, in a non-Western "B," Lewis even anticipated Hitchcock's ten-minute takes in *Rope* by a whole decade.) Nor were these just

Wanderer of the Wasteland (Paramount, 1935), another superior Zane Grey Western: Gail Patrick, Erville Anderson, Philo McCullough, and Larry "Buster" Crabbe

First and biggest of the Jack Randalls: *Riders of the Dawn* (Monogram, 1937); Ed Coxen is the varmint on the right

Arizona Frontier (Monogram, 1940): Tex Ritter, Indian athlete Jim Thorpe, and Slim Andrews

171

tricks to garner attention for Lewis and earn him promotion to better product, though they served that purpose, too. In many cases, Lewis's colorful framings (shooting through wagon wheels, for example) took attention away from overly familiar situations, and one extremely elaborate circular tracking shot around a card table (in a later Baker Western) meant that a great deal of dialogue and plot exposition could be dealt with in one single shot, with no cuts or multiple camera setups, simply because the actors' faces were not shown and they could *read* their lengthy dialogue if necessary rather than having to memorize it.

Lewis's virtuosity garnered a great deal more drama and punch from these Baker Westerns than their easygoing scripts might have promised. The Bakers weren't lacking in action, but they did lack the rugged and even frenzied quality of the Jones films they were replacing. Baker himself, though never given too much opportunity to shine in the action department, was a handsome and likeable fellow and an expert rider who could occasionally be seen doing his own stunts. By the end of the thirties however, Universal was to revert to type, first costarring Baker with Johnny Mack Brown, and then starring Brown solo in the early forties. Lewis was to direct several of these, too, and his visual and editing punctuations when aligned with a much stronger action content was to result in some really top-notch "B" Westerns. In the thirties Universal also experimented with a handful of slightly bigger budget "B's" starring Noah Beery, Jr. Usually given an extra reel of running time, films like *Stormy* and *Forbidden Valley* were merchandised as "outdoor adventures" or "horse pictures" rather than orthodox Westerns. They were a natural for rural exhibitors, and their slightly extended running times plus the fact that they were individual films, not associated with a regular series, meant that they could play top of the bill in the right situation.

The only other major company with a regular schedule of "B" Westerns was RKO Radio, which had presented a Tom Keene series early in the thirties. Keene, who had begun his film career as George Duryea, and concluded it under the name of Richard Powers, was one of the more genuinely handsome Westerners, and a reasonably good if sometimes over-hearty actor. He handled his action well enough, although he was never wholly at ease with horses. His RKO films were carefully made, and sometimes quite offbeat in their content. *Scarlet River* was a Western built around the making of Westerns, and even managed to rope in Joel McCrea, Myrna Loy, and other RKO stars as guests. Others like *Freighters of Destiny* and *Come On Danger* were notable for their large scale action climaxes. Lon Chaney, Jr.,

appeared in some as the villain, and the omnipresent Yakima Canutt in a bit role was always a tip-off that lively stuntwork was on the way. For their period, they were superior to the Waynes at Warner Bros., but they did lack polish, and comedy interpolations from the likes of Edgar Kennedy tended to be obtrusive. While an interesting group, they date rather badly. Keene went on to be one of several stars featured in Paramount's Zane Greys, and he later did a pedestrian series for the Poverty Row Crescent company, and a much better but still undistinguished one for Monogram.

However, RKO's follow-up series with George O'Brien was a huge stride forward, not only for the studio, but also for O'Brien. He had followed his independent series for Sol Lesser, releasing through Fox, with another (not wholly Western) action series for George Hirliman, releasing through RKO. The biggest of these, a near special, *Daniel Boone*, was so well received that the studio put O'Brien into his own Western series starting with *Gun Law*. Rather surprisingly, for the first in a series, it did not try too hard to impress either audiences or exhibitors with its quality, probably (and rightly) reasoning that it would automatically look bigger and better than the Hirliman series it was replacing. Actually a remake of a silent Tom Tyler for FBO, it was stronger on plot than action, but as always in any O'Brien, when the action came it was beefy and believable. The film was also exceptionally well photographed, with atmospheric desert scenes at the opening, and an effective night ride near the climax, when O'Brien uses a relay of hidden horses to thwart the villains' plans and still get back to town sufficiently ahead of them to provide an alibi for himself. *Gun Law* got the series off to a solid start, and it would maintain an unusually high standard until its cessation in the early forties, when O'Brien left for wartime naval service.

All of the RKO O'Briens were obviously more expensive and carefully made than the average "B." They were never in the front rank of juvenile favorites, since the youngsters were less impressed by good stories, bantering comedy, and pleasing if lightly-handled romantic elements, preferring the uncomplicated and more direct action of a Ken Maynard. Conversely, it was these very qualities that enabled the O'Briens to appeal to adult audiences as well, and as a result they got far better bookings, often at the big circuit houses (in England, as well) than most "B's." *Racketeers of the Range* and *Lawless Valley* were probably the best of this very distinguished series. The former contained some amusing comedy with the headstrong heroine, and a lulu of a running battle conducted on a locomotive, as the rustlers try to steal an entire consignment of cattle bound for market, as the film's climax. The latter, apart from being

Border Café (RKO Radio, 1937): Harry Carey and John Beal

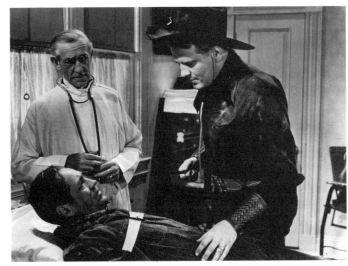

Empty Holsters (Warner Bros., 1937): George Chesebro, Earl Dwire (lying down), and Dick Foran

Wildcat Trooper (Ambassador, 1936): Kermit Maynard

Swifty (Diversion, 1935): Some obviously posed action with George Hayes (left foreground), Robert Kortman, Hoot Gibson, Wally Wales, and William Gould

Cheyenne Tornado (Kent, 1935): Reb Russell, ex-football player, had a brief tenure of Western stardom in the thirties. (At right, production manager Bartlett Carre also plays a character role)

Drums of Destiny (1937): One of Tom Keene's historical but actionless series for Crescent

much more serious and something of a murder mystery to boot, offered the unique spectacle of Fred Kohler, Sr. and Jr., as father and son villains, and more than worthy opponents for George in the fistic encounters. Although he always had a slight waistline problem, O'Brien was in superb physical condition in these films, and loved to prove it in scraps where his shirt was literally torn off his back. (There had been a priceless moment in one of the early Fox Zane Greys, *The Lone Star Ranger,* in which a shirtless O'Brien stops a runaway stagecoach. As the heroine, Sue Carol, steps out to thank him, one can clearly see O'Brien, perhaps subconsciously, sucking in his stomach to make a better impression!)

The most prolific producer of Westerns during the thirties (or any other period) was Republic Pictures, initially a small independent company that grew out of the even smaller Mascot Pictures. Through a concentration on quality Westerns and serials, Republic amassed profits that ultimately enabled it to expand to major company status. Even when it did so, and was able to support bigger films from the likes of John Ford, Fritz Lang, Hecht and MacArthur, and Orson Welles, it sensibly maintained a large schedule of bread-and-butter product, while adding many big-scale Westerns in its Trucolor process as well. However, like Paramount, Republic seemed to lack the happy knack of transposing the speed, slickness, and energy of its smaller Westerns to the bigger ones. With the exception of a brace of specials by John Ford and Raoul Walsh, most of its large-scale Westerns tended to be slow moving, studio bound, and bogged down by too many characters and too much decor, coming to life in the big action highlights that were usually orchestrated by Yakima Canutt. Those bigger Westerns, though, followed in the wake of John Wayne's success in *Stagecoach* (1939) and more properly belong in a discussion of the forties.

But Republic's "B" Westerns were perfect examples of ultraefficient assembly line product. Factory products they certainly were, formularized in both cast and plot. Plots at Republic were conspicuous not only for their lack of originality but also for the number of times they could be remade and made again as non-Westerns before reverting to type once more. One could take an early John Wayne scenario and follow its loyal service through the years as it was adapted to the needs of Roy Rogers, Bill Elliott, and others, ultimately winding up with Wayne again. Key action footage was recycled endlessly, and even songs were doctored, sometimes just by one word, so that an "old" Roy Rogers song like "Roll On Texas Moon" would come back five years later as "Roll On Border Moon" for Rex Allen. But if one can carp at this economy-minded pillaging of content, no such complaint could be lodged against the films' most important ingredients—action and production values.

From the beginning, Republic got more excitement into its chases, more pep into its stunts, and more punch into its fights than any other studio. Camerawork was always clean, sharp, and in crystal clear focus, and locations—at least until the very final years, when the drab Chatsworth trails and hills were overused just because they were so close to home—were often unfamiliar and always first class. Republic also built up an outstanding library of musical themes: mysterioso, agitato, pastorale, menace. The studio's musical scores were among the best in the business, and certainly put to shame the tuneless collections of blasts and horn blowings that characterized the Frank Sanucci "scores" over at Monogram. Few "B" Westerns could long escape the taint of standardization, but since the key audience requirement of the Western was action, it hardly mattered that Republic's machinery showed. It was exceptionally well-oiled machinery, operated flawlessly by master mechanics. And to Republic's credit, the formularization varied with each specific series. Republic produced many different series and introduced many different star personalities. Each star had a formula tailored to his particular specialities, and while there might be an underlying common denominator in the *efficiency* of each series, the style of a Johnny Mack Brown was as different from that of a Gene Autry as Autry's was from that of the Three Mesquiteers.

Republic first got under way with straightforward action series starring Johnny Mack Brown, Bob Steele, and John Wayne (Wayne's an extension, in fact, of a Monogram series), but soon establishing its own and superior character. But audiences and exhibitors really began to sit up and take notice with two new series in the 1935–36 season. *The Three Mesquiteers,* based on characters in the William Colt MacDonald novels, launched one of the most expert and enjoyable of all Western series. Even the stories, based initially on some of the original MacDonald books, were a decided cut above the Republic average. The characters were obviously harmlessly plagiarized from Dumas's *Three Musketeers,* and they enjoyed a similar romantic and adventurous camaraderie. As ranchers, they were their own bosses and had a home base, but unlike Hopalong Cassidy's Bar 20 base (he was the foreman, not its owner), we rarely saw it. At most we might see them breaking a horse in their corral or out on a roundup, until a message arrived (usually within the first minute or so of playing time) summoning them to help a distant friend in trouble. More usually time would be saved by having them arrive in the territory that needed cleaning up.

Ray Corrigan, Bob Livingston, and Max Terhune played the heroic trio in the early and best entries in the series, though later on John Wayne, Tom Tyler, Bob Steele, Duncan Renaldo, Raymond Hatton (and sundry unfunny transients in the comic corner of the triangle) were utilized, too. In terms of their period, the films were inconsistent to say the least: the very first in the series was set in the immediate aftermath to World War I, and the heroes were veterans making a rather incongruous covered wagon trek Westward in search of new homes. Other installments in the long-running series were set in the Old West with its Indian raids, in Civil War days, and, in the mid-forties, in films like *The Phantom Plainsmen,* in contemporary World War II, since the West was then (according to imaginative Hollywood scenarists) overrun with Axis spies seeking either valuable mineral deposits or wild horses for use on the battlefields! Some would *seem* to be period Westerns until fast cars and planes were introduced unexpectedly.

The Purple Vigilantes seemed to be another post-Civil War adventure, dealing as it did with a KKK-like band of hooded terrorists; then in one scene, the Mesquiteers ride down a Western street and we see a one-sheet poster advertising Johnny Mack Brown's *A Lawman Is Born* prominently displayed on a hoarding! But at least the Three Mesquiteers films were consistent where it really mattered, in their fast, clean, uncomplicated action entertainment. And while the Mesquiteers were certainly role models, and their films had an appropriate quota of widows and crippled orphans, they made their own allowable mistakes, had occasional weaknesses, and generally were more human and less rigidly enthroned on a pedestal than William Boyd's Hopalong Cassidy.

The stuntwork, usually organized and performed by Yakima Canutt, was of the highest calibre, and contained some spectacular horse action, falls, and wagon crashes that were *so* realistic that they would probably have been disallowed in "A" films lest audiences thought they were dangerous for the animals involved. The chases, shot from a new camera truck of which Republic was very proud, were unusually smooth and exhilarating. Carole Landis, Jennifer Jones, and Rita Hayworth were among the more prominent of several leading ladies who found them useful stepping-stones to stardom, while William Witney and George Sherman were the best of a handful of directors who guided the series. *Heart of the Rockies, Range Defenders,* and *Outlaws of Sonora* were outstanding in a spirited and deservedly popular series.

Even more far reaching in its influence and impact was a Gene Autry Western that Republic offered in 1935, *Tumbling Tumbleweeds.* Autry was a former singer of cowboy songs on radio and had starred in Mascot's decidedly peculiar but most ingenious science fiction Western serial, *Phantom Empire,* as well as (with his perennial sidekick, Smiley Burnette) having a prolonged musical specialty interlude in Ken Maynard's *In Old Santa Fe. Tumbling Tumbleweeds* was a fairly straightforward Western, though on a bigger scale than most, unusual in that it *opened* with an elaborate mass action sequence, and kept going at a lively clip until its stunt chase climax. It also had a large quota of songs. Music wasn't entirely new to the Western, but it had never been stressed and exploited as it was here—perhaps because at this juncture in his career, Autry's singing was superior to his action capabilities. This first release was so successful that Republic immediately devised a new and unique formula for him. Songs and hillbilly comedy, largely supplied by Smiley Burnette, to be a fixture in all but one of Autry's Republic series, were given equal prominence with action, and indeed in many rural areas it was these elements that were the key box office attractions.

The remarkable thing about the Autry Westerns is how quickly they, and Autry, improved and acquired a definite style of their own. The initial films, still produced by Nat Levine of the old Mascot Company, were very rough around the edges, seemingly uncertain as to what direction to take, and disjointed and clumsy in their welding of action and music. Autry's riding and athletic abilities were limited at first, though this was not too apparent, even in the first film, as unusual skill was brought to bear in the use of doubles and clever editing and camera angling often made it look as though Autry was pulling off tricky action stunts. But within two years, a bright, breezy, thoroughly engaging formula had evolved. Autry had increased his riding and other action skills considerably, and while a series of acting lessons had not changed him into a performer of any depth, at the same time his rather colorless personality had been transformed into a most appealing one. He never aspired to the acting standards of a Buck Jones, but on the other hand, his scripts never required that of him. Warmth and geniality were enough. The character that gradually evolved for Autry also became of itself a kind of launching pad for most of his plots. Invariably, he was the unofficial leader of his community, the most successful of the ranchers not only because he was hardworking and smart, but also because he had good judgment and had always helped *others,* so that he had plenty of friends to call on. Everybody liked him and trusted him, so that in time of crisis his fellow ranchers would come to him for advice. To help them, he'd not only put his own fortune and future on the line, but he'd urge them to stick together and hold on, no matter what the banks or the landowners threatened. (Autry's period of peak popularity was in the Depression, so rural audiences could take to their hearts films which seemed to understand their problems and offer possible solutions).

Invariably of course, some underhanded work by the villains, who sometimes had the deceived and uninformed heroine working for them, would undermine Autry's work and make it seem that he had sold out his

Romance of the Rockies (1937): Tom Keene (with Franklyn Farnum) in a modest but much better series for Monogram

Toll of the Desert (Commodore, 1935), a cheapie with ambitions and a good script: Left to right in foreground are Edward Cassidy, Fred Kohler, Jr., Tom London, and John Elliott

Border Brigands (Universal, 1935): Buck Jones subduing Fred Kohler

Secret Valley (Fox, 1936): Virginia Grey and Richard Arlen

friends. This state of affairs usually came to a head about two reels before the End title, allowing Autry to straighten out matters by a combination of strategy, technology (bad guys in his films were often foiled by Autry's cunning use of newspapers, radio, and even television) and the more direct means of fists and guns. An offshoot of this formula was for Autry to have to go to the big city to either seek out the head of a cattle or land combine, or the politicians who could do something about his local problem, as in *Rovin' Tumbleweeds,* which was literally an Autry parallel to Capra's *Mr. Smith Goes to Washington.* Throughout all of these travails, Autry always remained a symbol of personal integrity, physical courage and American enterprise.

To offset expected criticisms that this new brand of musical Western was a travesty of tradition, Republic set them in their own Never Never Land, keeping them quite apart from other Westerns. The few early "histor-ical" Westerns that Autry had made, cavalry-versus-Indian actioners like *Ride Ranger Ride* and *The Singing Vagabond,* were quickly abandoned in favor of entirely modern Westerns. Always playing under his own name, Autry was often cast as a radio or rodeo star; the props included high powered cars, trucks, army tanks, air-planes, and radio stations, while the plots touched on contemporary politics, big business, social problems (the Dust Bowl), and dairy farming as opposed to cattle ranching, and problems of soil erosion, flood control, and crop destruction by weeds. Against this thoroughly modern background, the traditional action ingredi-ents—runaway coaches and barroom brawls, to say nothing of cowboys toting six guns and engaging in full scale range wars—were incongruous indeed, but here the musical elements came to the rescue. Short-skirted, glamorous cowgirls paraded down Western streets urg-ing the populace to vote for Autry; the villains operated

The Rainbow Trail (Fox, 1932): Sex—or at least, nudity—in this Western with Cecilia Parker and George O'Brien

Lawless Land (Republic, 1937): Louise Stanley and Johnny Mack Brown

lavish Broadway-style nightclubs in small Western towns where their potential customer list must have been nil; ranch owners invariably had palatial homes back East where their pretty and spoiled heiress daughters lolled around swimming pools. All of this obvious artifice, glamour, and song put the Autry films into a deliberate kind of horse operetta framework that disarmed criticism. Admittedly, at times the song and frolic aspect dominated out of all proportion, and trade press reviewers were quick to be scornful, especially of those films that had virtually no action at all.

On the whole, the balance was well maintained and Autry soon became not just the biggest moneymaking Western hero, but one of America's top ten stars, right up there with Gable and Mickey Rooney. Autry's stock company of directors, cameramen, musicians, and players (June Storey was a lovely and partly modern leading lady in many of his films) knew what was expected, and they always delivered. Autry's peak was reached in 1937, and was maintained through 1939 with such films as *Home on the Prairie, The Yodellin' Kid From Pine Ridge,* and *Colorado Sunset. South of the Border* (1939), a big

Rose of the Rio Grande (Monogram, 1938): John Carroll could never remember his lines, but he looked good on a horse

Gun Packer (Monogram, 1938): This Jack Randall Western showed that "B's" could still afford good locations

hit because of its wildly popular title song and added production values, caused the Autrys to be upgraded into bigger, slower, more musically-oriented productions temporarily, but without any lessening of his popularity. While some of his Westerns were relatively serious in theme—*Sierra Sue* for example—the biggest successes were those which most fully exploited their freedom from convention, such as *South of the Border,* with its improbable tale of South American revolution, espionage linking up with the war in Europe, and a heroine who enters a convent.

The same year, however, Autry also made *In Old Monterey,* which, despite the U.S. neutrality act and Hollywood's supposed strict adherence to it, managed to be quite stirring and convincing preparedness propaganda, using footage from the Far East and Spanish war fronts to get across the message that it could all happen at home unless America was fully prepared. And while some of the plots of the Autry films seemed a little outlandish, probably in their forced juxtaposition of old and new, more than once life itself seemed to be following an Autry plot. The story line of *In Old Mon-*

Rose of the Rio Grande: An extremely unlikely piece of action choreography for publicity stills

The Cowboy and the Bandit (Argosy, 1935): Rex Lease with grand old-timer Lafe McKee, who never seemed to age over a three-decade career

Breed of the Border (Monogram, 1933): George Hayes and Bob Steele

terey was virtually repeated intact during the Vietnam period, when the Army sought to oust ranchers from their land near Santa Fe, because it was needed for bombing and other training purposes, and like Gabby Hayes in *In Old Monterey,* the ranchers refused to move, claiming angrily that they'd fight if necessary to keep what was theirs.

The incredible public response to Autry produced singing cowboys from all sides. Some of them were better singers or actors—or both—than Autry while others took to the action elements more naturally, but lacked the magic combination of Autry's personality, a carefully planned formula, and Republic's production know-how. Tex Ritter could have been one of the best, for he had a likeable personality and a Western singing style now regarded as classic, and for a newcomer, he put on a very good show in the riding and scrapping department. But most of his films, initially for Grand National and later for Monogram, were too scrappily put together to do him justice, though there were certainly some entertaining ones among them. Bob Baker, Dick Foran, Smith Ballew, Jack Randall, and Fred Scott were among the many post-Autry hopefuls, and still more followed in the forties: Jimmy Wakely (who copied Autry slavishly, even to using identically designed shirts and costumes), Eddie Dean, Monte Hale, James Newill, and Rex Allen.

Even the little seen (outside of their own specialized territories) all-black Westerns created their own singing cowboy in Herb Jeffries. Bearing titles like *Harlem Rides the Range* and *The Bronze Buckaroo* they were Westerns singularly lacking in the fast action their audiences expected. The producers took their small units out to good locations and then lacked the expertise to follow through. The sparse fights were clumsily staged and the chases no better. The plots were the standard Western themes, with stock dialogue amplified and exaggerated until it reached the proportions of near parody. Interestingly enough, there was no inverted racism in these films. The stories unfolded in a totally black West; there were no whites in them at all, even as villains. Yet the prolonged comedy relief consisted of the kind of material (the comic pal scared of ghosts, the chicken-stealing cook, the lazy roustabouts) which black audiences understandably objected to when it appeared in a more restrained form in regular Hollywood films. Apart from the "personality" stars like Herb Jeffries, the acting quality was low, with the casts remaining fairly constant from film to film with the same comics and heavies. While the veteran Sam Newfield directed one or two of them, most of these Westerns were made by inexperienced black directors and on very meager budgets. The musical element was not stressed, and Jeffries was really the only singing cowboy that this small group produced.

The most successful of them all, however, and the only one ever to challenge Autry's supremacy, was Roy Rogers, who had played singing and other bits in earlier Autry and Mesquiteer (and outside) Westerns, and who was developed by Republic in 1938 as a second-string Autry at a time when Autry was showing signs of dissatisfaction and in fact kept himself off the screen until his demands for better material and salary were met. At first the Rogers films had a laid back quality of their own; although some were modern—probably because they were inheriting Autry scripts—they were primarily historical and action Westerns with songs introduced casually. Rogers had a likeable personality, but was youthful and of slim build, hardly seeming much of an opponent for the formidable array of villains that Republic lined up for him: Fred Kohler, Noble Johnson, and Cyrus Kendall, among others. Nevertheless, the early Rogers Westerns had flair and style, and benefited a great deal from the presence of George "Gabby" Hayes doubling in both comedy relief and straight dramatic chores. In the early '40s, they began to emulate the Autry films more openly, although with such a minimizing of action and often such a total avoidance of fisticuffs that juvenile support was slow in coming.

When Autry joined the Armed Forces during World War Two, Republic got behind the Rogers films with a big "King of the Cowboys" campaign and built him into a major star. His films, many of them remakes of earlier Autry successes, were given far bigger budgets than had ever been allocated to Autry and for a time the formula was almost destroyed through imbalance. Too great an emphasis on music, not just songs but mildly spectacular production numbers, long fiesta and nightclub sequences, and miniature "shows" to conclude the films, often crowded the action content out almost entirely. Such Westerns as *Idaho* and *The Cowboy and the Senorita* could far more honestly have been labeled merely musicals. The costumes employed by Rogers, heroine Dale Evans, and the singing group, the Sons of the Pioneers, became more reminiscent of uniforms or Broadway chorus line costumes than of authentic Western regalia.

With Rogers firmly established, however, the always economy-conscious Republic saw no need to continue with these musical spectaculars indefinitely. Gradually the budgets were lowered and the musical elements reduced. Toward the end of his contract at Republic, when his films were being made in color, there was even a drastic shift of emphasis so that music almost disappeared, and action for its own sake became the norm with fight scenes becoming suddenly savage, realistic, and bloody.

The Rogers Westerns never quite duplicated the

The Man From New Mexico (Monogram, 1932): Tom Tyler and Robert Walker

The Silent Code (International/Stage and Screen, 1935): Kane Richmond (being pummeled) and Blanche Mehaffey in a scene that the kiddies probably complained had been cut; there's more action in this still than in the entire movie

John Wayne with Marion Burns in two pleasing scenes from *Randy Rides Again* (Monogram, 1934)

The Lawless Frontier (Monogram, 1935): Wayne with Yakima Canutt, Jack Rockwell, and George Hayes

The Wayne fights with Yakima Canutt go on . . . and on

Thunder Trail (Paramount, 1937), a Zane Grey that's one of the very best of the "B's" of the thirties: Gilbert Roland, Marsha Hunt, and Charles Bickford

freshness of the Autrys, and could be *very* variable, a particularly neat little Western like *Young Buffalo Bill* (1940), one of the best of the early Rogers films, being followed only two months later by *The Ranger and the Lady,* one of the *worst.* But at their best, in the 1942–43 years, when Rogers was being built up, his budgets increased, but the inflated musicals hadn't yet come on the scene, they had a sober and relatively realistic quality and a neat blending of song and action with cinematography that was enhanced by new, different locations. *Heart of the Golden West, Silver Spurs, The Man From Music Mountain,* and, a little later, *Utah* were the best from this period. Rogers himself was not necessarily better than Autry, though he was a better and more naturalistic actor. They complemented one another rather well; both had the common denominator of sincerity, but Autry was somewhat more obviously a showman, while one felt that Rogers probably cared a little more about Westerns as an entity rather than merely a box office product. Either way, both made many and major contributions to the genre.

One should not leave the Republic Westerns of the thirties without turning a spotlight on one of the studio's key directors, William Witney. A former editor, Witney was still in his early twenties when codirecting the serial, *The Painted Stallion,* and although he was so expert at serials that he continued to direct them well into the forties, he was promoted to full directorial charge of Westerns with one of the earlier Three Mesquiteers films, *The Trigger Trio* (1937). Witney's contribution to the art of the Western was a major one. He had long been dissatisfied with the way fights and other action scenes were staged. Even with the expertise of a Yakima Canutt, there was still a tendency to shoot fight scenes in long takes. The stuntmen would fight and roll all over the set, virtually destroying prop furniture so that retakes were difficult, and making the use of doubles sometimes too obvious. Witney was impressed watching Busby Berkeley stage and shoot one of his huge production numbers for a Warner musical. There was little actual dancing in the accepted sense of the word; but Berkeley would fragment the routine, shooting individual pieces of movement and alternate angles. When it was all pieced together, it not only looked like a superbly choreographed example of massed dancing, but also was neat and uncluttered, directing the collective audience eye only to what Berkeley wanted it to see.

Witney reasoned that Western action, and especially fights, could be shot this way, too. So smooth is the action and the relationship of one shot to another, and so expert is the stuntwork involved, that it is sometimes difficult to realize that a piece of Witney action is as complex a mosaic of visuals as an Eisenstein sequence.

Nor was Witney *just* an expert at the mathematical construction of action. He was also a good dramatic director, an excellent writer, and, important to a company like Republic, fast and efficient. He made notable contributions to the serial field via at least two of the finest Western serials ever made, *The Lone Ranger* and *Zorro's Fighting Legion,* and certainly (at least) three of the finest non-Western serials: *Drums of Fu Manchu, Daredevils of the Red Circle,* and *Spy Smasher.* In his own way, he was every bit as responsible for the unique "look" and tempo of Republic films from 1937 on as director Michael Curtiz and art director Anton Grot were for the overall "look" of Warner Bros. films of the thirties and forties. Some of Witney's most impressive work awaited the fifties, and will be discussed in the appropriate chapters. It included the superb second-unit work on Frank Lloyd's *The Last Command* wherein Witney directed virtually all of the Alamo sequence, and his own very personal little masterpiece, *Stranger at My Door.* Witney did not work with Roy Rogers until 1946 and *Roll On Texas Moon,* but he then directed all twenty-six of Rogers's remaining Westerns for Republic and had a great deal to do with changing, reshaping, and improving them.

Witney raised horses and dogs himself, and had worked them in films other than his own; the animal thrill scenes in his Rogers films often looked almost too grimly realistic, yet any illusion of harsh treatment was *purely* an illusion, created by brilliantly creative editing and trickery. While Witney made many major "A" films, and in television many of the best entries in the *Tarzan, Bonanza,* and other popular series, his best work was almost certainly in the serial and the Western, and in more recent years has been properly acclaimed at archival homages in Paris, Zurich and Munich, as well as in Luxembourg and elsewhere. But his contribution to the films of Republic is almost too large to assess; without it, their quality would have been less, and their life span possibly shorter.

The final major purveyor of Westerns in the thirties, Monogram Pictures, had a long history with its roots in the old Rayart Company of the late twenties, in a sense paralleled Republic but never equaled it. Monogram's first sound Westerns with Bill Cody, Bob Steele, Rex Bell, and Tom Tyler were no different from most other independent Westerns of the period, though their plots were sometimes a cut above the average. Tom Tyler's *Partners of the Trail,* for example, was unique in having no villains, an element of mysticism, a hero who is accused of the murder of his wife, and a powerful prison cell scene of the hero going to pieces—shot in a style at least approaching that of German expressionism. Monogram drew its stars from the ranks of those who had slipped slightly, or newcomers on their way up, and it was unusual indeed for Monogram to inherit John Wayne *after* Columbia and Warner Bros., a sure sign of the lack of faith or interest that most studios placed in Wayne. His Monogram series was of decidedly uneven quality. Some, like *The Trail Beyond,* were virtual marathons of action, with locations well chosen to simulate (in this case) Canadian terrain, since it was a Mounted Police story. Yet others were dull and pedestrian. If nothing else, they were unique in their stunt action. Yakima Canutt was pressed into service as character player, villain, and double for Wayne. As a double, he was often photographed in semi close-up, and in climactic episodes, he could sometimes clearly be seen leaping into the saddle (as Wayne) and literally chasing himself. Monogram, not too concerned with production polish, would frequently leave in the finished film stunts that went wrong. Thus in *The Trail Beyond,* Canutt, doubling for Wayne, miscalculates a leap from horse to wagon, is knocked to the ground, gets up, dusts himself off, remounts, gives chase again, and this time makes the transfer with room to spare, the camera recording the whole procedure and adding a touch of unexpected realism.

Also during the later thirties, Monogram turned out enjoyable series with Tom Keene, Tim McCoy, Tex Ritter, and Jack Randall. The studio had one of the best Western town locations of any studio, located in Newhall, and in Harry Neumann it had an excellent cameraman, too. Its basic weakness, shared by all studios except possibly Warners, but indulged in more ruthlessly by Monogram, was in allocating a bigger budget than usual to the first one or two films in a series, and then cutting back as soon as the series was established.

This was especially true of the Jack Randall series, which started out under producer Scott R. Dunlap with *Riders of the Dawn* in mid-1937. Here was a small Western with real class, and a brilliantly staged and photographed climax. It is a running battle between a posse of lawmen and the villains, some of whom are in a stagecoach. The effectiveness of the climax was increased by a reshaping of the Hopalong Cassidy formula, a slow and methodical buildup to a climax in which background music was suddenly introduced to underline the action. But in this instance the climax itself was subjected to a repetition of that formula: a street gun duel, the hero riding off to collect his waiting posse, the baddies' bank holdup and escape, this *then* merging into the pitched running battle. This final chase, staged on salt flats and with much unusual angling in the camerawork, would have done credit to a much larger production. Since the location appears to have been at least partially the same, and Yakima Canutt performs similar

stunt work in both films, one must assume that somehow this sequence came to John Ford's attention, for its similarities to his salt flats chase in *Stagecoach* are unmistakable.

Despite the budget cutting in later films in the series, the Jack Randall group did maintain a high standard, with *Riders From Nowhere* and *Gunsmoke Trail* particularly good follow-ups. Randall (the brother of Bob Livingston) unfortunately had a tragically short career. No other series was offered when his Monogram group came to a close, and he was killed in a horse action accident while appearing in one of the starring roles of a 1945 Universal serial, *The Royal Mounted Rides Again.*

Monogram was to make substantial improvements in the overall quality of its "B" Westerns in the forties, and later on would make isolated "A" Westerns superior to the average Republic "A" product, but Monogram was to remain permanently in Republic's shadow. However, with the emergence of a new—and cheaper—company in the '40s, Producers Releasing Corporation (PRC), Monogram was put into a better light.

One tangentially interesting offshoot of Western "B" production in the thirties was Columbia's decision to make several of its Buck Jones, and later Charles Starrett, films, in Canada. A quirk in British law made any film produced on British soil technically a British picture, and by law, British exhibitors *had* to show a certain percentage of British films every year. Columbia felt that American "B's" with all their zip and pace would be vastly preferable to the often crudely made and pedestrian British "B's" that were pressed in to service to meet legal requirements. But the experiment was not a success. For one thing, Canadian facilities just across the border did not match Hollywood's, and good locations often weren't equipped with good camera truck roads. Those that were had been used too much and the Westerns that emerged from this experiment—Buck Jones's *McKenna of the Mounted,* Charles Starrett's *Secret Patrol,* among others—were invariably inferior to their Hollywood counterparts. Too, the Western market in Britain was not very flexible. There was only room for a certain number of Westerns every year, and many series got no release there at all, odd samples trickling through years later via independent distributors. The British "pedigree" of some of Columbia's Westerns made no difference at all to their marketability, just as attempts to widen Westerns' usability by experimenting with a four-reel format in the forties was doomed to failure, if for no other reason that reduced budgets made their threadbare cheapness all the more visible. The one innovation that did increase the marketability of the "B" Western was the widespread application of the cheap color processes like Cinecolor and Trucolor. There had been some minor experimentation along these lines in the thirties, via Republic's Zorro adventure, *The Bold Caballero,* and totally independent ventures such as *Lure of the Wasteland,* but the application and workability of the small-budget color Western would have to await the 1940s.

Cherokee Strip (Warner Bros., 1937): Dick Foran, here with a new leading lady, Jane Bryan, on the way to better things at Warners

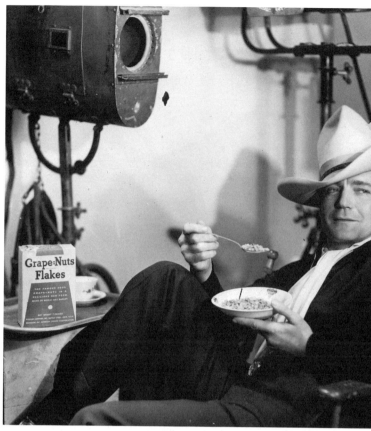

Pre-television commercials: According to the caption on this still, Buck Jones "frequently" asked for Grape-Nuts Flakes as a morning snack on the set, attributing his "marvelous stamina" to the product

Rhythm of the Saddle (Republic, 1938): A good stunt action scene from the stagecoach race climax

Union Pacific: The linking of the rails

ELEVEN

The Thirties

The spectacular upsurge in both quantity and quality of the "B" Western throughout the thirties was hardly matched by a corresponding increase in the big-scale Western. In fact, apart from a flurry of activity at the beginning of the decade, and the launching of the biggest-ever cycle of super-Westerns at the *end* of the decade, not until 1939, in fact, so that they properly belong with the Westerns of the forties, most of the major companies virtually ignored the "A" Western.

Fox, even though it had John Ford under contract for the entire period, offered him not a single horse opera, and indeed shunned the genre almost entirely. *Ramona,* the old Indian romantic tragedy was remade (by Henry King) primarily because it afforded an excellent opportunity for displaying the versatility of the newly perfected three-color Technicolor system. The studio also brought Warner Baxter back for another and diminished-in-size Cisco Kid adventure *Return of the Cisco Kid,* but this not until early 1939, and useful mainly as a segue into a "B" series of the forties in which former comic pal Cesar Romero took over as The Kid. Fox's dalliance with Zane Grey was limited to only one new property, *King of the Royal Mounted* which independent producer Sol Lesser turned into a pleasant but not very lively melodrama. Presumably it was successful enough

to spur Fox into considering a series—a follow-up "Northern," *The Country Beyond,* a much better film and also starring Robert Kent as the Mountie hero, had all the earmarks of a successor, but presumably Grey was not going to let the rights go for more than the one film, and the credits for *The Country Beyond* played safe by assigning its story origins to James Oliver Curwood. Otherwise, Fox's contribution to the genre—until the big landrush of super-Westerns following *Stagecoach,* when the studio's major contribution was *Jesse James—* was limited to *Frontier Marshal,* another go-round for the Wyatt Earp story with Randolph Scott as Earp and Cesar Romero as Doc Holliday. A decent production but far from an "A," it was relatively short, but Allan Dwan's experienced direction and a good cast turned it into a surprisingly successful film that was *sold* as an "A." Although it kept most of its action within the confines of the Western town, it was consistently lively and its box office performance undoubtedly helped by the dearth of good bigger Westerns at that time.

The same dearth undoubtedly helped MGM's *The Bad Man of Brimstone,* another largely studio-bound Wallace Beery vehicle that also served to introduce Dennis O'Keefe as a new star of note. Even more sentimental than most Beery vehicles, it was helped by a good cast of veteran character actors (Noah Beery, Lewis Stone, Guy Kibbee, Joseph Calleia) but hindered by a budget that apparently ran out at the critical moment, so that the long awaited confrontation climax was presented as a somewhat frustrating montage. Its success paved the way for Beery's return to Westerns with more frequency in the forties. Two of the Nelson Eddy–Jeanette MacDonald operettas, *Rose Marie* and *The Girl of the Golden West*, could pass as fringe Westerns, and Laurel and Hardy's *Way Out West* was one of their very best and funniest comedies, though its actual satire of Western conventions was minimal. The two best MGM Westerns came from the mid-thirties, William Wellman's romanticized but still very rugged biography of the bandit Joaquin Murietta in *Robin Hood of El Dorado*, with Murietta well played by Warner Baxter, and Richard Boleslawsky's surprisingly gritty and unsentimental *Three Godfathers* with Chester Morris and Lewis Stone, one of the most effective of many versions of the Kyne story because its running time was relatively short, not allowing for its theme of self sacrifice to become cloying. Also worth noting from MGM, if only because its dreadful reputation has prevented its revival, and because it is a far more deserving film than its devastating and dismissive reviews indicate, is *Laughing Boy* (1934). Like the same year's (admittedly much better) *Massacre* from Warners, it was an attempt to focus attention on the problems and hardships of contemporary Indian life. Based on a mildly celebrated novel by Oliver La Farge, it was slightly changed and compromised in its screen adaptation, but not drastically so. Although some Indian-white relationships were involved, it dealt primarily with intertribal life, and was particularly interesting in stressing the role that Indian *women* played in their culture and day-to-day living. Its principal drawback, perhaps even stronger today when he no longer has much of an audience following, was the inadequate performance of Ramon Novarro in the title role. His career had slipped badly, and MGM was winding up his contract by putting him into films like this, *The Call of the Flesh,* and *The Barbarian,* hoping to eke out to the last vestiges of his exotic appeal, now sadly outdated in talkies. W. S. Van Dyke directed, doubtless hoping that he could turn the film into an Indian parallel to his not-unrelated *Eskimo.* It was a misfire, due mainly to Novarro, but not a dishonorable one.

Columbia's schedule was significantly shy of "A" Westerns, an area the studio wouldn't get into (and then would specialize in) until 1940. But some of its programmers had a quality indicating that more ambitious treatment might have turned them into substantial hits. Although allegedly based on a Zane Grey story, *The End of the Trail* (1936) was actually a reworking of an earlier gangster film, *The Last Parade,* with the same director and star combination in Erle C. Kenton and Jack Holt. It was unique in both its plot (starting with the Spanish-American war, it followed its protagonists through to the contemporary West) and in its use of an "antihero" long before the term or the type became commonplace. Until the much later *Tom Horn* (which had a different set of circumstances anyway) it must also rank as the only Western in which the hero (Jack Holt) went to the gallows at the end for killing the villain, an unusually poignant and well-played scene that must have wreaked havoc with unprepared juvenile audiences.

Universal's sole spectacular of the thirties was *Sutter's Gold,* a project at one time designed for the Russian director Eisenstein, who ultimately never worked in Hollywood at all. Drastically reshaped as a vehicle for Edward Arnold, and too similar in many of its ingredients to *Diamond Jim* and *The Toast of New York,* it was also hoped to reestablish James Cruze as a major sound director, and to be a talkie equivalent of *The Covered Wagon.* Unfortunately, it was just that. Despite a crowded canvas, it was a jerky, episodic tale, frequently held together by old fashioned inter titles, and with its action sequences set up on a big scale, but disappointingly and unexcitingly underplayed. Its length, its lack of really big star names, and its much higher than anticipated budget, the expenditure of which did not show up on the screen, all but wrecked Universal, a relatively small company, and would have done so had not *Show Boat* been both good enough and successful enough to bail it out at the right time.

The main disappointment with *Sutter's Gold,* however, was its dissipation of a big and fascinating theme. Sutter was an incredible man, a visionary, adventurer, politician, con man, pioneer, all rolled into one. Unfortunately, many of his visions were far greater than his ability to carry them out. Further, he was inclined to have no compunction about cheating the little people who had helped him, although he was smart enough never to renege on agreements with those in positions of greater power, and his relations with the Russian government, as it was about to abandon its holdings in California, were handled with skill and foresight. Far from a sympathetic man in his personal life, he had been forced into an unwanted marriage when he got his sweetheart pregnant, and finally abandoned a by now quite large family when debts and the threat of prison forced him to flee from Switzerland.

In America, he eventually became the most powerful man in California, ruler of a huge agrarian empire, only to lose it all when gold was discovered on his lands and he was stripped of his wealth by gold seekers and claim jumpers, even losing one of his sons in the mob turmoil that followed. The U.S. government recognized his claims to restitution but, apart from granting him a modest pension, did nothing to make amends, and he died in poverty, still waiting and expecting justice. In filmic terms, the basic problem with Johann Sutter was that he was a loser on a monumental scale, and, certainly in the Depression years, American audiences weren't particularly interested in the stories of losers. *Diamond Jim* was a big success the same year precisely because Jim Brady was an outgoing, optimistic, big spending entrepeneur of just about anything that would make money.

Universal may also have been chastened by the comparative failure of *Silver Dollar* (1932), a Warners biography of "Haw" Tabor, a relatively accurate but not very imaginative starring vehicle for Edward G. Robinson. Tabor's career not only paralleled, in a way, the story of William Randolph Hearst, and thus was an unofficial forerunner of *Citizen Kane,* but also reflected Sutter's career in miniature. Tabor was a silver tycoon who literally turned Denver from a small mining community into a major metropolis. Along the way, he followed the Hearst/Welles route of building an opera house as a shrine to his mistress. Tabor's fortune collapsed when gold eclipsed the value of silver. It was an interesting film, underrated because for its time it *was* surprisingly honest and un-Hollywoodian. But Tabor's loss of power seemed personal and relatively minor compared to the total collapse of Sutter and his literal empire.

Instead of coming to terms with this story, Universal chose instead to reduce it to the level of "B" melodrama, taking isolated incidents and characters from Sutter's life, and reshaping them into a typical Edward Arnold vehicle encompassing action, enterprise, romance, and disappointment. It started off on the wrong foot by having Sutter flee Switzerland to escape a trumped up political murder charge of which he was totally innocent. He doesn't even *learn* about California and its opportunities—the very thing that led the real Sutter to America in the first place—until he is in a New York hospital recovering from injuries received in a union fracas over the operation of streetcars! The only signs of historical accuracy in the Universal film are the care with which Sutter's Fort, located at Sacramento, is recreated. Even here however, historical integrity is short-lived. Before long, Sutter's Fort is engaged, Alamo-like, in a pitched battle with Mexican forces, and the day is saved only by the timely arrival of a United States cavalry troop headed by Kit Carson (Harry Carey) and General Fremont! In actuality, no battles or even mild skirmishes ever took place at the fort, its guns firing only in salute to visiting dignitaries.

The full story of Sutter's career—"adventures" would

The Golden West (Fox, 1932): Stanley Blystone and George O'Brien in a sequence deleted from the final version

The Mine With the Iron Door (Columbia, 1936): Henry B. Walthall, Cecilia Parker, Spencer Charters, Richard Arlen, and Stanley Fields in a loose adaptation of the Harold Bell Wright novel that provided an unusual mystery Western

Lobby card for the 1935 Harry Carey–Hoot Gibson Western that, despite its powerhouse cast, was a disappointment

be an equally appropriate word, though it tends to downgrade the material much as Universal's film did—has yet to be told in an American film. Ideally it would have made prime material for Orson Welles, John Huston, or Robert Rossen, all of them directors sympathetic to the theme of a fall from authority and power, and, unfortunately, all of them now gone. There is also ample material there for an extended television miniseries.

Coincidentally, the same year that *Sutter's Gold* was made by Universal, the German writer-director-star Luis Trenker made his own Sutter film, *The Kaiser of California.* Trenker was a unique moviemaker, a specialist in the mountain films that were as much of a national genre to Germany as Westerns were to America. Rugged, a good enough actor (for the kinds of role he always elected to play), a superb athlete and mountain climber,

Trenker was rather like a formidable combination of John Ford and John Wayne. His films contained many of the subthemes of Ford movies, most specifically the breaking up of families and sadness as old traditions give way to new.

Trenker's initial hopes had been to make his Sutter film as a coproduction with Universal, for whom he had made a brace of mountaineering action adventures earlier in the thirties. But because of the political situation in Germany by mid-decade, Hollywood studios were now wary of coproductions, and the deal fell through. Trenker, however, was still determined to make the film, and Paul Kohner, an old friend and Universal executive, partially assuaged his disappointment by promising to help out by acquiring photographic equipment and helping to underwrite the cost of whatever U.S. shooting Trenker could arrange. But

Trenker was out of favor with Dr. Goebbels for his refusal to join the Nazi filmic propaganda efforts; Goebbels had done his best to suppress Trenker's previous film (*The Lost Son,* his best work and an enduring classic) and had been forced to backtrack when it won international festival awards. On this occasion, Goebbels hit back by seeing to it that the German financing that Trenker was banking on was yanked. By raising money on his own, and shooting the film, very convincingly, in Italy rather than America, Trenker wrote, directed (and starred in, as Sutter) a remarkable movie that, despite some rough edges, was far more of an epic than Cruze's film.

Influenced at least partially by the writings of Karl May, a still-popular Germanic equivalent of Zane Grey (even though it was later established that May had never been to America), it may not have been more accurate in detail than *Sutter's Gold.* Opting for mysticism and poetry, instead, it conveyed admirably the European conception of the West as a land of opportunity and fulfilled destiny, and the creation of Sutter's great agrarian empire—surely his most expansive dream, and the one that he most succeeded in achieving—was given greater prominence in the German film. Superbly photographed by Albert Benitz, and with a richly romantic score by Giuseppe Becci—two of Trenker's frequent collaborators—*The Kaiser of California* made the most of the limited American locations he could afford, and integrated them brilliantly and seamlessly into the Italian footage. A highlight was a stylized sequence in which Sutter, dying of thirst in the desert, is "drowned" in images of waterfalls and crashing waves. A later one allowed Trenker to demonstrate his mountaineering skills as he climbed up and out of the Grand Canyon, while the mob turmoil of the closing scenes, the rioting in the streets and the burning of the town, were splendidly done. Only in its post-production work does the film indicate some of the problems it labored under due to its enforced shoestring budget. In its final form, the film is confusing at times. Too many of the bearded Western characters look alike, and should, in some cases, have been given an additional scene or two, or extra dialogue, to differentiate between them. Some of the mass action is confusing, too, and needs a little more motivation and explanation. Had Trenker been able to go back and do additional shooting, or had he had sufficient surplus footage on hand to doctor some of the scenes, it might have been a tidier film. But there was neither time nor money, so that it lacks the ultimate professionalism of most of Trenker's films. It *was* a success in Germany, and paved the way for more Germanic Westerns, particularly two vehicles for that country's biggest star, Hans Albers. *Sergeant Berry* was a

Sutter's Gold (Universal, 1936): Edward Arnold as Johann Sutter in a typical Hollywood rewriting of history

straightforward, often enjoyably vulgar, romp in which Chicago cop Albers goes West to round up the badmen there. One of its delights was the constant repetition by the Mexican villains and peasants of what was apparently their only expletive, the time-honored "Caramba!" *Water for Canitoga,* made in 1939 and set in Canada, was actually cunningly contrived as anti-British propaganda on the eve of the war. Dealing with the piping of water in to a remote outpost, it was a slow-moving, almost operatic story of heroism, sacrifice, and regeneration. Albers clearly enjoyed his incredibly protracted death scene (his lungs have collapsed while performing heroically to save the pipeline machinery far below ground level) as he staggers into the saloon and the miners speed him on his way to Valhalla by singing "Good-bye, Johnny!" to him.

Worthy of note while considering German Westerns of the thirties is *The Great Barrier* (1937), one of two made in Britain that year by the German producer Gunther Stapenhorst (the other being *The Challenge,* a remake of one of the Luis Trenker films about the Matterhorn). *The Great Barrier* was part of a concerted British effort to woo the U.S. market with action and genre themes considered surefire (horror, futuristic science fiction) and often with American stars. *Rhodes of*

Writer/director/star Luis Trenker as Johann Sutter in *Der Kaiser von Kalifornien* (1936)

Africa, starring Walter Huston—and replete with comparisons to *The Covered Wagon* in its advertising—had come first, and now *The Great Barrier,* the epic story of the building of the Canadian Pacific Railroad, and the first such film since Ford's *The Iron Horse.* Although the Canadians objected to the liberties taken with their history, it was an excellent film of its type, and considering that the British had no precedents in making such a film, surprisingly up to Hollywood standards. Stylistically, it was something of a mixture. Although based on a book, its script seemed to work on the assumption that all the clichés of the American Western were in fact a reflection of life and no more, and that in order to make them exciting and dramatic, they had to be exaggerated. This resulted in barroom brawling scenes and "Western" dialogue that at times approached parody. On the other hand, the location work in Canada was first-rate, though sometimes uneasily matched with London studio work and miniatures.

Milton Rosmer, a good but basically theatrical director, handled it all well enough, but presumably had a great deal of help from (uncredited) American second-unit directors. The action sequences, particularly an overland horseback pursuit when riders must overtake a train before it plunges into a just-discovered quagmire,

Scene from Trenker's Germanic approach to the Sutter story

192

were exceptionally well done and hinted at more than a little Hollywood expertise. Since there were many familiar American players in the cast—Richard Arlen in the lead, and J. Farrell MacDonald, Frank McGlynn, Tom London, Jack Rockwell, and many others in key support and bit roles—it had more the look of a coproduction than a British film done on location. Its finest asset was the superb mountain photography, the combined work of German, American, and British cameramen—one long sequence of the initial assault on rapids and mountains having the near mystical quality of so many of the German mountain films. And the climactic mob scenes of rioting railroad workers egged on by agitators to sabotage equipment and rolling stock was clearly imitative of the mob destruction scenes in Fritz Lang's *Metropolis,* saloon girl Lilli Palmer replacing Brigitte Helm, and carried aloft on the workers' shoulders, exhorting them to further violence. The triumphant discovery of the vital pass at the end of the film was actually a false climax; in actuality, Rogers' Pass, named after its discoverer, proved to be a death trap in the winter months, burying trains in avalanches of snow. Although only isolated British films in the thirties succeeded in making any kind of a dent in the American market, *The Great Barrier* was one that did, enjoying several profitable reissues (once under the title *Hell's Gateway*) and television usage in the fifties.

Until 1939, Warner Bros. shared the general apathy toward "A" Westerns, catering to the action market with their crime films and Errol Flynn swashbucklers, and making only a token gesture toward Western-oriented fare with rugged North woods and logging melodramas: *Valley of the Giants,* best of them all, with some blistering action sequences and stunt work; *God's Country and the Woman,* perhaps technically and geographically Western since it takes place in the California redwood forests; and *Heart of the North,* highlighted by an exceptionally spirited cliff-edge fight between Dick Foran and Joseph Sawyer. All of these films were designed primarily to exploit the new, improved Technicolor, and with green trees, blue lakes, red Mountie uniforms, fire scenes, and dynamited dams, they did so with a vengeance.

Warners turned its attention to one genuinely ambitious Technicolor Western, however, in Michael Curtiz's *Gold Is Where You Find It.* It too exploited color in obvious ways—Olivia de Havilland's cheeks and ripe red apples vied for attention in some scenes—but also in creative ways. The story dealt with hostility between California farmers and gold miners, and used dramatically effective shots of fields of golden wheat ruined by diverted rivers of mud and sludge, scenes that would have had little impact in black and white. Although not

The Plainsman (Paramount, 1936); Gary Cooper and Jean Arthur as Wild Bill Hickok and Calamity Jane

The Plainsman: Hickok greets Buffalo Bill (James Ellison) and his bride (Helen Burgess)

The Texas Rangers (Paramount, 1936): Hank Bell, Jack Oakie, Edward Ellis, and Fred MacMurray

planned or sold as an action film, and certainly able to hold its own with its plot, color, and cast, its Western classification made one expect a little more than the film managed to deliver in terms of excitement. Somehow the various confrontations produced little tension, anticipated large-scale action seemed to fizzle out, and the good guys seemed to have most of the brawn and brains on *their* side, although Barton MacLane was, as always, a tower of strength as the meanest of the villains, never merely talking when he can shout, and coming up with the most complicated and nefarious schemes at a moment's notice.

Dealing with the period some thirty years after the discovery of gold at Sutter's Mill, when mining had been totally mechanized with hydraulic drills, *Gold Is Where You Find It* is a useful piece of ecological history as well as an enjoyable if somewhat slowly paced film. (At ninety minutes, it was hardly overlong, but Warners' other three Technicolor actioners were all in the eighty-minute range or slightly less, and did move more briskly.)

By far the most unusual Warner Western of the thirties—though it is something of an injustice to describe it casually as one—was *Massacre* (1934), if not the

The Texas Rangers: Part of the big Indian battle

194

The Texas Rangers: The film's best-remembered scene with Lloyd Nolan about to shoot Jack Oakie from under the table

Three Godfathers (MGM, 1936): Chester Morris (above), Lewis Stone, and Walter Brennan (left)

best then certainly the most interesting sound film by Alan Crosland, the director of such silent Barrymore extravaganzas as *Don Juan* and *The Beloved Rogue*. A film which grew out of Warners' series of social protest melodramas, it dealt with the plight and exploitation of the American Indian in the Depression. In actual fact, the Depression had very little bearing on the story told,

since the injustices and indignities inflicted on the Indian had been his lot for years. But 1934 was a significant year in that government policy toward the Indian was supposedly changing, largely due to the work of John Collier, a sincere (if sometimes opportunistic and limelight-seeking) spokesman for the American Indian through the 1920s, and who was to become the commissioner for the Bureau of Indian Affairs under Roosevelt's New Deal administration. In the film, Henry O'Neill plays a character loosely based on Collier, but it is a minor role, and the story is really told through the eyes of Richard Barthelmess, playing a successful Wild West show Indian star, who returns to his reservation on the death of his father only to find his people cheated by their white overseers and dying of disease and malnutrition.

Although this is largely conjecture, it would seem that Warners probably bought the well-received book of the same name by Robert Gessner, knowing its basic contents but not its format. Expecting a novel like *I Am a Fugitive From a Chain Gang* that could easily be transformed into scenario form, the studio must have been somewhat dismayed to find that *Massacre* was virtually a documentarian book, full of facts and dates and figures, but with no continuity and no star roles. The solution was to reshape the chain gang story line to fit the contempo-

195

rary Indian situation, but to flesh it out with the most colorful and attention-getting data that could be lifted from the book. Though an almost mathematical procedure, it worked well; sometimes the film is too close to *Chain Gang* in terms of structure and individual incident (including an escape over the same bridge!) but it does have passion, integrity, and dignity. It should also have had a little more footage: at sixty-eight minutes, like so many Warner programmers of the period, it just moves too fast to do total justice to its theme. As with most other social essays of the thirties, its framework is a melodramatic one in which the scales of social comment are decidedly loaded. It does seem unlikely that *all* of the white Indian Affairs representatives were thieves, rapists, drug addicts, lechers, and corrupt in as many other ways as possible. No mention is made, for example, of the Indians' own self-destructive path via alcohol, a substance literally poison to their systems, and a theme not picked up until some hard-hitting documentaries of the late seventies.

Not an expensive film, *Massacre* is often quite creative in its production economies. Back projection is used inventively, and a climactic fire sequence cunningly achieves most of its effect through flickering shadows. The dialogue is frequently very much to the point, often seeming to fling speeches directly at the audience as it protests, for example, white attempts to suppress and obliterate Indian religious ceremonies. Like so many films of 1934, it seems to have managed to squeak through before the Production Code restrictions were limited, and to counterbalance its grim foreground theme, offers snappy dialogue and even some casual race humor (a colored valet constantly makes cracks about the Indians, whom he considers *his* social inferiors). But from its opening image—an Indian head on a drum being aggressively beaten—to its savage mob justice climax, it is a film of outrage. The optimistic happy ending strikes a somewhat false note, and there are certainly signs that it was planned otherwise. But the sad thing about the film is that so few of the improvements in the Indians' mode of living, planned so energetically in 1934, were ever implemented. Sadder still is the fact that the chain gang film *did* have some effect in bringing about needed reforms in the treatment of convicts, whereas this one, crusading for totally innocent victims, had no effect whatsoever.

RKO Radio maintained a regular output of medium budget Westerns, stronger on casts and plot than on action, but very pleasing though for the most part not hard-hitting or novel enough to make much impact today, even on television. A notable exception, however, was *The Last Outlaw* (1936), about an old-time outlaw returning from jail to his home in the modern West,

encountering prejudice, contemporary racketeers, and, an amusing and topical touch, a grown daughter entranced by a singing cowboy in the movies! The original story was by John Ford, who had made it as a silent, and had hoped to remake it at RKO. Instead it was handed to Christy Cabanne, who did a competent enough job with it, but totally failed to inject the kind of magic that Ford would have added intuitively. Harry Carey, returning to the location of a favorite old saloon, finds that it is now an art-deco bar on a busy street corner. One can well imagine what Ford would have done with that one shot, perhaps using a superimposed image of the saloon as it was, and the sound of its piano. But it was too good a plot, and too well cast, to be anything but a delight. Harry Carey and Hoot Gibson seemed to be carrying on exactly where they'd left off in *Straight Shooting* nearly twenty years earlier, neither of them showing anything like a two-decade advance in age, despite Gibson's constant referring to Carey as "Pop." Henry B. Walthall had one of his best roles in years as the former sheriff now demoted and being eased out of his job, while Tom Tyler, in one of the first of many villain roles (although he would continue as a cowboy hero through the forties) gave an early glimpse of the viciousness that made his Luke Plummer such a standout role in *Stagecoach*.

RKO's other medium-size Westerns fluctuated between Richard Dix (*The Arizonian, West of the Pecos*) and Harry Carey. Carey's *Powdersmoke Range*, based on one of William Colt MacDonald's "Three Mesquiteers" novels, gathered together such a remarkable cast of Western favorites and old-timers that just finding each of them something special to do used up so much time there was none left for either plot or action. Although it was billed as the Barnum & Bailey of Westerns, it was a novelty that didn't come off, but was an enterprising endeavor. Other Carey films included the less ambitious *Border Cafe*, an enjoyable time-killer that repeated the *Last Outlaw* formula to a certain degree, and *The Law West of Tombstone*, a curious attempt at an almost wholly comic Western (with Carey as a blowhard liar) that is heartily espoused by many, despised by others. Certainly it is a Western that offers *nothing* that is expected, and the success of which depends entirely on the mood of the individual viewer. If nothing else, RKO was prepared to explore new ground in its thirties Westerns, but in the forties, it would entrench itself more securely with traditional and bigger star vehicles for the likes of Randolph Scott, John Wayne, and Robert Mitchum.

The only remaining major company, Paramount, had no difficulty in effectively monopolizing the bigger Westerns in the thirties. There was just no competition. Also, as in the twenties, Paramount had the stars and

Robin Hood of El Dorado (MGM, 1939): Warner Baxter in a scene from the film as a rather whitewashed Joaquin Murietta and then watching the rushes with director William Wellman

Wells Fargo (Paramount, 1937): John Mack Brown and Frances Dee

directors—and owned properties by such writers as Rex Beach, Will James, O. Henry, and Emerson Hough. Even though there was apparently no great demand for the bigger Westerns, the studio owned its own theaters and so could be sure of an exhibition outlet. Its release

Way Out West (Hal Roach, 1937): Laurel and Hardy versus Jimmy Finlayson

Girl of the Golden West (MGM, 1937): Having done *Rose Marie* beautifully, Nelson Eddy and Jeanette MacDonald followed up with the more old-fashioned and far less successful horse-operetta

Heart of the North (Warner Bros., 1938): Designed to exploit the new Technicolor and doing it very well, this programmer starring Dick Foran—here with Anthony Averill, Allen Jenkins, Arthur Gardiner, and James Stephenson—was packed with action, including a rugged cliff-edge fight

schedule in the 1930s was peppered with epic Westerns from directors such as King Vidor, Cecil B. DeMille, and Frank Lloyd. Henry Hathaway, under contract too, was given the distant cousins—*Trail of the Lonesome Pine* and *Spawn of the North*—which while a yarn of the Alaskan fishing industry, was actually a very thinly disguised remake of *The Virginian*, with salmon poachers substituting for cattle rustlers. Some of the studio's more rewarding Westerns were the seventy-minute programmers such as *Lone Cowboy* (based on a Will James story, whose best-known work, *Smoky*, was filmed three times) and especially *Gun Smoke*, an overused Western title that in this, its first usage in the sound period, was attached to a 1931 film directed by Edward Sloman.

One of several thirties films that sought to find novelty in both the gangster and Western genres by linking them, *Gun Smoke* was also a member of the "vigilante" Westerns best exemplified by *Law and Order* of the following year. As in most films of this cycle, big town gangsters, headed here by William (Stage) Boyd and J. Carrol Naish, find the city too hot for them, and go west looking for a good hideout from the law, and easy pickings from the simple cattle folk. These Westerns equated the individual destiny of the old-time cowboy with the mass responsibility of the public to combat crime, and in *Gun Smoke* clearly and literally in as many words states that the only way to deal with killers is to kill them! Its climax is not so much a pitched gun battle as an orgy of slaughter, the chief gangster (Boyd) being thrown to his death from a mountain top via a grisly trick shot which follows his downward path. Very much a forerunner of such contemporary vigilante films as the *Death Wish* cycle, *Gun Smoke* is perhaps a little less disturbing because of its distancing from reality. A tough and lively film, it came at a time when too many Hollywood Westerns were still slow and talkative, as witness the same year's *The Conquering Horde,* from the same studio and director, and with the same star, Richard Arlen. Incidentally, the (fictional) Idaho town seemed, by geographic and signpost information provided in the film, to be an approximation of Ketchum, the small town about a mile away away from Sun Valley, a community that didn't exist then, having been developed as a tourist center by the Union Pacific railroad only in 1936. *Gun Smoke* was shown in the area in the summer of 1982, as part of an academic conference on the changing West. Richard Arlen's rousing speech about the East's infiltration into the West, and of cowboys looking forward sadly to the day when they'd have to trade in their horses for trucks (the sorest point of all with Western ranchers who long to cling, however unrealistically, to their old way of life, and to whom the inevitable truck is the symbol of the new) received a tumultuous ovation from all the ranchers and farmers present. It's a surprisingly prophetic and accurate speech, and much of what it predicted had happened right there, although not quite as devastatingly since Sun Valley was developed more for sports and tourism than industrialized ranching.

By far the best and most enjoyable of Paramount's quartet of mid-thirties epics was King Vidor's *The Texas Rangers,* his first Western since *Billy the Kid.* Paramount, so expert in the smaller Zane Grey and Hopalong Cassidy Westerns, never really mastered the art of the big-scale ones. The best were those done by directors like Vidor, or much the very personal but essentially independent Westerns by Ford and Hawks, merely released through Paramount. But by any standards, *The Texas Rangers* was an exception to the disappointing quality one learned to expect from the bigger Paramount Westerns, and a far more polished if less gripping work than *Billy the Kid.* While Vidor's 1935 Civil War film, *So Red the Rose,* suffered from too many good writers trying to transform merely good hokum into something worthy of literary respect, the script of *The Texas Rangers* was not ambitious enough. Vidor wrote it himself, officially basing it on Texas Rangers records, and, being a Texan himself, infusing it with a natural love of his state and its history. However, while the script does make use of a couple of well-known incidents in Ranger history (referred to in brochures issued by the very publicity-conscious Rangers headquarters in Amarillo), it falls back far more on the very standard movie plotting of the breakup of three badmen, two of them joining the Rangers as a hideout and being converted to the path of duty and, of course, eventually confronting and bringing to justice their old comrade. The dialogue is often as trite as the basic story line, but Vidor fills his film with enough incident, action, and well-developed characters for these flaws not to matter too much.

The merits of *The Texas Rangers* become all the more obvious when one compares it with its dull Technicolored remake, *Streets of Laredo,* from the forties. The Indians were gone from the second version entirely, along with any sense of history and Empire-building, and large doses of sex and brutality were added. A sadistic flogging became the key piece of illustrated art work in the advertisements, an element entirely absent from the original. After a stirring foreword, *The Texas Rangers* is full of images stressing heroism and self-sacrifice, and an inspiring musical score partially borrowed from the original "live" orchestral score for *Old Ironsides.* (This music was later used to add stature to many smaller Paramount Westerns). The staging of the action is splendid (many movie houses brought the old

Magnascope screen into play to enlarge the already spectacular Indian fighting highlight), the horse falls and stunts expertly done, and the editing sharp. The locations (more of them in New Mexico than Texas) are impressive and unfamiliar. Most of the film was shot out-of-doors, and the few studio "exteriors" are mainly for matching-up or cutaway purposes, and not jarring. Hollywood's attitude toward the Indian seemed to have changed again, though, and once more they are presented as warring savages who have to be suppressed and placed back on their reservations. There's one unintentionally amusing sequence in which the Ranger band, out *looking* for Indians to decimate them, suddenly comes across a large party of them, and takes refuge in mountainous rocks. The Rangers are well equipped with rifles, while the Indians, having only their knives and bows and arrows, very sensibly use the terrain itself as a weapon, and from higher ledges roll huge rocks down on the Rangers. "Only an Indian could think up a trick like that!" snarls the Ranger captain (Edward Ellis) in a tone of contempt rather than admiration.

Even though not a classic, *The Texas Rangers* is an exhilarating Western with a refreshing schoolboy vigor, excellent cinematography, and a strong supporting cast of good Western types: Fred Kohler, Charles Middleton, George Hayes, Frank Shannon. It was fortunate, too, in having one of those unexpected scenes that made such a vivid impression that it was constantly talked about and kept the film "alive," rather like Cagney's grapefruit scene in *The Public Enemy.* It was the scene of Lloyd Nolan's callous murder of his friend Jack Oakie, shooting him in the belly from under a table, while smiling and talking in terms of friendship.

Paramount's companion super-Western for 1936, and in its own eyes a much more important film, was DeMille's *The Plainsman* with Gary Cooper as Wild Bill Hickok. This was DeMille's first full-scale Western epic, and while it was a big popular success, this was due in no small measure to Cooper's incredible run of hits. In just two years, this was his sixth straight success: *Lives of a Bengal Lancer, Peter Ibbetson, Desire, Mr. Deeds Goes to Town,* and *The General Died at Dawn* had all been critical and box office winners. Hit number seven, Hathaway's *Souls at Sea,* would follow *The Plainsman* before the golden vein petered out, though only temporarily since a similar run of hits would begin with *Beau Geste* in 1939. *The Plainsman* restored Cooper to the Western, a genre he had not worked in since *Fighting Caravans* in 1931, and it also reunited him with Jean Arthur, who had been teamed so successfully with him in *Mr. Deeds Goes to Town.* DeMille's name was certainly a help too, but he had not had a hit of the stature of *The Plainsman* for some years. Unfortunately, its script was heavy-handed and obvious, getting off to a typical start with Abraham Lincoln being forced to interrupt a discussion of his plans to open up the West when Mrs. Lincoln hurries him along, warning that he'll be late for the theater.

Far too much of the film was marred by DeMille's fondness for shooting as much of it as possible within the confines of the studio. He was a director whose sense of efficiency—and perhaps a sense of power, too—demanded that every studio facility, every piece of equipment, and every department head be at his beck and call at all times. He was a showman like Ziegfeld rather than an artist like Hitchcock (whose need for studio control was more understandable, and was justified by the results it produced) and he only functioned well on his home studio ground. Major location action sequences were usually made by experienced second-unit directors like Arthur Rosson, their skill and the realism of their Indian battles and other action highlights minimized when later intercut with obvious studio-filmed inserts making excessive use of the back projection screen. Nevertheless, despite the omnipresence of the process screen and a few silent stock shots, *The Plainsman* was big and certainly entertaining, especially in view of the dearth of similar material from other studios. Jean Arthur, playing Calamity Jane for glamour, blond hair, and a snappy if unlikely Western costume, was a far cry from the homely, wizened woman who was the real Calamity Jane, and whose historically doubtful liaison with Hickok would be further romanticized in later years by Frances Farmer and Doris Day.

The first of four collaborations between Gary Cooper and the director, *The Plainsman* also introduced audiences to DeMille's curious fondness for casting totally unsuitable character actors as his lead Indians, in this case Paul Harvey (usually type cast as a blowhard businessman or politician) as Chief Yellow Hand, and the Hungarian Victor Varconi as Painted Horse. Leisurely in its pacing, but colorful in incident and peopled by an excellent troupe of character actors, the film may well have been all corn and contrivance, but its machinery worked well. *The Plainsman* was also a major landmark in the shifting Hollywood treatment of Wild Bill Hickok who, following William S. Hart and Gary Cooper, gradually lessened in box office stature (Richard Dix, Bruce Cabot, Roy Rogers, Ted Adams, Douglas Kennedy, Tom Brown) and heroic status until in fifties films like *I Killed Wild Bill Hickok*, he underwent a strange moral metamorphosis to become an unmitigated villain! Attempts by Western historians to demythify Hickok first set him up as merely a show-off and a bully, then as a lecher and a coward, and finally as a callous murderer. The ultimate was probably reached in 1953 with *Jack McCall, Desperado,* in which an upright

Frontier Marshal (20th Century-Fox, 1939): Cesar Romero as Doc Holliday (to Randolph Scott's Wyatt Earp) and Nancy Kelly

Let Freedom Ring (MGM, 1939), produced under the more traditional title of *Song of the West,* was nowhere good enough to warrant the honor of being the film that technically launched the new cycle of super Westerns. Here, left to right, are C. E. Anderson, Lionel Barrymore, Nelson Eddy, Edward Arnold, and H. B. Warner

George Montgomery (the very antithesis of the sneaking, cowardly McCall as played by Porter Hall in *The Plainsman*) bests and kills Hickok in a fair fight and is acquitted by the court and returned to his bride. Having distorted history to such an extent already, Columbia Pictures obviously didn't feel it necessary to add that in actuality McCall was retried by a different court, in itself an illegal act, and promptly hanged.

200

For all their (quite different) script weaknesses, both *The Texas Rangers* and *The Plainsman* had all the ingredients for box office success, and deserved their popularity. But Paramount was unable to duplicate that success in two follow-ups. *Wells Fargo* (1937) was long, carefully made, its historical background and data well documented, but it was also dull and stiff, long on romance and overdressed interiors, short on action and exteriors. Like so many Frank Lloyd epics (and one wonders why he was *constantly* given this kind of film to direct), it was treated in tableau form, with the characters rather lifelessly symbolizing progressive pioneering, self-centered greed, and so forth. It did introduce Joel McCrea effectively to the Western arena, though it would be some time before he specialized in the outdoor film, and its two major action sequences—an Indian pursuit of a stagecoach, and a Civil War skirmish in which Confederate troops raid a supply wagon train— saw frequent service as stock footage in subsequent Paramount Westerns. Later theatrical and then television revivals edited the film drastically, but such recut-

John Ford's classic *Stagecoach* (1939)

Stagecoach: George Bancroft, John Wayne, and Claire Trevor

Man of Conquest (Republic, 1939): Yakima Canutt taking a stunt fall in the Battle of San Jacinto sequence

Wasser für Canitoga (1939): Hans Albers in a German Western designed partly as anti-British propaganda

ting could only shorten the film, not accelerate its leaden pace. In many ways, *Wells Fargo* was rendered even duller in its shorter form, since one of its most interesting characters, a scheming banker played by Lloyd Nolan, was eliminated almost entirely.

The Texans (1938), another remake of *North of '36,* carried less prestige but considerable more animation. It was actually little more than a "B" given "A" status by its increased (though still brief) length and Randolph Scott and Joan Bennett as its stars. It was full of action, but most of it was clearly stock from older films and didn't match either in pictorial quality or speed, nor was much care exercised in shooting additional footage to round out the old. The villain was casually disposed of *only* via the footage from the silent version, for example. There was far too much of May Robson being tough and tiresome, and despite a potentially big canvas of postwar Texas, it never seemed very important. However, again, it was helped by the dearth of big Westerns in the thirties, and did better at the box office than it deserved to.

Paramount's last epic Western of the decade was not only one of its best, but also one of DeMille's best. The success of *The Plainsman,* and the only lukewarm popularity of an interim historical swashbuckler, *The Buccaneer,* prompted him to return, quickly, to the West—and *Union Pacific.* Although it covered the same historical ground as *The Iron Horse,* it had a better script and one in which personal relationships were more appropriately subordinated to the overall theme of Empire Building. Further, DeMille kept his action—a couple of fights, a train holdup, a wreck in a snowy pass, a big-scale Indian attack, and the traditional street stalking and shootout— fairly constant and regularly spaced, instead of compressing most of his action into a single highlight as he had done in *The Plainsman* and would do again in his dullest and slowest Western, *North West Mounted Police.* One reason for the unusual pace and vigor of *Union Pacific* may have been that DeMille was sick during much of the shooting and, showman that he was, released carefully lit publicity stills showing him directing from a cot on the set! Thus, far more responsibility was delegated to the second-unit director, Arthur Rosson, than usual, and the ratio of studio faking was much smaller. There were awkwardly obvious riding close-ups filmed against process screens in the night chase sequence, but otherwise *Union Pacific* has far more of a sense of the genuine outdoors than was usual in DeMille's Westerns.

Joel McCrea took a major step forward from *Wells Fargo* to establish himself in *Union Pacific* as an actor in the same league as Gary Cooper, and the overdone Irish blarney of Barbara Stanwyck apart, the acting from a

Destry Rides Again (Universal, 1939): Marlene Dietrich as Frenchy was restored to box office favor again with this comedy Western

Dodge City (Warner Bros., 1939): The first of the big town-taming Westerns, with Errol Flynn, Olivia de Havilland, and, as her brother, William Lundigan, just killed in a cattle stampede

The Oklahoma Kid (Warner Bros., 1939): Lola Lane and James Cagney

The Oklahoma Kid: Humphrey Bogart as the black-clad Whip McCord, second of his three Western heavies

first-rate cast (including Brian Donlevy as the now stock heavy of "A" Westerns) was uniformly good, and even the comedy, of which there was possibly a shade too much, at least arose naturally from the narrative. As always with DeMille and Paramount, economies reared their heads at the wrong moment. What could have been an exhilarating episode—the destruction of Donlevy's saloon by the railroad men, coming at a time when the audience was ready for Donlevy to be taken down a peg or two—was neatly sidestepped by having the whole

203

The bank holdup sequence in Henry King's *Jesse James* (20th Century-Fox, 1939) with Tyrone Power and Henry Fonda

sequence merely suggested by sound effects and one or two fragments of scenes. Had this been a Val Lewton production, one would have found this oblique approach fascinating, and Lewton would undoubtedly have done it better. From DeMille, it was patently an attempt to save time and money. Likewise the big set piece of the Indians attacking a train, and railroad men rushing to the rescue on another one—an episode copied from *The Iron Horse*—reduced the impact of its splendid and spacious location work by intercutting extremely ingenious but obvious combinations of studio back projection and miniatures as the Indians pull down a water tower, and set fire to the trestle across a chasm which the rescuing train must cross.

Union Pacific was one of the blockbusters of 1939, and at two hours and fifteen minutes, the longest talkie Western yet. In those days, with extended pre-release engagements, such major films were slower in getting into general release than is the practice today. Although initially released in April of 1939, by the time it had gone into general distribution the outbreak of World War II was that much closer. Few Americans believed that the United States would actually be embroiled in a war, but feeling against Nazi Germany ran high, none could deny that dark days lay ahead, and the patriotic zeal that had lain dormant for almost two decades was suddenly rekindled. Unwittingly, *Union Pacific* catered to that zeal, and its climax, promising toil and sacrifice, with some kind of Utopia "at the end of tracks" (a quick shot of a modern UP train roaring across the film into the End title helped to bring it up to date) was both prophetic and topical, if in an ambiguous way. British audiences, seeing it in the summer of 1939, knowing that war could come at almost any minute, found it additionally meaningful.

Good as *Union Pacific* was, it was too isolated a spectacle, too atypical of the Western genre, to bring the Western back to life on its own. That minor miracle was largely wrought by a less ambitious film, John Ford's *Stagecoach,* but that one Western, too, while deserving all the praise it received *as a film,* did not exist in a vacuum, and has been somewhat overrated as to its influence at the time. An outstanding year in many ways, 1939 was quite certainly the one of a major renaissance of the Western film, and of the launching of the biggest and longest sustained cycle of Westerns ever. At least ten deluxe Westerns were released throughout 1939, and the catalyst for *most* of them was the political climate in Europe. Half a century later, it is difficult to pinpoint exactly which film was conceived first. Release dates are relatively meaningless due to differing production methods, post-production delays and the working speeds of the studios involved. MGM could put a film into production early, fuss with it, rewrite, reshoot, and by the time it was ready to release find that Republic, geared to rapid production and distribution patterns, had written, produced, shown, and gone on to something else. Delays in waiting for sufficient supplies of Technicolor stock could well put back the release date on a color film, allowing a black and white competitor to get in first.

Regardless of the commercial success of *Stagecoach* (which initially was modest) and its critical reception (which was enthusiastic), there can be no doubt that films that immediately followed it into release, most notably Warners' *Dodge City* and Republic's *Man of Conquest* had been planned and were in production well before *Stagecoach* was released and its reception and impact anticipated. However, it was the Ford film that ensured that the new revival of interest was no flash in the pan but was here to stay, although it is curious that William Wyler's *The Westerner* (with Gary Cooper) was the only post-*Stagecoach* Western that aimed for its artistic qualities.

Chronologically speaking, the first big Western of 1939 was MGM's *Stand Up and Fight*. It was another of the studio's attempts to deglamorize Robert Taylor by putting him into action roles alongside his standard romantic ones. Costarring Wallace Beery, it was the first major Western to take up the social issue of slavery, although Warners' *Santa Fe Trail* a year or two later, with John Brown (Raymond Massey) stealing center stage away from Jeb Stuart and George Custer (Errol Flynn and Ronald Reagan) would do so in far more outspoken fashion. Twentieth Century-Fox's *Jesse James*, directed by Henry King, was also a January release, but one without any overt or implied allegorical connection to the European situation. It was first and foremost another Henry King–Tyrone Power collaboration, notable for its pleasing Technicolor and a strong cast—Tyrone Power and Henry Fonda as Jesse James and brother Frank, Randolph Scott as a fair minded marshal, John Carradine as Bob Ford, the ubiquitous Brian Donlevy as the railroad-employed villain, and such useful character players as Jane Darwell, Donald Meek, J. Edgar Bromberg, Lon Chaney, Jr., and Slim Summerville. More related to the Depression years than contemporary Europe, its whitewashed account of the James Boys' vendetta against the land grabbing railroads might have found greater parallels earlier in the thirties. Location work, always an asset in Henry King's Americana films, was extremely good, and the reconstruction of day-to-day Missouri farm life realistically done, but as a Western it was long drawn out and tame. The train robbing motif that dominated all the advertisements was dealt with in cursory fashion in the film itself—one holdup sequence, and a brief montage of others—but some of the surrounding horse action and stunt work (particularly jumping horses through store windows, and off a high cliff) was so vivid as to bring complaints from humane societies. In the long run, the main function of *Jesse James* was to establish the place of the badman "biography" as one of the three main thrusts of the upcoming Western cycle, and to pave the way for films on the Daltons, the Youngers, Billy the Kid, more on Jesse James, and the exploitation of such lesser Western outlaws as Sam Bass and Butch Cassidy.

The third big Western of 1939, *Let Freedom Ring*, lent credence to the possibility that MGM was using the Western for semipropaganda purposes, and thus by association gave a little more significance to the earlier *Stand Up and Fight*. In a secondary sense, *Let Freedom Ring* tried to do for Nelson Eddy what the earlier film had done for Robert Taylor, even to having him best Victor McLaglen in an unconvincingly staged (and speeded up) fistfight. But the main intent of its flag-waving script by Ben Hecht was to sell America, with Edward Arnold and Lionel Barrymore repeating their stock Capra roles as dictator-tyrant and homespun idealist. Nelson Eddy, as an underground "freedom fighter," publishing the truth in a clandestine newspaper, was a clearcut forerunner of Philip Dorn in *Underground,* and far from subtly concluded the film by singing the "Star-Spangled Banner." Once the war was officially on, however, MGM no longer had any need for neutral subterfuge, and switched to traditional anti-Nazi and pro-American movies, restoring the West to Wallace Beery and Robert Taylor, though no longer together.

Stagecoach, also a February release, marked John Ford's return to the Western fold and finally established John Wayne as a major star, though contractually he still had four "B's" to complete for Republic. (Wisely, they were upgraded slightly, and their release was staggered to capitalize on Wayne's new popularity). *Stagecoach* was based on an Ernest Haycox short story, "Stage to Lordsburg," which was actually little more than a detached account of a journey across hostile Indian territory, more tone-poem than story. Dudley Nichols's creative screenplay fleshed it out, created structure and characters, used landscape, built to two major climaxes. Both he and Ford readily admitted that they had been heavily influenced by Guy de Maupassant's short story "Boule de Suif," whose prostitute heroine was transformed into Claire Trevor's Dallas.

Superbly photographed and splendidly staged, its Indian pursuit across the salt flats immediately became an action classic, although the beautifully designed climactic sequence in Lordsburg, when Dallas's true profession is revealed to John Wayne's Ringo Kid, and he settles scores with the enemies sworn to kill him, is probably (and rightly) the most memorable portion of

Jesse James: The crew on location at Pineville, Missouri

the film. It was the combination of drama, excitement, visual poetry, and beauty (enhanced by Richard Hageman's score) that make *Stagecoach* seem so new and dynamic, for those qualities had not all been possible in the fine but technically crude Westerns of the early thirties, and as a combination, had not been tapped in the limited number of bigger Westerns made since. *Stagecoach* alerted critics, public, and Hollywood to the possibilities of the Western in films transcending action for its own sake, but although those possibilities were acknowledged, they were little acted upon.

Among the more unexpected examples of *Stagecoach*'s influence, however, was a French remake, by Christian-Jacque, of *Boule de Suif* in 1945. It would probably have been made anyway; its witty and sardonic view of an earlier Prussian occupation of France was made to measure for that country to take a departing kick at their hated and now defeated German conquerors. But *Stagecoach* had reached France before the war had cut off supplies of new Hollywood product, and Christian-Jacque had had ample time to study it. While he retained de Maupassant's original story line, he copied Ford's structure and even individual incidents entirely, enlarging the role of the stagecoach and his passengers. As it swayed across French skylines, accompanied by a score that was less Gallic than pseudo-Hageman, Christian-Jacque even copied many of Ford's specific images. The swish pan from the stagecoach to the shot of Geronimo's Apaches waiting to attack on a nearby ridge was copied exactly, though it now applied to sympathetic partisans rather than hostile Indians, and the fording of the river was paralleled in a sequence where the French stagecoach is mired in mud. Christian-Jacque had always shown a fondness for American cinema; his *Carmen* was likewise almost transformed into a Western in its sequences of mountain banditry. But his *Boule de Suif* remains a prime example of Ford's—and the Western's—influence on European cinema.

The Oklahoma Kid, a March release, was a follow-up to *Jesse James* in the badman sub-cycle, but little more than an outrageous though highly entertaining frolic, with Cagney and Bogart transferring their big city personas to the West without the slightest change of

Dodge City: The town's leading outlaws—Victor Jory, Bruce Cabot, and Douglas Fowley (right)—meet their first opposition in Errol Flynn and Alan Hale

Union Pacific (Paramount, 1939): The year's biggest Western finds Lynne Overman, Joel McCrea, and Barbara Stanwyck taking up a collection in the saloon for murdered railroad worker Regis Toomey

Union Pacific: Robert Preston and Joel McCrea, the best friend who suspects that he has just robbed the payroll

Union Pacific: The Indians attack

pace, and even squaring off for the time-honored climactic fistic sloshing match. Although there were certain elements of the Western—a landrush, expanding frontiers, town building, and appropriate pioneering platitudes uttered by Donald Crisp—it never for a moment took itself seriously and was all the better for it. Slick, fast, beautifully photographed by James Wong Howe (original prints were released in sepia form), Lloyd Bacon's film was thoroughly and enjoyably old-

Geronimo (Paramount, 1939): Andy Devine and Preston Foster leading a convoy that will be matched up with footage from *Wells Fargo*

fashioned, even to the utilization of frequent unnecessary but flavorsome inter titles.

Dodge City, one of three April releases (another was *Union Pacific*) was Warners's first entry into the Errol Flynn town-taming sweepstakes. Although audiences probably didn't stop to think about it in 1939, the town, an armed camp run by a despot, could be equated with Europe, and the soft-spoken, hopefully neutral marshal who brings law and order was a prophecy of America's potential role in the world conflict. Olivia de Havilland was the pioneer woman (told by Flynn that she should be at home having babies, not running a newspaper, a line that invariably raised hackles in later years) and the resolutely non-American-sounding Errol Flynn proved how effective he could be in transferring his swashbuckling manner to the West. Full of rough, brawling, expansive action—an outsize saloon battle and a climactic running gunfight on a burning train—were two of many highlights. Among other things, the film provided proof of the grandeur-inducing capabilities of Technicolor. *Seen* in color, it was a grand-scale epic; in black and white, as it was to be shown in reissue and in its early days on television, it became just another Western. Michael Curtiz, who directed, was to make many more super-scale Westerns, but few as successful at the box office as this one.

Man of Conquest, likewise an April release—the momentum was increasing now—is one of the most interesting (and most forgotten) of the revitalized epics, and a credit to a small company like Republic whose first really big production it was. Although Republic's success with bigger Westerns was variable, its first two (Raoul Walsh's *The Dark Command* was the second, and one of two John Wayne–Claire Trevor vehicles to follow *Stagecoach*) were exceptionally good. While the big mass action scenes of the fall of the Alamo and the Battle of San Jacinto don't have the spectacle that Warners could have given them, they do benefit from the ultra vigorous second-unit direction (Reaves Eason) and stuntwork (Yakima Canutt). Sam Houston, played at various times by Joel McCrea, William Farnum, and others, is one of the most potentially interesting (for movie biography purposes) of all the Western empire builders, and it is surprising that *Man of Conquest* is the only big film made on his life (Sam Elliott starred as Houston in an episodic, three-hour biographic television movie in 1986), though strong-jawed Richard Dix was an ideal choice for the role, backed by an interesting group of character actors playing, and not just as name-dropping background dressing, such key figures as Stephen F. Austin, Andrew Jackson, Jim Bowie, Davy Crockett, and Santa Anna. Again, the plight of refugees from Santa Anna's tyranny is made to equate that of refugees, and

oppressed minorities, in the Europe of 1939. *Man of Conquest* telescopes a great deal of time, and whitewashes under the guise of patriotism what could be considered a major unleashing of American colonialism in the great Texas land grab, but on the whole, it is honest and surprisingly strong in the stand it takes for the exploited American Indian, somewhat ignored of late though given negligible lip service in *Union Pacific.* It was the biggest and best film of a little-known director, George Nicholls, Jr. (son of the silent character actor), who died just a year or two later. Joseph August again was responsible for the excellent cinematography.

November's *Destry Rides Again* at the time annoyed Western purists for being essentially a James Stewart and Marlene Dietrich vehicle and for being too "gentle" and "comedic" and far removed from the spirit of Max Brand's original novel (filmed earlier with Tom Mix), but it has achieved its own rather special niche since and most of its detractors have since made their peace with it. Certainly it did much to restore Universal's fortunes as a major company, and reestablished Dietrich, if only temporarily, as a star of the front rank. Its wonderfully rhythmic, evocative score by Frank Skinner, one of the best ever written for a Western, seemed strangely inappropriate for a film that had only one brief long shot of Stewart riding to justify its title, and otherwise was essentially a town-bound Western. However, that same score did yeoman service when reused in other Westerns (almost immediately), adding stature to "B" Westerns and serials as well as bigger films. Friends of producer Joe Pasternak, a refugee from Nazi Germany who arrived at Universal in the mid-thirties, insist that he saw *Destry* as a very specific anti-Nazi allegory, and that it could be broken down point by point, character by character (including Brian Donlevy whose little mustache made his Hitler alignment at least plausible) to prove it. On paper, it made for interesting theorizing, but the ineptitude of Stewart's Destry and his reluctance to take *physical* action even though he might adopt a moral stance—and the stress placed on comedic and aggressive *women*—make it a dubious theory to support. Fortunately it doesn't need that rationale to enable it to survive as an interesting footnote to the 1939 renaissance.

Though hardly a bona fide Western, *Drums Along the Mohawk,* dealing with the Indian fighting along the Eastern seaboard during the Revolutionary War, is important in that it is the first Western (if one can term it that) to go into release after Britain and France officially declared war on Germany, and to address itself, obliquely, to that war. One of several films made at that time to remind American audiences that they had once been at war with Britain, and that perhaps they should not advocate rushing to her defence, it was also a film that seemed to see war as a kind of cleansing period. *Drums Along the Mohawk* was unusually harsh and realistic (despite its Technicolor photography) in establishing the pain, suffering, loss, and sacrifice of war. Although an empire building film, it does not gloss over the blood and sweat that will be involved. It does follow the war through to a successful conclusion, but does not deal with the *issues* or even the *justification* of the war, promising only that it will be worth the sacrifices. Often touted as a commercial failure, it was a solid money-maker and one of John Ford's bigger successes. It was, in any case, a particularly felicitous film with which to close the 1939 Western renewal.

The immediate cycle broke down into three basic groups: The "epic" themes of national progress, which would be continued via such films as *Western Union* and *Brigham Young, Frontiersman;* the town-taming Westerns with *Virginia City* spearheading many more to come; the badman cycle *(When the Daltons Rode, Bad Men of Missouri);* and of course many splinter groups once the momentum was established. There were Westerns in Technicolor, modern Westerns, historical Westerns, the beginning of a return to self-satire, Westerns with bigger name stars than had ever conde-scended to appear in them. The boom continued for a full three years, even upgrading the quality of "B" Westerns. While the freshness began to fade in 1942, the popularity of the genre had been too firmly reestablished and entrenched for it ever to disappear from the screen again. The history of the Western since 1942 has not been one of diminishing and subsequent revitalizing; it was instead, for thirty years at least, one of constant popularity if of changing attitudes, tastes and styles: Westerns with sex, sadism, psychology. A cycle of self burlesque in any genre is usually a sign that that genre has played itself out, but after the Western began to kid itself, it was followed by yet more cycles, including the unexpected popularity of the German- and Italian-made Westerns which merely confirmed that if the Western had nothing intrinsically new to say, it was constantly finding new ways to say it. Many of those new ways would come to light in the forties, with new directors (Jacques Tourneur, Fritz Lang) bringing fresh and sometimes European insights. Just as 1919 was a remarkable year that laid the groundwork for major changes and advances in the twenties, so had 1939 prepared the way for the Western's most prolific and distinguished decade, the forties.

The Westerner (Goldwyn-United Artists, 1940)

TWELVE

The Forties and Peak Popularity

Seeing a good Western in the early forties was an exhilarating experience. There was an excitement and a momentum that built from film to film. If *Jesse James* had disappointed somewhat in its action content, then the vigor and tongue-in-cheek quality of *The Oklahoma Kid* which followed it into release more than made up for it. One could sense the anticipation in an audience as soon as the main titles came on. Color was no longer new or even a novelty, but it wasn't commonplace either. Color in a film added immeasurably to its box office value, and even the pedestrian ones like *Belle Starr*, part of the "badman" cycle, gained from the use of color. Audiences weren't exactly discovering Westerns, but their size, their scope, and the big-name stars who were appearing in them were attracting audiences that normally did not attend Westerns. Younger audiences especially, used to seeing their "B" Westerns at Saturday matinees designed for them (and certainly not giving up that habit), were pleased that films of the calibre of *Dodge City* provided material for a whole family outing.

Destry Rides Again (1939), discussed in the previous chapter, deserves renewed attention here for some of its tangential aspects. Despite its tragic ending—a stock situation dating back to *Under Two Flags* and beyond—it was basically fairly lighthearted, and has some-

times been credited with introducing sex into the Western. Since many earlier Westerns, even smaller ones like *The Rainbow Trail,* had a much stronger sexual content, it's an inaccurate generalization. What is true however is that it introduced sex-*appeal* into the Western, as well as a "battle of the sexes" element into both the plotting and the advertising. Over the succeeding few years, other Westerns would take it several steps farther: the sensationalism of Howard Hughes's *The Outlaw* (the sex exploitation of which often seems muted to contemporary audiences, due to the many *much* edited versions were in circulation), the much underrated comedy western *Frontier Gal* (full of action despite its farcical plot), and the hard-breathing passion of the Selznick/King Vidor *Duel in the Sun. Destry Rides Again* was also instrumental in setting up a kind of acting-ensemble approach to the Western. This was nothing really new of course. *Stagecoach* had been termed a kind of *Grand Hotel* on wheels and had an outstanding cast of solid character players (George Bancroft, Andy Devine, John Carradine, Berton Churchill, and others) to support its stars. But *Destry Rides Again* was a Universal production, and Universal had a contract player roster bursting at the teams with character actors and comedians. The studio quickly devised a formula for using these players in support of one or two top names, but actually building the action and comedy *around* these players. The non-Western *Seven Sinners* (1940), a South Seas actioner with Marlene Dietrich and John Wayne, repeated the formula even more successfully, and then reverted to the West again. In that same year, and with some shuffling around to avoid total repetition, Universal put the same troupe (Broderick Crawford, Andy Devine, Mischa Auer, et al.) into *Trail of the Vigilantes,* a very lively Western spoof, and *When The Daltons Rode,* a more serious Western in which the frequently lighthearted ensemble playing effectively counterbalanced the sense of tragedy with which the story had to end.

Trail of the Vigilantes, underrated at the time (or possibly oversold), was released and advertised as a straight Western, perhaps because it seemed too soon for the big and profitable new cycle to be spoofing itself. It was directed by Allan Dwan, who only the previous year had made a satirized *The Three Musketeers* with the Ritz Brothers. Both films shared the virtue of being good spoofs *and* good examples of the genre they were kidding, not an easy feat to pull off. They likewise shared the trait of loading the scales in favor of the villains, who were allowed to play it straight, and making the heroes either inexperienced or inept, or both. In *Trail of the Vigilantes,* Franchot Tone played the Eastern detective, sent West to shut down a reign of outlawry although he couldn't even ride a horse, and Warren William was the suave villain who never once suggested his awareness of the whole film being a joke. Not only were the sight gags, which kidded familiar Western set pieces, very funny, but the dialogue was also surprisingly witty. Most of the comedy was concentrated into the first half of the brisk (less than eighty minutes) film, with the major action coming in the second half, though still sustaining a light touch. *Trail* also became a minor footnote to film history in that its plethora of stunt work, much of it performed by Tom Steele, expedited the formation of a stuntmen's union.

Stunt work also abounded in the more serious *When the Daltons Rode* (directed by George Marshall) which repeated the *Jesse James* formula of having the Daltons literally forced into outlawry to combat the land-grabbing machinations of the railroads. Tolerably accurate in its basic facts, it nevertheless killed off *all* of the Daltons in the climactic Coffeyville raid, even though in actuality one of them survived to write the book on which this film was based! For once, Brian Donlevy—as one of the Daltons—was a sympathetic outlaw, and yet again, Randolph Scott was in for name value only, having little to do except add box office value to the posters and be around to inherit Kay Francis following the bloodbath climax. Its main asset however was an astonishing

mid-movie sequence of nonstop action running for almost two reels. Starting with a montage of Dalton depredations, it picks them up in a big shoot-out in a small-town cafe from which they engineer their escape in a stagecoach, switch to the coach's horses when the sheriff's posse catches up, lead the posse a merry chase, abandon the horses in order to leap from overhanging cliffs onto a passing train which turns out to be full of lawmen, and from which they eventually escape via a stunt never duplicated since, leaping horses from the moving train. For twenty minutes, accompanied by Universal's best musical agitatoes and superb camera tracking, the pace never lets up, the tension wisely relaxed a little by a frequent return to bantering comedy interpolations. It's an excellent sequence, with far more vigor than one normally finds in an "A" Western.

Universal continued its "ensemble" format into 1941 with *Badlands of Dakota,* but the formula was beginning to wear a little thin. There was too much comedy from Andy Devine, Fuzzy Knight, and, of all people, Hugh Herbert, and for the first time, production values were bolstered by stock footage. However, Universal sustained the formula for a few more years, spread over minor but efficient programmers like *Men of Texas, The Daltons Ride Again,* and *Frontier Badmen,* the last rather straining for stellar prestige by giving Diana Barrymore one of the feminine leads, and by giving Lon Chaney's entirely routine if somewhat uncouth second-string villain special billing which promised as a kind of guest star bonus, "And Lon Chaney, Jr., as Chango the Mad Killer." Apart from a sustained high level in its "B" series, Universal's other Western output in the early forties was sporadic. The studio seemed satisfied to let its fairly small yet ambitious *sounding* programmers (*Men of Texas* dealt with post–Civil War conflicts, *Badlands of Dakota* brought in Hickok, Calamity Jane, and General Custer) coast on the reputations earned by its competitors' bigger product.

Universal's *The Lady From Cheyenne* (1941) was strong on names (Loretta Young, Robert Preston, and Edward Arnold, with Frank Lloyd directing) but weak in interest and drama despite its potentially novel story of a fight for women's rights in the West. *Ride 'Em Cowboy* was one of the most enjoyable Abbott and Costello frolics, but in spite of the presence of Dick Foran, Johnny Mack Brown, and Bob Baker, it was basically A & C slapstick and musical formula as before, with none of the inspired spoofing of *Trail of the Vigilantes.* Oddly enough, the film's one major action sequence near the end was cut in half for its British release, probably because it suddenly looked too much like a "B" Western and kept Abbott and Costello off the screen for too long a stretch. *Can't Help Singing* (1944), a pleasing Deanna

Durbin musical, was notable mainly for bringing the West and Technicolor together at Universal. Despite its theme of a wagon trek West, it was dull going, the panoramas of the wide open spaces only illustrating how little was happening in them. In the latter half of the forties, however, Universal would match medium budgets with medium stars (Rod Cameron, Yvonne de Carlo), and with the addition of Technicolor come up with a slick and agreeable "A" product which would remain a backbone of its output throughout the fifties.

Considering the enormous public interest in the Western in the early forties, it is surprising that so little real enterprise was shown in investigating and, if you like, exploiting the potential of the Western background. One cannot read a history book on the American West and the Indian without finding frequent reference to, and discussion of, Manifest Destiny. Whether Hollywood was afraid of the term as sounding too intellectual, or figured that by killing off Indians en masse it was covering the same ground anyway, it certainly never even referred to the phase as an explanation or apology for the decimation of the Indian. And the awesome space of the West was seldom used as anything but a dramatic and exciting backdrop. True, in that context, it was sometimes used creatively. The forbidding, unassailable cliffs of New Mexico in which the hero is trapped and killed in Raoul Walsh's *Colorado Territory* are in a sense a parallel to the Great Wall in Fritz Lang's silent *Destiny*. The framing of space, as we have noted earlier, was used in different ways and for different purposes, by William S. Hart and John Ford. No Western, however, used the awesomeness of Western space as a theme in itself. Perhaps only the Europeans, used to the more confined and boundaried space there (the Lake District in England, the Swiss Alps), were *really* impressed by the West's breathtaking size. While American painters Charles Russell and Frederic Remington caught the excitement and poetry of the West, and in the case of Russell, a wonderful sense of immediacy and movement, it was the European painters like Bierstadt who captured its majesty and the wonderment of its sheer size. Indeed, it was the European painters and photographers, going into the West and creating stylized and sometimes romanticized images and panoramas, who sold Congress on the idea of establishing National Parks out of such major tracts of land as Yellowstone and Yosemite.

There's a tremendous story to be told of such vision and the problems of bringing it to reality, yet it never has been told on film. One would have thought that the forties, when a pride in one's country and heritage was again in fashion, was the ideal time to do that. After all, there was no drama whatsoever in the construction of the Western Union telegraph system. It was simply a matter of stringing wire, endlessly and boringly, without opposition, across a near wilderness. When 20th Century-Fox filmed *Western Union* in 1941, its Zane Grey source had to fake up Indian opposition and a William S. Hart type of redemption plot in order to add cinematic excitement to a bland historic event. But the development of the National Parks was hardly bland, even if lacking in traditional villains, and could have made, with or without interpolated Hollywood poetic license, an inspiring film. In fact it still could. But to Hollywood in the early forties, it was showmanship and excitement that came first and foremost.

Virginia City, Warners' follow-up to *Dodge City*, reverting to black and white, and a more historical Civil War milieu, starred Errol Flynn again, this time opposed by Randolph Scott, representing the South, and Humphrey Bogart, representing only himself as a none-too-convincing Mexican bandit. It was slow in getting underway, but the money saved on the Technicolor treatment was put to good use in better scripting and generally superior production values. Interestingly, Flynn seemed to be following the casting formula of the "B" Westerns by using tough but comic buddies. Alan Hale and Guinn "Big Boy" Williams had filled those roles in *Dodge City*, and did so again in *Virginia City* and a third entry, *Santa Fe Trail*, best of the three in terms of story and overall values, though highly suspect in its historic detail. Raymond Massey took center stage in the first of his two movie incarnations of abolitionist John Brown, and the film's climax was a well-staged reconstruction of the battle at Harper's Ferry. Curiously, *Santa Fe Trail* seemed unwilling to take sides on the slavery issue, conveniently having stars Errol Flynn (as Jeb Stuart) and Ronald Reagan (as Custer) offer opposing but nonpassionate views, and presenting Brown as a sincere zealot but also as something of a madman, so that the rights and wrongs of the matter from his point of view seemed almost irrelevant.

For sheer length and size, Warners outdid itself with its next Flynn epic, *They Died With Their Boots On*, incidentally the first big one that Flynn had done away from Michael Curtiz. He had had a falling out with Curtiz, primarily over that director's cavalier disregard for safety where extras and horses were concerned. Raoul Walsh took over, turning it into almost a companion piece to his 1939 film, *The Roaring 20's*. In that one, Walsh had taken a seminostalgic look back at the gangster era, tracing it from World War I, through the twenties and into the Depression. It was the first gangster film that wasn't in some way a contemporary story, using music and glasses that were a trifle rose-colored to look back with fondness at cause and effect. In *They Died With Their Boots On*, Walsh did much the same

Rangers of Fortune (Paramount, 1940): Albert Dekker, Gilbert Roland, Fred MacMurray, Richard Alexander, and player

Dark Command (Republic, 1940): John Wayne gets the drop on Roy Rogers and Walter Pidgeon

North West Mounted Police (Paramount, 1940): Gary Cooper and Madeleine Carroll

North West Mounted Police: Paulette Goddard and Robert Preston in a typical DeMille studio "exterior"

Arizona (Columbia, 1940): The Union troops retreat from Tucson

Arizona: Director Wesley Ruggles with star Jean Arthur

kind of thing, turning it into a colorful cavalcade that started with events leading up to the Civil War, the war itself and its aftermath, and the opening up of the West and gradually increasing warfare with the Indians.

The film was long, all of its major roles filled by major actors (including Sydney Greenstreet, Arthur Kennedy, Walter Hampden, and Anthony Quinn), its many sets handsomely and elaborately designed, its considerable action footage highlighted by Custer's Civil War glories and climaxed of course by the spectacle of the famous Last Stand, a sequence that lacked nothing in size and staging. Yet it somehow fell short of the similar climactic sequence in *The Charge of the Light Brigade,* which among other things was more creative in its use of glass shots and dynamic editing, though also far less humane in its treatment of the horses. Even though recent revisionist views of Custer have made the film's depiction of him seem even more distorted than it was conceded to be in 1941, much of it, due to skillful writing and playing, holds up surprisingly well. Particularly effective is the poignant farewell scene between Custer and his wife, played by Olivia de Havilland. Knowing that he is on a suicide mission from which he cannot return, Custer talks of their happy life together and of the happiness that still lies ahead, and contrives to tear a button from his tunic ostensibly for her to sew back on "later," but in actuality a remembrance of their last meeting. It may be Hollywood scripting rather than bona fide history, but it is a beautifully done scene. (Raoul Walsh was able to switch from rambunctious action and vulgarity to sensitive tenderness almost without pause; it's a scene that, even given the same script and players, Curtiz would probably not have pulled off nearly as well). It's also one of those scenes that often takes on a life and quality of its own, one peculiar to movies. Certainly today it has added meaning and sadness because it was the last scene that Errol Flynn and Olivia de Havilland—screen partners for eight movies ever since they were first united in *Captain Blood* (1935)—would ever play together. It was not known then of course that the vagaries of Hollywood casting and contractual destinies would prevent further costarring appearances. Thus, in its own way, the parting scene has a kind of truth that has surfaced only through the years, making it timelessly touching.

They Died With Their Boots On was the last of the Warner spectaculars for a long time, many of its Westerns soon becoming standardized products and, by the end of the forties (and into the early fifties) often mere programmers of seventy minutes or less—vehicles for such now slipping stars as Flynn, Dennis Morgan, and Gary Cooper (whose "slipping" periods were usually followed by "comeback" films like *High Noon*).

When the Daltons Rode (Universal, 1940): Excellent stunt work in a train holdup sequence from this George Marshall Western

215

Throughout the rest of the forties, the studio's best Westerns fell into groups other than historical ones: the action-oriented *South of St. Louis* with Joel McCrea, or *The Younger Brothers*, little more than a "B," but now spruced up with a new and increased use of Technicolor, and several by Raoul Walsh: *Cheyenne, Silver River* and two superb and genuinely *film noir* Westerns, *Pursued* (with *noir* icon Robert Mitchum in an almost Freudian Western) and better still, *Colorado Territory*, a faithful, undistorted remake of Walsh's own earlier Bogart gangster classic, *High Sierra*. Among other assets, *Colorado Territory* offered the best train holdup sequence since *When the Daltons Rode* and was almost documentarian in its detailing of how to pull off such a caper successfully. And while its climax was essentially a repeat of the ending to *High Sierra*, it seemed also to build on, and benefit from, audience foreknowledge that it was a hopeless climax, audience awareness partly based on the similarity of the interim-released *Duel in the Sun*. Above all, the basic decency of Joel McCrea as the Western badman, and the apparent freedom offered by the spaciousness of the West, made the inevitable doomed climax seem all the more tragic. The gangster film and the Western have always been closely related, and many crime and gangster films (*Kiss of Death, The Asphalt Jungle*) as well as films from other genres (*The Sea Wolf, House of Strangers, Sahara, The Lost Patrol*) have been effectively remade as Westerns. But few have made the changeover as *naturally* as *Colorado Territory* which is also unique in being at least arguably superior to the original.

Only in *San Antonio* (1945, directed by David Butler) did Warners return to the super-scale, nearly two hour Technicolor special format for Errol Flynn. It was too big and too long, and having Victor Francen play the chief villain, a role that would normally have been played by Harry Woods in a "B," couldn't conceal the fact that it was a "B" at heart if not in fact. But its climax, a huge-scale and even overwrought gun battle that starts in a saloon and spreads into the streets and the ruins of the Alamo is a real humdinger, and even follows the pattern of the "B" by letting the surviving villain (Paul Kelly) escape, allowing for a prolonged horseback chase as Flynn pursues and subdues him in a final stunt/horseback/fistic bout. Hardly an important Western, *San Antonio* was so big, so colorful, so full of favorite faces ranging from S.Z. Sakall to Monte Blue, that it left a pleasant taste in the mouth just as Westerns were beginning to get smaller and more serious.

The epics from the other companies were extremely variable. Columbia's *Arizona* (1940) not only was the studio's first super-Western, but also returned director Wesley Ruggles to the Western for the first time since *Cimarron*, and no more successfully. Its attention to detail was commendable, the reconstruction of old Tucson realistically done (it saw service in subsequent movies, and eventually became a tourist attraction), and some of the scenes of mass movement, the Union troops' evacuation of Tucson, for example, well organized. But it was a slow, tedious work, the footage devoted to the personal stories of the somewhat uninteresting principals swamping what should have been dominant themes: the development of the territory of Arizona, and the too-often overlooked contributions of *women* to the opening up of the West. Ironically, Jean Arthur, who had convincingly played standard Western ingenues in Wally Wales silents at the beginning of her career, was three times called upon to play pioneer women in major Westerns, and each time failed to shake her thoroughly modern image. Here, as freight-hauling business woman Phoebe Titus she was somewhat less artificial than she had been as Calamity Jane in *The Plainsman*, but not much. A decade later, she was considerably better in *Shane*, but still miscast. In the long run, the basic contribution of *Arizona* turned out to be as a supplier of stock footage for "B" Westerns and serials from its nighttime Indian raid and cattle stampede sequences.

Texas, which followed, also starred William Holden (partnered by Glenn Ford and Claire Trevor), and likewise played down its epic potential, but intentionally. Its plot had little to do with the growth of Texas as cattle country, and none of it was shot there, Columbia's studio Western street, carefully photographed from different angles, serving not only as Abilene, Kansas, but also as Texas trail towns. As if to make up for the plodding quality of *Arizona*, director George Marshall filled *Texas* with traditional Western action, including a spectacular town-wrecking stampede climax in which the hero's stunt double makes his way through the melee by hanging from the tail of a marauding steer, and with slapstick and grisly black humor. One of its most endearing qualities was the use of Edgar Buchanan (then less familiar as a Walter Brennan substitute) as the mastermind villain who also happened to be the town's dentist. Columbia was to make more and more grade "A" Westerns as the forties progressed, but all of them, despite the added use of Technicolor and star names in such films as *The Man From Colorado, The Desperadoes*, and *Renegades*, were as standardized, in their own way, as the studio's prolific output of "B's."

MGM's only genuine epic of the forties was King Vidor's *North West Passage*, hardly a Western in the accepted sense, though notable in its refusal to gloss over the horrors of any kind of warfare, and in repudiating the Seventh Cavalry romanticism in its grim Indian fighting scenes. The Robert Taylor "remake" of Vidor's *Billy the*

Kid was not only different but vastly inferior, notable mainly for its striking use of color and one lively chase sequence. MGM, as did RKO, made a number of "pocket" epics with James Craig, one of the forties' major hopefuls for replacing if not dethroning a called-to-the-colors Clark Gable. Through no obvious fault of his own, most of the Craig Westerns were total misfires, ranging from MGM's *Gentle Annie* to RKO's horrendously miscast and misguidedly comedic *Valley of the Sun,* which offered Lucille Ball and Cedric Hardwicke totally out of place in the West, and Tom Tyler as a grotesquely written Geronimo. MGM had much better luck with its periodic Wallace Beery Westerns such as *Wyoming* and *Bad Bascomb* which, even though often mawkishly sentimental (especially when Beery costarred with Margaret O'Brien!) were often superbly photographed (usually by Clyde de Vinna) and did have major action set pieces.

Fox's success with *Jesse James* naturally prompted a sequel, *The Return of Frank James,* likewise in Technicolor, and equally naturally, the two were eventually reissued together as a combination. In the original *Jesse James,* Tyrone Power was all warmth and nobility, with none of the mean killer instinct that apparently characterized the real Jesse, and it was easy for Henry Fonda's quiet, authoritative performance as Frank James (a more likable character in fact, and a more interesting one filmically) to take over the movie. That Fonda was a poor rider hardly mattered since the James boys were farmers until forced into outlawry. Fonda starred again in *The Return of Frank James,* one of a brace of Westerns made for Fox by Fritz Lang. Lang's black humor and his perennial habit of making his villains far more colorful than his heroes later brought some real style to *Western Union,* but he was hamstrung by the Production Code with *The Return of Frank James.* The story dealt with Frank's attempts to avenge the murder of Jesse by Bob Ford (John Carradine), but since the Code expressly forbade themes of revenge, Fonda was forced into a passive role and the retribution left to a lesser character, played by Jackie Cooper, who was allowed to be "amoral" since he paid for his indiscretions with his life. (Lang was able to redress the balance a little with a fifties Western, *Rancho Notorious,* in which the revenge theme was so dominant that it could not be diverted, and was allowable because virtually everybody wound up dead! It was surely no coincidence that a ballad sung during the credits concluded with the emphasized words ". . . *hate, murder* and *revenge*" just as the credit "Directed by Fritz Lang" flashed on screen!)

Fox also offered *Brigham Young*—quickly retitled *Brigham Young, Frontiersman* to snare the action crowd along with the Mormons—a reasonably accurate account of the Mormon wagon trek to Salt Lake, with Dean Jagger cast as Young, though Tyrone Power, in a smaller role, got top billing. Its opening sequences of religious persecution were far more dramatic and powerful than the later pilgrimage footage, although director Henry Hathaway made smooth use of interpolated footage from *The Big Trail.* Harry Sherman's production of *Buffalo Bill,* directed by William Wellman, included a well-done battle in a river between Indians and cavalrymen (later included as stock in many other Westerns, and always recognizable because of the water splashing right on to the camera lens!) but otherwise was slow, sentimental, and historically suspect, though at least partially salvaged by the dignity of Joel McCrea's playing. Wellman also directed Fox's *The Ox-Bow Incident* at this time, based on the Walter Van Tilburg Clark novel, and one of the few socially conscious Westerns of the early forties. It came into being partially because both Henry Fonda and William Wellman wanted to do it, and made its production a condition of their signing for other commitments, and also because under a wartime economy, when the most unlikely films were being made, it stood a good chance of breaking even or perhaps showing a small profit. Although an interesting experiment, extremely close to both the spirit and content of the novel, and exceptionally well cast (with players like Jane Darwell, Dana Andrews, and Francis Ford playing against *type,* as opposed to William Eythe, Paul Hurst, and Frank Conroy, expertly cast *to* type), it didn't entirely come off. Its uncompromising study of a lynching was told mainly via dialogue in studio sets which didn't jell with the few action exteriors of the posse riding, presumably shot as a false come-on for the trailers. Its main weakness was a climactic scene designed to use Fonda (heretofore kept commendably on the sidelines, where his character belonged) in a mildly upbeat ending, by having him read aloud a letter written by one of the lynch victims. In the novel, the letter was never read, allowing the reader to use his own imagination and emotion. In the film, the viewer loses that privilege, and scenarist Lamar Trotti's letter becomes his personal and rather Hollywoodian letter, perhaps trading on Fonda's sincere delivery of a Sacco-Vanzetti letter as a climactic set piece of *The Male Animal.* It's a disappointing footnote to a remarkable (for its time) film, although one that now seems more self-indulgent than inspired.

Fox, too, tended to let its Westerns slide after the early forties. True, with John Ford's magnificent *My Darling Clementine* in 1946—one of the loveliest Westerns ever made, if already a legendary distortion of the Wyatt Earp story—the studio could afford to rest on its laurels. But most of their other Westerns of the period drifted into

217

Western Union (20th Century-Fox, 1941)

Virginia City (1940): Randolph Scott and Errol Flynn

Kit Carson (1940) highlighted by a much bigger Indian raid on a covered wagon train than these few wagons and extras would indicate.

Bad Men of Missouri (Warner Bros., 1941): Arthur Kennedy, Dennis Morgan, and Wayne Morris as the Younger Brothers

The Spoilers (Universal, 1942): Randolph Scott, John Wayne, and Marlene Dietrich

The Kansan (United Artists, 1943): Another town-taming Western and a good one, starring Jane Wyatt and Richard Dix, here with Willie Best

The Great Man's Lady (Paramount, 1942): Barbara Stanwyck, Joel McCrea, and player in William Wellman's arty, interesting misfire, more soap opera than epic

Honky Tonk (MGM, 1941): Clark Gable and Lana Turner

Go West (MGM, 1940): Indians were, as usual, used as stooges in this Marx Brothers comedy

The Lady From Cheyenne (Universal, 1941): Robert Preston and Loretta Young

Wallace Beery made a major return to big-scale "good badman" Westerns at MGM in the forties.

the expert but formula pattern of Wellman's *Yellow Sky* (which plagiarized a key early scene from *The Ox-Bow Incident*) and Bruce Humberstone's *Fury at Furnace Creek*.

With one notable exception, Paramount spent money, time, big stars, and prestige directors on their initial super-Westerns of the forties, though generally with results less satisfactory than those achieved on a far less prolific output in the thirties. The film that fired the opening salvo was *Geronimo*, rushed into production in late 1939 to cash in on the Indian warrior who, thanks to *Stagecoach*, had acquired a new fame and topicality. *Geronimo* was a fascinating example of millions of dollars of accumulated production values being squandered on a mere programmer. (There had been some precedent for this kind of film in *The Last Outpost* (1935), in which Paramount had built an entire movie around key sequences lifted from four earlier Schoedsack–Cooper productions, but at least there had been a serviceable new story, good location work, and star value in Cary Grant and Claude Rains.) Every foot of major action material in *Geronimo* was lifted bodily from *The Plainsman, Wells Fargo,* and *The Texas Rangers,* with shorter scenes and establishing montages going back to footage from the silent *The Vanishing American, The Pony Express,* and *The Thundering Herd.* The plot itself, and all of the lead characters *except* Geronimo, were reworked from *The Lives of a Bengal Lancer* (1935).

Nobody had the gall to claim an individual story credit for this mélange, so it was bestowed on the director, Paul Sloane, who probably more than deserved it for his cunning in maneuvering around the old footage, principally via intercutting between it and cramped new studio sets created in front of a back projection screen, so that cavalrymen in 1939 footage could shoot Indians from 1936 footage! Even though much of it used was only a few years old, apparently nobody tumbled to the deception, such total effrontery being virtually unheard of in a major studio film at that time. Matching up was sometimes minimal (Indians in medium shots were actually Confederate troops in long shots lifted from *Wells Fargo*), and it was considered sufficient to dress one character like Fred MacMurray in *The Texas Rangers* before segueing into a sequence from that film where the MacMurray character climbs down a tall fir tree adjacent to high cliffs, or to have Andy Devine rather too pointedly insist on hitching up *mules* to a supply wagon before cutting in a major sequence from *The Plainsman.* (Devine drives off *alone*, but when the wagon reaches its mid-river destination in the older footage, there are clearly *three* men in the wagon!) The cast, made up mainly of lesser Paramount contractees without a major

star name among them, was notable mainly for being one of the few non-"B" movies to give Indian player Chief Thundercloud, any kind of a role. He played Geronimo, as he was to do later in the quickie *I Killed Geronimo*, which pillaged not only *Stagecoach* for footage, including the salt flats chase, but also history itself since Geronimo was *not* killed but died peacefully in captivity.

Gene Lockhart, as a gunrunning renegade, was given another opportunity for cringing and whining as only he knew how, while leading lady Ellen Drew, second billed (to Preston Foster) in a long cast, surely had the most nontaxing role in movie history. Given a word or two of dialogue at the very beginning of the film, she was promptly involved in a stagecoach wreck lifted from *Wells Fargo* and spent the rest of the movie in a hospital bed, suffering a deep coma from which she emerged only in the fadeout to smile bravely as her fiancé (William Henry, repeating the old Richard Cromwell role) is decorated for bravery. However, with DeMille, Vidor, Cruze, Lloyd, Howard, and other top directors unwittingly (and if they knew about it, unwillingly) contributing to the excitement, *Geronimo*, if nothing else, was not a dull movie.

Paramount's more ambitious new Westerns were less stingy with their budgets but also less productive of excitement. DeMille's *North West Mounted Police* was a star-laden, top-heavy, studio-bound expansion of the relatively minor Louis Riel rebellion in Canada. It was his first in Technicolor, apart from color sequences in his silents, and from now on all of his films would be made in that process. Long enough to be single-billed in most areas, it was also very slow, and only on those few occasions when it ventured into the genuine outdoors did it come to life. One stunt—Gary Cooper's double roping a Gatling gun and yanking it downhill behind him while on horseback—was warned off by experienced stuntmen as being too dangerous, and did in fact misfire, but provided one of the film's few real thrills in the process. *Rangers of Fortune* tried, futilely, to repeat the basic idea of *Three Godfathers* but in a more light-hearted vein, and with Fred MacMurray, Gilbert Roland, and Albert Dekker enterprisingly costarred, but the leaden direction of one of the dullest directors of all, Sam Wood, did it in. Putting its hottest new star, Alan Ladd, into a Western—*Whispering Smith*—was also, despite a good cast and story, a disappointment, though other Ladd Westerns followed and all did well at the box office.

The new version of *The Virginian*, now in Technicolor, remained a slow and somewhat tame production, but benefited from the starring presence of Joel McCrea who, surprisingly despite his suitability for the genre, was still far from being associated with Westerns. From

American Empire (United Artists, 1942): Despite its comedic look, this pocket epic of post-Civil War Texas had Leo Carrillo (center) as the *villain*, with Preston Foster (left) and Richard Dix

The Ox-Bow Incident (20th Century-Fox, 1943): Hank Bell, Anthony Quinn, Dick Rich, Dana Andrews, and Francis Ford

The Outlaw (United Artists, 1941, though released much later due to censorship problems): Jack Buetel, Walter Huston, and Jane Russell

Dakota (Republic, 1945): John Wayne, Ward Bond, and Vera Ralston

Duel in the Sun (Selznick, 1946): Gregory Peck, Jennifer Jones, and Joseph Cotten

Duel in the Sun: Harry Carey and Otto Kruger await the onslaught of Lionel Barrymore's giant posse of ranchers

The Virginian on, however, and despite a newly discovered flair for comedy under Preston Sturges, he would tend to specialize, profitably, in Westerns. Eventually, Paramount turned over much of its Western schedule to its "B" unit headed by producers Bill Pine and Bill Thomas, who were in the process of expanding into fairly safe "A" product. Their Westerns, *El Paso* and *Albuquerque,* using the economic Cinecolor process, were no great shakes either, but they did have good casts of Western veterans, were unpretentious, and delivered the action that the market wanted.

Although a slight disappointment at the time, both critically and at the box office, Samuel Goldwyn's *The Westerner* (1940) proved to be one of the most durable of the new Western cycle. Going into release at almost the same time as *North West Mounted Police* (in which Gary Cooper had played a Texas Ranger whose manhunt had led him into Canada), it helped reestablish Cooper as the preeminent star of grade "A" Westerns until overtaken by John Wayne. Carefully directed by William Wyler, it provided Gary Cooper with one of his best roles in a long while, and earned Walter Brennan another Academy Award for his performance as Judge Roy Bean. (Bean was later to have his own television series, and to provide an offbeat starring role for Paul Newman in a 1972 movie). Exceptionally well photographed, with some of the finest running inserts ever seen in an "A" Western, *The Westerner* was a sober, naturalistic film in which action (which was not a dominant factor) was handled in a restrained, sometimes deliberately clumsy fashion, never becoming a circus for stuntmen.

Another independent producer, Edward Small, came up with the pleasingly unpretentious *Kit Carson,* although its script was cluttered with too many romantic and comic interpolations, and rather vague allusions to aspects of California history that were never really spelled out. Unfortunately the budget seemed to run out just when it was needed most, and its climactic battle sequence fizzles out in a mass of evasions, studio economies, and back projection. But at least at the midway point, director George Seitz had had his big Indian battle. Beautifully shot and staged in impressive Monument Valley locations, it was the best "traditional" Indian battle—hordes of warriors surrounding a ring of covered wagons—since *The Big Trail.*

Although RKO Radio made no major contributions to the Western field in the forties, it maintained a high standard in serviceable, popular "A's." When the badman cycle had run its allotted span at the other companies, RKO emulated Universal (which gave new life to its somewhat jaded horror monsters by costarring them all!) by putting Belle Starr, the Daltons, the James Boys, and other miscreants into single films like *Badman's Terri-*

tory, where even collectively they were no match for town marshal Randolph Scott. Actually the best RKO Westerns of the forties were offshoots of other cycles. *Station West* was a tough mystery from a Luke Short story in which Dick Powell merely transferred his Philip Marlowe persona (and dialogue) to the West. Even better was *Tall in the Saddle,* one of the most enjoyable Westerns of the forties. It was sold as a straightforward action Western (the ads showed John Wayne rescuing Ella Raines from a runaway horse, a sequence that didn't exist in the film), but was actually another very solid mystery yarn, though it certainly made its necessary concessions to the Western format via two bruising, realistic fistfights, one between Wayne and Ward Bond, and another between Wayne and Harry Woods. Best of all was *Blood on the Moon.* Apart from its relatively happy ending, it was in mood, photographic treatment, and character delineation very much *film noir,* its action sharp and vicious, and a particularly well-photographed Robert Mitchum–Robert Preston fight in a deserted saloon at night being an outstanding highlight. It was beautifully directed by Robert Wise in one of the most interesting phases of his career, when he had been promoted from "B's" and was being given his head in not-too-costly "A's" (his best film ever, *The Set-Up,* was from this period) before eventually going on to the big prestige films.

Another notable Western *noir* of the forties was *Ramrod,* a tough, austere Joel McCrea Western, with Veronica Lake as a typical *noir* femme fatale. Its producer was Harry Sherman, who, with the Hopalong Cassidy "B" series as a base, branched out into quite enterprising bigger Westerns during the forties. Apart from the earlier-mentioned *Buffalo Bill,* a Fox release, Sherman's work was done primarily for Paramount, although in the early forties the studio found that it had overproduced and sold much completed product to United Artists. The Sherman contract for upcoming films was also turned over to United Artists. The earlier Sherman Paramounts included the interesting if misfiring *The Parson of Panamint* (which needed a stronger lead than Phillip Terry); *Tombstone, The Town Too Tough to Die,* with Richard Dix in another variation on the Wyatt Earp story; and another Dix vehicle, *Cherokee Strip,* a refreshingly lean, clean, well-locationed town-taming Western, although its eighty minutes seemed a trifle excessive.

The films coming out under the United Artists banner were all upgraded in terms of budget and cast and included *American Empire, Buckskin Frontier* (a model of how to make a pocket *The Iron Horse,* though *not* a model of expert doubling since the very slim David Sharpe took over for the quite chunky Richard Dix in a spectacular climactic fistic bout), *The Kansan,* more large-scale town-taming, and *Woman of the Town.* All except the last-named starred Richard Dix, with an unofficial stock company usually headed by Victor Jory, Jane Wyatt, and Albert Dekker. *Woman of the Town* promoted Dekker to stardom as an unlikely Bat Masterson, but the film was in essence a vehicle for Claire Trevor and an attempt to make a Western that was also a "Woman's Picture." The trade press applauded the novelty; the lay press deplored it. Actually it had just enough orthodox action to retain the traditional male trade, while the use of Barry Sullivan (then being groomed, ultimately unsuccessfully, as a new romantic leading man) as a likeable villain, further helped the distaff appeal. Thanks to its generally unorthodox qualities, it survives the years extremely well—save for one appalling example of name-dropping cuteness. A young lady reporter in Bat Masterson's office is advised to stick to her gossip column, and a follow-up line as subtle as a sledgehammer informs us that her name is Louella Parsons!

Harry Sherman liked Westerns, was willing to spend more than a normal budget to get good results, and Hitchcock-like, often played bits in his own films, not as a trademark, but just for the fun of being part of the action. His standards were high, and one of his most satisfying films of the forties was the second he made for the short-lived Enterprise Company (the other was *Ramrod*) which released through United Artists in America, and via MGM throughout Europe. This was *Four Faces West,* directed by Alfred E. Green, no Western specialist but a good all-around journeyman director, and starring Joel McCrea, Frances Dee, Charles Bickford, and Joseph Calleia. Today it would be succinctly described as a "feel-good movie," an idiotic phrase that nobody would have dreamed of using in the forties when so many movies successfully pursued that intent. Advertised as a Western in which no shot was fired—true, though not as much of a novelty as might be supposed—its lack of traditional villainy and mayhem, and an above-normal quota of sentiment in no way lessened its tension and dramatic interest, thanks mainly to the playing of the four leads, and most specifically that of Joel McCrea.

However, as the forties progressed, and despite the merit of individual films like *Four Faces West,* the smaller "A" Western gradually came to need an extra ingredient to sustain its box office value, and so color came to be more and more of a staple. Universal and Columbia in particular increased their output of medium-budget Westerns in the eight-reel range and featuring such stars as Randolph Scott, Rod Cameron, and Joel McCrea, and some like *Saddle Tramp* (Mc-

My Darling Clementine (20th Century-Fox, 1946): John Ford's return to the Western, with Walter Brennan, Grant Withers, and John Ireland as the leader of the Clantons and Henry Fonda as Wyatt Earp

Pirates of Monterey (Universal, 1946): Rod Cameron, Maria Montez, and Gilbert Roland in one of the first of Universal's "minor A" Technicolor Westerns

Crea) and *Frontier Gal* (Cameron) were exceptionally good. *Frontier Gal,* made by the relatively new Fessier–Pagano writing and producing team, was a most enjoyable welding of fast and furious Western action with

The Virginian (Paramount, 1946): The second talkie version, with Sonny Tufts (seated left), Joel McCrea, and Brian Donlevy

Can't Help Singing (Universal, 1944): Deanna Durbin and Robert Paige

comedy and a not-overdone element of suggestive sex. Because the framing was so lighthearted and mildly self-mocking, it even allowed itself to go a mite overboard in its cliff-hanging climax, where the plight of the hero's young daughter—clutching a teetering log over a yawning chasm—was intercut with the chase and fight stuff. Made before television became a really serious form of competition, these expensive-looking Westerns were actually fairly economical to produce, and also proved useful experimental grounds for the various cheaper new color systems that were being introduced, among them Cinecolor, Anscocolor, and Trucolor. However, while overall they proved to be an effective answer to the cheaper Western fare seen on a television that was still in black and white in that medium's earlier days, their very quality, and the fact that they were used as double-bill fodder, especially in the bigger cities, hastened the decline of the standard "B" Western.

At the beginning of the forties, the "B" Western too had benefited from the resurgence of audience interest in the genre. It was still possible to make them economically, with style, and for every dollar expended to show up on the screen. Republic was at its peak, not only producing the Gene Autry series (including some of the best of them, such as *Call of the Canyon*), the Roy Rogers, and The Three Mesquiteer series, but also regularly introducing new stars (Sunset Carson, Allan Lane, Red Barry) and reutilizing well-established ones (Bob Livingston, Bill Elliott). They remained essentially formula movies, more action than originality of plot, but within their own self-imposed boundaries, they were expertly done and made by some of the best directors in the field, Lesley Selander and William Witney in particular, with John English, Frank MacDonald, Thomas Carr, and (occasionally) Yakima Canutt backing them up. And since Republic still had John Wayne for a series of big budget Westerns (*In Old Oklahoma, Dakota*) which occasionally offered a real surprise treat—Wayne's own production of *Angel and the Badman* was a minor classic—it remained very much the leader in the field.

Monogram was also improving the overall quality of its product, most notably in the *Rough Riders* series which costarred Buck Jones, Tim McCoy, and Raymond Hatton, and were initially produced by Scott Dunlap whose films, Western or otherwise, always had that little extra care and polish that makes all the difference in low-budget production. The *Rough Riders* series placed more emphasis on plot and characterization than action, but the first three at least—*Arizona Bound, The Gunman from Bodie,* and *Forbidden Trails*—had a nice balance of both, plus well chosen locations and a willingness to spend a little more money than usual on the

Canyon Passage (Universal, 1946): Ward Bond and Dana Andrews

creation of new musical scores. Though the later ones became disappointingly standardized, and the series was brought to a close by the tragic death of Buck Jones, it remains one of the most interesting of the newer series. Moreover, its popularity inspired a number of imitations, most notably Monogram's own *Trail Blazers* and *Range Busters* series. Both of these groups were lamentably lacking in the finesse of their Dunlap produced predecessor; production values were often slipshod, the musical scores by Frank Sanucci were repetitious and (to be charitable) unmelodic, and their stories merely pegs on which to hang action, many of them loose remakes of earlier Monogram "B's." However, they *were* fast-moving, and attracted a certain amount of loyalty from Western fans by their use of old favorites.

The *Range Busters* films, clearly a rip-off from Republic's *Three Mesquiteers* series, with the same kind of action-romance-comic relief ingredients built into the three-star lineup, even included two of the stars from the original Mesquiteer films, Ray Corrigan and Max Terhune. Rather better, thanks mainly to the stars involved, were the *Trail Blazers* films which initially costarred Ken Maynard and Hoot Gibson, and later added Bob Steele to make up a formidable trio. Although the publicity claimed that these veteran stars were still scorning doubles, the use of Cliff Lyons and other stuntmen in the action scenes was readily apparent, though Bob Steele was still in fine condition and produced some truly spectacular leaps into the saddle in *Death Valley Rangers*. Maynard was by now rather clumsy, and his dialogue delivery was more self conscious than ever, but Gibson had maintained a relatively slim build, a naturalistic acting style and his familiar sense of humor. Both he and Maynard still did much of their own riding, especially in the running inserts. Use of doubles in Westerns is, in any case, not entirely a matter of ability or lack of it. Expediency is also a consideration since a second-unit can be shooting doubles in long-shot action scenes while the main unit does the dialogue, close-up, and studio scenes.

Monogram's *Cisco Kid* series started off rather weakly with Duncan Renaldo in three lackluster entries, but for once Monogram reversed its usual procedure, brought in producer Dunlap, upped the budget, replaced Renaldo with Gilbert Roland, and not only salvaged the series but also turned it into an entirely superior one. The Ciscos of Roland had genuine charm, a quality not often found in smaller Westerns, pictorial qualities were often exceptional and even near-poetic in the first of the series, *The Gay Cavalier,* and action, while never excessive, was often extremely well staged. Together with the first one, *Beauty and the Bandit* was probably the best of this quite underrated series. (Duncan Renaldo returned

Blood on the Moon (RKO, 1948): Robert Mitchum and Barbara Bel Geddes

Pursued (Warner Bros., 1947): Robert Mitchum

Red River (United Artists, 1948): John Wayne and Montgomery Clift

Colorado Territory (Warner Bros., 1949): Henry Hull, Virginia Mayo (in an astonishingly good performance), and Joel McCrea in Walsh's remake of *High Sierra*

Raoul Walsh, director of some of the finest Westerns, from *The Big Trail* to *Pursued* and *Colorado Territory*

to the role for a later theatrical series, and also enjoyed a long-running popularity in a subsequent television series, many of the entries directed by the veteran Lambert Hillyer.)

Jimmy Wakely, in a variable and generally pedestrian, but at least smoothly produced group of musical Westerns, and later, Whip Wilson, in a so-so series, also bolstered the Monogram outdoor schedule in the forties, but Monogram's longest running series was one costarring Johnny Mack Brown and Raymond Hatton. Considering that they were specifically designed to replace the Rough Riders films following Buck Jones's death, and that in inheriting Brown, a top-liner, from Universal, it had a real prestige name to offer, the Monograms were surprisingly small scale and unambitious at the outset. Some sixty-six of them were made (Raymond Hatton dropping out toward the end) and the first ones were clearly inheriting scripts designed for the Rough Riders. Nevertheless, it was a pleasing series. The early ones such as *Outlaws of Stampede Pass* and *Six Gun Gospel* were somewhat shy on action, especially in comparison with Brown's frenetic Universal series, but later ones, influenced by the private eye films of the period, offered tougher pseudo-Chandler dialogue and rougher and more frequent action scenes. *The Gentleman From Texas,* produced by Dunlap and directed by

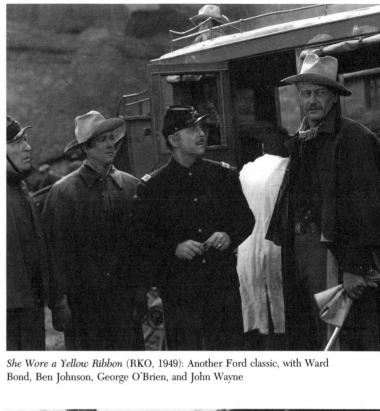

She Wore a Yellow Ribbon (RKO, 1949): Another Ford classic, with Ward Bond, Ben Johnson, George O'Brien, and John Wayne

The Kid From Texas (Universal, 1949): Audie Murphy as Billy the Kid and Albert Dekker

Colorado Territory: Joel McCrea in front of the forbidding, escape-proof rock cliffs that remind one of the expressionistic wall in Fritz Lang's *Destiny*

Massacre River (Allied Artists, 1949): This climactic shot from a good medium-budgeter was slightly different in the final release, since one of the four observers at right died in an alternate ending

Big Jack (MGM, 1949): Wallace Beery's last scene in his last movie, with Charles Dingle and Vince Barnett among the players on the left, Marjorie Main and Richard Conte flanking Beery, and Vanessa Brown at right

Lambert Hillyer, was exceptionally strong and quite the best of this interesting if unremarkable series.

RKO continued to make the best and most polished Western "B's." George O'Brien was still turning out exceptionally high quality films *(Bullet Code, Stage to Chino)* until he left for war service. Tim Holt took over, his slim build and extreme youthfulness making him seem at first a somewhat immature substitute for the beefy O'Brien. But the films themselves maintained the usual polished RKO production values, and as Tim Holt put on a little more weight, he became a more convincing opponent to RKO's crew of veteran heavies, headed by the venerable Harry Woods. The Holt films continued for more than a decade, and included some genuinely outstanding "B's," topped perhaps by *The Arizona Ranger,* giving costar billing to Tim's father, Jack, and casting them in father-son roles, and *Under the Tonto Rim,* bearing virtually no resemblance to the Zane Grey novel from which it claimed to be adapted, but an excellent job nonetheless. A brief Zane Grey series offered Robert Mitchum in two (*West of the Pecos* and the first-rate *Nevada*) and the unimpressive James Warren in several others. The series didn't run long, but Grey properties owned by RKO continued to turn up as titles, if not as bona fide adaptations, in the Holts.

Ownership of several Zane Grey properties also caused 20th Century-Fox to begin a fresh series of Westerns in the early forties to bolster the last days of the studio's Cisco Kid adventures with Cesar Romero, which were films strong in casts and elaborate production values, but by their very nature mild in action content. The first Zane Grey, the many-times-filmed *Riders of the Purple Sage,* was that rare animal, a remake superior to at least some of its predecessors. In less than an hour, it packed in all of Grey's complicated plot (the same basic script seemed to have been used for all four versions, but this one was easier to follow than the others, perhaps through familiarity), managed to prevent the unusually large collection of complex characters from getting in each other's way, and offered good photography and locations and plenty of action. It was a "class" production all the way, lacking (surprisingly) only the finesse of a musical score. George Montgomery, a former stuntman and Western bit player, starred, and was promptly put into another Grey, curiously not the *Sage* sequel, *The Rainbow Trail,* but the old reliable *The Last of the Duanes.* It was slightly below the standard of its predecessor, but was still well above average. However, Montgomery, like Mitchum over at RKO, was almost immediately elevated to bigger picture stardom. A new discovery, ex-footballer John Kimbrough, took over at Fox. His two, *The Lone Star Ranger* and *Sundown Jim,* sustained the same solid values, but he didn't click personally, and the series was dropped. *Riders of the Purple Sage* has not been remade in the more than half-century since, leaving perpetually unsolved the great mystery of how a single rock, toppled to start an

Arizona Bound (Monogram, 1941) launched the new Rough Riders series costarring Buck Jones, Tim McCoy, and Raymond Hatton

Blazing Guns (Monogram, 1943) brought old-timers Ken Maynard and Hoot Gibson together as the Trail Blazers, with Bob Steele later added to make a trio

avalanche, can so *totally* seal off an entire valley that hero and heroine must expect to spend the rest of their lives there, happily, but with little outlet for energy and enterprise. (The sequel *did* rescue them, hauling them up the sheer cliff face via ropes, but it didn't solve or explain that very unlikely geographic premise.)

Columbia continued to grind out strictly formula Westerns, in the early forties doubling up their stars so that Charles Starrett and Russell Hayden appeared in one group, Bill Elliott and Tex Ritter in another. Action fans had no complaints. There were often five or six fistfights per movie (usually without even a trace of blood or bruises) and as many chases, but not surprisingly the plots were not of the strongest. Also, one could always tell which company made a Western just by listening to the sound effects. Columbia's effects for gunshots, fisticuffs, and galloping hooves had a cheap, unrealistic sound to them, suggestive of amplification in an echo chamber. However, they did their job well enough and many of them are interesting today for the small part players and stuntmen who appeared in them—Lloyd Bridges and Ben Johnson, for example— before attaining stardom. Directors on the Columbias were workmanlike, usually chosen for their experience (Lambert Hillyer) or their speed (Sam Nelson, William Berke). The only one to show signs of real care and extra effort in editing and compositional effects was Joseph H. Lewis, who handled several of the Starrett and Elliott vehicles to notably worthwhile and upgraded results. In *Texas Stagecoach*, a Charles Starrett, he even brought a prosaic song number by the Sons of the Pioneers to creative life by having them sing it while digging holes for and erecting a fence, cheerfully plagiarizing the famous "Paris Awakening" sequence at the beginning of Rouben Mamoulian's classic *Love Me Tonight* by creating a symphony of fast-cut natural sounds (pick axes, hammers) to interweave with the song!

The quality of Columbia's Westerns declined steadily during the forties as production costs rose, until Gene Autry, forming his own production unit, transferred from Republic (where his postwar films were not befitting his status, and seemed deliberately designed to keep him a second-stringer to Roy Rogers) and launched a new series at Columbia. Not surprisingly they were designed to be entirely different from his Republic format: the plots were more sober, the musical element

Black Market Hustlers (Monogram, 1943): A new Range Busters trio cheerfully plagiarized the Three Mesquiteers, who were still going strong. Two of the original Mesquiteers, Ray Corrigan and Max Terhune, were teamed with Dennis Moore (right), though later both John King and David Sharpe filled in the third spot. Wartime Westerns had a lot of anti-Axis propaganda

whole was shoddy, and its Westerns fast but totally lacking in polish, let alone subtlety. The exploitation of Cinecolor gave PRC's Eddie Dean series a commercial edge over the others, and production values reflected the added box office expectations, but Dean was never as popular as anticipated and his films eventually reverted

Lone Star Trail (Universal, 1942). Three scenes from a typical Universal Western stress the series' rugged action content. In the first, Johnny Mack Brown battles newcomer Robert Mitchum; in the second, a bulldogging leads into a fight scene, the third, between Mitchum and Fred Graham (**below**) doubling the heavy

much reduced, the general tone subdued and realistic, and the action more elaborate. The first, *The Last Round-Up, Strawberry Roan,* and *Loaded Pistols,* were the best and at a time when production standards in Westerns generally were on a downhill path, impressed both exhibitors and audiences. Their extra length and budgets almost belied their "B" category, and in time, Autry was forced to curtail both. The films became more standardized, but he did maintain good quality until the end. Columbia's final Charles Starrett Westerns, shot in as little as three days, directed by the third-rate Ray Nazarro, and loaded with stock footage, seemed doubly poor in comparison with the Autrys.

PRC (Producers Releasing Corporation), a new company set up along the lines of Monogram, offering a more vigorous but distinctly cheaper product, established itself in the early forties. It attracted a large number of reputable Western stars—Tim McCoy, Buster Crabbe, Bob Livingston, Bob Steele, and Tex Ritter—along with some lesser ones—George Houston, James Newill, Dave O'Brien, Bill Boyd (a radio singer, not the still active Hopalong Cassidy star), Lash LaRue, and Eddie Dean. While some of the earlier McCoy and Crabbe Westerns were good, the studio's output as a

Hoppy Serves a Writ (United Artists, 1943): In one of the best of the Hopalong Cassidy Westerns, Jay Kirby and William Boyd rescue Andy Clyde from Robert Mitchum, in another early villain role

Man From Montana (Universal, 1941): Nell O'Day made a particularly attractive hard-riding heroine in several of the Johnny Mack Browns

Heart of the Golden West (Republic, 1942): The first of the upped-budget Roy Rogers specials was also one of several in which he was teamed with a pert firecracker of a heroine in Ruth Terry

Two of the most popular clichés of the "B" got a good going-over in the forties: in *Prairie Schooners* (Columbia, 1940), the villain is dunked in the horse trough by hero Bill Elliott, and in *Texas Trouble Shooters* (Monogram, 1942), bartender Dick Cramer watches suspiciously as hero Ray Corrigan pours a glass of milk

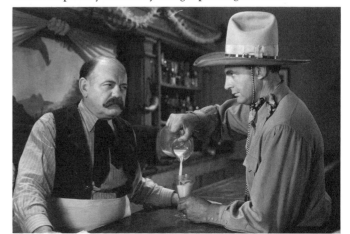

to black and white. Of this move, a blasé New York *Daily News* critic was moved to comment: "Eddie Dean's latest is in black and white rather than color, but the improvement is hardly noticeable; you can still see him." In retrospect, the lack of enthusiasm for Dean seems a

Murder on the Yukon (Monogram, 1940): James Newill and Dave O'Brien were a pleasing team in the economically-made but lively Renfrew series carrying over from the thirties

Sky Bandits (Monogram, 1940): Another Renfrew adventure, this was one of several Westerns sufficiently up to date to have a Death Ray. Dwight Fry (right), a *Frankenstein* graduate, seems more at home with the equipment than Kenneth Duncan, Bob Terry, and William Pawley, among other heavies

Texas Stagecoach (Columbia, 1940): One of the superior "B's" directed by Joseph H. Lewis, with Iris Meredith intervening between Charles Starrett and Bob Nolan, while members of the Sons of the Pioneers look on

Silver Stallion (Monogram, 1941): Interesting offbeat casting for a one-shot picture that might have been intended as a series, with Chief Thundercloud, stuntman David Sharpe, and LeRoy Mason (normally a villain) as an unusual costarring trio

trifle unfair. He *did* have a good singing voice, and had been around Westerns long enough (as a villain and support player in many of the Paramount "B's" of the late thirties) to seem at home in them. Certainly now he seems superior to many of the other late-comers like (particularly) Lash LaRue.

Like Republic, Universal was primarily concerned with a fast action format. Its Johnny Mack Brown series (which included an initial group with Bob Baker, and a final group costarring Tex Ritter) evolved an ultra-streamlined style in which such directors as Ray Taylor, Lewis D. Collins, and Ford Beebe slammed over the fights with tremendous gusto. Brown was in top form

and handled much of the action, including energetic leaps into the saddle and realistic fights, without an undue use of doubles. Universal built up an excellent library of chase and action music, made a fine art of the running insert, and for the most part didn't overdo the spasmodic interpolations of musical numbers and requisite, though seldom inspired, comedy relief from Fuzzy Knight. Nell O'Day, who appeared in many of the Brown Westerns (though surprisingly never as a romantic vis-à-vis) was pretty, a fine horsewoman, and a big asset to the series, a pleasant change from the usual passive and helpless heroine.

Although it was excellent entertainment for dyed-in-

The Topeka Terror (Republic, 1945): Frank Jacquet, Allan Lane, and Roy Barcroft in a typically slick Republic actioner

Red River Renegades (Republic, 1946): Sunset Carson and Edmund Cobb

the-wool fans, the sameness of this series was pointed up when a really imaginative director like Joseph H. Lewis—who had worked earlier on the Bob Baker films, and concurrently on some of the Columbia Westerns—was put to work in them. Lewis was a former editor, and it showed. In *Arizona Cyclone*, he broke down a simple confrontation between hero Brown and villain Dick Curtis into a series of tense shots, crosscut between hands poised over holstered guns, changed focus within a shot for added emphasis, and increased the speed and depth of his chase scenes by placing objects (trees, fences) between his camera truck on one level and his riders on another, higher one. *Arizona Cyclone* and others that he directed in the Brown series were perfect examples of how imagination and care could bring added excitement to familiar material without changing the script, though probably adding shooting time—which a man of Lewis's ingenuity could make up by later shooting a collection of scenes as one extended take. Best of the Brown series, apart from the Lewis entries, were *The Man From Montana, Stagecoach Buckaroo, West of Carson City, Law of the Range,* and *Riders of Pasco Basin,* though the overall standard remained remarkably high. As Universal gradually abandoned its "B" Westerns, the later ones starring Rod Cameron, Eddie Dew, and Kirby Grant were notably inferior, though a solitary Russell Hayden entry, *Frontier Law,* was an exception, and must have set some kind of record for virtually nonstop action.

By the end of the forties, the "B" Western scene had changed considerably. Independent Westerns had all but disappeared (though ultra-cheap ones would return briefly in the fifties, hoping to pick up the trade presumably left unserviced when all of the major Western series stopped entirely). Many of the former Western favorites

King of the Bandits (Monogram, 1947): Angela Greene with Gilbert Roland as The Cisco Kid

Sun Valley Cyclone (Republic, 1946): Edmund Cobb, Bobby Blake, and Bill Elliott in one of the Red Ryder series

Over the Santa Fe Trail (Columbia, 1947): Ken Curtis was wasted by Columbia in a series of weak hillbilly Western comedies; only later—and especially under John Ford—did his flair for action, *good* acting, *and* comedy become apparent

Wild Horse Mesa (RKO, 1947): Richard Martin, Nan Leslie, Tim Holt, and Jason Robards (Sr.) in the third filming of the Zane Grey story

were either dead, or in retirement. Quality had been seriously curtailed. Groups of eight per year had been cut to six, and one by one the series were being discontinued entirely, since, thanks to constantly rising production costs, it was impossible to maintain the former level of quality. The Hopalong Cassidy series that Harry Sherman had produced for United Artists earlier in the forties had been polished, actionful, well peopled with extras and good character actors, and shot in good locations. Now they were being produced by William Boyd himself with slim plots, meager action, a dearth of people and even livestock, and the skimpiest of sets. Boyd, older, went out of his way to turn over what action there was to his younger cohorts. Even the best of his own Hopalong Cassidys was barely up to the standards of the weaker Sherman produced entries.

Even the "look" of the "B" had changed: the bright, glossy, sunlit photography that had always characterized the Republics had been replaced by drab camera work in dull local locations, shot regardless of overcast skies, and apparently photographed (or processed) on cheaper film stock. A craftsman like William Witney could reject such standards on the still commercially important Roy Rogers films, but Republic had several Western series still running, and only *one* Witney. It was definitely the beginning of the end for the "B" Western.

Such handicaps were not, however, affecting the "A" Western as yet. (Indeed, another big boom period lay ahead in the fifties). The notoriety of Howard Hughes's *The Outlaw* (a slow film, sometimes an inept one, but by no means as bad as it is generally reputed to be) gained a further foothold for Sex in the West, and King Vidor's *Duel in the Sun* was a natural and superior successor to it. Forcibly expanded by producer David O. Selznick into becoming a would-be Western parallel to *Gone With the Wind*, it was literally too big and imbalanced a film for its own good—Vidor not helped by Selznick's constant tampering, bringing in directors like Dieterle and von Sternberg to shoot either tests or additional scenes, and having Orson Welles deliver a fanciful, semi-poetic spoken prologue. Nevertheless, the sheer size of *Duel in the Sun* for its own sake seemed not an inappropriate stance to take for a story about the growth of the great cattle empires in Texas. And its mass action scenes, particularly a huge-scale gathering of ranchers, to be confronted by a railroad gang and a troop of cavalry, were well organized and staged, while its sexual scenes had a raw, erotic flavor entirely missing from *The Outlaw*. Its use of color was daring and dynamic, and more intimate scenes, such as the impending execution of Herbert Marshall, and the death of Lillian Gish, showed Vidor at his sensitive best. And Jennifer Jones was never better photographed nor exuded more animal sexuality than as Pearl Chavez.

The film also included one masterly use of space. Midway, a long dialogue conversation takes place on the observation platform of a train. As the conversation, staged in tight close-up, comes to its conclusion, the train pulls slowly away to recede into endless space and towards the far horizon. Remaining in its fixed position, the camera picks up not only the vastness of the prairie, but also a herd of milling cattle which, previously unseen, now take over the foreground from the departing train. Thus in one single shot we see all the elements that sum up *Duel in the Sun*'s themes—land, cattle, the progress symbolized by the railroad. As Dimitri Tiomkin's music reaches a climax of its own, the scene fades to provide a superb natural chapter ending.

Rather surprisingly, for a film conceived with box office as its only aim, it forsook the traditional happy ending of the novel for a starkly tragic one, turning it into yet another Western *film noir,* if only partially so. A sweeping success with audiences, *Duel in the Sun* was reviewed scornfully and sarcastically. For that matter, even Ford's *My Darling Clementine* of the same year (1946) was received relatively coolly compared with the praises justifiably heaped on it in later years.

As far as the critics were concerned, there were only two Westerns with major artistic integrity in the '40s, ironically made by those two always juxtaposed directors, John Ford and Howard Hawks. The films were *Stagecoach* (even though a 1939 movie, its circulation and influence was still major in the forties) and, in 1948, *Red River.* United Artists built its whole advertising campaign around its (presumed) critical reception as a classic. The line "In thirty years, only three—*The Covered Wagon*—*Stagecoach*—and *Red River*" was the pitch used most frequently. Although a big critical and commercial success, *Red River* was (comparatively) forgotten rather quickly. It was long and its minimized or short-circuited action content disappointed fans who might well have paid it repeat viewings. Too, on the surface at least, it seemed to have nothing really fresh to say and to be merely an expert retraveling of familiar trails. Its impact was primarily via its stars. For perhaps the first time, John Wayne emerged (at least to critics unfamiliar with his entire body of work) as a serious and talented actor, and certainly his subsequent films for John Ford built very substantially on the persona that Wayne had created in *Red River.* And although the performance was less impressive, Montgomery Clift attracted favorable audience attention, too.

Death Valley (Screen Guild, 1946): Helen Gilbert, Russell Simpson, and Nat Pendleton in a real oddity—a *film noir* Western, filmed in far from perfected Cinecolor, and a remake of a silent with the same title

The sudden cult interest in director Hawks some fifteen years later caused *Red River* to be reacclaimed, reappraised, and probably over-analyzed. Hawks's films *are* complex in their character interrelationships and even in the thematic relationship of one film to another, but the revisionist and overintellectualized approach to *Red River* in later years seems a trifle ludicrous when one considers that it was originally conceived as a variation on—but still unofficial remake of—*Mutiny on the Bounty*. Remaking non-Westerns as horse operas (*Gunga Din* into *Sergeants Three, The Sea Wolf* into *Barricade, House of Strangers* into *Broken Lance*) has long been an old dodge, and *Red River* was an admittedly much more thoughtful application of the same method, a particularly adroit reworking of the 1935 film with the same conflicts, the same floggings, the same mutiny, and cattle making a more picturesque and flavorsome substitute for breadfruit trees. Hawks has never seemed enough of a sentimentalist to be as entirely at home with the Western as with the gangster film *(Scarface)* or the crackling satire of *His Girl Friday*. Perhaps more so than his later, more relaxed Westerns,

Red River is more in the anti-romanticist tradition of *The Covered Wagon* than in that of the warm idylls of John Ford. There is of course no criticism implied in this; there is certainly room for both, although it is difficult to be *passionately* fond of Ford Westerns *and* Hawks Westerns. In 1948, however, *Red River*, coming so close to the end of the decade, conveniently became the "milestone" Western of the forties.

Far from writing "Finis" to the Western, its dealing with familiar themes and incidents did nevertheless imply that the Western had little more to *say*. Yet how wrong such an assumption was. Less than two years away were two Westerns, both, perhaps coincidentally, from 20th Century-Fox: *Broken Arrow* and *The Gunfighter*, which not only would set new standards of maturity, honesty, and compassion, but also would launch new cycles along hitherto largely unexplored tangential paths. And waiting in the wings were the technological advances and innovations of the wide screen and three-dimensional processes to mirror changing content on a changing screen shape.

A birthday party for Roy Rogers on the set in 1947: from left, producer Edward J. White, Al Wilson, Roy, Dale Evans, and William Witney, Republic's most prolific serial, Western, and Rogers director

THIRTEEN

The Fifties and Sixties: Westerns Everywhere

Although the fifties and sixties are separated in one very key sense—in the fifties the old studio system began to die, and with it the assembly line production of all movies though Westerns especially, while the sixties ushered in a new era of independent production and a lack of studio "identity"—in most others they are linked together to form two solid decades of continuous if changing Western popularity. There was a greater emphasis on color, the introduction of 3-D, CinemaScope, and other wide-screen processes, and the replacement of the "B" Western with almost equally standardized "A" Westerns with big name stars—James Stewart, Gary Cooper, Robert Mitchum, John Wayne, Kirk Douglas, Rock Hudson—as well as the creation of enormously popular television series, initially at half-an-hour in black and white, but very soon full hours in color. All of these developments grew and reached their peak over a twenty year period in which the death of the studio system seemed to have only marginal impact.

The new decade started off neatly and decisively. The gradual decline and disappearance of the "B" Western (which would hang on grimly until the mid-'fifties) seemed hardly to matter, except to diehard fans, in the face of three of the finest "A" Westerns Hollywood had ever produced: John Ford's *Wagonmaster,* Henry King's

The Gunfighter, and Delmer Daves's *Broken Arrow.* While the forties had certainly seen a number of films in which the Indians had been treated sympathetically, most notably Ford's *Fort Apache* and even more so, his beautiful and sentimental if somewhat uneventful *She Wore a Yellow Ribbon,* none of them had been unreservedly pro-Indian. While *Broken Arrow*'s production may have been espoused by 20th Century-Fox because Darryl Zanuck wanted to sustain his reputation for socially conscious films, and it suggested more of the controversial but commercially successful race problem (Jewish and Negro in particular) ingredients of many films of the forties, it still managed to pull off the rare movie trick of making a valid social comment without overbalancing one side of the scales.

The side issues and byproducts of *Broken Arrow* were commercialized to the hilt. It established Cochise (played by Jeff Chandler), an Indian figure but little exploited in such earlier Westerns as *Valley of the Sun,* as a "regular" Western hero, prompted sequels in which Cochise's name was prominently featured in the title. It also set a pattern by which big male stars (Burt Lancaster, Robert Taylor, Rock Hudson, ultimately even Elvis Presley) could fashionably and profitably play Indians, and ushered in a whole new era of villainous whites and noble, misunderstood Indians. All of this was climaxed by a popular television series (with Michael Ansara as Cochise) with its attendant money-making merchandising of toy bows and arrows and Indian outfits. Its self-control in the area of melodrama, often approaching near documentarian values, was copied quite blatantly by lesser Westerns.

But the original *Broken Arrow*, despite almost universal complaints about Debra Paget's decidedly un-Indian looks, was good enough to survive all of this shameless exploitation. It was and is a warm, poetic film, with some of the best use of Technicolor to that date. Delmer Daves has always been an interesting and underappreciated writer-director, and there is little doubt that *Broken Arrow*, about which he cared deeply, and for which he prepared by living for many months in an Indian community, is his best film. Even James Stewart's mannered playing is held remarkably in check. Pictorially it is often superb, and the gentle beauty of its courtship scenes, and especially the simplicity of composition of the wedding night one—white horse, brown tepee, blue skies, and a scene that has the good taste to fade out just before it can be fully absorbed—are some of the most appealing images any Western has ever given us. If one has cause for complaint at all, it is only at the censorship-dictated compromise ending. Racial barriers being what they were at the time, an "important" white star still was not permitted to marry an Indian girl and have it turn out happily. One of them had to meet an untimely and often contrived end which could however be twisted to symbolic purpose, and it invariably proved to be the hapless Indian girl (who was also the lesser star). This was also the case in William Wellman's deeply felt but severely edited *Across the Wide Missouri*, although some forty years later its considerable values stand the test of time well. Samuel Fuller's *Run of the Arrow* a little later did allow such a union to survive. Had censorship's rigidity been relaxed a few years earlier, *Broken Arrow* might well have been the best, most honest, and most definitive movie on Indian-white problems. As it is, it is merely the best.

Many of the increasingly prolific Westerns of this type were directed by veterans like George Sherman, a graduate of Republic's "B" factory, a man who really knew how to keep his films on the move. One major new name to come to the fore in this period was that of Budd Boetticher, director of some of the best Audie Murphy films. A horse breeder, Boetticher made perhaps the only really good American documentaries and narrative films on Mexican and Spanish bullfighting, and also established his most notable relationship with Randolph Scott in a series of Westerns for Columbia and Warner release: *The Tall T, Ride Lonesome, Seven Men From*

Now, and others. Although making some concessions to Scott's increasing age, and dealing more with character studies and themes of revenge rather than offering more than a modicum of physical action, they were lean, gutsy, bitingly underplayed, the kind of films one might have expected had John Huston, in his prime, suddenly decided to specialize in Westerns.

The French critics discovered Boetticher first, and with the exception of one or two astute American critics who had been aware of him from the beginning— Andrew Sarris in particular—their American counterparts chorused their approval secondhand. This is not to undercut the merit of the Boetticher films, merely to stress that there was a great deal of luck in his critical success. His films happened to be made at a time when that budgetary classification of Western was getting a wider play and receiving the benefit of press showings, critical attention, and coverage in the more serious movie magazines. That same kind of arena just a few years earlier might well have given the medium-budget films of Lesley Selander *(Panhandle, Stampede, Shotgun)* equally favorable critical coverage, which they richly deserved.

John Ford's *Wagonmaster*, made in the wake of two big Indian-cavalry Westerns, was obviously a "little" picture that he wanted to do and which gave him the "breathing" period that he always needed between his more important films, and that was often productive of some of his best and most personal works. *Wagonmaster* was a simple yet poetic, vigorous yet at the same time easygoing apotheosis of Ford. Alan Mowbray's Shakespearean ham returned from *My Darling Clementine* and the Clantons from that film were reincarnated, too, this time via a religious patriarch with a brood of psychopathic sons. Ben Johnson and Joanne Dru, a dull actress who came to life for Ford, were Ringo and Dallas from *Stagecoach* all over again. Johnson, one of Ford's best players, gave an especially appealing performance. Then there were Ward Bond, Jane Darwell, and Russell Simpson as the leaders of the wagon train; Francis Ford, as another lovable wreck of a drunk; Jim Thorpe, happily sitting around a campfire, glad to be working again; and Harry Carey, Jr., doffing his hat for courtly bows to the ladies. It is a lovely, leisurely movie, a deliberately romanticized invocation of the pioneer spirit, all beautiful images and stirring ballads; in fact, the ballad is used to distance the audience from the movie, telling us from the outset that this is a story set "Back in 1849 . . ." and reminding us that we are looking at history from a vantage point a hundred years removed.

Photographically, *Wagonmaster* is deceptively simple. Ford seems to track his camera only two or three times in the entire movie, and then when it is so

Stars in My Crown (MGM, 1950): Dean Stockwell and Joel McCrea

Broken Arrow (20th Century-Fox, 1950: Debra Paget and James Stewart

Winchester '73 (Universal, 1950): Stephen McNally

Wagonmaster (RKO, 1950): Harry Carey, Jr., Ben Johnson, Charles Kemper, and Ward Bond

absolutely right that it is hardly noticeable. He never moves the camera when a lesser director would have done so merely for emphasis. Ford even resists the temptation to adopt smooth tracking shots in the twilight scenes of the women marching wearily along in the dust, behind their wagons. They come—and go—while the camera remains stationary, it, and the audience, a *spectator* to history parading by with dignity and courage, but not a *participant* in that bygone parade. When Ford *wants* to move his camera to involve his players and his audience as mutual participants, he knows just how to do it—but here all he was after was a fond, nostalgic look backwards, and the omnipresence of a Hollywood unit, suggested automatically by elaborate tracking shots, would have spoiled that viewpoint.

The frequently and casually applied term "adult" Western is a meaningless and even insulting phrase, since there have always been adult Westerns. Too often that description, or its companion, the "psychological" Western, are convenient labels to trot out when, by accident, a Western turns out to have few of the popular elements needed to make it a success. Television's constant use of the phrases have made them especially shallow. But if any films can be considered to have inaugurated trends towards more "adult" Westerns, then they are two related films from early in the decade: *The Gunfighter* by Henry King in 1950, and Fred Zinnemann's *High Noon* of two years later. By far the better of the two, *The Gunfighter* enjoyed only moderate success, and was so misunderstood (or potential public response to it held in such low esteem) that it was sold as a normal action Western, its trailer cunningly if somewhat dishonestly pulling together its sparse elements of action, emphasising its limited exterior scenes, slapping on a blood and thunder musical score (the film itself is most effectively almost devoid of music), and generally making it look like any one of a thousand other Westerns. In *The Gunfighter* (and many very similar though always inferior follow-ups), with its theme of a young hothead out to make his reputation by killing a notorious wanted man, sympathy has always been with the older outlaw (whose crimes have always taken place before the start of the film) and never with the younger gunfighter-to-be, who is invariably depicted as a sadistic, maladjusted troublemaker. While this whitewashes the older outlaw, especially as he is presented as a man weary of being forced to kill and aware that he and his way of life are doomed, at the same time violence, killing for the sake of "glory," and the taking of the law into one's own hands are heartily condemned. Nevertheless, in essence, one *is* asked to sympathize with a killer, and to reject a man whose actions, even if for the wrong motives, will benefit society, although it is to the film's credit that one never

realizes this until afterward. Beautifully acted and designed, literate in its writing, with welcome humor to offset the melancholy theme, it is also superbly and atmospherically photographed, mainly in low-ceilinged interior sets, by Arthur Miller, who carefully avoids the romantic warmth of his films for Ford. *The Gunfighter* creates such a mood of inexorable Greek tragedy that no matter how often it is seen, somehow one is always hoping subconsciously for that accidental change of circumstance that will bring about a happy ending. The falsely romanticized fadeout shot excepted (after he is gunned down by the young hoodlum, his ghostly image is seen riding into the sunset), *The Gunfighter* is a major classic among Western movies.

High Noon, which has usurped much of the innovational reputation that rightly belongs to King's film, was shaped into a substantial box office success partly because it is, within limits, a good movie, partly because of the exploitation help given it by its theme song as rendered by Tex Ritter (a much less familiar film-plugging gimmick then than now), and largely because it provided an Academy Award-winning comeback to its popular star, Gary Cooper, too long wasted in unimportant films (to which he would return, although there would be some interesting highlights, such as Anthony Mann's *Man of the West*, among them). Historians of the (non-movie) West disclaim the film, pointing out that in essential details it is false and that the ballad especially is both artificial and anachronistic. Movie critics tended to be misled, apportioning too much credit to producer Stanley Kramer (whose achievements rarely matched his honorable intentions) and director Zinnemann (never really comfortable with such essentially American subjects), and too little to the work of star Cooper and editor Elmo Williams. However, its twin themes of civic responsibility in time of crisis and latent courage in ordinary people of non-heroic stature (even if negatively and pessimistically deployed here) were soon taken over by such subsequent spin-off Westerns as *At Gunpoint* (with Fred MacMurray as a storekeeper largely replaying the Cooper role) and were rapidly absorbed as "new" clichés. Its commentary on the average citizen's determination *not* to be involved, and to abandon the helpless and victimized, unfortunately proved to be sadly prophetic as crime increased on the streets of America's cities. But in the Westerns themselves, one often found oneself going against the scenarist's intentions and feeling sorry for the outlaws, suddenly beset by an outnumbering group of petty, avenging townspeople, who seemed to find their social conscience only when they feel safe by being part of a mob.

The affection engendered by *Wagonmaster* (though it was not a box office winner) and the differing successes

The Gunfighter (20th Century-Fox, 1950): Harry Shannon, Gregory Peck, and Richard Jaeckel (on the floor)

of *Broken Arrow, The Gunfighter,* and later *High Noon* tended to take the spotlight away from another outstanding Western of 1950, *Winchester '73.* Originally intended for Fritz Lang, it used the story of the famous gun—and its theft from its winner in a shooting contest—as a peg on which to hand a fairly complicated story of a search and a planned revenge; ideal material for Lang. As directed by Anthony Mann, by 1950 already a specialist in atmospheric and violent *films noir,* it retained its grim, dog-eat-dog view of the West, but Mann made more of the outdoor locations and action scenes than Lang probably would have. It introduced James Stewart to Mann, paved the way for a string of outstanding collaborations (though not perhaps as striking as this first one) and generally was more influential on Westerns of the fifties than is often supposed. Its routine-*sounding* content (an Indian attack, a hero with an outlaw brother) made it seem less unique than the four big Westerns that surrounded it, but it certainly deserved to be placed in their company.

The proverbial "shot in the arm" that *High Noon* provided for the Western was followed up less than a year later with a booster shot in Paramount's *Shane,* directed by George Stevens. It confirmed the new prestige status of his career, only just secured via *A Place in the Sun,* and restored the sagging career of Alan Ladd. While a milestone movie rather than a permanent classic, it is a film of diminishing returns and succeeding viewings tend to leave one liking it a little less. (In the film's defense, it should be added that its pictorial splendors were designed for and need the big screen, and repeat viewings, for the average audience, tend to be on television or via videocassette, which hurt its appeal badly). A production that had gone alarmingly over budget and shooting schedules, and was not considered by Paramount executives to be worthy of such over expenditure, *Shane* could well have stalled the momentum of Stevens's career had it not been a hit. But to Paramount's surprise and relief, it rapidly achieved both critical and popular success. After the unsubtle onslaught of introspective and pedestrian Westerns that sought to cash in in the new "formula" of *High Noon,* it was a refreshing return to the simple themes on which the popularity of the Western had been built, man vs. man and man versus nature.

With its stunning Technicolor photography of the Grand Tetons territory, its "class" production all the way, its fine cast (with Ben Johnson especially effective among the supporting players, displaying a subtlety of acting style as a three-dimensional villain that had not been apparent in his effortless playing of his straightforward and likeable heroes for Ford), and sufficient tough action to satisfy those who didn't care about "class,"

Shane could hardly miss, and Paramount's lack of faith in it is hard to understand. However, it had the misfortune to go into release in the midst of a nationwide conversion to wide-screen presentation. When it premiered at the huge Radio City Music Hall, George Stevens's meticulously composed framings were hacked and elongated in order that it might qualify as a totally up-to-date production (although hardly "old," Paramount's indecision about it, coupled with Stevens's own postproduction tinkering, had delayed its release) and be sold *as* a wide-screen production. Even this merchandising development boomeranged to the film's advantage, enlisting the support and sympathy of movie purists, including the more sensitive critics, who otherwise might not have been too concerned with its success or failure.

Despite the disappointment one is likely to encounter on a repeat viewing today, much of *Shane* holds up extremely well as *film;* the realism of the unvarnished sets, the ritualistic sadism of Jack Palance's killer, the astounding impact of his shooting of Elisha Cook, Jr. After seeing good guys and bad by the thousand crumple comfortably and bloodlessly into the dust through thirty years of death being pantomimed in most Westerns, this sudden confrontation with the physical *force* of a gunshot blast comes as the shock that Stevens intended. But as a total entity, the film no longer seems to have the accumulated strength of its individual components, and the wonder is that its flaws were not recognized earlier. Alan Ladd is still the weakest of the impressive array of leading players when obviously he should be the strongest, and he is not helped by a too pretty buckskin outfit which lacks the dramatic flair of Palance's costuming or the conviction of the farmers' everyday work clothes. Victor Young's musical score is melodic, certainly easy to remember, but it is incurably romantic and parallel scenes in this film and *The Gunfighter* work far better in the latter, denied musical backing.

For all of the memorable use of landscape, what is really achieved by it is the sense of men dwarfed by nature or at war with it. While this is certainly part of the story that Stevens is telling, the sense of man's *relationship* to the land, an inherent part of any John Ford Western, is almost totally lacking, although there is an acknowledgment of the need for that relationship in the well-done sequence of the uprooting of the tree stump. Perhaps, in essence, the shortcomings of *Shane* boil down to the difference between Stevens and Ford. Stevens was always, and particularly from the mid-forties on, a meticulous craftsman who preplanned carefully, planned again, experimented, discarded, shot endlessly, and amassed miles of footage of alternate takes with just the slightest variance in angle or length, until he achieved a kind of mechanical perfection, a process that certain involves a great deal of art and skill. And then, in the time that it would take Ford to shoot an entire film, he would sit down to cut it to a preconceived mathematical pattern. The first time one sees it (and in fairness, most films are designed for that one exposure) its perfection takes one's breath away. But thereafter one notices more and more the cold calculation, the lack of warmth that comes from the unplanned "bit of business" dreamed up spontaneously or possibly suggested by a dedicated cast or crew member. Ford often liked to slow his Westerns down for a moment, to just mark time while he experimented with a specific act or movement: Fonda as Wyatt Earp in *My Darling Clementine,* leaning his chair back on a veranda, balancing himself by moving his feet, is a felicitous example. This "extraneous" quality of warmth, humanity and spontaneity is what makes the Ford Westerns, for all their occasional rough edges, so durable. *Stagecoach, My Darling Clementine,* and *Wagonmaster* get better with each viewing; *Shane,* and for that matter *High Noon* and *Red River,* do not. In a way, it's all John Ford's fault; if he had made no Westerns at all, there would be no basis for comparison, and everybody else's Westerns would look infinitely better!

While the deluxe and even ordinary "A" Western of the early fifties was in fine commercial shape, looking forward to nearly three decades of profitable life, the humble "B" was in less happy straits. Production expenses have risen to a point where they were costing more to make—and still looking cheap and showing their corner-cutting despite those slightly upped budgets. Nor was the added cost worthwhile, since they weren't bringing in any more at the box office. Television, with its free Westerns—the cheap ones made *for* that media, the old theatrical ones with their superior production values—was only just beginning to exercise its competitive threat, and things could only get worse. In the '30s, depending on the salary paid to the star (often much lower than might be supposed), decent looking "B" Westerns could be made for $25,000 or less. Now they were costing a *minimum* of *twice* that much, and coming up with an end result of *half* the quality. Action was avoided where feasible, cheaply staged where not, and as much footage as possible was borrowed from earlier Westerns. Even if they *didn't* talk more, they often seemed as though they did because of the proliferation of long dialogue takes, unbroken by time-consuming changes of camera angle or cuts for individual close-ups. Even a single bit of stunt action in an Allan Lane Western at Republic might be pieced together from as many as three different sources: an establishing scene from a Three Mesquiteers film for example, then a long shot, Gene Autry or John Wayne

footage supplying the next vital chunk of action, followed by Allan Lane in newly filmed insert footage, and yet another star in a fourth bit of action to wind it up.

In Republic's earlier Westerns, each star had his distinctive dress and hat, so identifying him in long shots that didn't match was not difficult. Moreover, Republic had a number of big scale action set pieces from their bigger Westerns: Quantrill's raiders storming through a Kansas town from *The Dark Command,* a wagon convoy and attack from *Wagons Westward,* John Wayne's men racing their oil wagons through a blazing canyon in *In Old Oklahoma.* Republic's writers would devise scenarios built around these sequences, the very superior quality of which made them instantly recognizable, especially as the repetition became so frequent. (When Republic moved into the television field, the procedure was repeated.) Newly-filmed action became ultra standardized. The substantial outlaw gang of old had now shrunk to a mere three riders, and it became an oft-repeated ploy for the undermanned chief villain to send one of his minions to bring in "the Baxter gang from across the border," paving the way for use of a much more menacing but totally unintegrated group of riders to be cut in so that the bad guys, thanks to the stock shot vault, could at least properly outnumber the good guys. Running inserts were always shot on the same stretches of road at Chatsworth and cut in regardless of continuity or other locales in use; studio "exteriors" got skimpier, with a few papier-mâché rocks, a bush or two in front of a white backdrop, and much back projection substituting for decent art direction.

Despite the writing on the wall, some companies *did* do their best to maintain quality, and even instituted new series. RKO maintained a high standard to the very end with its Tim Holt series, using almost no stock footage, continuing to use good locations and good casts, and not giving in to economy by staging its action or dialogue scenes with meager production values. But the studio had to pay for it, with budgets that were reputedly near the $100,000 mark. Republic's new Rex Allen series benefited from Allen's own likeable personality and agreeable singing voice, and expert direction from William Witney, who put astonishing vigor into Westerns like *The Last Musketeer* through sheer pace and liberal use of the mobile camera trucks in his chase scenes. Apart from the monotony of the conveniently nearby Chatsworth locations, there was no apparent sign of economy in the Allen Westerns, and their plots were surprisingly fresh (within the boundaries of the species) and even novel.

Monogram, in the process of changing itself into Allied Artists and concentrating on higher-bracket product, was phasing out its long-running but now somewhat

Wagonmaster: Alan Mowbray, Ruth Clifford, and Francis Ford

Gold Raiders (United Artists, 1951): Hardly deserving of its classic company, yet notable for George O'Brien's still virile appearance and his refusal to be fazed by the Three Stooges

tired Johnny Mack Brown series, but started an intelligent and interesting new one with Bill Elliott, fresh from bigger budget Westerns at Republic. *The Longhorn, Kansas Territory, Waco,* and *Fargo* provided a satisfying mixture of good scripts, slightly increased running times, production values initially at least higher than Monogram "B's" had offered for a long while, and generally good if unspectacular action content. Most of the Elliotts were written by Dan Ullman, a good screenwriter who managed to combine well drawn characters with fairly novel plots and a realistic knowledge of what could be accomplished within the budgetary allowance. More than any of his other series at Columbia and Republic, this series allowed Elliott to develop his affinity to the old William S. Hart character, frequently playing reformed badmen. *Topeka* seemed almost like a remake of Hart's *The Return of Draw Egan* and may well have been influenced by it, since it was one of the few Harts available for viewing at that time. *Topeka* also went berserk, fascinatingly but inexplicably, with the moving camera. On tracks or atop a crane, it delved into stagecoaches and bunk houses, circled poker players in a dizzying movement, zoomed upward to catch long-shot action, prowled restlessly back and forth during a bank holdup sequence. Not since the German-inspired films of the late twenties had the cinematographer moved his equipment so much purely for its own sake, and probably *never* so much in a humble program Western.

Unquestionably, the most surprising aspect of the Elliott series was the realistic quality of the hero's personal conduct, a far cry from the behavioral code instituted in the thirties that required a cowboy to abstain from drinking, smoking, and other more colorful vices, and to be virtually a saint in his obsessive need to help the underdog. While Elliott's screen character was to remain a man of integrity, at the same time he abandoned most of those Boy Scout inspired codes. Foremost among these was the taboo on alcoholic drinking. The standard Western hero often had to go to extreme lengths to even justify his presence in a saloon, and had to use unsubtle pantomime to play-act his deception of *seeming* to drink lest the villain immediately deduce from his teetotal state that he was automatically a Texas Ranger incognito.

The hero's obstinate refusal to drink anything stronger than milk or sarsparilla—the latter pointedly having the dust blown off it before the bottle was opened—was of course one of the standard methods by which saloon fights were provoked. But Elliott drank the hard stuff whenever it seemed appropriate and, to be fair, he frequented restaurants, too, something most cowboy heroes rarely found time for. When Elliott played an outlaw, he was just that, not a lawman posing as one.

While fair, he could also be ruthless and unsportsman-like when the occasion arose. One of the standard clichés of the Western, and one of the surefire ways of writing in some fistic action when there seemed no logical reason for it otherwise, was for the hero to hold the villain at gunpoint, and have the latter complain, "You wouldn't be so big if it weren't for them guns!" whereupon the hero would quite unnecessarily lay aside his guns—usually allowing the bad guy to get in a sneaky first punch while the hero was doing so—and then of course wallop the tar out of him. Elliott had had more than his fair share of such contrived fights at Columbia and Republic. But in at least one of the Allied Artists Westerns, Elliott responds to the time-honored statement with complete indifference, and proceeds to beat the information out of his captive with one hand, while continuing to keep him covered with the other!

Some of these clichés had a habit of contradicting themselves anyway. How many times has Hopalong Cassidy been introduced to the town by stopping an attempted killing and in steely tones telling the thwarted assassin, "Where I come from, we don't shoot men in the back!"? Yet such chivalry is usually forgotten in the final reel when the chief heavy tries to make his getaway. In *Silver on the Sage,* as villain Stanley Ridges tries to ride to freedom after the traditional outlaw roundup, both William Boyd *and* George Hayes shoot him in the back without a moment's hesitation! The added dimension of relatively realistic behavior brought to the Elliott Westerns arrived too late to have much effect on the "B's," but it is interesting that this innovation should come *via* the "B's," which from the forties on were much influenced by the *film noir* and private eye cycles. The heroes of the "A" Westerns were still basically hewing to traditional codes of honorable behavior, and it was only later that the Waynes and the Widmarks followed in Elliott's realistic footsteps.

Inevitably, the care lavished on the earlier Elliotts

High Noon (United Artists, 1952): Grace Kelly and Gary Cooper

Callaway Went Thataway (MGM, 1951): Glenn Strange being bested by Hollywood cowboy Howard Keel, as Don Haggerty, Dorothy McGuire, and Fred MacMurray look on

245

Across the Wide Missouri (MGM, 1951): Clark Gable returns to the Westerns in a much underrated William Wellman-directed film

Stagecoach Driver (Monogram, 1951): A new "B" series with Whip Wilson (here with Jim Bannon and Fuzzy Knight on the coach) arrived too late to beat rising production costs, but it tried hard

Lone Star (MGM, 1952): Gable with Ava Gardner and Broderick Crawford

Rancho Notorious (RKO, 1952): Fritz Lang's Western with Arthur Kennedy, Marlene Dietrich, and Mel Ferrer

Son of Paleface (Paramount, 1952): Bob Hope, Roy Rogers, and Jane Russell

Sitting Bull (United Artists, 1954): Douglas Kennedy as Custer

Naked Spur (MGM, 1952): Janet Leigh and James Stewart

Two Guns and a Badge (Allied Artists, 1954): Morris Ankrum and Wayne Morris in the last of the "B" series Westerns

Johnny Guitar (Republic, 1954): Nicholas Ray's bizarre allegorical Western with Sterling Hayden and Joan Crawford

Gunfight at the O.K. Corral (Paramount, 1956): Burt Lancaster as Wyatt Earp

247

eventually petered out, and the last entries in the series—films like *Rebel City*—were short in length, short on action, and lower on good stories and production values, though still given distinction by the Elliott presence. One by one, the series Westerns dropped by the wayside. Johnny Mack Brown, Tim Holt, Rex Allen, Whip Wilson, Bill Elliott, Monte Hale, Charles Starrett, Allan Lane, Roy Rogers, and Gene Autry, all regularly making "B" Westerns in 1950, had stopped by 1954. In New York, it was possible to witness the death throes of the genre week by week at a Times Square movie house that for years had shown Westerns on every program. At first it had done sellout business by coupling two of the best current Westerns; gradually it was forced to take two of anything it could get, then one Western plus some other "B" movie, by now of such humdrum quality that it couldn't hope to survive for a week without a third feature being added as a "Special Preview." (The preview usually turned out to be a twenty-year-old Ken Maynard or Bob Baker Western!) Eventually the bottom of the barrel had been scraped and there was nothing left to play, although there was some coincidental poetic justice in the fact that its final Western was also Gene Autry's last theatrical Western, appropriately titled *Last of the Pony Riders*. The last "B" Westerns to go into production were a series—if one can call a quartet a series—of Wayne Morris films for Allied Artists. When the last of those, *Two Guns and a Badge*, went into release in mid-1954, the "B" was dead permanently.

Many of us who had grown up on and with "B" Westerns had sometimes, as children, indulged in masochistic fantasies in which we dreamed that one day they would be no more. We never really believed that that day could ever dawn because if it did there would be nothing left to make life worthwhile. But when that Doomsday did come (even making allowances for the fact that we were older and possibly wiser), it wasn't as difficult to live with as we'd feared. Most of our older favorites had died or gone into retirement, and it required no great fortitude to say farewell to Lash LaRue. The last "B's" were, for the most part, so poor (always excepting those directed by William Witney!) that it was far better to have no Westerns at all than ones that were such pale shadows of former glories. The fact that many of the stars—William Boyd, Rex Allen, Roy Rogers, Gene Autry—had taken their boots and saddles over to television was but minor compensation. Although they varied in quality, these television Westerns were generally substandard. Autry probably maintained the highest standards, not only in his own starring series, but also in the others that his company produced, including an *Annie Oakley* series with Gail Davis, and most notably *The Range Rider* series which spotlighted that remark-

able stuntman, Jock Mahoney. But even these contemporary equivalents of the "B's," running only half an hour, less with commercial time subtracted, had a relatively short life span before they gave way to the equally standardized but more dialogue-controlled, ostensibly more "adult," and eventually longer series like *Gunsmoke*. Certainly these were more elaborately produced than the cheaper half-hour action shows. *The Lone Ranger*, for example, had been done almost entirely on cramped studio sets, with the same stock riding close-ups and exterior scenes cut in once or twice per episode. And for every series that made it, such as Guy Madison's popular *Wild Bill Hickok*, there was another that never got past the single pilot stage, as for example, a *Buffalo Bill* series in which James Ellison reprised his Cody role from DeMille's *The Plainsman* but on a *considerably* smaller budget.

Passing with the "B" Western but far less mourned since its quality had fallen even lower was the serial film, which naturally included many Westerns. In the silent period, starting in 1913—though it would take several years for the traditional cliff-hanger ending to evolve—the quantity of Western serials produced ran second only to the Mystery, a genre that, despite its need for exposition via lengthy dialogue titles, proved well suited to the silent film. With the coming of talkies, however, the Western serial had moved into first place. In a way, and not discounting the popularity of Westerns generally, this was surprising. For although the fragmented form of the serial lent itself well to the protracted telling of a certain *kind* of Western story—the building of a railroad, or a covered wagon trek—it offered no special opportunities that the regulation Western did not also offer. By its very nature, a matter of tried and true formulae, the Western was limited in its action: dynamited shacks, lynch mobs, stampeding herds of cattle or buffalo, wagon crashes, tumbles from cliffs or into mine shafts, stake burnings by Indians, an occasional flood or avalanche, falls from or under an Iron Horse or, once in a while, an ore-crushing machine—that about summed up the climactic perils that could be presented. Not only is the list so circumscribed that the average twelve- or fifteen-chapter serial found itself repeating situations within its own span, but naturally those same situations were duplicated in *other* serials and in regulation Westerns.

Moreover, the serials required some four hours of footage but were usually budgeted at the cost of about two features. Not only were they made quickly but they had to be made cheaply—and one obvious way to economize was to reuse big scenes from other serials and Westerns, so that the same burning barns, avalanches, and stagecoaches crashing over cliffs turned up time and

Lesley Selander, director of some of the very best "B's" of the thirties and forties, and in the fifties of such unusual "A's" as *Shotgun* and *Short Grass*

The Searchers (Warner Bros., 1956): Wayne with Natalie Wood and Jeffrey Hunter

Jubal (Columbia, 1956): Glenn Ford at the head of the posse

Ride Lonesome (Columbia, 1959): Randolph Scott and James Best in a taut, lean Budd Boetticher film

The Return of Jack Slade (Allied Artists. 1955): Mari Blanchard and John Ericson

249

Badman's Gold (Eagle Lion, 1951): Johnny Carpenter (landing one on Kenneth Duncan's jaw) parlayed a slight resemblance to Montgomery Clift and a desire to make strong, adult Westerns—with other people's funding—into a series of curious, overwrought, often ludicrous but well-intentioned independent Westerns in the fifties

Broken Lance (20th Century-Fox, 1954): Spencer Tracy and Katy Jurado in Edward Dmytryk's Western remake of Joseph L. Mankiewicz's non-Western *House of Strangers*

The Outriders (MGM, 1950): Joel McCrea, Ramon Novarro (with gun), Arlene Dahl, and cast confront Barry Sullivan (back to camera)

Shane (Paramount, 1953): A George Stevens-staged barroom brawl

Gun Fury (Columbia, 1953): Depending on 3-D for its novelty, a lesser work for director Raoul Walsh and star Rock Hudson, here with Phil Carey, Leo Gordon, Donna Reed, and Forrest Lewis

Hiawatha (Allied Artists, 1952): A well-intentioned peace-propagandizing version of the Longfellow work with Vince Edwards and Yvette Dugay, done in by a naive script and too meager a budget

time again. Considering the pressures of time and money, it's remarkable that the Western serials, in their peak period from the mid thirties to the early forties, turned out as well as they did, although there was some lamentable "cheating" in getting the heroes out of their predicaments, the entirely fallacious belief being that children wouldn't remember specific details a week apart (they certainly would and did) and that adults wouldn't care (wrong again). Yet despite a format that permitted less deviation, variety and imagination than the adventure or science-fiction serial, the Western serial always flourished, especially when they were lucky enough to have a Buck Jones or a Johnny Mack Brown as the star. Occasionally the Western serial allowed itself the luxury of stepping outside its already strained boundaries of logic and mixing in science-fiction, lost cities, Nazi spies, and other melodramatic ingredients into the hopper.

The best Western serials managed to exploit their format intelligently by borrowing a device from the silent Mystery serials—that of the masked Mystery hero or villain. Audiences were neatly led up and down the garden path all through the serial, red herrings abounded, cheating was sometimes outrageous (the Masked Man was often shown in the same scene with the character who finally turned out to be *under* that mask!), but suspense was neatly sustained. Chapter endings would break off *just* as an unmasking was about to take place; or leading contenders for Mystery Man honors would be killed off, and a new set of red herrings introduced. The Masked Mystery Hero also made doubling by a stuntman an easier task, and Republic's Mystery Men in particular usually looked suspiciously like slim and lithe Tom Steele. Best of the masked heroes was undoubtedly *The Lone Ranger,* who was either George Montgomery, Hal Taliaferro, Lee Powell, Bruce Bennett, or Lane Chandler. Most colorful villain was undoubtedly Don Del Oro (the list of suspects was much greater) in *Zorro's Fighting Legion.* Both of these were outstandingly well-made serials, among the best of many great ones (*Drums of Fu Manchu, Daredevils of the Red Circle, Spy Smasher, The Perils of Nyoka,* and *The Adventures of Red Ryder* are just those at the top of the list) directed by William Witney. If we can thank the silent two-reel comedies for Chaplin and Keaton, then we can thank the sound serials for William Witney—and his presence in such august company is fully warranted.

From a purely action point of view, Republic made easily the best Western serials just as they made the best "B" Westerns. Universal, particularly in its earlier days made some good ones, too, and early in the forties made a real effort to put bigger production values into them. *Riders of Death Valley* had an exceptionally strong cast,

and though not quite as good, *Winners of the West,* a railroad-building story, had an unusually elaborate first chapter. Columbia was more concerned about unmotivated action for its own sake, and many of their plots just went around in circles. But—something serial purists never forgave them for—they also had a sense of humor about the basic idiocy of some of their creations. *Deadwood Dick* goes overboard in its absurd climactic cliffhangers, and everybody rushes from scene to scene hustled along by undercranked camerawork. But it was all great fun, even though it ignored the fact that the *real* Deadwood Dick was black, and that the supposedly hidden identity of the mysterious *The Skull* was obvious from the beginning, as was that of *Pegleg* in *Overland With Kit Carson.* Even more than the "B" Westerns, the serials suffered from pinched economy, rising production values, and the lack of good stars (Gene Autry, Ken Maynard, Bill Elliott, Johnny Mack Brown, Buck Jones, Tom Tyler, John Wayne, Tim McCoy, serial stars of the thirties and forties, had been "replaced" by Dennis Moore, Lee Roberts, Marshall Reed, Richard Simmons, and Keith Richards by the fifties). By the time Westerns were ready to give up the ghost, they were so dull, so padded (and at Republic so short, the average "two reel" episode now running a mere twelve minutes) that even the most dedicated aficionado found it a chore to sit through them. There's some minor satisfaction perhaps in that the very last serial released, *Perils of the Wilderness* (1956), was a Western.

The television Western has its own history and warrants its own full-scale documentation, but through the years, progressing from the thirty-minute actioner in black and white to shows in color, documentaries, bigscale specials, and eventually elaborate mini-series, it never once produced a single episode or single show to match a *My Darling Clementine* or a *Gunfighter.* Despite the occasional half-hour TV film by Ford, or the more regular television work by such accomplished filmmakers as Joseph H. Lewis, Sam Peckinpah, William Witney, or Budd Boetticher, the television movie always seemed hemmed in by restrictions, compromises, limitations in time or money, regimented fragmentation for the commercial breaks, and a kind of "in house" censorship inflicted not only by television's own restrictions—or "guidelines" as they preferred to call them, but also by those imposed more irrationally by sponsors. This is perhaps an unfair generalization, since, as in theatrical Westerns, there have to have been exceptions to the rule, and it is these exceptions that keep the genre flourishing. But the very essence of television, which is, after all, basically that of illustrated radio, works against the genre in that particular medium, as does television's conception of its audience. Too many television documentaries (*especially* those with a Western-oriented theme) fall short of expectations merely because of an ill-conceived notion that they should include elements that an audience *expects* to see, whether appropriate or not.

As far back as 1951 (when television was still regarded as an enemy, and Hollywood sought to belittle it at every opportunity), MGM made an amusing spoof of the whole television Western situation in general, and the remarkable Hopalong Cassidy renaissance in particular, in a film entitled *Callaway Went Thataway*. It zeroes in with some accuracy on the hype employed to merchandise toy six-shooters, cowboy hats, and other accessories, and was more honest than most Hollywood satires perhaps because, in knocking a competitor rather than itself, it didn't feel the need to pull any punches. It still remains one of the best films of its kind, later ventures into the same field tending to cash in on nostalgia rather than sharp observation. However, even in the early fifties, *Callaway Went Thataway* didn't *quite* have the courage of its own convictions, dissipating some of its bite with a post-End title follow-up in which a longer title explained that it had all been offered in fun and with no disrespect for the many cowboy stars who had for so long displayed civic awareness, social responsibility, and generosity to charities. This provided a further touch of irony, since the cowboy stars who really lived up to those claims were few and far between. Buck Jones, in whose name a youth organization, the Buck Jones Rangers, had been sustained, and who died a heroic and tragic death in the Coconut Grove fire in Boston in the early forties, was a major exception.

To most studios, the making of Westerns was purely and simply a lucrative business, their public image important commercially but not necessarily morally. Wonderful outtake footage exists of Jack Randall, a Western star who had apparently great problems in remembering his lines, exploding with frustration and using a flow of expletives that would have shocked his youthful admirers had it been made public at the time. (Amusingly, the Western heavies—especially Charles King and LeRoy Mason—were quite gentlemanly and restrained in their use of language to express dismay at a fluffed line!) William Boyd, embodiment of all of the known virtues in his Hopalong Cassidy films, regarded them so totally as merchandise pure and simple that when he took them over for television release, and found it expedient to edit them down to a standardized length, he didn't do so with time-consuming care, editing a snippet here, a bit of comedy business or a song there, but merely lopped off the excess minutes in *one chunk* from the head of each movie. On rare occasions, and notably when the film was short to begin with, this

worked well enough. But on most of the films so cut, one was thrust immediately into unmotivated action and a plot well under way. At least one major Western star of the forties and fifties—Allan Lane—was so consistently egotistical and commercially minded that he was universally hated by his directors and coworkers. (Which is undoubtedly why, unlike Rex Allen, Roy Rogers, and others, his employment since the cessation of his starring series was virtually nil, until his death limited to providing the voice of a talking horse in the *Mr. Ed* television series in the sixties).

But if the "B" Westerns, bad as they had become, were missed, there was a good deal of compensation in the greatly increased number of "A" Westerns, and in the way in which they were now catering far more to the action requirements of longtime Western addicts. These new "A's" were made very largely to combat television, which was still limited to old black-and-white theatrical Westerns, particularly the creaky independent ones of the early thirties, and the unimpressive new made-for-television variety. They could offer size, color (still seeming much further away from television than it actually was), and respectable star names of the calibre of Randolph Scott, Jeff Chandler, Sterling Hayden, Charlton Heston, and Dale Robertson. Universal worked out an especially satisfying formula, its approximately eighty-minute "A" programmers, not only welding star names and Technicolor production values to enable them to appeal to most general audiences, but also adding the slick, fast tempo action of the vanishing "B's." Budd Boetticher's *The Man From the Alamo*, a 1953 vehicle for Glenn Ford, had a sturdy plot line and some exceptionally polished and ably performed stunt work by David Sharpe. In terms of pure speed and (literally) cliff-hanging action it compared favorably with the best of Republic, while its writing and other values were somewhat superior.

Allied Artists, which had ventured into the bigger-budget Westerns in the late forties with two extremely good Rod Cameron vehicles, *Panhandle* and *Stampede*, maintained an interesting though inconsistent record thereafter. *Bad Men of Tombstone* and a would-be satire *The Dude Goes West* disappointed; *Cavalry Scout* and *Wagons West* were little more than "B's" given some class by Rod Cameron and the use of Cinecolor; *Son of Belle Starr* and *The Return of Jack Slade* did little to live up to their titles; and *Arrow in the Dust* was concerned mainly with matching up to the Technicolor stock footage of Indian attacks that it had bought from Paramount. But there were some likeable highlights: *Short Grass, Cow Country,* and especially *Shotgun,* all directed by Lesley Selander, and one of the best of the pocket-epic railroading films, *Kansas Pacific.* Sterling Hayden, never quite regaining the momentum of his brace of prewar service films, made an interesting offbeat hero in several of these fifties Westerns—antisocial, cigar-chewing, deliberately unromantic in costume. One of the best and certainly most bizarre of Hayden's Westerns in this period was *Terror in a Texas Town* (1958, and a United Artists release), Joseph H. Lewis's final theatrical film before retirement, and specifically designed to help break down the never-acknowledged but nonetheless real blacklist imposed on politically suspect actors and writers in those Red-baiting McCarthy years. Screenwriter/actor Nedrick Young was one of several who used this film as a stepping stone back to industry acceptance. Hayden, playing a bowler-hatted Scandinavian seaman, now a Texas settler, undertakes the traditional last-reel street confrontation with the villain armed with a whaler's harpoon!

Other than for the lazy borrowing of the *High Noon* thematics and the post-*Broken Arrow* sympathy towards Indians, there were no specific trends during the fifties. *Colt .45* and *Springfield Rifle* tried to pass themselves off as descendants of *Winchester '73*, but the influence didn't go much further than the titles. A tentative return to the whitewashed badman vehicles never really got past the level of medium budget films like *Jack Slade, Wyoming Renegades, Jack McCall, Desperado,* and *Al Jennings of Oklahoma.* Jennings, one of the last and certainly one of the lesser old-time outlaws, had perpetrated little real damage and had been pardoned before his jail term was up. Despite being an authentic badman, he decided against returning to train holdups and became a movie cowboy himself. He played himself in a series of shorts supposedly based on events in his brief career, rather consciously modeling his screen image after the sentimental/heroic one popularized by William S. Hart, then at his peak. However, they were interesting little films—*When Outlaws Meet* is one of the few that has survived—and had a certain amount of documentarian quality in depicting the day-to-day pattern of outlaws on the run, and the details of the life style of the farm and mountain people who befriended and helped them. (Although too little of this silent material survives, there's a wonderful documentary to be made, some day, from the little films made by men like Jennings, Jesse James's son, and the surviving Dalton brother, to explain and justify their lives, and hold themselves up as warning examples to others). Columbia's version of Jennings's life, done in Technicolor, followed the usual stereotyped movie pattern. He had been a somewhat inept outlaw, and was physically something of a runt. As a realistic ideal, he should have been played by Elisha Cook, Jr., or lesser known character actor Lou Lubin. *Al Jennings of Oklahoma* almost doubled his physical size to that of

The Spoilers (Universal, 1955): Rory Calhoun and Jeff Chandler in the fifth rendition of the classic scrap

Man From God's Country (Allied Artists, 1957): George Montgomery

Dan Duryea (still an interesting piece of casting, however) and gave his outlawry the importance and crusading stature of a Jesse James, doubtless because, at the time, Jennings was still very much alive.

Son of Belle Starr (Allied Artists, 1953): Peggie Castle and a newcomer who didn't last too long, Keith Larsen, in yet another fictionalized account of the outlaw's undocumented offspring

Stranger at My Door (Republic, 1956): Macdonald Carey and Patricia Medina in a little gem from director William Witney and writer Barry Shipman

Badlanders (MGM, 1958): Alan Ladd and Ernest Borgnine in Delmer Daves's Western remake of John Huston's non-Western *The Asphalt Jungle*

The Last Sunset (Universal, 1961): Director Robert Aldrich and writer Dalton Trumbo's psychological Western with Kirk Douglas and Rock Hudson

The Misfits (United Artists, 1961): John Huston's Western with Clark Gable and Marilyn Monroe in their last roles

Outrage (MGM, 1964): Paul Newman and Laurence Harvey in the Western remake of Kurosawa's *Rashomon*

Stagecoach (20th Century-Fox, 1966): First of two remakes of the John Ford classic; Ann-Margret in the Claire Trevor role and Bing Crosby in Thomas Mitchell's

The War Wagon (Universal, 1967): John Wayne and Kirk Douglas planning a big heist, and Wayne aboard the war wagon itself

Ride the High Country (MGM, 1962): Joel McCrea and Randolph Scott in the Sam Peckinpah classic

The renewed but minor interest in the Badman Western—the only impressive one was Nicholas Ray's late 1950s remake of Henry King's *Jesse James*—soon dwindled down to the "B" level. While no more series Westerns were produced, sporadic "B's" continued to be made on an individual basis, but usually in color, with a minor "name" star and an exploitation gimmick by which they could technically be sold on the "A" level, at least to the smaller theaters. The outlaw vehicle, generously laced with violence and as much sex as was permissible (still not much, though one would never know it from the lurid advertising) proved a useful if short-lived mini cycle in this period via such cheap and tawdry films as *Outlaw Women* and *The Daltons' Women*.

Supplementing the already large numbers of big Westerns being produced in the fifties were the technological advances affecting the movie industry at that time. Three-dimensional films and CinemaScope offered new visual possibilities for the Western. Shooting in CinemaScope did not materially affect its budget, but did give it a superficially spectacular aura, although most directors and cinematographers worth their salt professed their dislike of the system and its artificially elongated frame, pointing out that none of the great artists of history, all of whom had the freedom to paint in whatever framings they chose, had ever elected to use the equivalent of the CinemaScope shape. 3-D provided extra excitement in fight scenes, remarkable depth to chases, and sometimes real beauty in panoramic long shots, but the novelty gimmicks of flaming arrows shot *at* the audience soon became over familiar. However, 3-D in the fifties was killed off not so much by uninspired application of the device as by inadequate presentation on the nation's screens. Movie projection was in a deplorable state at that particular time, and aging and sometimes half-blind projectionists who could not even project a flat film in focus, could hardly hope to maintain *two* synchronized projectors in good focus. (Some of the fifties' 3-D films, revived as a novelty in the nineties, were absolutely breathtaking in their clarity thanks to careful projection, and had *never* seemed that good on the occasion of their first release.) CinemaScope allowed for greater exploitation of panoramic landscape, although *White Feather* (1955) was one of the few to take full advantage of this. The good Westerns were usually good in spite of their new processes, not because of them.

Several like *Hondo* of 1953 (probably the best John Wayne film *not* directed by Ford) though shot in 3-D were released in flat versions, and would probably enjoy a whole new lease on life if rereleased today with the improved projection facilities now available. It and Ford's *The Searchers* stood out among the scores of "A"

Westerns produced during the fifties. In terms of quantity, the fifties represented a kind of peak for the sustained production of "A" Westerns by the best directors: John Ford, King Vidor, Robert Wise, Jacques Tourneur, Henry Hathaway, Henry King, John Sturges, Raoul Walsh, William Wellman, Andre de Toth, Howard Hawks, Anthony Mann, Fritz Lang, Allan Dwan, Sam Fuller, Delmer Daves, William Wyler, Edward Dmytryk, and Michael Curtiz all returned to the Western either periodically or regularly. And the reigning "name" stars—Gregory Peck, William Holden, Ray Milland, Cornel Wilde, Jeff Chandler, Tyrone Power, Kirk Douglas, Burt Lancaster, Robert Taylor, James Stewart, Gary Cooper, Alan Ladd, Joel McCrea, John Wayne, Charlton Heston, Richard Widmark, Robert Mitchum, Henry Fonda, even Marlon Brando, Spencer Tracy, and James Cagney, made Westerns now as a matter of course, or as highlights in their careers, not as a kind of interim novelty.

The end of the decade could not begin to match its beginning in terms of truly outstanding Westerns, although in 1958 the veteran Henry Hathaway came up with an unsung beauty in *From Hell to Texas*. By then, the great boom in Westerns had begun to diminish ever so slightly, and by virtue of its size, William Wyler's multi-starred *The Big Country* stole most of that year's thunder, helped, as *High Noon* had been, by Elmer Bernstein's memorable and much broadcast musical score. *From Hell to Texas* with a cast of lesser names and a title that unfortunately suggested a cheaper kind of picture, was lost in the shuffle. This was a pity, for not only was it one of the few Westerns to use the ultra-wide screen really creatively, but together with *Hondo* and *The Searchers*, it helped form a small, selective high water mark of outstanding Westerns between *Wagonmaster* in 1950 and *Ride the High Country* in 1962.

The script for *From Hell to Texas* was an unusually literate one, coming up with the expected action yet at the same time avoiding hackneyed characters and situations. Even the badmen, as vicious a family as we had seen on the screen since Ford delighted us with the Clantons and the Cleggs, act with a certain logic and justification, and aren't even villains in the strictest sense of the word. Don Murray was particularly well cast in the lead, the kind of role that Audie Murphy was always looking for at Universal and never quite finding. Even Chill Wills, normally given his head by the Johns Wayne or Ford (or taking it, if it was not given) to the detriment of the movies involved, managed to tone down his obnoxious qualities here (or if Hathaway was responsible, it was one of the crowning achievements of his career) and was even quietly effective at times. Perhaps the biggest surprise of all was in Hathaway's work and that he could come up with so totally different a Western, especially one with a revenge theme. Despite the mysticism of his one really offbeat work, *Peter Ibbetson*, Hathaway till now had been essentially a straightforward director of the old school, brought up in the thirties via such action films as *Lives of a Bengal Lancer, Spawn of the North*, and *The Real Glory*. His one major foray into the "serious" (i.e., nonaction) Western was in the Tyrone Power–Susan Hayward *Rawhide* (1951), an interesting "mood" remake of the 1935 gangster film, *Show Them No Mercy*. In *From Hell to Texas*, he seemed to have combined, successfully, much of the old William S. Hart sentiment and austerity with the slickness of John Ford, which is perhaps why in "look" and appeal it so much resembles Ford's late Western silent, *Three Bad Men*. The film has some magnificent outdoor locations—ramshackle towns and single frame buildings rising starkly out of the dust—that rival those of *Shane*, and are more effectively dramatic because they are less studied. Although Hawks's *Rio Bravo* and Ford's big but disappointing *The Horse Soldiers* followed it a year later to round out the fifties, it was superior to both of them, even if remembered less.

Equally ignored, and equally deserving of recognition, is a smaller black-and-white "A" Western from Republic and director William Witney, *Stranger at My Door* (1956). Dramatic, charming, leisurely, though with some splendid action sequences, it was, like Jacques Tourneur's Joel McCrea film, *Stars in My Crown*, a Western with religion and redemption as subthemes. However, for all of its sensitivity and warmth, it cannot help but stake its claim for fame on a memorable action sequence of a rampaging horse, and its one-on-one fight with the minister (played by Macdonald Carey, and in this sequence of course helped out by a number of stuntmen doubles). There are three basic ways to shoot such a sequence. One, as employed in the 1932 *The Devil Horse*, was to have Yakima Canutt hang doggedly to the neck of the horse, staying in place even when rolled on and shaken vigorously. (It was an astonishing sequence, but would have been frowned on in the fifties by the ASPCA who could not have been expected to admit that there was far more cruelty to the man than to the horse.) A second way was the method used in *Duel in the Sun*, where Gregory Peck and double fight an untamed horse. There the physical action was far less explicit (and exciting) than in *The Devil Horse*, with cutting and sound effects (an art for which there was little time in the earlier, cheaper film) making all the difference. Witney chose a third path: to shoot it in fragmented form, as he had the fight scenes in his Westerns and serials. Shot over a period of days, and always for a limited period when the horse was fresh and

Blue (Paramount, 1968): Joanna Pettet and Terence Stamp

full of energy, it is a mosaic of action of which Eisenstein might have been proud, brief fragments, reactions, a dummy dog thrown at the horse's flank in one scene, a dummy hoof obliterating a fence in another, all intercut with very real and unfaked footage of man versus horse. It is a sequence of such stunning fluidity that one is almost unaware of the editing process, and totally unaware of the painstaking trickery and illusion that went into the sequence.

Witney also directed the second-unit action scenes for *The Last Command*—virtually the entire climactic Alamo battle—and created some outstanding stunt action scenes in his Roy Rogers films of the fifties. His running fight between two wagon loads of cowboys in Roger's *Spoilers of the Plains* is a classic. The cameras record the action from the wagons themselves, and from parallel camera trucks as cowboys jump back and forth between the careening wagons. A potential accident—one stuntman's timing is slightly off and he falls under the wagon wheels—was prevented from being turned into tragedy through the presence of mind of fellow stuntman David Sharpe who saw what was about to happen and gave his colleague an extra push so that he was able to *just* roll clear of the wheels. The episode is in the finished scene, though the action is so fast that it's easy to miss. One who *didn't* miss it was France's current leading director, Bertrand Tavernier, who cites this

Hang 'Em High (United Artists, 1968):
Clint Eastwood

Hang 'Em High: Pat Hingle, typical of the
Broadway and even Method actors who
took over from the familiar but fast
disappearing character players associated
almost exclusively with Westerns

remarkable action scene as one of the highlights of American cinema as reflected in his early nineties book of opinions and reflections on the Hollywood films that formed his tastes and enthusiasms.

By the end of the fifties, the Hollywood studio system that made possible such enjoyable and worthwhile "little" films as *Stranger at My Door* was on the way out. It would be a long time before we would again see such satisfying and personal films, perhaps not until the nineties and such (commercially unsuccessful) films as *1000 Pieces of Gold.* Republic closed its production doors in the sixties, concentrating solely on selling its huge accumulation of product throughout the world for reissue, television, and videocassette markets. It's interesting that in the early nineties Republic was to make something of a comeback first via the television miniseries route with a Western on Custer, *Son of the Morning Star,* and then in 1992 with a modern Western, *Rope of Sand*—a "cheapie" by nineties standards with a "small" budget of only $6.5 million—roughly about fourteen times as much as *Stranger at My Door* had cost the same studio. Rather sheepishly explaining why the Western should provide the studio's reentry vehicle into the theatrical market, a studio executive was to announce:

> When things get bad economically and politically everybody has a tendency to look backwards towards something good. In this country, which is founded on the Western motif people like to look backwards at Westerns. That's why *Dances With Wolves* did so well.

As of this writing, *Rope of Sand* hasn't gone into release to either confirm or disprove the wisdom of that somewhat obvious but not necessarily commercially sound prophecy.

It is sobering, if not downright depressing, to realize that despite the continued large-scale production of deluxe Westerns during the sixties, the overall standards fell drastically from the fifties. At the beginning of the decade, we had two of the best (and saddest) of sixties Westerns: Sam Peckinpah's *Ride the High Country* and John Ford's *The Man Who Shot Liberty Valance.* In the last three years of the decade, we had three more: *Will Penny,* a magnificent film (with Charlton Heston's best performance) on the sadness of the "loner," something of a companion piece to *The Gunfighter,* less dramatically tragic yet somehow sadder because it deals with the loneliness brought on by age and disappearing way of life, not by retribution for a life thrown away in criminal pursuits. Rounding out the trio the more spectacular, certainly more popular, but generally less impressive *The Wild Bunch* and *Butch Cassidy and the Sundance*

Kid. In between lay the last hurrahs of directors like Ford, the squandering of major acting talents like Robert Mitchum's in too many undistinguished—and indistinguishable from each other—Westerns like *The Way West;* brief enthusiasms for Italian- and German-made Westerns; a flurry of now largely forgotten satires; and an increase in modern and socially-conscious Westerns. But on the whole it was a leveling off process, rather like a jumbo jet coming in for a landing over the sixties and gliding to a complete stop, with all safety belts securely fastened, over the seventies and eighties.

In general, Westerns of the sixties tended to stress the age of their protagonists, partly for comedy purposes, but largely from necessity since many of the bigger Western "names" had aged, and in order to use a sixty-year-old star and retain some sense of logic, that age had to be reflected in their story lines. *Ride the High Country* took Joel McCrea and Randolph Scott (whose physical appearances quite belied the infirmities attributed to them by the script) as two veteran misfits in a changing, more lawful, more modern West—one trying to perform an honest if menial job with dignity, the other out to make one last haul in order to retire with a measure of comfort. The story had a number of subplots—perhaps a shade too many in the middle portions of the film—and an earthy but tasteful approach to sex. Its strength, however, lay in the sincere performance of the two stars, and in the beauty and poignancy of its final scene wherein McCrea dies quietly and with the dignity he had sought, as his head sinks out of the frame, the camera panning over to the rugged skyline, emphasizing once more this man's affinity to the land. *Ride the High Country* was not only one of the best Westerns of the sixties, but one of the best from any period. The same year, 1962, saw another commendably off-center Western in *Lonely Are the Brave,* in which veteran nonconformist and small-time outlaw Kirk Douglas finds his freedom and indeed his whole way of life threatened first by the simple expedient of fenced-in range and then by larger technological encroachments. An interesting if not wholly successful effort, it possibly seemed forced and pretentious only by direct comparison with the simplicity and naturalistic values of *Ride the High Country.*

John Ford, older, tired, sadder about the changing and disintegrating values of life in the sixties, began to reflect that sadness in his movies. He continued to work right through the decade, but much of the old spirit had gone. He had become lazy, if a working director in his seventies *can* be termed "lazy." But directing film is an arduous, exhausting job; fun for a younger man, a chore for an older one. Ford became less of a perfectionist in his visuals and shot too much of his films in the studios. *The Man Who Shot Liberty Valance* is thematically one of his most important works, but filmically it moved in spurts—moments of poetry here or excitement there, his always interesting use of background music well in evidence. But the artifice of too many obvious studio exteriors and a minimal use of good sets and sufficient extras, giving it a threadbare look *except* when it got out into the genuine outdoors, worked against it. Nevertheless, his obviously sincerely felt *Cheyenne Autumn,* despite being badly and inconsistently edited down prior to release, made a graceful and appropriate farewell to the Western genre for this grand old warrior.

The more ambitious the Western of the sixties, the more it seemed to fail. John Wayne's personally directed (with unofficial help from Ford) *The Alamo* was overwrought, overlong, and not well cast. Cinerama's *How the West Was Won,* far from being the "definitive" Western it set out to be, was merely a kind of circus, sobered briefly by Ford's sad, introspective Civil War episode, though otherwise notable for an exceptional cast, fine locations, and exciting stunt action sequences, but somehow never even achieving much conviction let alone poetry or the genuine epic stature it strove for. The most ambitious of all the Andrew McLaglen films, *The Way West,* merely proved that he was better off sticking to imitation Ford or Walsh "fun" Westerns and star vehicles. Its long running time exceeded that of *The Big Trail,* but there was no sense of hardship or pioneering dedication at the end of it, merely the feeling of having been off on a Hollywood junket (except for two moments of unexpected, sudden death). Despite extensive location work, the awesome space of the West seemed to be used as illustrations for chapter pages, the stars posing meaningfully and inspiringly against skylines or vistas of pastures and rolling hills, before being reclaimed by the plot and proceeding with further adventures. It was one of far too many Westerns of the sixties to waste the superb, relaxed, and always underestimated acting talent of Robert Mitchum, actually served better by small roles in "B" westerns in his first year in the business (*Colt Comrades, Beyond the Last Frontier*) and the bigger films that followed before the end of the decade.

The most enjoyable Westerns of the sixties were, on the whole, those that aimed at being nothing more than serviceable star vehicles, Howard Hawks's *El Dorado,* for example, with Mitchum quite easily stealing the show from Wayne. Westerns generally seemed to be taking themselves less seriously, to be playing themselves tongue-in-cheek. This mood was accelerated by the fluke success of *Cat Ballou,* a Jane Fonda vehicle considered a misfire disaster until someone had the bright idea of an advertising campaign selling the film as the last word in spoofs of all Westerns, an idea that, despite some good sight gags and Lee Marvin's comic

playing, had not been its intention during production. Its success prompted further and fairly continual levity in the Western, extending to the heavyhanded *Support Your Local Sheriff* (1969) with James Garner, and on into the vulgarity of *Blazing Saddles* in the seventies.

If this slide into Westerns as self-parody was not markedly successful, however, at least the results were a little more entertaining than those from Westerns that became over-obsessed with the notion of taking themselves completely seriously. To enjoy a belated "cult" status because of its director (Arthur Penn) and star (Paul Newman), *The Left-Handed Gun* (1958), a Billy the Kid saga, introduced both Method acting and writing and Broadway stage directorial styles to the Great Outdoors, even trying to reduce that great outdoor stage to the stylized and limited confines of artificial theater sets. One of the most pretentious Westerns ever made, it even seemed to be influenced by the surreal visuals of Luis Buñuel at times. While there should certainly be no rules concerning new approaches to the Western—after all, German director Frank Wysbar once made a Hollywood Western, *The Prairie,* entirely on cramped sound stages—it does seem likely that if there is ever to be "new blood" in the Western, it is unlikely to come via chi-chi theatrics like this, but more probably from major directors who have never yet made a Western but *do* respect the genre. Orson Welles and Alfred Hitchcock, more's the pity, never did get to make a Western. Stanley Kubrick seemed *about* to in *One-Eyed Jacks* (1961), but was fired before it got properly under way. Star Marlon Brando took over, turning it into a superbly located and photographed but overly mannered and ponderously paced movie. Quite incidentally, *most* newer Westerns have been hurt, to a degree, by a surfeit of Broadway actors. All of our old familiar friends are gone now: badmen Fred Kohler and Harry Woods; old-timers George Hayes, Tully Marshall, and Si Jenks; granite-jawed sheriff Jack Rockwell, the heroine's father; morally strong but physically feeble Lloyd Ingraham or Edward LeSaint. Typecast they may have been, no more than adequate actors some of them certainly were, but their faces merged naturally into Hollywood's West. We knew them, accepted them, and by their very presence they imparted a kind of instant realism which the newer breed of character actor like Pat Hingle can never duplicate.

Lowering of censorship barriers in the mid-sixties also opened up the West to exploitation by the fast-buck producers of "nudie" features, which in the course of time developed into near pornographic features in which graphic violence and equally graphic sex became the norm, although admittedly the exhibition outlets for these films were limited. The West, apart from supplying outdoor locations (and the cutting of studio rental costs) and a logical showcase for color, also provided the opportunities for sex (rape, nude swims) and violence (ritual and revenge rape, hangings, whippings). *The Bushwackers* of 1969 was only one of the earlier films to begin running this gamut. During the same year, the so-called Underground cinema also discovered the erotic possibilities of the West, *Lonesome Cowboys* by Andy Warhol adding degeneracy and artistic vacuity in the name of experimentation.

The one dominant trend of the sixties was the unexpected commercial and artistic popularity of the European-made Western. Europe had made them before, but always as the occasional novelty and as a vehicle for big stars like Hans Albers and Luis Trenker. Inordinately rising production costs made it an economically sound move for Hollywood to begin shooting Westerns (and indeed many action films with outdoor locales) in Europe where the production dollar went much further. But this minor trend was soon seized on by the Germans and Italians who began to specialize in their own full-blooded Westerns, taking every Hollywood cliché seriously, enlarging on them, displaying wildly imaginative ideas about costuming and the interior design of saloons, and adding liberal doses of sex and violence. Hollywood players who had never quite made it at home—Clint Eastwood and Lee Van Cleef—suddenly found themselves stars overnight once they began to play in the Italian spaghetti Westerns, while talented American directors like Monte Hellman, finding it tough to get a job in Hollywood, had less trouble working out of Rome—or Yugoslavia.

The hybrids that resulted were mixed breeds indeed. The Italian *A Fistful of Dollars* was a careful, precise remake of Kurosawa's Samurai film, *Yojimbo*, itself equally careful and precise in adapting the style and visuals of John Ford's Westerns to the Japanese idiom. So popular did the European Westerns become that Sergio Leone became a major directorial cult figure with American audiences, and major American stars, including Henry Fonda, felt privileged to appear in his unique, highly personal, and usually excessively protracted and paced films such as the three-hour-plus *Once Upon a Time in the West*. Hollywood began setting up coproduction deals and sending its own stars over and finally, as with *Hang 'Em High*, a Clint Eastwood Western for United Artists, shooting its Westerns on its own home ground again, but in the new terse, violent, almost grotesquely "realistic" style made popular by the Italians.

Germany, on the other hand, falling back on the many works of their own Karl May—a homegrown James Fenimore Cooper—embarked on a series of elaborate color specials, all very much in the Hollywood style of the twenties, but undeniably spectacular and full of mass action. (No simple three-man gangs for *these* Westerns; the outlaw gangs usually ran to at least fifty riders, and there were always as many in the pursuing posses). Since these genuinely epic (in size) films could be made for a fraction of the cost of a Hollywood equivalent, they made it increasingly difficult for the Hollywood producer to come up with a saleable product that could compete with them in the open market. And since the German Karl May Westerns, many of them based on his famous *Winnetou* stories (never out of print, but popular all over again when the movies appeared), used well-known Hollywood stars in the leads, Stewart Granger and Lex Barker in particular, they had little trouble gaining U.S. release through such major companies as Fox and Columbia. Even so, there were too many of them for the American market to accommodate, especially as some that were *not* released in the United States followed the old German semiserial tradition of being two-parters, each one complete in itself, but the second an extension of the first. Such a double-barreled attraction was one (or more correctly two) directed by Robert Siodmak, now back in Germany again after a highly successful Hollywood career in the forties and early fifties. His 1964–65 duo *The Treasure of the Aztecs* and its sequel *The Pyramid of the Sun God*, was a wildly extravagant adventure in which a Dr. Sternau (one of May's favorite characters, played here by Lex Barker) is sent into Mexico by President Lincoln to assist Juarez in his problems with Maximilian. Although Dr. Sternau is supposedly working undercover, he seems—like *The Lone Ranger*—to be recognized by everybody with whom he comes in contact, including one of the virgins in a hidden lost temple, a young lady who supposedly has had no contact whatsoever with the outside world!

Unfair competition or not, the Western was too ingrained a part of Hollywood production for it ever to be abandoned. John Wayne went on grinding out inexpensive but commercially successful medium-scale actioners like *The War Wagon*, while an enterprising independent producer, Alex Gordon, with *The Bounty Killer* and *Requiem for a Gunfighter*, provided yeoman service to tradition, nostalgia, and expertise by restoring old-timer Spencer Gordon Bennet to the directorial helm and uniting such veteran Western players as Tim McCoy (still as virile-looking in the sixties as he had been forty years earlier!), Johnny Mack Brown, Buster Crabbe, Bob Steele, Richard Arlen, Rod Cameron, and even Broncho Billy Anderson, whose bright, piercing eyes and striking if battered profile had weathered almost seven decades!

But the credits and plots of the last Westerns of the

Butch Cassidy and the Sundance Kid (20th Century-Fox, 1969): The train robbery and the escape

sixties were reflecting many changes. In *Once Upon a Time in the West,* Henry Fonda, the erstwhile Wyatt Earp, was now a vicious and unshaven badman. The musical Western, *Paint Your Wagon,* featured a heroine with the thoroughly "mod" idea of maintaining two husbands simultaneously. Undoubtedly the most acclaimed, most criticized, and generally most controversial Western of the decade was *The Wild Bunch,* which revived and recycled most of the complaints about excessive violence that had greeted *Bonnie and Clyde,* a gangster movie, two years earlier. Directed by Sam Peckinpah, who had started the decade off so promisingly with *Ride the High Country,* much of *The Wild Bunch* was still Peckinpah at his best: the reconstruction of a changing period, the attention to realistic detail, the wry and sad commentary on the plight of men, good and bad, who had, in their own way, helped to build a West that was now passing them by. But the film also became a kind of paen to violence, and neither the insistence of its stars and director that it *had* to depict violence graphically in order to condemn it, nor the unquestioned virtuosity of its pictorial style (ritual and choreographic depiction, often in slow motion, of graphic blood letting and slaughter) could really counteract or justify the effects of revulsion that it created, and that caused considerable censorship problems and reediting both at home and in Europe, although ultimately a full version

Butch Cassidy and the Sundance Kid: Paul Newman and Robert Redford as Butch and Sundance in the climactic shoot-out

was put into release. There had often been excessive (but totally unreal) violence even in the "B" Western, yet it played as a kind of charade. But in its obsession with violence and in the shock tactics employed, *The Wild Bunch* took the charade to the opposite extreme, becoming a Western equivalent of the Hammer Frankenstein blood-baths and setting up new standards which, inevitably, would be copied and enlarged upon by subsequent Westerns.

Some of the traditionalist approach remained, however. *True Grit* presented John Wayne with makeup and costuming that emphasized rather than minimized his years (and girth) as an aging deputy marshal. Based on a novel that was a sixties' best-seller, its first hour suffered from a too faithful adherence to its source material. Although the 1880 Arkansas period was well recreated, there was perhaps too great an emphasis on "characters," most of them played by contemporary stage actors with both eyes firmly fixed on the horizon of the 1970 Best Supporting Actor Oscar. The novel's heroine, teenage Mattie Ross, may have made good and colorful reading, but when transposed to the screen, Mattie in the person of mannered and aggressive Kim Darby, came across in far too strong a fashion, forever reminding one of a 1938 Judy Garland looking for an excuse to burst into song. Significantly, Miss Darby's subsequent career floundered and petered out quite rapidly. Fortunately, in its second half the film segued into its manhunt theme and maestros Henry Hathaway and John Wayne took over, pushing Miss Darby into the background, albeit never quite far enough.

Beautifully photographed in breathtaking California and Colorado locations, *True Grit* has only one short studio "exterior," and while its action content is restricted to the closing reels, it is sharp, vicious (excessively bloody at times, it must be admitted), and well staged. Wayne, unexpectedly playing some scenes for pure comedy, did some of his best acting in any non-Ford film. One scene, in which he half humorously, half wistfully described his brief married life and the son who didn't like him, revealed a subtlety and a controlled warmth in Wayne that had rarely been displayed so well before. Wayne's charisma, popular sentiment for him, and his Academy Award for *True Grit* understandably though rather unfortunately tended to blot out memories of the similar but much superior *Will Penny* of just the year before. *True Grit*'s reception, and Wayne's rightness for the role, would have made it a perfect and graceful farewell to the Western scene, an ideal climax to an almost forty year career that had nominally begun with *The Big Trail*. (The two films, side by side on one bill, would complement one another perfectly and make a most felicitous Wayne homage; a pity it was never done.)

Paint Your Wagon (Paramount, 1969): A singing Clint Eastwood with Jean Seberg

263

But with Gary Cooper gone, Wayne not only became Hollywood's Western figurehead, but also remained a box office giant. Obviously he intended to go on making Westerns as long as his failing health permitted him to sit a saddle. If it seemed that he had passed up a good bet by not quitting while he was ahead, with his *True Grit* Oscar tucked into his belt, fortunately events proved otherwise. After a string of pleasant, profitable, but generally routine Westerns in the early seventies, he was to bow out not only gracefully but also poignantly with *The Shootist* (1976), the story of which—an aging Western gunman, already almost an anachronism, is dying of cancer, but wants to meet death on his own terms—so sadly reflected Wayne's own personal situation.

FOURTEEN

The Seventies and Eighties: The End of the Trail

The two decades beginning with 1970 represent the saddest period in the whole history of the Western movie, yet in a way it was also a period marked by a dogged tenacity and a determination that the Western *should* survive in one form or another. When sci-fi and outer space spectacle seemed to render the Western obsolete, then—as in *Outland* (1981, almost an outer space–futuristic remake of *High Noon*)—the Western formula would be transferred. The year 1980 saw both *Heaven's Gate*, the most self-indulgent, pretentious, and costly Western ever made, so expensive that it literally wrecked its sponsor, United Artists, and *The Long Riders*, a well-intentioned return to the austerity and realism of William S. Hart. Neither worked—at least, not at the box office. Nor did wholesale lampoon (*Blazing Saddles*, 1974), tongue-in-cheek adventure (*Silverado*, 1985), a return to simplicity and nostalgia (*The Legend of the Lone Ranger*, 1981), attempts at contemporary social protest (*Tell Them Willie Boy Is Here*, 1969), spoofs of the Western filmmaking process (*Hearts of the West*, 1975), increasing numbers of cowboy films with black actors as leading protagonists (*Take a Hard Ride*, 1975), and resettings in the contemporary West (*Comes a Horseman*, 1978). It should not be inferred that all of these were both critical and box office

failures. Some did very well, indeed; others—individually—were fine films. But it comes as something of a shock to realize that these last twenty years of Westerns have not produced one *classic* of the caliber of *Wagonmaster* (1950) or *Ride the High Country* (1962).

Perhaps the last really successful Western until 1991's *Dances With Wolves*, in terms of both critical and public response, was *Butch Cassidy and the Sundance Kid* (1969), and possibly that film, coming so close to the end of the sixties, provides something of a clue to the problems of the ensuing twenty years. For one thing, its plot was a fashionable mixture of traditional Western ingredients with something then still fairly new—civilization and mechanization overtaking the West. Too, it had popular stars at the peak of their careers in Robert Redford and Paul Newman. More important, perhaps, it was an echo of the fast-disappearing studio system. In earlier days, when the studios made a turkey—as they frequently did—they could salvage it to a large degree because they owned their own theaters and could get it preferred playing time or double-bill it with another of their films to make an attractive package. Today the double-bill is gone, and so are the chains of studio-owned theaters. Too, the mass-production methods of the studios ensured a measure of control: if the budget was getting out of hand, it could be curbed before it was too late—or expanded if the potential of the film seemed to justify it. A surprise success could be acted upon promptly, and sequels or similar films put into production right away, striking while the iron was hot, yet avoiding the machine-tooled sequels of today, which usually have only a number—two through a possible ten and up—to distinguish the subsequent *Rocky* and *Friday the 13th* follow-ups from their originals.

Many of today's films *have* to aim at blockbuster status or they would never get made. Too often they are overblown monuments to the egos of their directors. And when they fail, they do so so disastrously (witness both *Heaven's Gate* and *The Legend of the Lone Ranger*) that they discourage any attempts to retrench and try again in the same genre. John Ford's *Wagonmaster* (1950) was a commercial failure, but it was undeniably a fine film, and its losses were so comparatively slight that Ford had no problem making *Rio Grande* the same year. *The Legend of the Lone Ranger* on the other hand failed largely because of its total ineptness: a "hero" so poor an actor that all of his dialogue had to be redubbed, and an obvious indecision as to whether to play it straight or for serial-like fun. Perhaps its greatest folly was the building of a much publicized Western town set near Santa Fe. And a magnificent set it was, long, with a wide street, a church at one end and the sheriff's office at the other, with a remarkable variety of stores and dwellings in between. Surrounded as it was by the New Mexico foothills, it could have served as a basic set and point of reference for the whole film. Yet it was seen only briefly: once at night, when its fiesta lights and a few outlines of buildings were all that was visible, and during the Lone Ranger's daytime rescue of Tonto from the gallows, all centered at one end of the street. For all that was used of the set, they could have shot those scenes at Universal's Western street and shaved a couple of million dollars from the budget. That kind of extravagance would never have been countenanced in the old studio days, nor would it have come up.

Perhaps the greatest contribution to the generally lackluster look of the Westerns of the seventies and eighties was the passing of the "old guard": directors and stars who had made Westerns all their lives, and in many cases had personal and affectionate connections with the real West before they entered their movie careers. Directors John Ford and Howard Hawks died in 1973 and 1977 respectively; Henry Hathaway, Henry King, Jacques Tourneur, Raoul Walsh, Delmer Daves, and King Vidor followed at shockingly rapid intervals. John Wayne died in 1979, and virtually all of the major stars of Westerns, "A" and "B," have likewise passed on over these two decades: Randolph Scott, William Boyd,

George O'Brien, Tim McCoy (a living link of the Old West and Hollywood, since his career included cavalry service, an Indian agent and representative, an association with the Wild West shows that glamorized the West, and the movies, silents and talkies, that perpetuated that image), Ken Maynard and his brother Kermit, Charles Starrett, Bob Steele, stuntman and rodeo rider Yakima Canutt (who contributed superb second-unit direction to so many Westerns, big and small), Johnny Mack Brown, Buster Crabbe, Tim Holt. Even some of the lesser lights—Allan Lane, Tom Keene, Sunset Carson, and Whip Wilson—have gone too, as have most of those grizzled sidekicks, many of them fine actors away from their comic chores, exemplified best by George "Gabby" Hayes and Raymond Hatton. Even the first Western star of them all, Gilbert M. "Broncho Billy" Anderson, came to the end of the trail at the beginning of this period—in 1971.

Not all of these actors and directors were necessarily active or at their best in this period. Although he continued to work into the seventies, Henry Hathaway never again made a film to top *True Grit*. Bob Steele was an excellent example of a former cowboy hero who made an excellent villain: dirty, unshaven, menacing, he made a major contribution to many later Westerns by his mere presence. *All* of them made contributions just by *being there* and available for consultation, for participation in conferences and festivals, by keeping *their* West alive.

In the mid-1970s, Buster Crabbe made a curious little film called *The Comeback Trail.* Its bizarre and quite amusing premise was that of an independent schlock producer who conceives the idea of luring an old, retired cowboy star back into the fold to make a new Western—intending to heap so much strenuous action on him that he is bound to collapse of a heart attack, thereby allowing the company to collect the insurance. But the cowboy star, even in his sixties, is so hale and hearty that the plan misfires. Buster Crabbe, too, was in such magnificent form in his sixties, that it was hard to accept him as being as old as the script insisted. Unfortunately, the film was such an atrocious mishmash of misfiring inside jokes, poor timing, and an excess of foul language that it was little released. But it had its moments and some highlights of almost inspired insanity; with more care and a better budget, it could have made a delightful swan song for Crabbe's career.

However, as these directors and stars died, their actual and subliminal influence vanished. Of the genuine greats of the Western, only Joel McCrea (who had never been exclusively a Western star, and whose interest in ranching came *after* film stardom made it possible), and those two pioneers of the musical Western, Gene Autry and Roy Rogers, survived into the nineties.

266

High Plains Drifter (Universal, 1973), with Clint Eastwood, star and director, the only serious contender for the John Wayne mantle.

Blazing Saddles (Warner Bros., 1974): Gene Wilder and Cleavon Little in Mel Brooks's Western spoof that went way over the top

Bite the Bullet (Columbia, 1975): In one of the best Westerns of the seventies, James Coburn encounters his first auto

Bite the Bullet: Candice Bergen in one of the deglamorized saloon-bordello scenes

(McCrea died in October 1990.) Successors were generations away: whereas Ford, Walsh, and McCoy had based their possibly romanticized films on a West they'd *known*, the new directors based *their* Westerns on the Hollywood Westerns *they* knew. There was too much intimacy of detail and too much affection in the films of Ford and Walsh for them to be copied well. Steven Spielberg's films, whether the Indiana Jones adventures which were openly copied from highlights in the William Witney serials of the thirties and forties, or *Always*, his unbalanced tribute to *A Guy Named Joe*, were all homages to old-time Hollywood, overproduced, insensitive, and often missing the very point of the films that he admired so much. Spielberg has yet to make a genuine Western, although some of the films in which he has been involved as supervisor or executive producer—such as *Back to the Future, Part III* (1990)—suggest that it is not necessarily an event to look forward to. (Although one must admit that if he *did* turn his talents to a Western, it would probably be exciting and almost certainly profitable.)

The one major figure, both as actor and director, to dominate the Western film in the last twenty years undoubtedly had been Clint Eastwood. He has never been as charismatic a figure as Wayne, probably because he has never chosen to concentrate on the Western as much as Wayne did. By the same token, through not specializing, he has been able to carve a niche in the field of tough thrillers and *film noirs* as well, thus taking over the mantle not only of the departing Wayne but also of Humphrey Bogart . . . no mean feat. In his earlier films, his direction was a shade too tricky, aiming for instant recognition as a director by copying the methods of Hitchcock. But in later years, his work has become lean and laconic, almost as one with the character he plays. Though not a Western, his *White Hunter, Black Heart* (1990) demonstrates this admirably. One thing has helped the quality of Eastwood's thrillers and Westerns enormously: the relaxing and now virtual disappearance of the strictures of the Production Code. Revenge is a dominant motif in many recent Westerns, but especially in Eastwood's—and in his "Dirty Harry" city thrillers.

"Revenge" was an absolute taboo during the days when the Code ruled supreme, and many a film was all but ruined because of the its inflexibility. Too, the growing toughness, violence, and explicit brutality allowed by the increasingly powerless Code enabled Eastwood's character to mete out justice—sometimes in cold blood—and to go unpunished for it.

And though not necessarily an overall asset since it quickly became overdone, the permissiveness in depicting the *act* of killing (in Westerns usually by gun, though also by knife and by the hangman's rope) did replace the

Bite the Bullet: Ben Johnson, a familiar face, and Gene Hackman, a relative new one, fitted smoothly and convincingly into the Western scene

fairly bloodless pantomime of the average Western with a greater sense of reality. Even the classic 1932 Western *Law and Order* contains a singularly unconvincing scene in which Ralph Ince is fatally shot in the back. Yet although the scene is in near close-up, nary a bullet hole or a drop of blood appears on the coat adorning his broad back. Such Westerns as Robert Wise's *Blood on the Moon* (1948) among the "A's," and William Witney's Roy Rogers and Rex Allen "B's" of the late forties and early fifties were influential in introducing blood, bruises, and far more realism into fistfight scenes. George Stevens's *Shane* (1953) and its scene of Elisha Cook, Jr., being literally blown away by Jack Palance, was a pioneer in establishing the *force* of a gun and the pain and damage it could inflict. It began to take the gunfight out of the pantomime stage and prepare it for the gut-ripping technology of exploding blood-belts that would punctuate the Westerns from the seventies on—and especially Eastwood's.

If the last twenty-five years contained many Westerns *trying* to be modern, different and significant, then the average one still concentrated on traditional action, with an added bonus in that many top-line stars were beginning to slip, and could be added with minimal expense to a medium-budget Western. John Wayne and Kirk Douglas teamed up for *The War Wagon*, for example, Rock Hudson and Dean Martin for *Showdown*, and Henry Fonda and James Stewart for *The Cheyenne Social Club*. There was an interesting teaming of (relative) old-timer James Garner and newcomer Bruce Willis in *Sunset*, an amiable and well-intentioned fable about Wyatt Earp and Tom Mix getting together in Hollywood in the 1920s to solve a murder mystery. Blake Edwards's dull direction and Willis's even duller portrayal of Mix were luckily offset by a beautiful performance from Garner as Earp, and since he was on screen most of the time, he managed to inject both life and flavor into it.

Over that period, some of the most interesting Westerns, all of them falling somewhat short of being classics, included:

• *Bite the Bullet* (1975). An interesting comeback for writer-director Richard Brooks, and an unusual, realistic, and superbly photographed (in wonderful locations) Western centering around a horse race at the turn of the century, when the auto was on the way in. Among the best things about it were the relaxed, natural performances from Ben Johnson and Gene Hackman, and the rough-hewn charm of a deglamorized Candice Bergen.

• *Bronco Billy* (1980). One of Clint Eastwood's best as both actor and director. Not really a legitimate Western, it had something of the quality of Capra's *You Can't Take It With You* in its tale of a modern Western showman, part con man, yet concerned with upholding the image of the old-time Westerner. Although not more than superficially related in plot, and certainly

Hearts of the West: Westerns director Alan Arkin coaches new Westerns star Jeff Bridges in the art of the fast draw

Hearts of the West (MGM, 1975): A stunt that was a Ken Maynard specialty is reproduced in this likable spoof of the making of "B" Westerns

less self-indulgently "profound," it makes an interesting comparison with Robert Altman's *Buffalo Bill and the Indians* (1976). Charm was a quality that didn't rear its old-fashioned head too often in the seventies, let alone the eighties, but *Bronco Billy* had it. So did *Mackintosh and T.J.* (1975) and *The Grey Fox* (1982). The former (directed by Marvin J. Chomsky) was one of the most underrated and little seen Westerns of its decade; starring Roy Rogers as an aging ranch hand, and spinning a pleasing tale of his friendship with a young boy (with one good fight scene thrown in to keep the diehard Western fans happy), it was probably a boon to the rapidly disappearing small-town movie houses, but was virtually unseen in the big cities. The latter (directed by Phillip Borsos) was a curiosity that didn't quite come off, a part documentary, part narrative film on the career of Bill Miner, a lovable old chap who was inspired to become a train robber after seeing Edwin S. Porter's *The Great Train Robbery* in 1903. The Canadian-made *The Grey Fox* properly starts off with footage from that earlier film, but thereafter makes the mistake of trying to maintain a documentary flavor by backing up Miner's exploits with footage from silent movies. None of it matches and the device doesn't work, but the film is successful to a large extent through the remarkable performance of Richard Farnsworth, a former stuntman who late in life transformed himself into an excellent dramatic actor. What a pity that the discovery of his acting talents (and a wonderful grizzled Western face) wasn't made in time for the likes of John Ford and Raoul Walsh to have used him.

Butch and Sundance: The Early Days (1979). Another of those recent oddities, the prequel (as opposed to sequel) to a successful film where the plot didn't allow for a follow-up chronologically (usually because the leads were dead!) so had to go back to an earlier period. As directed by the always offbeat and unpredictable Richard Lester, it didn't really mesh and certainly didn't rekindle the magic of the original, but it did offer some excellent Colorado location photography, much of it during the winter snows, and included some sequences shot in the Rocky Mountain town of Telluride, where Butch and Sundance staged their first bank robbery. The building is there still, its red rock and brick facade unchanged, though it is no longer a bank. (That you'll find further down the street, a new modern building, one of many that is sadly changing the look of Telluride into that of another Aspen.)

The Long Riders (1980). Directed by Walter Hill, this got good enough reviews to suggest that it might usher in a whole new cycle of Westerns. Three Carradine

Breakheart Pass (United Artists, 1976): Charles Bronson and Jill Ireland in a unique combination of mystery and Western genres

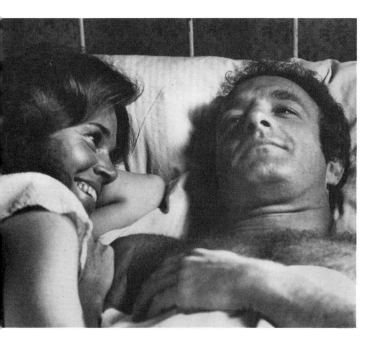

Comes a Horseman: Jane Fonda and James Caan in a traditional Western plot transferred to the West of post-World War II

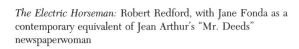

The Shootist (Paramount, 1976): John Wayne's last film . . . and a memorable one

The Electric Horseman: Robert Redford, with Jane Fonda as a contemporary equivalent of Jean Arthur's "Mr. Deeds" newspaperwoman

Butch and Sundance: The Early Days (20th Century-Fox, 1979): Tom Berenger as Butch Cassidy in the midst of a train robbery, and with William Katt as his outlaw buddy, Sundance

The Electric Horseman (Columbia, 1979): Robert Redford in an almost Capraesque contemporary Western in which the hype of modern journalism and commerce is defeated by a simple love of and adherence to old Western traditions

The Long Riders (United Artists, 1980): Brothers James and Stacy Keach as brothers Jesse and Frank James, assisted in a bank holdup by Randy Quaid (second right) as Clell Miller, a lesser outlaw

The Legend of the Lone Ranger (AFD, 1981):
Klinton Spilsbury as the Masked Man and
Michael Horse as Tonto

Bronco Billy (Warner Bros., 1980): Clint Eastwood in the title role

273

brothers, two Keaches, two Quaids, and other brothers convincingly played the James boys, the Younger Brothers, Bob Ford and his brother, and assorted old-time badmen in a Western unusually strong in realistic sets, costuming, makeup, and other matters. It had plenty of action and more than enough of the currently fashionable violence, in addition to the novelty of its casting. Yet somehow it didn't click, and while there were periodic attempts at repeating the experiment, such as the 1988 *Young Guns* and 1990's *Young Guns II* (with contemporary teen stars and unfortunately *too* contemporary dialogue), none of them worked as well.

The Grey Fox (United Artists, 1983): Richard Farnsworth as the real (if never very menacing) "badman" Bill Miner

The lack of influence of *The Long Riders* on subsequent Westerns was one of the major disappointments of the eighties. Almost certainly the *definitive* Western of the period—not necessarily the best, but one of them—was Don Siegel's *The Shootist* (1976). A climax of a sort to the kind of Western that began with Henry King's *The Gunfighter* and continued through Ford's *The Searchers* and *The Man Who Shot Liberty Valance* and Peckinpah's *Ride the High Country,* Siegel's film dealt with the last days of an aging gunfighter, dying of cancer in a West that is changing, and seeking to go on his own terms. Although adapted from a novel by Glendon Swarthout, *The Shootist* took on a life of its own, peopled as it was by actors from the Westerns' past—James Stewart, John Carradine, Richard Boone, Hugh O'Brian, and others, and telling a story that was, in a sense, John Wayne's own. It was a tragic though fitting climax to his career. Ironically, it was Wayne's own death less than three years later that gave it real power and poignancy. Had Wayne lived, the film, good as it was, would have seemed inferior to both *The Man Who Shot Liberty Valance* and *Ride the High Country.*

In passing, one might also mention some tangential pleasures of the two-decade season. Though certainly not a Western, the Australian *The Picture Show Man* (1977), based on an autobiography by an old-time showman, drew interesting parallels in its depiction of the traveling exhibitors, roaming the vast outback covered-wagon-style, to bring silent movies to wilderness communities in the teens and 1920s. Interestingly, one of the films used was a Jack Holt Zane Grey Western, long since lost in this country, but apparently surviving in Australia. And one might also point to two interesting documentarian newcomers, Nancy Kelly and Gwen Clancy, who together and singly have produced a number of affectionate documentaries on the West. *A Cowhand's Song* (1982), which they created over a two-year period while they were working cowgirls, was a striking film with many Fordian images, about contemporary ranchers striving to retain the way of life that they love against increasing odds. And Miss Clancy's *The Man They Call Will James* (1990) is a fascinating study of the famous writer-painter-actor, actually Canadian and never quite the authentic Westerner he claimed to be, and wanted to be. Appearing in the documentary, Richard Farnsworth helps to establish it as a major piece of Western folklore.

The disappointments of the same twenty-year period were perhaps fewer, because after the first five years or so we weren't expecting too much. *Rooster Cogburn* (1975), uniting Wayne with Katharine Hepburn, was neither a good *True Grit* sequel nor an interesting *African Queen* rip-off. *Bad Company* (1972), a Civil

Silverado (Columbia, 1985): Kevin Costner and Kevin Kline in Lawrence Kasdan's peculiar mixture of realism and send-up

Silverado: Kevin Costner

Pale Rider (Warner Bros., 1985): Director-star Clint Eastwood shows that death in a Western is no longer bloodless pantomime

War-era Western highly touted at the time as something of a classic dated very quickly like so many films of the period that tried for "significance" by building in too many contemporary references. *Hearts of the West* (1975) was a highly enjoyable little trifle about making "B" westerns in the thirties. Unfortunately it was made by people who at best had major company orientation and who knew nothing about genuine "B" Westerns, the last of which had been made nearly twenty years before. Earlier "B's" like Buck Jones's *Hollywood Roundup* had much more automatic honesty and realism. Nevertheless, it was a pleasing film, and, if nothing else, showed a kind of secondhand knowledge of the facts gleaned from old stills and maybe the screening of a Western or two. Other disappointments were not so much in the films themselves as in the treatment accorded them. *Heartland* (1979) was based on pioneer-woman diaries, and if a shade too neat and tidy in its design, was a worthwhile, unvarnished account (filmed in Montana) of the harsh lifestyle of frontier ranchers and farmers. Apart from a few festival showings, it went largely unseen. Disappointing, too, was the career of interesting maverick director Monte Hellman, who was a Westerner himself, and wanted nothing more than to make good, off-beat Westerns. The somewhat pretentious *The Shooting* out of the way, he seemed set for an erratic but at least interesting career. But at a time when Hollywood was losing interest in Westerns as a genre, there seemed no room for him, and he joined the trek to Italy. His 1978 *China 9, Liberty 37* offered Warren Oates (one of the best of the newer Western actors, whose career was tragically brief), Sam Peckinpah (in an acting role) and

Jenny Agutter—*and* some nice commercial nudity—but it, too, never surfaced beyond a few film festivals.

One of the more interesting developments of the period was the breaking down of boundaries of the genre—or the fusing of genres. *Breakheart Pass* (1976) was based on an Alistair MacLean novel and was essentially a *Lady Vanishes* kind of mystery set on a train. The period setting, the Western locale, the characters themselves (and the players included Charles Bronson and Ben Johnson), and certainly the breathtaking scenery and incredible stunt work staged by Yakima Canutt were all traditionally Western. Yet the concentration on intrigue and murder on the train itself was certainly a case of a cross genre. How different is it, for example, from *The Narrow Margin* (1990), an expanded remake (of sorts) of the 1952 film of the same name? The new version starts out with a murder in the big city, and both cops and badmen are from the city, but otherwise the action is like that of *Breakheart Pass* limited to the train itself, with similar stunt action on its roof, as the train passes through rugged Western scenery on its trip from the Canadian wilderness down to New York. And though dealing with an Australian outlaw, *Ned Kelly* (1970) was simply Jesse James transferred down under.

A renewed interest in movie history generally saw television more willing to underwrite and exhibit documentaries exploring this field. Tom Trusky, mentioned earlier for his valuable work in getting the silent Nell Shipman films better known, also rediscovered much of an early Western feature, *Told in the Hills* (shot in Idaho), the bulk of which was residing in archives in the old Soviet Union. In the course of his investigations into the details of its production, Trusky also uncovered the (till then) obscure fact that one of its players, later better-known as the Western star Jack Hoxie, while still a teenager, killed his brother! The whole complicated story, sounding like something out of *Tol'able David*, had been very much hushed-up when a sympathetic community closed ranks around the young Hoxie. In 1990, Trusky presented the story of the making of *Told in the Hills* in a lengthy and detailed local television program, and later still, was able to restage the premiere of the partially reconstructed film.

Such specialized researches into the history of the Western film became possible in the seventies and eighties thanks to a renewed academic interest in film history, and particularly into areas that had hitherto been granted little respect. The Institute of the American West, operating out of Sun Valley, Idaho, established a series of annual events, the first two of which were essentially film festivals. Soon they became more educationally and culturally-oriented conferences devoted to ecology, the National Parks, the American Indian, agri-

culture in the West, and other themes that drew educators and specialists together. The first conference, taking place in 1976, was virtually a last stand for many of the Western film pioneers who attended: Tim McCoy, Buster Crabbe, King Vidor, Henry King, Delmer Daves, Blanche Sweet (heroine of many a D. W. Griffith Western in the 1910–12 years), the Indian actor Iron Eyes Cody, and newer Hollywood representatives—Clint Eastwood, Warren Oates, Peter Fonda. Tim McCoy riding a stagecoach into the local rodeo was a sight to behold—and fortunately British film historian and TV producer Kevin Brownlow was there to interview them and preserve it all on film.

When, just a few years later, the Santa Fe Film Festival devoted its annual event to the Western, of that remarkable group of veterans only King Vidor, Buster Crabbe, and Iron Eyes Cody survived or were well enough to attend. Even those representing the new Hollywood—Sam Peckinpah, Warren Oates, Lee Marvin, Niven Busch—had since had their ranks severely depleted. But the genuine interest, academic as well as popular, that those festival/conferences reflected, seems to have increased in momentum. August archival institutions like the Pacific Film Archive in Berkeley, or Chicago's Art Institute, or the Film Forum in New York, run not only Westerns but "B" Westerns regularly. Gene Autry, at the end of the 1980s, opened his Western Heritage Museum in Hollywood's Griffith Park. It shows Westerns regularly in its theater, and the museum (devoted to the West, its artifacts and its art and history generally, not just to the Western film) has an excellently organized section outlining the history of the genre via props, stills and posters, costumes, and a series of film exhibitions which zero in succinctly on such areas as The Stuntman, The Singing Cowboy, The Early Westerns and so forth. Roy Rogers likewise has a fine museum, but its essential appeal is to Western fans, while Autry's approach is broader and more serious.

An odder phenomenon of the last two decades has been the proliferation of Western conventions—spaced all over the country—which meet over weekends to show Westerns nonstop, and to allow dealers to sell or trade Western movies on 16-mm and tape, posters, stills, and anything and everything catering to the Western nostalgia market. On the face of it, there's certainly nothing wrong with groups of enthusiasts getting together to pursue a hobby and to look at the films they love. But there's a sad side to these conventions, too. They display an almost obsessive need for hero worship. Had these conventions existed twenty years ago they would have provided a welcome reminder to stars like Ken Maynard and Hoot Gibson in their twilight years, how much their films had meant to their audiences, and

Young Guns (20th Century-Fox, 1988): Emilio Estevez and William H. Bonney, aka Billy the Kid, in a pose and costuming identical to that seen in the most famous shot of the notorious outlaw (who was, however, not quite as good looking)

Pale Rider: A reworking of *Shane* duplicates one of its most famous scenes, but on a more violent level

Sunset (Tri-Star, 1987): James Garner (left) and Bruce Willis as Wyatt Earp and Tom Mix

277

how much they were loved and remembered. But by the time the conventions were established, very few of the filmmakers or stars who *deserved* such admiration and respect were left. Charles Starrett and Sunset Carson were two who appreciated such attention, and undoubtedly these conventions enriched their last years. Ben Johnson and William Witney, both fortunately still hale and hearty, continue to genuinely enjoy such events—which in 1990 also expanded to include a pilgrimage to Lone Pine, California, location site of many Westerns. But for the rest, the conventions have made idols out of nonentities—the tangential villains, character players, lesser comics, and leading ladies—who are feted merely because they have survived, and have acquired a kind of glory by association. They appeared *with* Tex Ritter or Johnny Mack Brown, and that is enough. There is no point in causing pain by mentioning names, but it seems to belittle the Western itself by honoring (at least on a grand scale) those to whom it was merely a bread-and-butter business.

Even sadder perhaps is the fact that these conventions tend to attract the older people who were losers in life. For a long weekend, they can take themselves back to their youth, when Westerns were their favorite diversion, when life was simpler, and when their future held the promise of enterprise and success matching that of their "B" Western favorites. For many that future held either failure or compromise. The conventions provide solace if not renewed hope . . . and when one is over, there is always another one to look forward to. There's the making of a great movie in this situation itself, but it would probably be fully understood only by the *successful* convention attendees. But perhaps such a movie, if made, could be *The Last Picture Show* of the 1990s.

The industry is changing, and those changes do not bode well for the Western. Twenty years ago, a movie like *Ride the High Country* at least had a chance to build an audience. Even if the major houses shunned it, the critics would usually call attention to it, and a whole sub-circuit of second-run houses, neighborhood halls and revival houses would be available to give it a slightly extended life, time at least for the word-of-mouth to get around, and for interested parties to seek it out. Today those second-run houses are largely gone. If a film doesn't make it in its initial outing, capturing the fancy of both critics and public, it's gone, almost beyond recall. True, television awaits it—it can still be seen, but not in the media it was intended for, and not in a way that allows it to make any impact. (Television is too busy plugging its own often very ambitious Westerns—such as periodic Louis L'Amour ones—and mini-series—like *Lonesome Dove*—to care about its possible role as an alternate to the old second-run movie house). And after

television, there is the videocassette market. But again, it denies the shared enjoyment of a film in a large audience and changes—or *short*-changes—its impact. True, the videocassette market has been a veritable boon for the old "B" Western fancier. Many of the older (and especially the independent) Westerns have fallen into the public domain, and those of Ken Maynard, Hopalong Cassidy, Buck Jones, and others of the thirties and forties, including most of the serials, are sold with impunity.

Even if the rights are still intact and the films cannot *legally* be offered, they often are, in the fairly safe knowledge that the legal owner is not going to bother himself about a forty-year-old "B" when he has newer, bigger product to protect. Happily, many of the older Westerns are being offered at economical prices and in first-rate tape transfers. Less happily, many of them are of abysmal pictorial and sound quality and virtually unrunnable. Sadly, many younger Western fans may run across these and jump to the conclusion that "B" Westerns were crude. Some of them, like the memorably inept *Call of the Coyote,* certainly were. Others, though, had a quality and a visual beauty to match the best of the "A's." But if television and the videocassette market have a negative aspect, they also provide a kind of insurance, a guarantee of a filmic afterlife where initial losses can be recouped. If it were not for that guarantee, we might have far less Westerns in our future than we suspect. Even though the great directors and the great stars have gone, the tradition of the Western—and the belief that it can one day, with luck, retrieve its once guaranteed moneymaking potential—live on.

Fortuitously, as these closing notes were written in 1991, the big filmic event of the year, and the movie to sweep the Academy Awards (as no Western had done before) was Kevin Costner's *Dances With Wolves.* Paralleling but surpassing *They Died With Their Boots On* in scope, and dealing with the same period—the Civil War and the Indian wars that followed—it was one of the most ambitious Westerns ever planned or achieved, covering so much ground that even after final editing it ran for more than three hours. (Less than a year after its release, there was already talk of a restored "director's cut" version, running for up to five hours, though presumably intended primarily for the videocassette market). Critical reception, especially from reviewers with conveniently short memories, was rhapsodic. It is of course no discredit to the film that it was covering ground that *had* been covered before, in Delmer Daves's *Broken Arrow,* and far more specifically in Samuel Fuller's *Run of the Arrow,* which managed to tell exactly the same story (historically as well as personally) in less than ninety minutes. What was more important

Young Guns: An enterprising but controversial Western, an unromanticized though but none-too-accurate version of the Lincoln County Wars, with a cast of popular young stars: (from left) Casey Siemaszko, Charlie Sheen, Kiefer Sutherland, Emilio Estevez, Lou Diamond Phillips, and Dermot Mulroney

than the film's content was the faith that it displayed in the Western genre, since at the time of its conception it could hardly have seemed like the box office blockbuster that it ultimately became not just in America but throughout the world.

In some ways its length was its undoing. The first third of *Dances With Wolves*, dealing with the hero's disillusionment during the Civil War, and his (somewhat unmotivated) determination to see the Western frontiers while they were still there, at which time he became a staunch advocate of Indian rights, was frankly unnecessary. As Fuller's film had shown, the point could be more effective if it was made quickly, and the basic stance of the movie approached more rapidly. (Although not released as of this writing, the elongated version is said to contain still more detail in this opening section). Too, *Dances With Wolves* contains absolutely stunning photography in its panoramas of the West and in its rightly-praised buffalo hunt sequence. However, as though the grandeur of the West could not stand alone, its beauty is often enhanced and actually enlarged by the use of glass shots and matte paintings, so well done as not to be obvious, yet somehow symbolic of the film's need to overawe and impress with its importance.

The film, though, like *Massacre* (1934), is totally unbalanced in its attempts to address the wrongs inflicted on the Indian. Kevin Costner, producer and director as well as star, appears as a somewhat surly, Christ-like figure opposed by Indian-hating white Union officers and men who are insane, coarse, murderous, and generally so ill-disciplined that it's surprising that the majority of them hadn't been court-martialed and

Back to the Future, Part III (Universal, 1990): In one of the year's most elaborate (though not particularly successful) Westerns, time traveler Christopher Lloyd is on a locomotive about to transport him back to modern times—but even the spectacular action and stunting of this climactic sequence had a ho-hum quality

279

executed long before they got to Indian country. This lack of balance, coupled with the film's ecstatic collection of reviews and awards, caused a backlash surprisingly quickly, with historians of the West generally and Indian history in particular jumping in to point out the film's many inaccuracies. (Scrupulous accuracy, including the use of authentic Indian language, was one of the assets most claimed and self-praised in the film's advance publicity). The backlash is probably as unfair as were the rave reviews written without any knowledge of movie history or the film's honorable ancestors.

If nothing else, *Dances With Wolves* has undone much of the damage inflicted on the cause of the epic Western by *Heaven's Gate*. Whatever its shortcomings, and they tend to be relatively minor in light of its considerable achievements, the cost, time, and energy were proven worthwhile. Ironically, the film's success seems to have sidetracked Costner's career as an actor-director. The carefree bravado that he had exhibited in *Silverado*, which suggested that he might be ideal for the kind of lighthearted and near legendary heroes so often played by Errol Flynn, was suppressed instead of utilized when Costner played in the post-*Dances With Wolves* reworking of *Robin Hood*. His bandit of Sherwood Forest became dour and dull, a crusader for human rights and racial equality at a time in history when, in England at any rate, racial problems didn't exist. (Apparently, too, his serious mien disrupted the

official director's ability to control *Robin Hood*.) However, the release and success of *Dances With Wolves* coincided with other renewed energy and activity in the Western field. *Son of the Morning Star*, an elaborate two-part television special, dealt with the Custer story from two viewpoints, the Indian and the White. Not as well received as was hoped, it still had a satisfying reception from critics and audiences, enough to convince the television impresarios that there was still room for experiment in the Western.

The Black Robe, a film very similar in content and intent to *Dances With Wolves* though dealing with Canadian Indians, was actually superior to it, and planned sufficiently early that it could not be accused of cashing in on its success, but unfortunately it came too close on the heels of Costner's movie for its own merits to outweigh what seemed to be familiarity of theme.

The days of huge cycles of Westerns are clearly gone forever along with the studio system that made them feasible. But the success of *Dances With Wolves* has shown that the public will respond to the genre whenever it is treated with care, respect and integrity, even the kind of lopsided integrity that Costner brought to it. And after all, the best directors of the day—Stanley Kubrick, Bertrand Tavernier, Martin Scorsese, Lindsay Anderson (not an arbitrary selection, merely a cross-sectional one to indicate the possibilities)—have yet to make their first Western.

Kevin Costner in *Dances With Wolves* (1990)

Index

PUBLIC LIBRARY
Stoneham, MA